MW01050779

TExES Social Studies 7-12
232

Teacher Certification Exam Guide
By: Sharon Wynne, M.S.

XAMonline, INC.
Boston

Library of Congress Cataloging-in-Publication Data

Wynne, Sharon A.

TExES Social Studies 7-12 Teacher Certification / Sharon A. Wynne.
ISBN 978-1-60787-451-5

1. Social Studies   2. Study Guides.   3. TExES
4. Teachers' Certification & Licensure   5. Careers

Disclaimer:
The opinions expressed in this publication are solely those of XAMonline and were created independently from the National Education Association, Educational Testing Service, and any State Department of Education, National Evaluation Systems or other testing affiliates.

Between the time of publication and printing, state-specific standards as well as testing formats and website information may produce change that is not included in part or in whole within this product. Sample test questions are developed by XAMonline and reflect similar content to real tests; however, they are not former tests. XAMonline assembles content that aligns with state standards but makes no claims nor guarantees teacher candidates a passing score. Numerical scores are determined by testing companies such as NES or ETS and then are compared with individual state standards. A passing score varies from state to state.

Printed in the United States of America
TExES Social Studies 7-12 232
ISBN: 978-1-60787-451-5

About XAMonline

Founded in 1996, XAMonline began with a teacher-in-training who was frustrated by the lack of materials available for certification exam preparation. XAMonline has grown from publishing one state-specific guide to offering guides for every state exam in the U.S., as well as the PRAXIS series.

Each study guide offers more than just the competencies and skills required to pass a certification exam. The core text material leads the teacher beyond rote memorization of skills to mastery of the subject matter, a necessary step for effective teaching.

XAMonline's unique publishing model brings currency and innovation to teacher preparation:

- Print-on-demand technology allows for the most up-to-date guides that are first to market when tests change or are updated.
- The highest quality standards are maintained by using seasoned, professional teachers who are experts in their fields to author the guides.
- Each guide includes varied levels of rigor in a comprehensive practice test so that the study experience closely matches the actual in-test experience.
- The content of the guides is relevant and engaging.

At its inception, XAMonline was a forward-thinking company, and we remain committed to bringing new ways of studying and learning to the teaching profession. We choose from a pool of over 1500 certified teachers to review, edit, and write our guides. We partner with technology firms to bring innovation to study habits, offering online test functionality, a personalized flashcard builder, and eBooks that allow teachers-in-training to make personal notes, highlight, and study the material in a variety of ways.

To date, XAMonline has helped nearly 500,000 teachers pass their certification or licensing exams. Our commitment to preparation exceeds the expectation of simply providing the proper material for study; it extends from helping teachers gain mastery of the subject matter and giving them the tools to become the most effective classroom leaders possible to ushering today's students toward a successful future.

Three full Practice Tests

Now with Adaptive Assessments!

Adaptive learning is an educational method which uses computers as interactive teaching devices. Computers adapt the presentation of educational material according to students' learning needs, as indicated by their responses to questions. The technology encompasses aspects derived from various fields of study including computer science, education, and psychology.

In Computer Adaptive Testing (CAT), the test subject is presented with questions that are selected based on their level of difficulty in relation to the presumed skill level of the subject. As the test proceeds, the computer adjusts the subject's score based on their answers, continuously fine-tuning the score by selecting questions from a narrower range of difficulty.

The results are available immediately, the amount of time students spend taking tests decreases, and the tests provided more reliable information about what students know— especially those at the very low and high ends of the spectrum. With Adaptive Assessments, the skills that need more study are immediately pinpointed and reported to the student.

Adaptive assessments provide a unique way to assess your preparation for high stakes exams. The questions are asked at the mid-level of difficulty and then, based on the response, the level of difficulty is either increased or decreased. Thus, the test adapts to the competency level of the learner. This is proven method which is also used by examinations such as SAT and GRE. The Adaptive Assessment Engine used for your online self-assessment is based on a robust adaptive assessment algorithm and has been validated by a large pool of test takers. Use this robust and precise assessment to prepare for your exams.

Our Adaptive Assessments can be accessed here:
xamonline.4dlspace.com/AAE
You will be presented with a short form to complete for your account registration. You will need an active email address to register.

Table of Contents

DOMAIN II   U.S. HISTORY

COMPETENCY 5   EXPLORATION AND COLONIZATION: THE TEACHER UNDERSTANDS SIGNIFICANT HISTORICAL EVENTS AND DEVELOPMENTS IN THE EXPLORATION AND COLONIZATION OF NORTH AMERICA AND THE DEVELOPMENT OF COLONIAL SOCIETY.

COMPETENCY 12   **TEXAS IN THE TWENTIETH AND TWENTY-FIRST CENTURIES:** THE TEACHER UNDERSTANDS SIGNIFICANT HISTORICAL DEVELOPMENTS AND EVENTS IN TEXAS FROM 1900 TO THE PRESENT.

DOMAIN IV   **GEOGRAPHY, CULTURE, AND THE BEHAVIORAL AND SOCIAL SCIENCES**

COMPETENCY 13   **PHYSICAL GEOGRAPHY CONCEPTS, NATURAL PROCESSES, AND EARTH'S PHYSICAL FEATURES:** THE TEACHER UNDERSTANDS BASIC GEOGRAPHIC CONCEPTS, NATURAL PROCESSES INVOLVING THE PHYSICAL ENVIRONMENT, AND EARTH'S PHYSICAL FEATURES.

DOMAIN I WORLD HISTORY

COMPETENCY 1: ANCIENT WORLD CIVILIZATIONS

THE TEACHER UNDERSTANDS SIGNIFICANT HISTORICAL EVENTS AND DEVELOPMENTS IN ANCIENT WORLD CIVILIZATIONS, FACTORS INFLUENCING THE DEVELOPMENT OF ANCIENT WORLD CIVILIZATIONS, AND MAJOR CHARACTERISTICS AND CONTRIBUTIONS OF ANCIENT WORLD CIVILIZATIONS.

SKILL 1.1   Analyze the influence of various factors (e.g., geography, processes of spatial exchange [diffusion], development of agriculture) on the development of ancient civilizations.

Emergence of Human Civilization: 10,000–5000 BCE

Spatial exchange (diffusion) is defined as the way people and things are distributed, or located, over the earth. It involves migration within an area and between areas. During the early ages in history, for example, people moved from caves where they had been living to areas where they could build houses.

The **geography** of an area is a factor in the settlement and growth of civilizations. Mountainous regions tend to be isolated and difficult to reach, resulting in smaller and more scattered settlements. Valleys in mountainous regions, however, tend to attract settlements because the land is more fertile and can be used for agriculture.

The **development of agriculture** was the result of people having tools with which they could grow crops. Usually, agricultural areas developed in fertile river valleys.

Prehistory is defined as the period of human achievements before the development of writing. In the Stone Age cultures, there were three different periods: the **Lower Paleolithic Period,** characterized by the use of crude tools; the **Upper Paleolithic Period,** exhibiting a greater variety of better-made tools and implements, the wearing of clothing, a highly organized group life, and blossoming skills in art; and the **Neolithic Period,** characterized by domesticated animals, food production, the crafts of knitting, spinning, and weaving cloth, starting fires through friction, building houses rather than living in caves, developing institutions including the family, religion, and a form of government or the origin of the state.

The Neolithic Period is also referred to as the **New Stone Age** and began about 10,000 BCE. It ended from about 4500 to 2000 BCE, ending at different times in different parts of the world. During this time, farming was the primary means of subsistence in Western Asia, while hunting and gathering predominated elsewhere. Over the next five thousand years, farming became established independently in other areas. This Agricultural Revolution had monumental impact on the lives of humans because:

- Farming could support much larger populations.

- Sizes of settlements became increasingly larger.
- Larger communities generated new needs and new opportunities that gave rise to new activities.
- Trade in raw materials and finished goods developed between communities.
- Cooperation became normalized through communal efforts.

Some people were able to develop craft skills, engage in long-distance trade, and experiment with technology such as pottery kilns, metallurgy, and irrigation. Communities established permanent villages with material goods and equipment, which led to the beginnings of social differentiation. Various regions developed a dependence on different staple crops. Animals were domesticated, and selective breeding began to enhance useful traits. Permanent dwellings were constructed. Communities created identifying symbols and rituals, including burial customs. Communal living, however, also exposed people to disease and epidemics.

This period was also typified by active trade across constantly increasing spans of distance and culture. Religions flowered throughout the world, becoming, in many cases, truly global in their influence. Religion and politics began to influence one another in new ways, and these great world religions came into conflict. The period was rich in the development and rapid advance of various technologies, fields of learning, and the arts.

Communities in west Asia and southeastern Europe discovered independently that metals could be extracted from rock by heating. The first metals used were copper, gold, and lead. Tools made of these soft metals could not compete with flint and stone for durability. Copper and gold came to be used for decorative items.

Agriculture and Trade

Americas

Potatoes, squash, and beans were cultivated and began to supplement hunting and gathering. People living in the Andes Mountains began harvesting grains and vegetables, and squash, avocados, and chilies were staples in the Central American diet.

Europe

By 7000 BCE, farming had reached southeast Europe, spreading west along the Mediterranean and north into central and northwest Europe. New strains of cereals were developed in northern Europe, and cattle and pigs replaced goats as the main domestic animals. Two thousand years later, farming had spread to central Europe and fishing supplemented hunting and gathering in northern Europe. Cereal-farming villages arose in much of Western Europe at this time. Farming villages in southern Anatolia (Turkey) traded flint, obsidian, timber, shells, and copper.

West Asia

The earliest farmers settled in a fertile arc of land from the Persian Gulf to the eastern Mediterranean, an area known as the **Fertile Crescent.** Mesopotamia was located in the Fertile

Crescent between the Tigris and Euphrates rivers. This area is referred to as the **"cradle of civilization"** and produced agriculture because of the fertile ground. The Mesopotamians harvested wheat and cultivated large-seeded grains. The farmers used irrigation in southern Mesopotamia, and the goat was the primary domesticated animal. Anatolian and central Mesopotamian villages consisted of mud-brick houses, and craftsmen smelted copper and lead and painted pottery in northern Mesopotamia.

East Asia

Agriculture developed in northern China, and grain was kept in storage pits. Pigs and dogs were domesticated. Rice was cultivated in lowlands of the Yangtze River delta, and in 5000 BCE, jade was imported into northern Manchuria from Central Asia and Siberia.

South and Southeast Asia

New Guinea practiced drainage and cultivation during this time, and in 6000 BCE, pottery appeared as grave goods, indicating that there was trade with central Asia. Wheat and barley were cultivated in northern India and rice was cultivated south of Ganges River valley.

Africa

Hunters and gatherers moved into the Sahara Desert as the Ice Age ended in 9000 BCE. Rock art was developed and way-line pottery was produced. Cattle were domesticated in northern Africa, but by 6000 BCE the Sahara became arid again and people departed. At this time the cultivation of wheat and barley spread to the Nile Valley of Egypt from the Middle East.

Accomplishments of Civilizations

Africa

Egypt made numerous significant contributions that included construction of the great pyramids, the development of hieroglyphic writing, preservation of bodies after death, making paper from papyrus, developments in arithmetic and geometry, the invention of the method of counting in groups of ten (the decimal system), completion of a solar calendar, and the laying of the foundation for science and astronomy.

West Asia

The **Sumerians** lived in southern Mesopotamia. They invented the wheel, developed irrigation through use of canals, dikes, and devices for raising water, devised the system of cuneiform writing, and learned to divide time. They also built large boats for trade. The Babylonians were another group living in southern Mesopotamia (present-day Iraq). They devised the **Code of Hammurabi**, a system of laws.

The **Assyrians,** who lived in northern Mesopotamia, created complex societies and developed the fundamentals of human civilization such as agriculture, kilns, and smelting.

The **Hebrews,** another ancient Semitic people, occupied Canaan and are considered to be the ancestors of the Israelites. They migrated from Ur about 2000 BCE. The Israelites were first known to develop monotheism, one God.

The **Phoenicians** lived in the Fertile Crescent along the coast of present-day Lebanon. They were sea traders and were well known for their manufacturing skills in glass and metals and the development of a widely used purple dye. They became proficient enough in the skill of navigation that they were able to sail by the stars at night. They devised an alphabet using symbols to represent single sounds, which was an extension of the Egyptian writing system.

India was the birthplace of Siddhartha Gautama (Buddha) on whose teachings Buddhism was founded. The caste system was developed in India, and the major religion of Hinduism was founded here. The Indians also discovered the principle of zero in mathematics.

The **Persians,** who lived in present-day Iran, developed an alphabet and contributed the religions/philosophies of **Zoroastrianism, Mithraism,** and **Gnosticism.** The Persians allowed conquered peoples to retain their own customs, laws, and religions.

East Asia

China began building the Great Wall to protect its northern border. The Chinese practiced crop rotation and terrace farming, established the silk industry, and developed caravan routes across Central Asia for extensive trade. They also increased proficiency in rice cultivation and developed a written language based on drawings or pictographs.

Europe

The **Minoans** lived on the island of Crete in the Mediterranean Sea. They were predominantly farmers in 7000 BCE, but by the Bronze Age (approximately 2700 BCE) they developed commerce and a trade network. The Minoans devised a system of writing and used symbols to represent syllables in words. They also built palaces having multiple levels containing many rooms, water and sewage systems with flush toilets, bathtubs, hot and cold running water, and bright paintings on the walls

The **Mycenaeans** who lived in the Peloponnese in Greece conquered the Minoans in the 1400s BCE. They changed the Minoan writing system to suit their own language and used symbols to represent syllables. They developed commerce with their pottery, wine, and oil, and they made beautiful jewelry. They were warriors and after they destroyed the famous city of Troy during the Trojan War, they largely disappeared.

SKILL 1.2 **Demonstrate knowledge of individuals, events, and issues that shaped the development of ancient civilizations.**

The years between 500 BCE and 500 CE witnessed the rise of several great empires. Periods of creativity and accomplishment alternated with periods of **intense conflict** between rival empires.

This was the period of the full flourishing of classical Greece. Rome transitioned from Republic to Empire. The amazing empire of Alexander the Great brought many values from Asia, such as the values of ideas, wisdom, curiosity, and the desire to learn as much as possible about the world and not only became the largest empire but accomplished in its wake the fertile cultural cross-pollination that changed the world. It was a climactic period for the Persian Empire. The Byzantine Empire arose. The birth of the first Chinese Empire was followed by many internal struggles in China. In Africa and the Americas, other political structures united people previously isolated from one another. India and Africa were deeply impacted by the rise and growth of the Islamic Empire. In the Americas the Mayan culture entered its classical period.

Classical Greece

Greece developed a series of independent, strong city-states. The **Peloponnesian War** (431–404 BCE) was fought between Athens and Sparta and significantly weakened both of the major city-states, enabling **Philip of Macedon** to conquer them in 338 BCE.

Alexander the Great (356–323 BCE) was a Macedonian who was tutored by the Greek philosopher Aristotle. Alexander became one of the greatest conquerors in history. Alexander was the son of Philip of Macedon, who had united the various Greek city-states into one kingdom. When Philip died, these states again sought independence but they were conquered and reunited by Alexander. Alexander **expanded his empire** to the east and south, reaching as far as Egypt and India. At its peak, Alexander's empire covered most of the known world.

As Alexander conquered and moved through foreign regions, he increased his forces by absorbing foreign officers and soldiers into his own army. He also encouraged his own soldiers to marry into local populations. This **policy of inclusion and expansion** had the effect of bringing Greek culture to the East with its ideals of learning and inquiry. Alexander founded the city of Alexandria in Egypt, which became a major center of learning. Alexander was affected by Persian culture after he conquered part of that region and, for a time, took to wearing Persian-style clothing and adopting some of the Persians' customs, which made him unpopular with some Greeks.

Alexander died mysteriously at the age of 33, after a sudden illness. He left no heir, and his empire was split into four kingdoms. He had conquered the **Persian Empire**, creating the most important empire to date in history, and his Hellenizing policies made Greek culture the predominant force in the empire. His reputation persisted, and Greek culture in general served as the inspiration for the Roman leaders who would eventually recreate much of his empire in the following centuries. The conquests of Alexander the Great spread Greek ideas to the areas he conquered.

Greek **philosophers** contributed to the field of philosophy. **Socrates** is credited with laying the foundations of Western philosophical thought. His method of questioning and answering to arrive at a conclusion is called the **Socratic method**.

Plato and **Aristotle** were students of Socrates. Aristotle is considered "the father of political science" because of his development of systems of political order, a scientific system to study justice and political order. Plato founded one of the first schools.

Ancient Rome

Rome was one of the early cities on the Italian peninsula conquered by the **Etruscans** who ruled Rome until 509 BCE when the Roman Republic overthrew the monarchy. The period prior to the establishment of the republic remains a mystery to modern historians. However, it is known that Rome was composed of three tribes, each divided into clans. Clans were composed of groups of families. There was a division into a class of nobles and the class of commoners very early.

The nobles, called **patricians** (fathers), appear to have been the privileged class that functioned as an advisory council to the king and had certain political rights. There was no protective function in the government, and thus there was no army. Protection of the citizenry was the responsibility of the father of the family, who was also the priest of the religious cult of the home.

The father was also a patron to commoner clients. In exchange for services to the family, these clients were given political and legal protection. The family unit, then, was composed of the family itself, free clients, and slaves who were taken captives in wars of conquest.

The early kings were elected by the nobles and ruled with supreme power in legal matters and in time of war. The kings were advised by the council, or Senate, which was composed of thirty senators (ten from each tribe).

The Roman Republic

The primary factors that led to the overthrow of the last king and the establishment of the Roman Republic appear to been: (1) a desire to be free of the Etruscans; (2) a desire to put an end to the tyranny of the last king; and (3) the kind of political evolution that occurred elsewhere as the noble classes want to cast aside the control of the monarch and establish an aristocratic form of government.

The factors that enabled the Romans to conquer Italy were:

- Geographical location in the center of the peninsula with no mountain barriers
- A sturdy citizen army and superior military tactics
- The disunity of their enemies
- The use of a superior form of imperialism, by which military veterans settled in conquered areas, providing structure and guidance that allowed self-government to local peoples
- A highly disciplined family structure with a very powerful father
- A superior form of government, the republic

The structure of the early Roman Republic was clearly aristocratic. The nobles subjugated the commoners and dominated both the consuls and the Senate. In 450 BCE, a written law gave new rights to the common people—the right to popular assembly, the creation of *tribunes* to protect the rights of all citizens, and the creation of special new officials (judges and treasury officials) who were to make government more fair and more efficient. By 287 BCE, nobles and commoners were permitted to intermarry and commoners were allowed to hold public offices.

For approximately the next 275 years there was great **expansion**. This involved numerous wars of conquest. The Romans began their quest to become a great power after 300 BCE. They wanted to conquer territory but the Phoenician settlement of Carthage (in present-day Tunisia) was in the path of expansion because it was the largest power in the Mediterranean. Carthage had a strong naval fleet and controlled Sicily, which the Romans wanted in their expanded territory. A series of three wars took place between Rome and Carthage. The wars are known as the **Punic Wars** because "Punic" means "Carthaginian" in the Latin language. Rome defeated Carthage in the Third Punic War and became a powerful city.

After the fall of Carthage, Rome began a period of constant expansion, eventually controlling all of the Greek territories and reached as far north as Gaul (present-day France, Luxembourg, Belgium, Switzerland, parts of Germany and the Netherlands, and northern Italy). A period of brief **civil wars** in which various military leaders attempted to control Rome occurred in the first century BCE.

By 100 BCE, Rome controlled most of the Hellenistic world. This rapid conquest was one of the factors in the decline of the Republic. The republic did not have the infrastructure to absorb the conquered people. In addition, there was political decay, vast economic and social change, and military failure. In politics, the Senate refused to grant rights to the mass of the populace. A civil war erupted between rival factions. And, lacking adequate infrastructure, Rome was unable to provide good government to conquered territories. **Heavy taxation** of these territories, **oppression** by the government, and **corrupt resident government officials** led to decay.

Critical social and economic changes included the ruin of small farmers by **importing slaves** from conquered areas, a vast **migration** of the poor to the city of Rome, a failure to encourage and invest in industry and trade, the dissatisfaction of the new business class, and a general decline in morale among all classes of citizens. At the same time, the republic experienced a vast slave uprising in southern Italy and faced the first attacks from **Germanic invaders.**

The end of the Republic was marked by two significant power struggles. The first was the grasp of power by the **First Triumvirate** in 59 BCE. The First Triumvirate consisted of Caesar, Pompey, and Crassus. Caesar eliminated Pompey and attempted to establish a dictatorship. Caesar made many reforms, including reducing the power of the Senate, but he was killed in the Senate in 44 BCE.

The following year experienced the rise of the **Second Triumvirate,** which was composed of Octavian, Mark Antony, and Lepidus. Octavian (later called Augustus) emerged victorious from the ensuing power struggle in 31 BCE.

The Roman Empire

In 27 CE, **Octavian (Augustus)** became emperor and reunited the Roman Empire, creating a period of **peace** and prosperity that lasted for two centuries. From 1 to 250 CE, **uprisings and internal strife** began to weaken the structure of the Roman Empire. Octavian established a "disguised monarchy" in which he appeared to share power with the Senate but in which he withheld most power. He established the boundaries of Rome on the Rhine and Danube rivers, improved government, and extended citizenship rights to all Roman soldiers. The power of the emperor was gradually enlarged by his successors. The height of the empire was achieved under "the five good emperors"—Nerva, Trajan, Hadrian, Antoninus Pius, and Marcus Aurelius.

The major contributions of the Roman Empire were:

- Peace and prosperity (the *Pax Romana*)
- The codification of Roman law
- A unified empire that allowed much self-government to component city-states
- The introduction of the idea of separation of powers and popular sovereignty
- The development of the "science" of public administration
- Formalized methods of tax collection
- Construction of an extensive civil service program
- Tolerance and the granting of citizenship rights to all inhabitants
- Engineering and construction of excellent roads, bridges, aqueducts, and sanitation systems
- Construction of massive buildings—coliseums, public baths, and basilicas
- Architectural innovations such as the use of vaults and arches
- Preservation of Greek artistic techniques
- Development of education
- Refinement of rhetoric
- Literature: Cicero, Caesar, Lucretius, Virgil, Juvenal, Livy, Plutarch
- Extension of philosophy in the Greek tradition

Pompeii was destroyed by a volcanic eruption and famine and disease began to spread. Weak emperors began to lose control of the vast empire from 250 to 500 CE when there were various migrations and attacks by nomadic peoples, including the **Huns and the Goths**, who eventually destroyed the great empires.

In 284 CE, Emperor **Diocletian** divided the Roman Empire into Eastern and Western sections. The influence of Christianity and the **founding of Constantinople** moved power to the eastern part of the empire. Germanic and Slavic peoples infiltrated and conquered much of the Roman Empire, and the Western Empire collapsed in 476 CE.

The Persian Empire

During the period between 490 and 331 BCE, the Persian Empire in western Asia was **weakened by strife and rebellion**. Darius I of Persia attacked Athens and other Greek cities but was defeated at Marathon. In 331 BCE, Alexander the Great defeated Darius III and ended the Persian Empire. During the struggle for succession after Alexander's death, most of western Asia became part of the Seleucid Empire. About one hundred years later, the Parthian dynasty was founded. This dynasty lasted about five hundred years, holding off Rome and controlling the Silk Road that linked China and Rome.

By the end of the fourth century CE, Persia reached from the Euphrates to the Indus. Social stability in the empire was fostered by a strong bureaucracy, a healthy agricultural economy, and the state religion of **Zoroastrianism.**

Persia posed a threat to Rome's interest in Asia, and the two were in conflict for two hundred years, especially over Armenia. In the fifth century Persia was attacked by the "White Huns" but the Persian Empire survived. By the end of the seventh century, all of western Asia had been overrun by Arabian armies that spread the Islamic Empire.

The Byzantine Empire

The **Byzantines** (the eastern, Greek-speaking Roman Empire) and the **Saracens** (the common Greek name for Arabs) had civilizations that were dominated by religion (Christian Orthodox and Islam, respectively). The Byzantine Empire prevented Islamic Saracen expansion into Europe for centuries after the fall of the Western Roman Empire.

The years between 350 to 500 CE saw vast **migrations and invasions**. The migrations occurred for a number of reasons, including famine, population density, and the search for a better life. Major migrating groups included the Huns, Goths, Ostrogoths, Visigoths, Alans, Vandals, Burgundians, Franks, Jutes, Angles, Saxons, Irish, and Picts. By 526 CE, the map of Europe had been completely redrawn by migrations.

Southeast Asia and the Chinese Empire

Until 250 BCE, the Russian steppe was occupied by **nomads** who hunted and herded animals and practiced agriculture with their chieftains, possibly acting as middlemen in the trade between Europe and China. Alexander invaded northwestern India. Greek and Indian cultures blended, and much of **Southeast Asia** fell under Indian cultural influence as Hinduism and Buddhism spread eastward. Korea came to be controlled by small local states. Japan became a unified state.

China was absorbed by **internal conflict**. By 220 CE, the Chinese Empire had collapsed and regional warlords had created three kingdoms. China remained divided for more than three hundred years. China was reunited under the Jin dynasty, which retained control over southern China. Northern China was invaded several times by nomads. During the period of political uncertainty, Buddhism flourished, and many people were drawn to the monastic life. China's internal struggles came to an end with the rise of the Tang and Song dynasties after 618 CE.

Africa

Egypt was conquered by Alexander the Great and the Greeks ruled Egypt until the Romans defeated Carthage in the Third Punic War and brought North Africa into the Roman Empire. In 31 BCE, Octavian's army defeated Antony and Cleopatra, and Egypt became a Roman province.

Between 1 and 250 CE, Egypt underwent remarkable economic recovery under Roman rule. As ancient Egyptian cults and traditions declined, **Christianity** found many converts in Egypt. The Romans extended their control to the Berber kingdoms and Mesopotamia.

About 100 CE, **Alexandria** (Egypt) emerged as a center of Christian scholarship and became the seat of one of the first Christian bishops. Christianity spread westward to Roman provinces, and between 250 and 500, Christian Egypt linked the Mediterranean world with the various kingdoms of the Upper Nile.

Camels revolutionized the **trans-Sahara trade** in West Africa, and the Berber nomads dominated the trade, bringing West African gold, ivory, and ostrich feathers to the Mediterranean coast. The Phoenician city of Carthage controlled the trans-Sahara trade.

From 311 to 400 CE, the **Christian Donatist controversy** led African bishops to rebel against the Christian church. The controversy stemmed from the issue of whether certain people should be accepted back into the church after a period of persecutions took place in the fourth century. The controversy was centered in Roman Africa. In 397, the Berbers rebelled against Roman rule. Later, in 429, nomadic Vandals invaded North Africa from Spain, resulting in the fall of Roman Carthage in 439 and the establishment of a North African Vandal Kingdom.

The Americas

Between 500 BCE and 600 CE the Adena **mound-building culture** in North America merged into the Hopewell culture. Distinct local cultures emerged in Central and South America. The early **Zapotec** culture was flourishing, and the **Mayans** and Zapotecs continued to flourish until 900 CE. **Teotihuacan** in Mexico became one of the most populous cities in the world. The inhabitants of Teotihuacan controlled production and distribution of obsidian, and constructed the Pyramid of the Sun, the third largest pyramid in the Americas. The Mayan civilization, the only fully literate culture in pre-Columbian America, also built pyramids.

The **Nazca** culture lived along the coast in southern Peru and the **Moche** lived on Peru's northern coast. The Moche civilization thrived and expanded through military conquest.

SKILL 1.3   **Understand major political, economic, and cultural developments in the civilizations of Africa (e.g., Egypt, sub-Sahara), the Mediterranean Basin (e.g., Greece, Rome), Mesoamerica (e.g., Maya), Andean South America (e.g., the Inca tradition), the Middle and Near East, and Asia (e.g., India, China, Japan).**

Africa

Sub-Sahara

The civilizations **south of the Sahara** refined and developed the use of iron, especially for farm implements and later for weapons. They traded overland, using camels and they also traded at important seaports. Their **trading activities** were probably the most important factor in the spread of and assimilation of different ideas and the stimulation of cultural growth.

Egypt

Egypt became an organized and important Hellenistic kingdom after it was conquered by Alexander the Great. It became a Roman province in 31 BCE after the Egyptian army was defeated. The country exported grain to Italy during Roman rule. Alexandria was an important **commercial and cultural center** and stimulated cultural growth. Egypt became an important center of Christianity for groups that opposed the church in Constantinople.

Mediterranean Basin

Greece

Greece reached the pinnacle of the classical period in the fifth century BCE. Greece was built on the foundations laid by the Egyptians, Phoenicians, Minoans, and Mycenaeans. It contributed the Greek **alphabet,** which was derived from Phoenician letters. This alphabet later formed the basis for the Roman alphabet and our present-day alphabet. Extensive **trading and colonization** resulted in the spread of the Greek civilization. The Greek love of sports, with emphasis on a sound body, led to the tradition of the **Olympic Games.**

The Greeks influenced the Western traditions of **drama**, **lyric poetry**, and the **epic**. Their fables and myths centered on gods and goddesses and were later adopted by the Roman culture. The Greeks discovered ways to understand disease and developed the basis of **scientific medicine**. They developed theories about astronomy, mathematics, and philosophy. Doric, Ionic, and Corinthian were orders of **architecture** developed by the Greeks, and columns in each style remain classic today. The Greeks also invented **democracy**.

Eratosthenes calculated the circumference of the earth, and the difference between his calculations and those made in present times that referred to the distance between the earth and the sun differed only by one percent.

Homer, the Greek poet, is considered to be the founder of geography because of all the geographical details in his works, the *Iliad* and the *Odyssey*.

Rome

The **Etruscans** absorbed and modified Greek civilization. Such elements of the Greek culture as writing, certain religious practices, and engineering skills were passed on to the Roman peoples during the rule of the Etruscans.

The **religion** of the early Romans was animistic. The Romans believed that a spirit/soul inhabited everyone and everything. The spirits/souls were not personified or anthropomorphic until just prior to the birth of the republic. The religion absorbed a number of Greek and Etruscan elements. The household religion was devoted to household gods, called *lares* and *penates,* who were believed to protect the household. Ancestors were worshiped and their death masks were maintained in an in-house chapel.

Byzantine and Saracen Civilizations

Contributions of the **Byzantines** included written religious literature and preservation of the Greek language. The Byzantines (Christians) made important contributions in art and the preservation of Greek and Roman achievements, including **architecture** (especially in Eastern Europe and Russia), the **Code of Justinian**, and Roman law. The major contributions of the Saracens were in the areas of science and philosophy, including accomplishments in astronomy, mathematics, physics, chemistry, medicine, literature, art, agriculture, trade, and manufacturing. These advances had a marked influence on the Renaissance period of European history.

Mesoamerica and Andean South America

In **Mesoamerica**, the **Mayans** developed a written language and a calendar. Trading and cultural exchanges were instrumental in developing their art and architecture.

In **Andean South America**, the Nazca culture communicated through symbols and markings on pottery because they did not have a written language as the Mayans did. The Nazca built an irrigation system that consisted of underground channels that carried water for agricultural purposes. Some of the channels are in existence and continue to work today. Their civilization had begun to decline about 500 CE. The Nazca culture drew lines referred to as Nazca lines (geoglyphs) that were carved into the surface of the southern Peruvian desert. The Moche civilization was known for beautiful murals, pottery, and gold work. They also used irrigation systems for agricultural purposes. The Moche culture declined about 500 CE. Later, from the 1430s to 1530s CE, the Incas formed the largest empire in Andean South America.

Asia, the Middle East, and Near East

In **India,** Hinduism was a continuing influence along with the rise of Buddhism. The Ganges River, which is 1,560 miles long and runs northeast through India across the plains to the Bay of Bengal in Bangladesh, is considered to be the most sacred river in India according to the Hindus. **China** is considered by some historians to be the oldest, uninterrupted civilization in the world because it was in existence around the same time as the ancient civilizations in Egypt, Mesopotamia, and the Indus Valley. The Chinese studied nature and weather and stressed the importance of education, family, and a strong central government. Buddhism, Confucianism, and Taoism—each of which emphasized harmony between man and nature—influenced the Chinese. The Chinese invented things such as gunpowder, modern paper, printing, and the magnetic compass.

In 221 BCE, the Qin dynasty unified China, and the ruler took the title of "First Emperor." In 210, there were widespread revolts after his death. The Han dynasty achieved power and became prosperous through a state monopoly of iron and salt. The Han dynasty also opened the Silk Road to Central Asia.

The Chinese began building the Great Wall in 221 BCE as a defense against nomadic infiltration and attack. In 136 BCE, **Confucianism** became the state religion of China.

Japan imported rice cultivation from the Korean peninsula. As Japan became a unified state, it began to import weapons and other manufactured items from China. Japan adopted a code of laws similar to China's, and as the Japanese used, accepted, and copied Chinese art, law, architecture, dress, and writing. The Japanese incorporated the religion of **Buddhism** into their culture.

The **Near East** consisted of Mesopotamia, Syria, and Lebanon. Today the area is referred to as the **Middle East.** Industry and commerce developed along with extensive trading among the countries. Outstanding advances in the fields of science and medicine were made along with early advances in navigation and maritime enterprises.

SKILL 1.4   Apply knowledge of the location, political organization, cultural characteristics, and contributions of ancient civilizations.

Athenian democracy was a direct form of democracy, with every male citizen above the age of twenty being able to vote in the legislative assembly. The assembly was made up of a minimum of six thousand members who voted on proposals made by a council of five hundred citizens, who were chosen by lot. Within the council of five hundred, one person was chosen each day to serve as the head of state. Trials were held by jury, without judges, with jurors being chosen from the pool of citizens. Athenian democracy differed from representative democracy in that each voter had the right to vote directly on public issues and no formal leaders were elected.

The concept of "one person, one vote" was the basis of **Greek democracy** and is still the primary ideal behind all modern democracies. Direct democracy after the Greek method has not survived as a national form of government although smaller groups, such as town meetings, still practice a form of direct democracy over some matters. The Greeks provided the philosophy of democracy, but the modern form of national democratic government owes much to the Romans.

Democracy in the **Roman Republic** was an indirect form. Citizens were classified into groups based on economic status or tribal affiliation and were allowed to vote within that group. The majority vote of the group then determined how the group would vote in the assembly.

There were three voting assemblies in the Roman Republic—the Curiate Assembly, which was made up of elite Romans; the Centuriate Assembly, which was made up of elite and common citizens; and the Tribal Assembly, which represented all citizens and conducted most trials. The Roman Republic also had a Senate made up of appointees who served for life. The Senate had no direct legislative power but was nonetheless influential in its ability to recommend or oppose action by the assemblies. The highest elected office in the Roman Republic was consul. Two consuls were elected by the Centuriate Assembly annually, each with veto power over the other's actions. The consuls held considerable administrative power, and acted as military leaders in times of war.

Like the Roman Republic, the **United States** has an indirect form of democratic government with representative assemblies, including a Senate, whose members serve for six-year terms, and the more "common" House of Representatives, whose members serve two-year terms. Instead of consuls, the United States has a president who oversees the executive function of the country and represents the nation to the world. The president is elected in a national election but it is the Electoral College, overseen by the Senate that formally elects the national leader. Unlike the early Roman Republic, the United States has established a permanent independent court system. Unlike the complex Roman system that had conflicting powers among the various political bodies that made it difficult for one body to gain complete control over the others, the American system has built into it a series of "checks and balances" that ensures that no one branch of the government will become dominant.

COMPETENCY 2: WORLD HISTORY FROM 600 TO 1450 CE

THE TEACHER UNDERSTANDS SIGNIFICANT HISTORICAL EVENTS, DEVELOPMENTS, AND TRADITIONAL POINTS OF REFERENCE IN WORLD HISTORY FROM 600 TO 1450 CE.

SKILL 2.1   **Demonstrate knowledge of individuals, events, issues, and traditional points of reference that shaped the development of world civilizations from 600 to 1450 CE (e.g., Mongol conquests, the founding of Islam, Charlemagne, the Norman Conquest, Silk Road).**

The Age of Empires: 600–1000 CE

Europe and Africa

From 500 to 1000 CE, the Franks became the most powerful of the Germanic tribes. Constantinople became the Christian capital of the Byzantine Empire, and the emperor Justinian reconquered North Africa and most of Italy, although most of this territory was lost to the Islamic Empire or to Slavic peoples over the next two hundred years. **Charlemagne** brought most of Western Europe into a single kingdom of Franks. Charlemagne is known as the "father of Europe," and after his death the empire was divided into three parts—the Saxon Kingdom, the Holy Roman Empire, and the Carolingian Empire. In 711, the Arabs conquered Spain.

In 969 CE, Fatimid rulers of North Africa declared Egypt independent of Baghdad and made Cairo the capital. Kingdoms of West Africa become prosperous on caravans that crossed the Sahara to provide gold to Arabs. Arab trading settlements reached Zanzibar and Madagascar.

The Middle East and Asia

The teachings of Islam were developed by the prophet **Muhammad,** who was born in 570 CE. The year 622 is designated by non-Muslims as the **founding of Islam.** The word "Islam" means "to surrender or submit" and it is to the will of Allah that Muslims submit because of the belief that Allah is the creator of the world. The Quran is the sacred text of the Muslims that contains the teachings of Muhammad. Saudi Arabia, and more particularly Mecca, is recognized as the birthplace of Islam.

In 656 CE, Arabians overran Persia. The Umayyad dynasty began in 661 with Damascus as the center of the Islamic Empire. In 698, Arabs captured Carthage. In 750, the Abbasid dynasty came to power in the Islamic Empire but its legitimacy and authority were not universally accepted. Persian administrators were ruling much of the Islamic Empire. By 969, the **Byzantine Empire** peaked under a new dynasty of Macedonian rulers who came into conflict with the Arabs and regained control of Anatolia and Antioch.

After centuries of conflict, China was united by the Sui dynasty in 581 CE. From 581 to 617 CE, Chinese territory was expanded into Central Asia, and the Chinese gained control of most of the **Silk Road.** The Silk Road was not just one road but a series of routes across Asia that traders used to market goods. In addition to linking areas economically, the routes were also channels for communication and transmitting culture. The routes composing the Silk Road were about four thousand miles in length and they connected China with Persia, Europe, India, and Arabia. The Chinese expanded the length of the Great Wall to protect the goods and traders who used the route.

The Tang dynasty began in 618. During the eighth century, an internal rebellion weakened the Tang dynasty, which eventually collapsed in the ninth century. From 960 to 979, China was divided into ten separate states until it was reunified by the Song dynasty. Buddhism reached **Japan** from China in 538. Under Chinese influence, Japan underwent a series of reforms— abolishing slavery, adopting a modified form of written Chinese, and creating a civil service. Japan and Korea were governed by strong Buddhist dynasties by 1000.

The Americas

Between 500 and 750 CE, two cities emerged in **South America**—the city of Tiahuanaco, near Lake Titicaca, and Huari, which was well fortified. In about 1200, Incas settled in the Andean valley and local rulers organized independent states. The Incas began territorial expansion and continued until in 1438. Thirty years later, the kingdom covered 2,500 miles along the Andes and the west coast of South America, and all settlements were linked by a system of roads. The Incas were consolidating their empires when the first European contact occurred.

In **Central America**, Teotihuacan collapsed, yet it remained a pilgrimage center until the Spanish conquest in the sixteenth century. From 750 to 1000 CE, the Mayan civilization began to decline. The Toltecs migrated into central Mexico and developed a state. The Chimu rose to prominence with their capital at Chan Chan and were ruled by semidivine kings. The empire expanded by military conquest, exerting firm economic control of conquered territories and linking them with a system of roads. In Central America, Chichimec tribes sacked the Toltec city of Tula and established several small city-states that were constantly at war with one another. By the 1200s, many city-states were competing for power in central Mexico. People entered the Mexican region, laying the foundation for what would become the Aztec Empire. The Aztec Empire reached its height in the later 1400s, and through trade, its influence extended across most of Central America to the pueblo farmers north of the Rio Grande River.

In **North America**, the Pueblo culture began about 700 CE. The Mogollon, Anasazi, and Hohokam cultures emerged and they built pueblos in the desert canyons. In 750 CE, the first towns appeared in the Mississippi Valley, and in 900 CE, an advanced culture was developed by the Inuit of

Alaska. In about 1000, **Leif Ericson** (son of Eric the Red) sailed from Greenland to North America. North America's first true towns were established in the Mississippi Valley. Around 1100, the Anasazi (a Navajo word meaning "enemy ancestors") of the Southwest built cliff dwellings at Mesa Verde and Chaco Canyon. During the 1200s, the woodland peoples east of the Mississippi River built increasingly elaborate ceremonial centers. In 1492, **Columbus** landed in Cuba and Hispaniola.

The Era of Trade, Conflict, and Exploration: 1000–1450 CE

During the first millennium, **navigation of the seas** became possible. Three civilizations explored the seas and used the seas to reach and claim new territories. The Vikings used the rivers of Russia to reach the Black Sea and crossed the Atlantic to Iceland and North America. The Arabs discovered a sea route to China in the eighth century and began a new age of trade. They also reached the East Indies and East Africa. The Polynesians expanded from island to island throughout the Pacific, colonizing every island by the year 1000.

Religious conflict and **territorial wars** were intense in many parts of the world. As marginal land was cleared for agriculture, populations expanded and demanded new territory. **Trade routes** developed across Europe and Asia, and a mercantile economy developed. The growth of Christianity in Europe caused conflict with the Islamic Empire and led to the Crusades which were military efforts to regain or control the Holy Land between 1050 and 1350. For the most part, the Crusades were not successful, but Christian progress was made in Spain and Portugal. Northern India fell into Muslim control, and Buddhism was driven from the Indian subcontinent. Nomadic invasions from the north of China shrank the Song Empire.

In 1066, the Normans under the leadership of **William, Duke of Normandy**, invaded England. William believed himself to be the heir apparent to the English throne and decided the invasion was necessary when he was denied the throne. William defeated English troops at the **Battle of Hastings.** The **Norman conquest** and subsequent victory were significant because they brought a French-speaking monarch to the throne and infused new concepts into the English language and culture. The defeat of the English resulted in more connections to the French and to continental Europe. In 1091, the Normans conquered Sicily.

In Asia, in the thirteenth century, **Genghis Khan,** a Mongol horseman, and others emerged from Central Asia and began to conquer large regions of Eastern Europe and Asia. The **Mongol conquest** resulted in a huge empire. By 1300, the empire had split into four large empires reaching from China to Eastern Europe. The Mongol attacks were particularly destructive in China and in the Islamic states of southwest Asia. Once the Mongols controlled these regions, however, trade and travel were restored. The Muslim Abbasid Caliphate was ended, but Islam continued to spread as it was adopted by the Mongols. New Muslim states arose in Egypt and India. Europe continued to try to defend itself against both Muslim and Mongol incursions. Venice and Genoa flourished because of trade connections with the East.

Epidemics of bubonic plague moved from China and Korea to the west coast of Europe. Massive deaths led to economic and social devastation that weakened states throughout Europe, Asia, and North Africa. The "Little Ice Age" (which lasted until the nineteenth century) brought bad weather to these plague-devastated areas, causing poor harvests. Mongol empires began to decline and crumble in many areas. The Khanate of the Golden Horde, however, continued to rule in southern Russia until the fifteenth century.

In China and Persia, the Mongols were assimilated into the local populations. In China, the Ming dynasty introduced a Han Chinese aristocratic regime. Imperial expansion, mass migration, cross-cultural trade, and long-distance travel enabled the **spread of agricultural crops**, domesticated animals, and diseases. Chinese rulers extended their authority south of the Yangtze River. Muslim armies penetrated India, Persia, and North Africa. Bantu-speaking peoples migrated throughout the sub-Saharan Africa. The exchange of culture and biology dramatically changed societies throughout the eastern hemisphere.

The **Ottoman Empire** began in 1299 when Osman I declared independence for the Turkish principalities that gathered under his name. The Ottoman state followed a policy of steady expansion and was soon encroaching on the borders of the **Byzantine Empire**. In 1453, under the command of their leader Mehmed II, the **Ottomans captured Istanbul**, which later became the capital of the growing empire.

SKILL 2.2   **Demonstrate knowledge of major developments in the civilizations of Africa (e.g., Egypt, sub-Sahara), Mesoamerica (e.g., Aztec tradition), Andean South America (e.g., Inca tradition), Europe (including Western and Eastern), and Asia (e.g., Islamic civilization, China, India, Japan).**

Africa

Sub-Sahara

During the fourteenth and fifteenth centuries, the Islamic Empire experienced great expansion. The conquest of areas in the **sub-Sahara,** such as Ghana by Muslim Berbers in 1076, permitted rule to devolve to a series of lesser successor states. The Mali Empire conquered the Kingdom of Ghana in the 1250s and took control of the West African gold and slave trade with huge camel caravans crossing the Sahara to North Africa.

In 1150, the Zagwe dynasty emerged in Ethiopia and revived sea trade.

In 1324, Mansa Musa (the Mali ruler) made a pilgrimage to Mecca and word spread about his wealth. Swahili cities in East Africa escaped the plague but suffered economically due to a slowdown of trade. In 1344, Ethiopia was at its height.

The Mali Empire

By the thirteenth century, the successor state of Kangaba established the **Kingdom of Mali.** This vast trading state extended from the Atlantic coast of Africa to beyond Gao on the Niger River in the east.

Islamic scholars preserved much of the history of Mali after the Mali rulers converted to Islam. These scholars were responsible for the spread of Islam throughout Africa. The expansion of the Mali Kingdom began from the city of Timbuktu and gradually moved downstream along the Niger River. This provided increasing control of the river and the cities along its banks that were critical for both travel and trade. The Niger River was a central link in trade for both West African and North African trade routes.

Military power and trade held the government of the Mali Kingdom together. The kingdom was organized into a series of feudal states that were ruled by a king. Most of the kings used the surname Mansa (meaning "sultan"). The most powerful and effective of the kings was Mansa Musa.

The religion and culture of the Kingdom of Mali was a blend of Islamic faith and traditional African belief. The influence of the Islamic Empire provided the basis of a large and structured government that allowed the king to expand both territory and influence. The people, however, did not follow strict Islamic law. The king was thought of in traditional African fashion as a divine ruler removed from the people. A strong military, control of the Niger River, and control of the trade that flourished along the river enabled Mali to build a strong feudal empire.

Farther to the east, the king of the **Songhai** people had converted to Islam in the eleventh century. Songhai was at one time a province of Mali. By the fifteenth century, Songhai was stronger than Mali, and it emerged as the next great power in western Africa. Songhai was situated on the great bend of the Niger River. From the early fifteenth to the late sixteenth century, the Songhai Empire stood as one of the largest empires in the history of Africa. The first king, Sonni Ali, conquered many neighboring states, including the Mali Empire.

This gave him control of the trade routes and cities, including Timbuktu. Askia Mohammad, who initiated political reform and revitalization, succeeded him. Askia Mohammad also created religious schools, built mosques, and opened his court to scholars and poets from all parts of the Muslim world.

During the same period, the Zimbabwe Kingdom was built. "Great Zimbabwe" was the largest of about three hundred stone structures in the area. This capital city and trading center of the Kingdom of Makaranga was built between the twelfth and fifteenth centuries. Makaranga is believed to have housed as many as twenty thousand people. The structures were built entirely of stone, without mortar. The scanty evidence available suggests that the kingdom was a trading center and that is was part of a trading network that reached as far as China.

In 1050, Berber Muslim Almoravids controlled northwest Africa and part of Muslim Spain. The Berbers invaded Ghana in 1076, and in 1147 another Berber religious group, the Almohad, took control and unified the Maghreb (North African states, except Egypt, that bordered the Mediterranean Sea).

Swahili city-states on the East African coast exported goods through Indian Ocean trade routes. Rulers of Mali and Swahili city-states adopted Islam and built mosques and religious schools.

Islam did not reach central or southern Africa but trade led to the development of several wealthy states such as the Kingdom of Great Zimbabwe.

In 1270, the Christian Kingdom of Ethiopia was expanding. In the fourteenth century, the Mali Empire dominated West Africa because its empire was based on trade of gold and slaves for salt, textiles, horses, and manufactured goods from the north.

In 1390, the Kingdom of Kongo was formed.

The Portuguese explored the west coast of Africa where African rulers had laid the foundations for the Akan and Benin states. Sailors from the Swahili states in East Africa helped Vasco da Gama understand local monsoon winds and finish his voyage to India.

Egypt

In 1174, Saladin became ruler of Egypt, ending the Fatimid dynasty and founding the Ayyubid dynasty. In 1250, the Mamluk military caste took over Egypt.

Asia

Islamic Civilization

In the eleventh century the Byzantine Empire lost much of its Asian territory to the Seljuk Turks. In 1055, Islamic Turks became established in Baghdad and formed a partnership with Persians and Arabs. In 1099, the first Crusade retook Jerusalem and established small crusader states. In 1187, Muslims led by Saladin and others reclaimed Jerusalem. Mongols sacked Baghdad and overthrew the Abbasid Caliphate in 1258, establishing themselves as Il-Khans, subordinate to the Great Khan in China. By 1300, most of the people in these areas had accepted Islam.

In 1299, Osman founded the Ottoman state. In the late fourteenth century, the Turkish warrior Timur claimed a large empire in Central Asia, invaded India, and was planning to attack China. However, he died. The Ottoman Empire expanded during the fourteenth century but by 1400, the Byzantine Empire was reduced to Constantinople and a few coastal areas in Greece and western Anatolia. In 1347, the plague reached Baghdad and Constantinople. In 1405, Timur's sons divided his empire. At this time, the Shi'ite Safavids were a new power that was rising in Persia. In 1453, the Ottomans captured Constantinople and ended the Byzantine Empire.

The Ottoman Empire united a highly varied population as it grew through conquest and treaty arrangement. This unification is attributable to military strength, a policy of strict control of recently invaded territories, and an **Islamic-inspired philosophy** that stated that all Muslims, Christians, and Jews were related because they were all "People of the Book." The major religious groups were permitted to construct their own semi-autonomous communities. Conquering armies immediately repaired buildings, roads, bridges, and aqueducts or built them where needed. The armies also built modern sanitary facilities and linked the conquered cities to a supply structure that was able to provide for the needs of the people. This religious and ethnic tolerance was the basis upon which a heterogeneous culture was built. It quickly transformed a Turkish empire into the Ottoman Empire.

Respect for diverse ethnic and cultural groups in time produced a rich mix of people that was reflected in multicultural and multi-religious policies based on recognition and respect for different perspectives. Ottoman architecture, although influenced by Seljuk, Byzantine, and Arab styles, developed a unique style. Ottoman classical music and folk music developed as two primary styles of music, each reflecting a basis in the diversity of influences that came together in the unified empire.

The Mongol Empire

The Mongol Empire was founded by Genghis Khan in 1206 and included the majority of the territory from Southeast Asia to central Europe during the height of the empire. One of the primary military tactics of conquest was to annihilate any cities that refused to surrender.

Government was by decree on the basis of a code of laws developed by Genghis Khan. One of the tenets of this code was that the nobility and the commoners shared the same hardships. The society—and the opportunity to advance within the society—were based on a system of meritocracy. The carefully structured and controlled society was efficient and safe for the people. Religious tolerance was guaranteed. Theft and vandalism were strictly forbidden. Trade routes and an extensive postal system were created, linking the various parts of the empire. Taxes were quite onerous but teachers, artists, and lawyers were exempted from the taxes. Mongol rule was absolute. The response to resistance was collective punishment in the form of destruction of cities and slaughter of the inhabitants.

China

By 1110, Song China was the most advanced, wealthy, and populous state in the world. In 1045, moveable type printing was invented in China. In 1211, Genghis Khan invaded northern China, but the southern Song dynasty did not fall until 1279. In 1264, Kublai Khan became emperor. Six years later he founded the Yuan dynasty. Marco Polo left China in 1292 and two years later Kublai Khan died. During the fourteenth century, plague, floods, and famine raised Chinese resentment of Mongol rule. In 1356, a rebellion that arose in southeast China put the Ming dynasty in power. Mongols were eventually driven out of China.

The Ming dynasty in China was followed the Mongol-led Yuan dynasty. In addition to its expansion of trade and exploration of surrounding regions, the period is well known for its highly talented artists and craftsmen. The Hongwu emperor rose from peasant origins. He distributed land to small farmers in an effort to help them support their families. To further protect these family farms, he proclaimed title of the land non-transferable. He also issued an edict by which those who cultivated wasteland could keep the land as their own property and not ever be taxed. Among the major developments of the time were systems of irrigation for farms throughout the empire. Hongwu maintained a strong army by creating military settlements. During peacetime, each soldier was given land to farm. If he could not afford to purchase equipment, the government provided it.

The legal code created during the period is generally considered one of the greatest achievements of the dynasty. The laws were written in understandable language and in enough detail to prevent misinterpretation. The law reversed previous policy toward slaves and promised them the same protection as free citizens. Great emphasis was placed on family relations. The code was clearly based on Confucian ideas. The other major accomplishment of this dynasty was the decision to begin building the Great Wall of China to provide protection from northern horsemen. During the fifteenth century, the Ming dynasty consolidated its power in China.

Japan

In **Japan,** the emperors had lost power to the Fujiwara family in the mid-twelfth century, triggering a period of internal warfare that ended with the victory of the Minamoto clan as Shoguns. The year 1191 was the beginning of Zen Buddhism in Japan. In 1333, Japan's Kamakura shogunate collapsed. In 1351 the Yellow River had massive floods. In 1392, the Yi dynasty began in Korea.

India

During the eleventh and twelfth centuries the Khmer Empire in India was at its height. During the eleventh century, northern India was repeatedly invaded by Ghazni Muslims of Afghanistan. In 1186, the last Ghazni ruler was deposed by the Turkish leader Muhammad al Ghur. Southeast India was controlled by the Chola dynasty, which also controlled the sea route between west Asia and China. The Khmer Empire and the Kingdom of Pagan experienced a golden age.

In 1206, Qutb al-din and his Islamic raiders, after terrorizing northern India for thirty years, established a new sultanate with its capital at Delhi. During the fourteenth century the sultanate of Delhi reached its greatest extent, but it lost control of most of the peninsula by century's end.

In 1398, Delhi was sacked by Timur. In the fourteenth century, Southeast Asia was increasingly controlled by the Majapahit Empire in Java.

The Mughal Empire reached its height during the reign of Akbar, who is considered to be India's greatest ruler. He began his rule in 1556 and combined a drive for conquest with a magnetic personality and went so far as to invent his own religion, Dinillahi, which was a combination of Islam, Christianity, Zoroastrianism, and Hinduism. In the administration of the empire, Akbar initiated two approaches that are notable. First, he studied local revenue statistics for the various provinces within the empire. He then developed a revenue plan that matched the revenue needs of the empire with the ability of the people to pay the taxes. Although the taxes were heavy (one-third to one-half of the crop), it was possible to collect the taxes and meet the financial needs of the empire. Second, he created a rank-and-pay structure for the warrior aristocracy based on number of troops and their obligations.

Akbar introduced a policy of acceptance and assimilation of Hindus, allowed temples to be built, and abolished the poll tax on non-Muslims. He devised a theory of "rulership as a divine illumination" and accepted all religions and sects. He encouraged widows to remarry, discouraged marriage of children, outlawed the practice of sati (burning of the widow), and persuaded the merchants in Delhi to recognize special market days for women who were otherwise required to remain secluded at home. Policies supported a strong cultural and intellectual life. Akbar sponsored regular debates among religious and scholarly individuals with different points of view.

The unique style of architecture of the Mughal Empire was its primary contribution to South Asia. The Taj Mahal is one of many monuments built during this period. The culture was a blend of Indian, Iranian, and Central Asian traditions. Other major accomplishments were:

- Centralized government
- Blending of traditions in art and culture
- Development of new trade routes to Arab and Turkish lands
- Unique style of architecture
- Landscape gardening
- Unique cuisine
- Creation of two languages (Urdu and Hindi) for the common people

The Americas

Some of the earliest people of record in **Mesoamerica** were the Olmec who left behind little to reveal their existence but for a series of huge, carved figures.

The most advanced Native American civilization was the **Mayan** in Central America. They were the only Native American civilization to develop writing. Their writing consisted of a series of symbols that has still not been completely deciphered. The Mayans built huge pyramids and other stone figures and sculptures, mostly of the gods they worshiped. The Mayan calendar was accurate and was a complex system of distinct calendars. The Mayans also invented the idea of zero, a significant advancement in mathematics. Mayan worship resembled the practices of the Aztec and Inca, although human sacrifices were rare. The Mayans traded heavily with their neighbors.

The **Aztecs** dominated Mesoamerica. The Aztec had access to quantities of metals and jewels. They used the metals to make weapons and the jewels to trade for items. The source of much of the Aztec riches was from conquering neighboring tribes and demanding tribute from them. The Aztec believed in a handful of gods and believed that these gods demanded human sacrifice in order to continue to favor the Aztecs. The center of Aztec society was the great city of Tenochtitlan which was built on an island to make it easier to defend. Tenochtitlan boasted a population of three hundred thousand at the time of the arrival of the conquistadors. Tenochtitlan was known for canals and pyramids, none of which survive today. The city was located a little south of present-day Mexico City.

The **Inca Empire** stretched across a vast period of territory down the western coast of South America and was connected by a series of roads. A series of messengers ran along these roads, carrying news and instructions from the capital, Cuzco. Cuzco was a large city similar to but not as spectacular as Tenochtitlan. The Incas are known for inventing the *quipu,* a string-based device that provided them with a method of keeping records. The Inca Empire, like the Aztec Empire, was very much a centralized state, with all income going to the state coffers and all trade going through the emperor. The Incas worshiped the dead, their ancestors, and nature.

Europe

Western Europe

In the eleventh century, the consolidation of Poland, Hungary, and the Scandinavian regions into the world of western Christianity resulted in a new peak of power and influence. **Western Europeans** began to take control of the Mediterranean area from the Arabs and Byzantines, and a new era of prosperity based on trade began.

In 1016, Canute the Great united England, Denmark, and Norway. The final split between the Roman and Orthodox churches took place in 1054.

Bologna University was founded in 1119. Chartres Cathedral was built in France in 1154. In the thirteenth century, the feudal monarchies of England and France consolidated large regional states. This did not occur in Italy and Germany due to conflicts between church and state. In 1236, Christians took Cordoba and Seville in Spain, leaving only Moorish Granada under Islamic control. The year 1237 marks the beginning of the Mongol conquest of Russia.

Religious divisions brought conflict. Rival popes in Rome and Avignon split the church. The Lollards in England challenged the doctrine and the authority of the Catholic Church. In 1337, the Hundred Years War between England and France began. Ten years later, in 1347, the bubonic plague (Black Death) reached Italy. The fourteenth century was a time of plague and recovery, and the Black Death resulted in many changes, including labor-saving innovations.

The Peasant Revolt occurred in England in 1381. The Union of Kalmar placed Norway, Denmark, and Sweden under a single ruler in 1381.

The fifteenth century marked the beginning of the Renaissance in Italy, and city-states of Italy were the cultural leaders of Europe. Political power shifted to the "New Monarchs" who ruled strong centralized kingdoms in England, France, and Spain.

The Hundred Years War erupted between France and England. Joan of Arc appeared and was burned at the stake in 1431, and the English used cannons for the first time during this war.

Eastern Europe

The **Slavs** lived in what is today southern Russia. It is believed that they moved into **Eastern Europe** and settled in the Balkans, Hungary, and Bohemia and Moravia which later were part of Czechoslovakia in the sixth century. They assimilated into the culture of Western Europe but eventually their lands were invaded by other groups and they did not continue to maintain close contact with other Europeans.

The **Magyars** invaded Eastern Europe in 889, captured Slavic tribes, and occupied their lands. The pronunciation of their name led to the name "Hungary." The Germanic tribes moved east in the ninth and tenth centuries to capture more land. They clashed with the Slavs and Magyars. Many of the Slavic leaders were Greek Orthodox Christians while some of the leaders, in what is today

Hungary, were Roman Catholic. The areas of present-day Russia and Bulgaria were Greek Orthodox while the areas of Poland and Czechoslovakia preferred Roman Catholicism.

The Ottoman Turks and Mongols entered the Slavic area of Russia in the thirteenth century. They also moved into areas occupied by the Polish and Hungarians. The Mongols left the area and returned to the east when they learned their great leader had died. The Slavic influence remained dominant.

SKILL 2.3   **Know how new political, economic, and social systems evolved in Western Europe after the collapse of the Western Roman Empire (e.g., feudalism, manorialism).**

Collapse of the Western Roman Empire

The reasons for the decline of the Roman Empire are still a matter of debate but politics, economics, social issues, and invasions were causes.

The **political reasons** included a period of anarchy and military emperors led to war and destruction. Diocletian reconstructed the empire, establishing a "divine-right" absolute monarchy, a new imperial bureaucracy, and new administrative divisions to lessen the burden of ruling. Diocletian also reorganized the army and established a new efficient, but very oppressive, taxation system. Constantine reunited the empire but moved the capital to the East. All of this reform demoralized the city-states.

There was an increase in the number of large villas owned and controlled by landlords who settled poor people on the land as hereditary tenants who lived under conditions of partial servitude. Other **economic reasons** for the decline of the Roman Empire were the use of wasteful agricultural methods, a decline of commerce, skilled workers who were bound to jobs and forced to accept government wages and prices, corruption, lack of productivity, inadequate investment of capital, and the draining gold resources from the western part of the empire through unfavorable trade balances with the East.

There were a number of biological, ecological, and **social reasons** for the decline of the Roman Empire. These included deforestation, harmful agricultural methods, diseases (particularly malaria), earthquakes, immorality, brutalization of the masses in the cities, demoralization of the upper classes, and the decay of pagan beliefs and Roman ideals with the rise of Christianity.

The beginning of the barbarian infiltrations and **invasions** further weakened the sense of the Roman identity and contributed to an empire that was ill-equipped to contend with invaders.

Feudalism

In feudal societies few people, if any, owned land. Instead, they held it as a hereditary trust from a social or political superior person in return for services. The superiors were a small percentage of the people, a fighting and ruling aristocracy. The vast majority of the people were simply workers. Feudalism was an important aspect of European life from the ninth to fifteenth centuries. One of the largest landowners of the time of feudalism was the Roman Catholic Church. It is estimated that during the twelfth and thirteenth centuries, the church controlled one-third of the useable land in Western Europe.

During this time, the system of feudalism became a dominant feature in the way of life. Feudalism was a system of loyalty and protection. The strong protected the weak, and the weak returned the service with farm labor, military service, and loyalty. Life was lived on vast estates owned by noblemen and their families, called "manors." The manor was a complete village supporting a few hundred people, mostly peasants. Improved tools and farming methods made life more bearable— although most never left the manor nor traveled from their village during their lifetime.

Feudalism was also present in **Japan**. From its feudal beginnings, Japan transformed into an imperial form of government, with the divine emperor as ruler. **Kyoto**, the capital, became one of the largest and most powerful cities in the world. Slowly though, as in Europe, the noble landowners grew powerful. Eventually, the nobles had more power than the emperor, which required an attitude change in the minds of the Japanese people.

The nobles represented the highest social class, were lords of great lands, and were called **Daimyos**. People of lower social classes, including peasants who had few privileges, worked for them. Warriors known as **Shoguns** served the Daimyos, and the Shoguns were answerable only to the Daimyo. The Shogun code of honor was an exemplification of the overall Japanese belief that every man was a soldier and a gentleman.

The main economic difference between imperial and feudal Japan was that the money that continued to flow into the country from trade with China, Korea, and other Asian countries and from plundering on the seas. The money made its way into the pockets of the Daimyos rather than into the emperor's coffers.

Feudalism developed in Japan later than it did in Europe and it lasted longer as well. Japan escaped a huge Mongol invasion which was driven away by the famed **kamikaze**, or "divine wind," in the twelfth century. Japan was thus free to continue to develop in relative isolation until the nineteenth century.

Manorialism

Manorialism also arose during the Middle Ages. It was similar to feudalism in structure but consisted of self-contained manors that were often owned outright noblemen. Some manors were granted conditionally to their lords and some were linked to the military service and oaths of loyalty required in feudalism.

Manors usually consisted of a large house for the lord and his family, were surrounded by fields and a small village that supported the activities of the manor. The lord of the manor was expected to provide certain services for the villagers and laborers associated with the manor, including the support of the church.

Land is a finite resource, and as the population grew in the middle centuries of the Middle Ages, the manorial/feudal system became less and less effective as a system of economic organization.

The end of the manorial system was sealed by the outbreak and spread of the Black Death, which killed over one-third of the total population of Europe. Those who survived and those who were skilled in any job or occupation were in demand. Many serfs and peasants found freedom, which resulted ultimately in a decidedly improved standard of living for them.

Also, coming into importance during the Middle Ages was the era of **knighthood** and its code of chivalry along with the tremendous influence of the Roman Catholic Church. Until the Renaissance, the church was the only place where people could be educated. The **Bible** and other books were hand-copied by monks in the **monasteries**. Cathedrals were built and decorated with art that depicted religious subjects.

With the increase in trade and travel, cities sprang up and began to grow. Craftworkers in the cities developed their skills to a high degree, and they eventually organized **guilds** to protect the quality of the work and to regulate the buying and selling of their products. City government developed and flourished, and government was centered on strong town councils. The wealthy businessmen who made up the rising middle class were active in city government and the town councils.

SKILL 2.4 **Understand the influence exerted by the Roman Catholic Church and the Eastern Orthodox Church in medieval Europe.**

The rise of Christianity in early modern Europe was due as much to the iron hand of feudalism as it was to the church itself. Feudalism, more than any other element, helped the church to dominate Europe. Like the caste system in India, feudalism kept people in strict control according to their social class. Born a peasant, one would likely remain so for a lifetime. The rich and powerful were the highest class in society and maintained close ties to the clergy.

Through its warnings of death and damnation without salvation, the church maintained rigid control of the belief systems of most of the people throughout Europe. Thus, the church was able to assume more than a traditionally religious role in people's lives. Clergy were respected and trusted members of society, and people consulted them on secular matters as well as religious ones.

Also, at this time a desire emerged to travel to the Holy Land, Palestine, and Jerusalem. The church encouraged this, and pilgrimage routes sprang up.

Bordering Eastern Europe was the Byzantine Empire, which was the Eastern Roman Empire. The Roman Empire had been split into two by Emperor Diocletian. Diocletian's successor, Emperor Constantine, changed the name of the eastern capital—Byzantium—and renamed it **Constantinople,** after himself. With the fall of western Rome in 476 CE, the Byzantine emperors, starting with Justinian, attempted to regain the lost western territories. Due to ineffective rulers between the seventh and ninth centuries CE, any gains were completely lost, resulting in the territorial limits reverting to the eastern Balkans of ancient Greece and Asia Minor. The late ninth through eleventh centuries was considered the **Golden Age of Byzantium.**

The Byzantines (Christians) made important contributions in art and in the preservation of Greek and Roman achievements, such as architecture (especially in Eastern Europe and Russia), the Code of Justinian, and Roman law. Byzantium was known for its exquisite artwork, including the famous church Hagia Sophia. Perhaps the most wide-ranging success of the Byzantine Empire was in the area of trade. Uniquely situated on the Bosporus Strait, Byzantium was at the gateway to both West and East. Byzantium could control trade going north to the Black Sea and south to the Aegean and Mediterranean Seas. Indeed, the Eastern Empire was much more centralized and rigid in its enforcement of its policies than the feudal West.

Although Constantine made Christianity the official state religion of Rome, there remained an unresolved conflict between Christian and classical (Roman and Greek) ideals for the Byzantines. There were points of contention between the Pope in Rome and the Patriarch of Constantinople— including the celibacy of priests, language of the Liturgy (Latin in the West, Greek in the East), religious doctrine, and other unresolved issues. These issues led to the **Great Schism** that permanently split the church into the **Roman Catholic Church** and the **Eastern Orthodox Church.**

In a way that governments never could, Christianity unified Europe. With the Pope at the head of the religion, all areas of Europe could correctly be called "Christendom" because people all had the same beliefs, the same worries, and the same tasks to perform in order to achieve the salvation that they sought. The church capitalized on this power, and the power increased throughout the Middle Ages until it met resistance from Martin Luther.

SKILL 2.5 Compare social, political, economic, and religious aspects of medieval Europe with previous civilizations.

The **High Middle Ages** refers to the period in Europe between the Early and Late Middle Ages, spanning approximately the eleventh, twelfth, and thirteenth centuries. The rapid increase in population contributed to dramatic changes in society, culture, and political organization. The concept of the nation state took hold as populations became more stable and people began to think of themselves as belonging to a larger group of ethnically similar cultures.

The "divine right" of kings was the key **political characteristic** of the Age of Absolutism and was most visible in the reign of King Louis XIV of France as well as during the times of English King James I and his son, Charles I. The divine right doctrine claims that kings and absolute leaders derive their right to rule by virtue of their birth alone. They see this both as a law of God and of nature.

In Italy, the independent nation states such as Venice, Pisa, and Florence were established and provided a basis for the **Renaissance**. The concept of inherited nobility gained wide acceptance, and knighthood and chivalry developed as virtuous codes of conduct.

The **Crusades** took place during the High Middle Ages, further strengthening the importance of these orders of knights and solidifying the strength of the western church throughout Europe. As the power and influence of the church grew, it contributed to the growth of art and architecture, particularly in the development of the great Gothic cathedrals, most of which were constructed during this era.

The routes opened by Crusaders marching to Jerusalem opened the way for an increase in **trade** and contributed to the growth of many cities. A merchant class developed and began to exert its influence on political and economic affairs.

Crucial advances in thinking and technology occurred during the High Middle Ages. Improvements in shipbuilding and clock-making led to advances in navigation and cartography, setting the stage for the Age of Exploration. Printing, while not yet to the stage that Gutenberg was to take it in the fifteenth century, expanded the availability of texts serving a growing educated class of people. Thomas Aquinas espoused the philosophy of Scholasticism, which emphasized empiricism and opposed mysticism in Christian education. He combined Aristotelian ideas with Christianity, which helped lay the ideas of modern constitutionalism.

As the concept of the nation state arose, so did the idea of national borders and national sovereignty. This led to numerous wars which, in turn, had deleterious effects on the economy. These events are now used to mark the period of transition between the High Middle Ages and the Late Middle Ages.

SKILL 2.6   Demonstrate knowledge of the political, economic, religious, and social impact of the Crusades and other religious interactions.

The **Crusades** were a series of military campaigns beginning in the eleventh century against the encroaching Islamic Empire, particularly in Palestine and the city of Jerusalem. The Christian Byzantine Empire was centered in Constantinople. The empire was under attack from Seljuk Turk forces that had taken Palestine. The eastern emperor Alexius I called on his western counterpart, Pope Urban II, for assistance. Urban II saw the situation as an opportunity to reunite Christendom, which was still in the throes of schism between the Eastern Orthodox and the Roman Catholic sects and to invest the papacy with greater religious authority.

In 1095, Urban II called on all Christians to rally behind the campaign to drive the Turks out of the Holy Land. Participation in the crusade, the Pope said, would count as full penance for sin in the eyes of the church. A force of crusaders marched to Jerusalem and captured it, massacring the inhabitants. Along the way, several small crusader-states were established. A second crusade was led against Damascus in 1145 but it was unsuccessful.

In 1187, the Sultan of Egypt recaptured Jerusalem and Pope Gregory VIII called for a third crusade. This crusade was joined by the combined forces of France, England, and the Holy Roman Empire but fell short of its goal to recapture Jerusalem.

The fourth crusade took place in 1202, under Pope Innocent III. The intention of this crusade was to enter the Holy Land through Egypt. The plan was changed, however, and forces were diverted to Constantinople.

Crusades continued into the thirteenth century as Jerusalem and other holy cities changed hands between Christian and Muslim forces. Several crusades took place within Europe, as well, and were efforts made to reconquer portions of the Muslim-occupied Iberian Peninsula.

The crusades established and reinforced the political and military authority of the Roman Catholic Church and the Pope. The religious fervor spurred on by the Crusades would eventually culminate in such movements as the Inquisition in Spain and the expulsion of the Moors from Europe. The marches of the crusaders also opened new routes between Europe and the East along which culture, learning, and trade could travel.

COMPETENCY 3   WORLD HISTORY FROM 1450 TO 1750 CE

THE TEACHER UNDERSTANDS SIGNIFICANT HISTORICAL EVENTS, DEVELOPMENTS, AND TRADITIONAL POINTS OF REFERENCE IN WORLD HISTORY FROM 1450 TO 1750 CE.

SKILL 3.1   **Demonstrate knowledge of individuals, events, issues, and traditional points of reference that shaped the development of world civilizations from 1450 to 1750 (e.g., the fall of Constantinople, Martin Luther, the Black Death, Leonardo da Vinci).**

The Development of World Civilizations

During the fifteenth century, Portuguese mariners settled the Atlantic islands, explored the west coast of Africa, and made a sea voyage to India. Columbus crossed from Spain to the Americas where the Aztec and Inca empires ruled over complex agricultural societies. A new era of exploration had begun, paving the way for further expansion. Each of the major cultural regions had its own unique view of the world.

Trade, migration, and cultural and political expansion spread ideas, religions, and technologies. Buddhism, Christianity, and Islam each had wide areas of influence. Mapping was practiced in some form by almost all cultures.

By the eighteenth century new ideas began to emerge in science, philosophy, and politics. The Enlightenment fermented rebellion in many places. Agriculture increased food production which, in turn, fueled population growth. Technological innovations led to the Industrial Revolution and urban growth. European expansion continued, and Britain continued its trade with India that was carried on through the East India Company. Britain also established its power in India and Australia.

Africa

Between 1460 and 1490, the Songhai ruler Sunni Ali conquered Mali and took over the Saharan caravan trade. The Songhai were later defeated by the Ottomans who also gained control of the trans-Saharan caravan trade

The Portuguese explored the west coast of Africa where African rulers had laid the foundations for the Akan and Benin states. Sailors from the Swahili city-states in East Africa helped Vasco da Gama understand local monsoon winds and finish his voyage to India. In 1505, the Portuguese established the first trading posts in East Africa. In 1570, Portugal established a colony in Angola.

Today the Republic of Benin was the site of an early African kingdom known as Dahomey. By the seventeenth century, the kingdom included a large part of West Africa. The kingdom was economically prosperous because of slave-trading relations with Europeans, primarily the Dutch and Portuguese, who arrived in the fifteenth century. The coastal part of the kingdom was known as "the Slave Coast." This kingdom was known for a distinct culture with unusual traditions related to **Dahomean Vodoun**. In 1729, the kingdom started a female army system. A law was passed stating that females would be inspected at the age of fifteen. Women deemed beautiful were sent to the king's palace to become his wives. Those who were sick or considered unattractive were executed. The rest trained as soldiers for two years. Human sacrifice was practiced on holidays and special occasions. Slaves and prisoners of war were sacrificed to gods and ancestors.

The slave trade affected African politics and society in the 1600s. Two million slaves were exported and in 1620, African slaves were taken to the English colony at Jamestown. A Dutch colony was established at the Cape of Good Hope in 1652.

West Asia

The Fall of Constantinople

Constantinople was the capital of the Byzantine Empire in 1453. It had become the capital when Rome fell and it was a large and wealthy city by the 1100s. The city's walls made it a heavily fortified area. In 1453, the Ottoman Turks laid siege to the city. The Ottoman Turks were led by Sultan Mehmed II. His troops consisted of more than one hundred thousand men and they used cannons to open the walls and warships to stop the city's defense of the sea. The siege lasted fifty days before the Turks captured the city. After the capture, the city was renamed Istanbul and it became the Islamic capital.

In 1517, the **Ottomans** conquered Egypt, and the Ottoman navy ruled the Mediterranean Sea until 1571. The Muslims dominated commercial shipping.

South and Southeast Asia

By 1500, most of the eastern hemisphere had recovered from the population losses caused by the plague. In southwest Asia, two Turkish groups established strong empires—the Ottomans in Anatolia, and the Safavids in Persia. European states were beginning to build central governments with standing armies and gunpowder weapons. In 1520, **Suleiman the Magnificent** ruled Ottoman Empire. In 1523, the Chagatai Turks invaded northern India, creating the Mughal dynasty of Muslim rulers. Portugal gained control of the Spice Islands, and Burma remained the leading power in Southeast Asia, conquering Siam (present-day Thailand) and Laos. English and Dutch trading companies consolidated their holdings in the Indian Ocean. In 1619, the Dutch founded

Batavia as a trading center in Southeast Asia. The Dutch expelled the Portuguese from Ceylon in 1663.

East Asia

In 1644, a Manchu army defeated the Ming dynasty and established the Qing dynasty which endured until 1911. In 1603, the Tokugawa dynasty introduced a centralized government in Japan. Foreign trade was carefully controlled by China and Japan

Europe

Poland dominated Eastern Europe until power quickly shifted to Muscovy when Ivan III claimed the title "czar" in 1472 and began Russia's expansion.

The long schism in the Catholic church ended in Europe. Ferdinand of Aragon and Isabella of Castile married in 1469, and in 1492, Muslim Grenada fell to Spain. In 1494, Charles VIII of France invaded Italy. By the end of the fifteenth century, Europe was on the cusp of rapid territorial expansion. Europeans had become technically advanced and resourceful, and they had amassed an amazing knowledge of much of the world through travel and trade.

Between 1500 and 1600, Spain seized a huge land empire that included much of South and Central America, the Philippine Islands, and the West Indies. Portugal built a sailing empire that reached from Brazil to Malacca and Macao, and Magellan proved that the oceans were linked. Sea lanes were established through the Indian, Atlantic, and Pacific Oceans, marking the beginning of truly global trade. Portugal traded with China and Japan but cultural contact between Europe and East Asia was minimal.

European contact barely reached beyond the coast in Africa. Missionaries took the Catholic faith to many parts of the Spanish and Portuguese empires and the church faced the threat of the Protestant Reformation in Europe. Catholic kingdoms struggled to halt the expansion of the Ottoman Empire into the Mediterranean area and Central Europe. The Dutch and English began to build their overseas empires.

Russia's territory expanded to the Caspian Sea and to western Siberia. The Protestant Reformation was the primary concern, with Scandinavia, England, Scotland, and many German states abandoning Catholicism, taking over church lands and monasteries, and governing state religions.

Martin Luther

Martin Luther, a German ordained priest, taught theology at a university in Wittenberg. As a teacher, he studied the Bible and decided that he objected to several of the Catholic church's practices, including the sale of indulgences and the belief of the church regarding individual salvation. In 1517, he published his objections in a document called *95 Theses* and posted the document on the church door in Wittenberg. The leaders of the Catholic church asked him to retract his statements but he refused. The Catholic church declared him an "outlaw" and a friend of Luther's helped him take refuge in a castle in Germany. Luther lived in exile for approximately one year but he continued to study the Bible and he translated it into German. It is believed by many that the publication of the *95 Theses* was the beginning of the Protestant Reformation.

Leonardo da Vinci

The Renaissance, a rebirth of cultural activity began in Italy during the fourteenth century. The Renaissance served as the transitional period between medieval and modern Europe.

Leonardo da Vinci was an Italian who is referred to as the "Renaissance man." He apprenticed as an artist at a young age and became a master artist in a guild by the age of twenty. His best-known paintings are *The Last Supper* and the *Mona Lisa.* In addition to being an artist, da Vinci was an inventor, scientist, and mathematician.

The year 1527 marks the end of the Italian Renaissance.

In 1543, Nicolaus Copernicus published his theory that the earth revolves around the sun. Ivan IV (the Terrible) was crowned in Russia in 1547. In 1580, Francis Drake circumnavigated the globe, and in 1588, the English navy defeated the Spanish Armada. The Edict of Nantes ended three decades of religious fighting in France in 1598, and in 1600, the English East India Company was formed.

England was involved in a civil war between 1642 and 1648. In 1665, the Great Plague killed seventy-five thousand people in London.

Black Death

The Bubonic Plague swept across Europe during the mid-1300s. It was believed to have been caused by parasites on small rodents that were transported by trading ships. People in many trading ports were affected by the mysterious disease and nearly one-third of Europe's population died from the plague.

The plague was referred to as the "Black Death" in the 1700s to distinguish the plague that struck many parts of Europe in the 1300s from the one that struck London in 1665. The term may refer to the blackened tumors that appeared on bodies but more likely stems from the Latin word for plague which means "terrible" or "black." The plague continued into the 1770s and is believed to be the pivotal point in the economic development of Europe because wages increased due to the loss of the workforce. The plague is also believed to have been a factor in the development of universities and higher learning because of the desire and need to study medicine.

The Thirty Years War took place in Germany between 1618 and 1648. The Treaty of Westphalia ended the war and established a system of states based on a balance of power which maintained relative stability until the French Revolution. The Russian Empire expanded to the Pacific Ocean by mid-century. In 1643, Louis XIV became king of France. In 1682, Peter the Great became czar of Russia, and the following year, 1683, the siege of Vienna ended the Ottoman Empire.

Between 1600 and 1700, Dutch, French, and British explorers created settlements and trade networks. British and French seamen searched for northwest and northeast passages from Europe to Asia. During this time, they founded settlements on the North American continent. In 1701, the War of Spanish Succession began. In 1707, the United Kingdom of Great Britain was formed (England, Wales, and Scotland). The Seven Years War (Europe) and the French and Indian Wars (America) began in 1756. In India, more than one hundred British prisoners died in the "Black Hole of Calcutta."

The Americas

The **Spanish** arrived in Mesoamerica and South America with horses, iron weapons, and guns. In 1501, they brought the first black slaves to the Americas, and they introduced devastating diseases to the native populations. By 1511, the Spanish had control of all of the major Caribbean islands. Between 1519 and 1522, Cortés conquered the Aztecs. Pizarro defeated the Incas in South America between 1531 and 1532, and in the 1530s, Portugal gradually began to colonize the coast of Brazil.

The 1600s was a period of rapid colonization. Spain controlled much of Central America and the Andes, and the Portuguese built a plantation society along the coast of northeastern South America. English colonies were planted along the east coast of North America and the English developed sugar plantations in Jamaica and other Caribbean islands. French and Dutch colonists built forts and trading posts in North America and developed sugar plantations in the Caribbean and Guiana. French hunters and traders explored the Great Lakes regions and the upper Mississippi Valley. Indigenous peoples remained independent. In 1604, the French founded the colony of Arcadia. Massachusetts Bay colony was founded by the English in 1630, and in 1654, England seized Jamaica from Spain. Ten years later, in 1664, England gained control of New Amsterdam (New York) from the Dutch. In 1695, gold was discovered in Brazil.

During the 1700s, the American possessions provided wealth to their European rulers. South America provided riches from mines. North American colonies provided lumber and other products as part of the mercantile trade. Furs were sent to France from the Ohio and Mississippi river valleys and Canada. In 1728, the Danish-born Russian navigator Vitus Bering explored Alaska.

SKILL 3.2   **Demonstrate knowledge of major developments in the civilizations of Africa (e.g., Egypt, sub-Sahara), the Americas (e.g., Inca, Aztec, Maya), Western and Eastern Europe, the Middle East, and Asia (e.g., China, India, Japan).**

Americas

Differences in geography, economic focus, and the preponderance of visitors from overseas produced differing patterns of occupation, survival, and success among natives of North and South America.

In North America, the landscape was much more hospitable to settlement and exploration. The North American continent, especially in what is now the United States, had a few mountain ranges and a handful of wide rivers but nothing like the dense jungles and staggeringly high mountains of South America. The area that is now Canada was cold but otherwise conducive to settlement.

As a result, the Native Americans in the northern areas of the Americas were more spread out and their cultures more diverse than their South American counterparts.

The **Pueblo**, who lived in what is now the American Southwest, are perhaps best known for the villages that they constructed from the sheer faces of cliffs and rocks and for *adobes,* mud-brick buildings that housed their living and meeting quarters. The Pueblos chose their own chiefs. Theirs was perhaps one of the oldest representative governments in the world.

The **Iroquois**, who lived in the American Northeast, are noted for their organized government. The famous Five Nations of the Iroquois made treaties among themselves and shared leadership of their peoples.

For the North Americans, life was centered on finding and growing food. The people were proficient farmers and hunters. They grew crops such as maize (corn), potatoes, squash, pumpkins, and beans. They hunted animals for food, including deer, bear, and buffalo. Despite the preponderance of crop-growing areas, many Native Americans did not domesticate animals, except for dogs.

The Native Americans who lived in the wilds of Canada and in the Pacific Northwest lived off the land and the nearby water. Fishing was important in these places. Trade involved others who lived as far away as what is now Alaska, California, and Missouri. Religion was a personal affair for nearly all of these tribes, with beliefs in higher powers extending to spirits in the sky and elsewhere in nature, with a conception that sacred power is celebrated spatially and related to place—unlike religions that are set to time (Sabbath day, for example), and with the belief that spirituality is never something apart from the person or the community or nature.

The **Mayan** civilization reached its peak about 900 CE. The Mayans left little traces of their civilization after the Spanish arrived but today descendants of the early Mayans live in Belize, Guatemala, Mexico, Honduras, and El Salvador.

The **Aztec** civilization flourished up to the point in time that the Spanish arrived in the 1500s. Their civilization was defeated by Cortés and never regained its former glory.

The **Incas** also became victims to the Spanish *conquistadores* in the 1500s. The Incas did not leave a written history and the story of their civilization has been assembled by archaeological discoveries. When the Spanish arrived they have a vast empire in South America, but their empire declined during the Spanish conquest.

Middle East

The **Ottoman Turks** dominated the Middle East during this period. They expanded into the Balkans, conquered Egypt, Mesopotamia, and the Persian Gulf coast.

Europe

Much of the development in **Western Europe** was the result of the Renaissance, Protestantism, and scientific and technical inventions, such as the printing press. England became a naval power after defeating the Spanish Armada, and England, France, and the Dutch expanded their colonial holdings. The English were also involved in the Triangular Trade that moved slaves from Africa to the Caribbean islands and British colonies in North America.

In **Eastern Europe**, Russia continued to expand its territories from the Crimea but attempted to avoid confrontations with the Ottomans. The Russians were heavily involved in trade, extending routes from the Caucuses into Asia where they could sell Siberian furs and luxury textiles.

Africa

Trade routes connected the **sub-Sahara** with northern Africa, India, China, and the Indies. European missionaries and traders used the shoreline of Africa to spread their wares and teachings. The Swahili culture thrives, and the 1700s saw the beginning of the spread of Islam south of the Sahara. In 1517, the Ottoman Turks extended their empire and captured **Egypt**.

Asia

The Ming dynasty expanded its territory in **China** and developed a trade network. The Yangtze River and other rivers formed a transportation system that carried good long distances. China's trade also developed because of its long coastline and other advances commercial networks. The Silk Road transported goods and ideas and created a route for culture to spread. **Japan** entered into a period of warlords, warriors, and wars. The rules outlawed Christianity during this time period but the country's economy grew. They traded with the Dutch and British and developed weaving and farming. The country also developed a merchant class. In **India**, the Mughal Empire grew in size and covered most of the Indian peninsula. Several architectural wonders were constructed during this time. The Taj Mahal is an example.

SKILL 3.3   Understand the importance of the European Renaissance and Reformation eras in shaping the modern world.

The Reformation Era

The Reformation era consisted of two phases—the Protestant Revolution and the Catholic Reformation. The **Protestant Revolution** came about because of religious, political, and economic reasons. The religious reasons stemmed from abuses in the Catholic church, including fraudulent clergy, the sale of religious offices, indulgences, dispensations, different theologies within the church, and frauds involving sacred relics.

The political reasons for the Protestant Revolution included the increase in the power of rulers who were considered "absolute monarchs" because they wanted all power and control, especially over the church. The growth of **nationalism** or patriotic pride in one's own country was another political reason for the Protestant Revolution.

Economic reasons for the Protest Revolution included the desire of ruling monarchs to possess and control lands and wealth owned by the Roman Catholic Church, deep animosity against the burdensome papal taxation, the rise of the affluent middle class and its clash with medieval church ideals, and the increase of an active system of "intense" capitalism.

The Protestant Revolution began in Germany with the revolt of Martin Luther against church abuses. It spread to Switzerland where it was led by John Calvin (*Jean Chauvin*). In England, King Henry VIII wanted to have his marriage to Catherine of Aragon annulled so he could wed Anne Boleyn and father a male heir. Common people, nobles, and some rulers supported the idea despite the church's attempts to stop their support. The Pope excommunicated King Henry in 1533. Queen Elizabeth I was the daughter of Henry VIII and Anne Boleyn.

The **Catholic Reformation** was undertaken by the church in response to growing criticism. This intent of this reformation was to slow or stop the Protestant Revolution. Major efforts to this end were made by the Council of Trent and the Jesuits. Six major results of the Reformation included:

- Religious freedom
- Religious tolerance
- More opportunities for education
- Power and control of rulers limited
- Increase in religious wars
- Increase in fanaticism and persecution

The Renaissance

The Renaissance ushered in a time of curiosity and learning. The desire for trade was sparked to procure new exotic products and to find better, faster, and cheaper trade routes to get to them. The work of geographers, astronomers, and mapmakers made important contributions, and many studied and applied the work of such men as Hipparchus of Greece, Ptolemy of Egypt, Tycho Brahe of Denmark, and Fra Mauro of Italy.

The word **Renaissance** literally means "rebirth." It signaled the rekindling of interest in the glory of ancient Greek and Roman civilizations. This period in human history marks the start of many ideas and innovations leading to our modern age. The Renaissance began in **Italy** with many of its ideas starting in **Florence**, a city that became controlled by the Medici family. Education, especially for some of the merchants, required reading, writing, mathematics, the study of law, and the writings of classical Greek and Roman writers.

Contributions to the Renaissance period included:

- **Art:** A number of Italian artists pioneered a new method of painting and sculpture—that of portraying events and people as they really looked. The more important artists were Giotto and his development of perspective in paintings; Leonardo da Vinci, who was not only an artist but also a scientist and inventor; Michelangelo, a sculptor, painter, and architect; and others such as Raphael, Donatello, Titian, and Tintoretto. The effects of the Renaissance in the Low Countries can be seen in the art of van Eyck and Breughel the Elder. In Spain, the art of el Greco and de Morales flourished.

- **Literature:** Humanists such as Petrarch and Boccaccio (the "founders of humanism.") as well as Erasmus advanced the idea of being interested in life on earth and the opportunities it can bring rather than constantly focusing on heaven and its rewards. The monumental works of England's Shakespeare, Italy's Dante, and Spain's Cervantes also found their origins in the awareness of humans at center and a theme of justice. In addition, in England, Sir Thomas More and Sir Francis Bacon wrote and taught philosophy, and great literature was created by Spenser, Marlowe, and Johnson. In Italy, Machiavelli's works developed political philosophy. French writers Rabelais and Montaigne also contributed to literature and philosophy.

- **Science:** Copernicus, Kepler, and Galileo (the "father of modern science") led a scientific revolution in proving that the earth was round and not the center of the solar system—an earth-shattering claim to those who clung to medieval ideals of a geocentric, church-centered existence.

- **Medicine:** The work of Brussels-born Andrea Vesalius (Van Wesel) earned him the title of "father of anatomy." He had a profound influence on the Spaniard Michael Servetus and the Englishman William Harvey.

The Renaissance changed **music** as well. No longer just a religious experience, music could be composed for its own sake, to be enjoyed in fuller and more humanistic ways than in the Middle Ages. Musicians worked for themselves rather than for the churches and so they could command higher pay for their work, increasing their prestige.

In Germany, Gutenberg's invention of the **printing press** with movable type facilitated the rapid spread of Renaissance ideas, writings, and innovations, thus ensuring the enlightenment of most of Western Europe. Contributions were also made by Durer and Holbein in art and by Paracelsus in science and medicine.

SKILL 3.4   **Understand the causes of European expansion and the effects of expansion on European and non-European societies (e.g., Columbian Exchange, Atlantic slave trade).**

In the 150 years following 1520, European nations began to reap the benefits of the Age of Exploration. They began a period of economic and colonial expansion that spread European civilization throughout the world. Europeans invaded the Far East and the unknown areas to the West, pillaging, trading, colonizing, and introducing Christianity to native peoples. Capitalism spread to an extent that essentially dominated the economic activities of the nations.

Causes of European Expansion

Considering the rate of expansion of overseas trade, the great increase in the volume and variety of goods transported, and the resulting increase in the wealth of European nations, it seems appropriate to speak of a "commercial revolution." Several factors, including the desire for knowledge, the desire to convert natives to Christianity, the lust for gold and silver, and the desire to reap the benefits of trade, fueled the desire for expansion.

In the early years of expansion, the most active groups were the Spanish, the Portuguese, and the Dutch. In 1494, the Pope divided the planet between Spain and Portugal.

The French and English did not become active players in the competition for foreign colonies and domination until the seventeenth century when foreign trade was becoming more important to both nations. The English East India Company, a chartered company rather than a government effort, became an agency of expansion and typified the way this expansion occurred.

Portugal made a start under the encouragement, support, and financing of Prince Henry the Navigator. The more successful explorers who sailed under the flag of Portugal included Cabral, Diaz, and Vasco da Gama. Vasco da Gama was the first to successfully sail all the way from Portugal and around the southern tip of Africa to Calcutta, India.

Christopher Columbus, sailing for **Spain**, is credited with the discovery of the "New World." Magellan is credited with the first circumnavigation of the earth. Other Spanish explorers made their marks in parts of what are now the United States, Mexico, and South America.

For **France**, claims to various parts of North America were the results of the efforts of such men as Verrazano, Champlain, Cartier, La Salle, Marquette, and Joliet.

Dutch claims in North America were based on the exploration of Henry Hudson.

John Cabot gave **England** its stake in North America along with John Hawkins, Sir Francis Drake, and the half-brothers Sir Walter Raleigh and Sir Humphrey Gilbert.

The first Europeans in the New World were Norsemen led by the explorer Eric the Red and, later, by his son Leif Ericson. However, before any of the Europeans arrived, the ancestors of present-day Native Americans in North, Central, and South America had most likely arrived by crossing the Bering Strait from Asia to Alaska. They eventually settled in all parts of the Americas.

Competition for trade monopolies in the East led to a struggle between the English and the Dutch. England's first **Navigation Act** (1651) was directed against the Dutch. There was rivalry between Spain, the Netherlands, and England for control of various areas. This eventually led to the Anglo-Dutch Wars. The slave trade of Africa, Atlantic fisheries, North American settlements, and trade were all issues that resulted in the wars. The Dutch East India Company had shut off the Spice Islands from the English, and the English began focusing on trade with India.

England and France stood together to evict the Dutch from the North American mainland. Numerous changes were occurring within England and eventually William of Orange was brought to the throne. William and Louis XIV were bitter enemies, and opinion turned toward the view that the true enemy of England was France. This resulted in the Anglo-French War. Both nations had adopted mercantilist policies. Both countries had competing colonies and trading interests in the New World, Asia, and the West Indian islands.

On the North American mainland, English settlements essentially controlled the Atlantic coast from Maine to Georgia. These areas were well-populated and provided fish, tobacco, and trade. Although less densely populated, the French had claims to a large area of land. The Louisiana Territory was under French control. Competition between England and France for land, sugar, and furs was intense. The English colonies were barred from westward expansion by French territory, which was being protected by a strong line of military defenses.

India, which was densely populated and in possession of a strong culture, was also highly prized by both France and England. By 1689, the English had established outposts at Bombay, Madras, and Calcutta. The French had come to India somewhat later and established their outposts in two areas near Calcutta and Madras. Both nations saw these outposts as entry points for greater penetration of India. These areas were the loci of the conflicts that ensued.

Effects of European Expansion

The Columbian Exchange

The Columbian Exchange connected the Old World and the New World by the exchange of plants, animals, technology, and disease. Columbus took horses, dogs, chickens, pigs, and sheep on his second voyage in 1493. In 1521, the Spanish took cattle into Mexico. The animals were used for farming, clothing, and food. Animals such as squirrels and turkeys were exported from the New World but had little impact on the Old World's economy.

European colonists took seeds with them to the New World and planted wheat, apples, and other crops. They developed profitable sugar cane plantations that added to the economic value of Caribbean islands. The New World exported potatoes and maize, both of which were important contributions to European agriculture.

Settlers transported technology with them to the New World. The written alphabet was used as a tool for educating the Native Americans and introducing them to the Old World's religious beliefs. The plow was an important tool for farming, and weapons became desired items for the Native Americans because the weapons could be used for hunting and fishing. The European weapons could kill larger animals more quickly because Old World knives were made of steel and were stronger than Native Americans' knives. The settlers also brought the wheel, maps, and architectural technology that permitted them to build homes and communities.

In addition to plants, animals, and technology, the Columbian Exchange included disease and bacteria. Europeans carried smallpox, typhus, malaria, and other communicable diseases. Smallpox killed more Native Americans than any of the other diseases.

Atlantic Slave Trade

The Atlantic slave trade began in the 1300s and continued for approximately four hundred years. It reached its peak in the 1700s. The Portuguese began the slave trade as they attempted to find a route to Asia by sailing around Africa. Africans were accustomed to tropical climates, could be trained to become excellent workers, and had experience with agriculture. As a result, the Portuguese realized the Africans could provide the workforce for plantations in the New World.

The difficult voyage across the Atlantic Ocean was called the **Middle Passage.** The Atlantic slave trade was known as the **"triangular trade"** because ships sailed from Europe to Africa and to North and South America before returning to Europe. Ships departing from Europe and going to Africa carried weapons and trade goods such as textiles. Slaves were exchanged for those items and were then transported to plantations in Brazil, the Caribbean, and the American colonies. From America, agricultural products such as tobacco, sugar cane, and rice were shipped to Europe. Approximately seventeen million slaves were removed from Africa for the Atlantic slave trade operations. The Spanish, Portuguese, Dutch, French, and English were the primary participants in the slave trade. Most of the slaves were transported to Brazil, and the American colonies received the fewest.

SKILL 3.5   **Analyze the impact of political, economic, and cultural imperialism (e.g., conquest of the Aztec, expansion of the Ottoman Empire) on both colonizers and the colonized.**

Imperialism

In Europe, Italy and Germany each were totally united into one nation from many smaller states. There were revolutions in Austria and Hungary. The **Franco-Prussian War** took place during this time period, and Africa was divided among the strong European nations. Western nations interfered and intervened in Asia, and Turkish dominance was broken up in the Balkans. **Otto von Bismarck** is the man most often credited with the unification of Germany. Bismarck became the first Chancellor of a unified Germany.

France, Great Britain, Italy, Portugal, Spain, Germany, and Belgium controlled the entire continent of Africa except for Liberia and Ethiopia. In Asia and the Pacific Islands, only China, Japan, and present-day Thailand (Siam) kept their independence. The other countries were controlled by the strong European nations.

One reason for **European imperialism** was the urgent demand for the raw materials that were needed to fuel and feed the great Industrial Revolution. These resources were not available in the huge quantities needed. Therefore, European nations rationalized the necessity of partitioning the African continent and parts of Asia.

In turn, these colonial areas would purchase the finished manufactured goods. Europe in the nineteenth century was a crowded place. Populations were growing, but resources were not. The peoples of many European countries were also agitating for rights as never before. To address these concerns, European powers began to look elsewhere for relief.

One of the main places for European imperialist expansion was Africa. Britain, France, Germany, and Belgium took over countries in Africa and claimed them as their own. The resources (including people) were then shipped back to the mainland and claimed as colonial gains. The Europeans felt they were "civilizing the savages," reasoning that their technological superiority gave them the right to rule and "educate" the peoples of Africa.

Southeast Asia was another area of European expansion at this time, with France in Vietnam, Spain in the Philippines, and Great Britain in Burma, Malaysia, and Singapore.

Expansion of the Ottoman Empire

The Ottoman Empire continued its remarkable expansion in the early sixteenth century under the Sultan Selim I. Selim expanded his borders to the east and south, taking control of Persia (Iran) and Egypt and establishing a naval foothold in the Red Sea. This naval strength was built upon by Selim's successors until the controlled not only the Red Sea but also the Black Sea, the Persian Gulf, and a large section of the Mediterranean. By the late sixteenth century, the Ottoman Empire had also expanded inland to control all of southeast Europe, and it took advantage of its location between Europe and Asia to control access to the spice and silk trade routes. Maintaining such a large frontier far from its capital proved to be difficult, and beginning in the early seventeenth century Europeans made successful inroads along the western Ottoman borders. The technological advantages that the Ottomans had once held over Europe disappeared as the West made significant advances of its own and gained access to ancient learning from China and other regions to which the Ottomans had restricted access.

Conquest of the Aztec Civilization

During this period, the Spanish began their conquest of the Aztec civilization. Hernán **Cortés** arrived in Mexico in 1504. He lived peaceably with the Aztecs in their capital city of **Tenochtitlan** for several months in 1519. At the time, the Aztecs were led by **Montezuma** and had the most powerful empire in North America. Their capital city was large, prosperous, and beautiful. The Aztecs also had a large and experienced army, and Cortés had hoped to conquer the Aztecs peacefully and with diplomacy.

When rumors spread that the Aztecs were plotting against the Spanish **conquistadores**, some of the Spaniards massacred Aztec priests. The Aztecs drove the Spanish from their capital and Cortés spent the next year preparing to attack the city. Cortés convinced some Native American tribes to become allies of the Spanish, and with an army of approximately five hundred men, Cortés defeated the Aztecs in 1521.

COMPETENCY 4: WORLD HISTORY FROM 1750 TO THE PRESENT

THE TEACHER UNDERSTANDS SIGNIFICANT HISTORICAL EVENTS, DEVELOPMENTS, AND TRADITIONAL POINTS OF REFERENCE IN WORLD HISTORY FROM 1750 TO THE PRESENT.

SKILL 4.1   **Demonstrate knowledge of developments, events, issues, and interactions that shaped the development of world civilizations from 1750 to the present (e.g., the Great Depression, the Holocaust, decolonization).**

North America

In 1775, the **American Revolution** began. In 1783, there was division between the United States and Canada. Territorial expansion began with the settlement of the Northwest Territory and the purchase of the Louisiana Territory. As the country expanded its territory to the Pacific Ocean, the industrial power of America grew. Communicating from one coast to the other became easier with the invention of the telegraph and telephone. Completion of the transcontinental railroad increased the speed of transportation and made getting products to markets and urban centers easier and faster. The United States entered World War I but did not become a member of the League of Nations that Woodrow Wilson had proposed.

After World War I, the United States economy appeared prosperous and people were optimistic. Many people had believed that the stock market was an easy way to become wealthy very quickly. Land prices were increasing, and "speculation" was a common vocabulary word. However, on October 29, 1929, the American stock market crashed and the country was thrown into an economic depression known as the **Great Depression.**

The day the market crashed was referred to as "**Black Monday.**" Stock values hit bottom and people panicked. People had invested heavily in the market, but so had financial institutions. Stocks became worthless, people lost their savings, and banks were forced to close. Businesses closed or cut back on the number of workers. People remained out of work and without incomes. The depression began to be felt worldwide. When Franklin Roosevelt became president, he implemented the **New Deal** to bolster the economy and put people back to work.

South America

In the 1700s and early 1800s, the Portuguese and Spanish rivaled over territory in South America and both countries tried to control gold mines in Brazil. There were also struggles between settlers and native peoples. The Latin American countries were unhappy with Spanish restrictions on trade, agriculture, and the manufacture of goods. The turning point toward independence occurred in 1807, when Napoleon led the French army onto the Iberian Peninsula to capture Spain and Portugal.

Europe

Throughout Europe governments became stronger, particularly Peter the Great's in Russia and Frederick the Great's in Prussia. The Bourbon monarchy reached its peak in France. In France in

1789, the **French Revolution** began, and in 1799, a coup brought Napoleon to power in France. Napoleon expanded the French Empire. In 1793, Louis XVI and Marie Antoinette were executed, and the reign of terror began. Britain's empire in India began in 1757. During the mid-1700s, the steam engine was invented and the production of the spinning machine marked an early step in the Industrial Revolution.

Between May 1810 and July 1811, the *juntas* in Argentina, Chile, Paraguay, Venezuela, Bolivia and Colombia all declared independence from Spain. Fighting erupted between Spanish authorities in Latin America and the members and followers of the *juntas*. In Mexico City another *junta* declared loyalty to Ferdinand and independence.

Decolonization in Africa and Asia

The achievement of independence by the colonies and protectorates of European countries in Africa and Asia is called **decolonization**. Most of the decolonization occurred in the period following the conclusion of World War II. Decolonization was achieved in one of three ways:

- Attaining independence
- Establishing a "free association" status
- Integrating with the governing or administrative power of another state

Decolonization is a process rather than an event. Colonial areas tend to move through a series of steps that provide increasing autonomy. Decolonization may be peacefully negotiated or may result from revolt and armed struggle of varying degrees of intensity. The reasons for decolonization are primarily a matter of investing the former colonies with independence and self-determination. The colonizing countries benefit, however, from the ability to free themselves of the costs of maintaining the colonies. In many cases, a relationship continues to exist between the two countries.

The beginning of a movement toward decolonization followed World War I and the creation of the League of Nations. In theory, there was an intention to prepare the colonies for self-government. In fact, however, the League merely redistributed the former colonies of Germany and the Ottoman Empire.

Russia

Karl Marx (1818–1883) was an influential theorist of the nineteenth century, and his influence has continued in various forms until this day. He was not the first to believe in socialist ideas but was the first to call his system truly "scientific" or **Scientific Socialism**. His system is also called Marxian Socialism, widely known as **Marxism.** It was opposed to other forms of socialism that had been called **Utopian Socialism**. Marx expounded his ideas in two major theoretical works, *The Communist Manifesto* (1848*)* and *Das Kapital* (Volume 1, 1867*)*.

Until the early years of the twentieth century, **Russia** was ruled by a succession of czars who ruled as autocrats or, sometimes, despots. Society was essentially feudalistic and was structured in three levels. The top level was held by the czar. The second level was composed of the rich nobles who held government positions and owned vast tracts of land. The third level of the society was composed of people who lived in poverty as peasants or serfs. There was discontent among the peasants, and their several unsuccessful attempts to revolt during the nineteenth century were quickly suppressed.

The revolutions of 1905 and 1917 in Russia, however, were quite different. The causes of the 1905 Revolution were:

- Discontent with the social structure
- Discontent with the living conditions of the peasants
- Discontent with working conditions despite industrialization
- General discontent aggravated by the Russo-Japanese War (1904–1905) with inflation and rising prices. Peasants who had been barely able to earn a living began to starve.
- The deaths of many fighting troops in battles that Russia lost to Japan because of poor leadership, lack of training, and inferior weaponry
- The refusal of Czar Nicholas II to end the war despite setbacks
- The fall of Port Arthur in January 1905

A trade union leader (**Father Gapon**) organized a protest to demand an end to the war, industrial reform, more civil liberties, and a constituent assembly. Over 150,000 peasants joined a demonstration outside the czar's Winter Palace.

Before the demonstrators even spoke, the palace guard opened fire on the crowd. This destroyed the people's trust in the czar. Illegal trade unions and formed and organized strikes to gain power. The strikes eventually brought the Russian economy to a halt. This led Czar Nicholas II to sign the **October Manifesto**, which created a constitutional monarchy, extended some civil rights, and gave Parliament limited legislative power. In a very short period of time, the czar disbanded the parliament and violated the promised civil liberties. This violation fomented the 1917 Revolution.

The Holocaust

The Holocaust was the mass murder of Jews during World War II that was carried out by the Nazi leaders in Germany and in areas controlled by Germany. Laws were enacted before the outbreak of the war to exclude Jews from society. Jews were concentrated in parts of cities that were called ghettos but were removed from these areas when the Nazis decided to removed them to concentration camps.

Concentration camps were constructed as work and death centers for Jews, political dissidents, and others who the Germans wanted removed from society. The inmates of the camps became slave laborers or were killed in gas chambers. Approximately six million Jews were killed in the Holocaust.

Africa

Islamic influence spread in North Africa. The slave trade flourished in West Africa, with over 13.5 million people transported from Africa. African resistance in the south limited British and Dutch expansion, and between 1779 and 1780, war was fought between Boers and Bantu in southern Africa. In 1795, the British took over the Cape of Good Hope, and three years later, in 1798, the French Napoleon occupied Egypt.

The slave trade provided economic stability for parts of Africa for almost three hundred years. The continuing need for human sacrifices caused a decrease in the number of slaves available for export. As many colonial countries declared the trade of slaves illegal, demand for slaves subsided steadily until 1885 when the last Portuguese slave ship left the coast.

With the decline of the slave trade, the West African kingdoms began a slow disintegration. The French took over parts of West Africa in 1892.

Asia

In the early nineteenth century, under Mahmud II, the **Ottoman Empire** adopted a policy of modernization based on European customs, architecture, and legislation. The rise of nationalism throughout Europe affected the empire as well, and former sovereign states that had been conquered began to express nationalistic goals. These developments marked the beginning of the end for the empire. Despite several attempts to reform the government, economic depression and political unrest plagued the declining state.

The Ottomans fought in World War I in alliance with Germany and were defeated in 1918, when the army was disbanded. The harsh peace terms led to an upsurge in Turkish nationalism and revolution. Turkish revolutionaries abolished the Ottoman sultanate in 1922, and members of the family were expelled from Turkey.

SKILL 4.2   **Analyze the causes and effects of major political revolutions and independence movements of the eighteenth through the twentieth centuries (e.g., the American Revolution, the French Revolution, Napoleon, Simón Bolívar, Latin American wars of independence, Russian Revolution).**

American Revolution

The American Revolution was the efforts of the colonists in America to win their freedom from Great Britain. After more than a hundred years of mostly self-government, the colonists resented the increased British meddling and control. They declared their freedom, won the Revolutionary War with aid from France, and formed a new independent nation. The defeat of the British at **Saratoga** was the overwhelming factor in the Franco-American alliance of 1777 that helped the American colonists defeat the British. Some historians believe that without the Franco-American alliance, the American colonies would not have been able to defeat the British and America would have remained a British colony.

French Revolution

The **French Revolution** was the revolt of the middle and lower classes against the gross political and economic abuses and excesses of the rulers and the supporting nobility. Conditions leading to revolt included extreme taxation, inflation, and lack of food. During the first year of the revolution, 1789, members of the assembly, The Estates-General, agreed they would draft a new constitution. Their oath is known as the Tennis Court Oath because, having been locked out of their meeting place, they met in a make-shift conference room on a tennis court near the court of Versailles.

On July 14, 1789, partisans stormed the Bastille, the medieval fortress and prison in Paris. The prison contained only a few inmates but its capture was symbolic and served as momentum for the revolution. Approximately one month later, the **Declaration of the Rights of Man and of the Citizen** was adopted by the national assembly and is considered as the first step the French took in writing a constitution. The Declaration was influenced by ideas of the Enlightenment and the doctrine of natural rights of man. The Declaration was inspired by the American Declaration of Independence and has been used as the preamble of later French constitutions.

The revolution ended with the establishment of the First Republic in 1792. King Louis XVI was executed the following year. A **reign of terror** took place between 1793 and 1794 until Robespierre and other Jacobins were overthrown and executed. A group of five men ruled as a **Directory** until the end of the revolution in 1799.

Napoleon

Napoleon Bonaparte was a French army commander who expanded the French Empire in the late 1790s and early 1800s. **Napoleon** overthrew the Directory and established the **First Empire.** That empire is also referred to as the Napoleonic Empire. In 1802, he became the Emperor of France.

During the time Napoleon was emperor of the empire, he won victories throughout Europe. The wars, which were called the **Napoleonic Wars,** extended French influence throughout the continent. The **Napoleonic Code,** a civil law code, was introduced and abolished many of the feudal laws.

In 1807, Napoleon led the French army onto the Iberian Peninsula to capture Spain and Portugal. The war that resulted was called the **Spanish War for Independence** and the **Peninsular War.** Napoleon wanted to conquer Portugal because the British had used the country's shores to land troops. He wanted to conquer Spain because of the unrest and instability there. His main purposes for the war were to block the British from Spain and to gain additional access to the sea.

Napoleon's imprisonment of King Ferdinand VII made the local agents of the Spanish authorities in South America feel that they were in fact agents of the French. Conservative and liberal locals joined forces, declared their loyalty to King Ferdinand, and formed committees (*juntas*).
Napoleon's invasion of Russia in 1812 was disastrous for the French, and the French were defeated by the Germans in 1813. The German defeat led to Napoleon's abdication and exile in 1814.

Russian Revolution

The Russian Revolution occurred in the spring of 1917 with the abdication of Czar Nicholas II and the establishment of a democratic government. The **Bolsheviks,** extreme Marxists who had a majority in Russia's Socialist Party, overcame opposition and approximately six months later did away with the provisional democratic government and set up the world's first Marxist state.

Russia's harsh climate, tremendous size, and physical isolation from the rest of Europe, along with the brutal despotic rule and control czars held over peasants, contributed to the final conditions leading to revolution. Despite the tremendous efforts of Peter the Great to bring his country up to the social, cultural, and economic standards of the rest of Europe in the early 1700s, Russia always remained a hundred years or more behind. Autocratic rule, the system of serfdom, lack of money, defeats in wars, lack of enough food and food production, and little industrialization were conditions that contributed to revolt.

By 1914, Russia's industrial growth was even faster than Germany's and agricultural production was improving, along with better transportation. However, the conditions of poverty were horrendous. The Orthodox Church was steeped in political activities, and the absolute rule of the czar was the order of the day. By the time the nation entered World War I, conditions were just right for revolution. Marxist socialism seemed to be the solution or answer to all the problems.

Russia had to stop participation in the war. Industry could not meet the military's needs. Transportation by rail was severely disrupted, and it was most difficult to procure supplies from the Allies. The people were tired of war, injustice, starvation, poverty, slavery, and cruelty. Support for and strength of the Bolsheviks existed mainly in the cities. After two or three years of civil war, fighting foreign invasions, and opposing other revolutionary groups, the Bolsheviks were finally successful in making possible a type of "pre-Utopia" for the workers and the people.

As Marxist or communist leaders came to power, the effects of this violent revolution were felt all around the earth. The foreign policies of Western nations were directly and immensely affected by the Marxist-communist ideology. Its effect on Eastern Europe and the former Soviet Union was felt politically, economically, socially, culturally, and geographically. The people of ancient Russia had simply exchanged one autocratic dictatorial system for another.

Latin American Wars of Independence

The **Mexican Revolution** was a response to Mexico's long history under Spanish control that placed power, control, wealth, and land in the hands of a small minority, leaving the majority in poverty. Under General **Porfirio Diaz,** the distinction grew between rich and poor, and with this growing divide, the lower classes were losing any voice in politics. Opposition to Diaz began when **Francisco I. Madero** led a series of strikes throughout Mexico. Madero gained a following and brought pressure to bear on Diaz until an election was held in 1910. Madero won a large number of votes. Diaz had Madero imprisoned and claimed that the Mexican people were not prepared for democracy.

As soon as Madero was released from prison, he began an attempt to have Diaz overthrown. At about this time two other local heroes emerged—**Pancho Villa** and **Emiliano Zapata.** Villa and Zapata harassed the Mexican army and eventually won control of regions in the north and in the south. Unable to control the spread of the insurgency, Diaz resigned in 1911. Madero and Zapata ran for president of Mexico; Madero won but his plan of land reform was too slow in Zapata's opinion. Within a matter of months, Zapata denounced Madero and claimed the presidency. With control of the state of Morelos, he deported the wealthy landowners and divided their lands among the peasants. He was assassinated in 1919.

Many factions began to arise, and guerilla units roamed the country pillaging and destroying large haciendas and ranchos. Madero was executed, and the country remained in disarray for several years, allowing Pancho Villa free reign in the north. Various factions vied for control of the government until **Venustiano Carranza** emerged and became president. He called a constitutional convention, resulting in the 1917 Constitution which is still in effect. One of the provisions of the Constitution was land reform. The Constitution created the *ejido,* a farm cooperative program that redistributed much of the land among the peasants.

Society in Latin America was sharply distinguished according to race and the purity of Spanish blood. **Miguel Hidalgo**, a sixty-year-old priest and enlightened intellectual, disregarded the racial distinctions of the society. He had been fighting for the interests of the Indians and mestizos (part Indian, part European) as citizens of Mexico and called for the return of land stolen from the Indians. In 1810, he called for an uprising.

Simón Bolívar

Simón Bolívar had been born into Venezuela's wealthy society and educated in Europe. With Francisco de Miranda, he declared Venezuela and Colombia to be republics and removed all Spanish trading restrictions. They removed taxes on the sale of food, ended payment of tribute to the government by the locals, and prohibited slavery. In March 1812 Caracas was devastated by an earthquake. Statements of the Spanish clergy in Caracas that proclaimed the earthquake was God's act of vengeance against the rebel government provided support for the Spanish government officials, who quickly regained control.

When King Ferdinand of Spain was returned to power in 1814, it was no longer possible for the rebel groups to claim to act in his name. Bolívar, a Venezuelan, was driven to Colombia where he gathered a small army that returned to Venezuela in 1817. As his army grew, Spain became concerned and the Spanish military moved into the interior of Venezuela. This action aroused the local people to active rebellion. As Bolívar freed slaves, he gained support and strength. Realizing that he did not have the strength to take Caracas, Bolívar moved his people to Colombia. Bolívar's forces defeated the Spanish and he organized **Gran Colombia** (which included present-day Ecuador, Colombia, and Panama) and became president in 1819. When King Ferdinand encountered difficulties in Spain, the Spanish soldiers who were assembled to be transported to the Americas revolted.

Several groups in Spain joined the revolt and, together, drove Ferdinand from power. Bolívar took advantage of the opportunity and took his army back into Venezuela. In 1821, Bolívar defeated the Spanish, captured Caracas, and established Venezuelan freedom from Spanish rule.

In Peru, **San Martin** took his force into Lima amid celebration. Bolívar provided assistance in winning Peru's independence in 1822. Bolívar now controlled Peru. By 1824, Bolívar had combined forces with local groups and rid South America of Spanish control.

Whereas Chile, Argentina, and Venezuela continued to have histories marred by civil wars, dictatorships, and numerous violent coups during their quests for independence, Brazil experienced a more rapid independence from Portugal in a bloodless revolution in 1889 that officially made Brazil a republic with economic stability from a strong coffee- and rubber-based economy.

Iranian Revolution

The Iranian Revolution in 1979 transformed a constitutional monarchy, led by the shah (king), into an Islamic populist theocratic republic. The new ruler was **Ayatollah Ruhollah Khomeini.** This revolution occurred in two essential stages. In the first, religious, liberal and leftist groups cooperated to oust the shah. In the second stage, the Ayatollah rose to power and created an Islamic state.

The shah had faced intermittent opposition from Islamic figures and from the middle classes in the cities. These groups sought a limitation of the shah's power and a constitutional democracy. The shah enforced censorship laws and imprisoned political enemies.

At the same time, living conditions of the people improved greatly and several important democratic rights were given to the people. Islamic Mullahs fiercely opposed giving women the right to vote. The shah was said to be a puppet of the U.S. government.

A series of protests in 1978 was sparked by a libelous story about the Ayatollah Khomeini that was published in the official press. The protests escalated until December of that year when more than two million people gathered in Tehran in protest against the shah.

On the advice of Prime Minister Shapour Bakhtiar, who was an opposition leader, the shah and the empress left Iran. Bakhtiar freed the political prisoners, permitted Khomeini to return from exile, and asked Khomeini to create a state modeled on the Vatican. Bakhtiar promised free elections and called for the preservation of the Constitution.

Khomeini rejected Bakhtiar's demands and appointed an interim government. In a very short period of time, Khomeini gathered his revolutionaries and completed the overthrow of the monarchy.

The revolution accomplished certain goals, including a reduction of foreign influence and a more even distribution of the nation's wealth. It did not change repressive policies or levels of government brutality. It reversed policies toward women, restoring ancient policies of repression.

Religious repression became rife, particularly against members of the Baha'i faith. The revolution isolated Iran from the rest of the world and has been rejected by both capitalist and communist nations. This isolation, however, allowed the country to develop its own internal political system rather than having a system imposed by foreign powers.

Chinese Revolution

The Chinese Revolution of 1911 was a response to imperial rule under the Qing dynasty. Numerous internal rebellions caused widespread oppression and death. Conflicts with foreign nations had tended to end with treaties that humiliated China and required the payment of reparations that amounted to massive cost. In addition, there were popular feelings that political power should be restored from the Manchus to the Han Chinese.

There was some attempt at reform, but it was undercut by the conservative supporters of the dynasty. The failures in modernization and liberalization and the violent repression of dissidents moved the reformers toward revolution.

The most popular of the numerous revolutionary groups was led by **Sun Yat-sen**. His movement was supported by Chinese who were living outside China and by students in Japan. He won the support of regional military officers. Sun's political philosophy consisted of "three principles of the people" that included:

- Nationalism that called for ousting of the Manchus and putting an end to foreign hegemony
- Democracy that would establish a popularly elected government
- People's livelihood, or socialism, which was designed to help the common people by equalizing the ownership of land and the tools of production

The revolution began with the discontented army units and was called the Wuchang Uprising. The uprising spread to other parts of China. The Qing Court suppressed the rebellion within fifty days. During this time, however, a number of other provinces declared independence of the Qing Dynasty. A month later Sun Yat-sen was elected the first Provisional President of the new Republic of China. Yuan Shikai, who had control of the Army tried to prevent civil war and possible intervention by foreign governments. He claimed power in Beijing. Sun agreed to unite China under a government headed by Yuan, who became the second provisional president of the Chinese republic.

Yuan quickly gathered more power than was controlled by the Parliament. He revised the constitution and became a dictator. In the national elections of 1912, Sung Jiaoren led the new Nationalist Party in winning the majority of seats in the parliament. A month later, Yuan had Sung assassinated. This increased Yuan's unpopularity. Several leadership missteps of a dictatorial nature aroused greater discontent. A second revolution began in 1913. This resulted in the flight of Sun and his followers to Japan.

While Yuan pursued an imperialistic policy, Sun gathered more followers. Yuan alienated the parliament and the military. When World War I broke out, Japan issued the "Twenty-One

Demands," and Yuan agreed to many of them, further alienating the people of China. Several southern provinces declared independence. In 1916, Yuan stepped down as emperor.

A period of struggle between rival warlords followed. By the end of World War I, Duan Qirui had emerged as the most powerful Chinese leader. He declared war on Germany and Austria-Hungary in 1917 in the hope of getting loans from Japan. His disregard for the constitution led Sun Yat-sen and others to establish a new government and the Constitutional Protection Army. Sun established a military government and the Constitutional Protection War continued through 1918. The result was a divided China, divided along the north-south border.

By 1921, Sun had become president of a unified group of southern provinces. He was unable to obtain assistance from Western nations, and turned to the Soviet Union in 1920. The Soviets supported both Sun and the newly established Communist Party in China. This set off a power struggle between the communists and the Nationalists. In 1923, Sun and a Soviet representative promised Soviet support for the reunification of China. The Soviet advisers sent **Chiang Kai-shek** to Moscow to be trained in propaganda and mass mobilization. Sun died in 1925. Chiang Kai-shek was commander of the National Revolutionary Army, and began to take back the Northern provinces from the warlords. By 1928 all of China was under his control, and his government was recognized internationally.

Africa

Opposition to colonial rule took several forms in Africa during the years between World War I and World War II. There were mass protests, demands for opportunity and inclusion, and economic and religious opposition.

The effect of World War II on Africa was profound. Not only were several important battles fought in Africa, but the English and French actively recruited soldiers from their African colonies. When the soldiers returned to their African homes they began questioning the reasons they took risks to protect Europe from fascism and Nazism when they were not free in their own country.

Further, the proliferation of news and information during and after World War II made many Africans, especially those who served in the military, aware of the content of the *Atlantic Charter*. The third paragraph of the charter states that the Allies "respect the right of all peoples to choose the form of government under which they will live; and they wish to see sovereign rights of self-government restored to those who have been forcibly deprived of them." Many Africans saw this as a commitment by the British to end colonial rule in Africa.

European colonies in Africa were demanding independence from Europe. In particular many Africans viewed the independence of India from British rule in 1947 along with the partitioning of India and Pakistan as a model of what could be achieved in their own countries. In the late 1940s and early 1950s, new political organizations emerged throughout Africa with the support of the broader populace. These organizations demanded political freedom and the end of colonial rule. Libya and Egypt were the first African nations to win independence. Ghana gained independence in 1957. Fourteen African countries won independence in 1960, and by 1966, all but six countries were independent. The events leading to the "Arab Spring" resulted in changes in government in North African countries again in late 2011 and early 2012.

SKILL 4.3   Understand the impact of political, economic, and cultural expansion (e.g., rise of the British Empire, Japanese imperialism).

In the United States, territorial expansion occurred in the expansion westward under the banner of Manifest Destiny. In addition, the United States was involved in the war with Mexico, the Spanish-American War, and support for the Latin American colonies of Spain in their revolt for independence. In Latin America, the Spanish colonies were successful in their fight for independence and self-government.

The period from 1830 to 1914 is characterized by the extraordinary growth and the spread of patriotic pride in nations along with intense and widespread imperialism. Loyalty to one's nation included national pride, an extension and maintenance of sovereign political boundaries, the unification of smaller states with common languages, histories, and cultures into a more powerful nation, or the unification of smaller national groups who, as part of a larger multicultural empire, wished to separate into smaller, political, cultural nations.

Rise of the British Colonial Empire

England began building its overseas colonial empire with the settlement the North American colonies. After the colonies gained independence, the British expanded into the Indian subcontinent and Africa. The end of the nineteenth and beginning of the twentieth centuries was the age of imperialism and expansion. After World War I, England obtained more territory, called mandates. Mandates were colonies of Germany or Turkey before the war. The League of Nations gave authority to a member nation to govern these former territories.

The League of Nations divided the mandates according to their stage or level of development and according to their location. England received Middle East mandates of Iraq, Palestine, and Israel which had been Turkish provinces and Tanganyika (part of present-day Tanzania), a German colony, in Africa.

It has been said that at one time the sun never set on the British Empire. By 1924, the colonial empire had peaked. Following World War II, the empire was reduced in size because colonies gained independence. Hong Kong, one of England's major colonies, became independent in 1997.

Japanese Imperialism

Japan began expanding its territories in 1853. The country had been isolated until Commodore Matthew Perry opened the country to the Western world. Taiwan was obtained after Japan's victory in the Sino-Japanese War of 1894 and 1895. Japan was one of the nations that participated in putting down the Boxer Rebellion in China in 1900. Japan defeated Russia in the Russo-Japanese War of 1904. Japan emerged as a military power and Korea became a Japanese protectorate. The southern area of Manchuria also became part of Japan's territorial properties. Korea remained under the control of Japan until 1945.

After World War I, Japan acquired former German colonies in Micronesia because it had fought on the side of the Allies. By the 1930s, Japan had a colonial empire that reached from mainland China to Micronesia. During World War II, Japanese territorial expansion increased farther into the South Pacific. At the conclusion of World War II, Japan was required to relinquish its territories.

SKILL 4.4   Analyze the causes and effects of the Industrial Revolution.

The Start of the Industrial Revolution

The Industrial Revolution began in Great Britain when the development of power-driven machinery fueled by coal and steam led to the accelerated growth of industry, with large factories replacing homes and small workshops as work centers.

The lives of people changed drastically, and a largely agricultural society changed to an industrial one. In Western Europe, the period of empire and colonialism began. The industrialized nations seized and claimed parts of Africa and Asia in an effort to control and provide the raw materials needed to feed the industries and machines in the "mother country." Later developments included power based on electricity and internal combustion, replacing coal and steam.

The Industrial Revolution in the United States

In the United States, there was a marked degree of industrialization before and during the Civil War, but at war's end, industry in America was small. After the war, dramatic changes took place. Machines replaced manual labor, extensive nationwide railroad service made possible the wider distribution of goods, new products were made available in large quantities, and large amounts of money were loaned by bankers and investors for expansion of business operations.

Impact on American Life

People's lives were dramatically affected by this phenomenal industrial growth. Cities became the centers of this new business activity that resulted in mass population movements and tremendous growth. This new boom in business resulted in huge fortunes for some Americans and extreme poverty for many others.

The discontent this caused resulted in a number of new reform movements—from which came measures controlling the power and size of big business. Other measures helped the poor.

Industry before, during, and after the Civil War was centered mainly in the north. The late 1800s and early 1900s saw the buildup of military strength as the United States grew into a world power.

The use of machines in industry enabled workers to produce a large quantity of goods much faster than by hand. With the increase in business, hundreds of workers were hired and assigned to perform a certain job in the production process. This method of organization, called **division of labor,** increased the rate of production and allowed businesses to lower prices for their products, making them affordable for more people. As a result, sales and businesses were increasingly successful and profitable.

A great variety of new products or **inventions** became available. Examples include the typewriter, the telephone, barbed wire, the electric light, the phonograph, and the gasoline automobile. From this list, the one that had the greatest effect on America's economy was the automobile.

The increase in business and industry was greatly affected by the many **rich natural resources** that were found throughout the nation. The industrial machines were powered by the abundant water supply. The construction industry as well as the manufacturing industry that created products made from wood depended heavily on lumber from the forests. Coal and iron ore in abundance were needed for the steel industry, which profited from and increased from the use of steel in skyscrapers, automobiles, bridges, railroad tracks, and machines. Other minerals such as silver, copper, and petroleum played a large role in industrial growth. Petroleum, from which gasoline was refined as fuel for the increasingly popular automobile and from which plastics and synthetic fabrics were created, pushed industrial growth forward.

Between 1870 and 1916, more than twenty-five million **immigrants** came into the United States, adding to the phenomenal population growth taking place. This tremendous growth aided business and industry in two ways. First, the number of consumers increased, creating a greater demand for products and enlarging the markets for the products. Second, increased production and expanding business meant more workers were available for newly created jobs.

The completion of the nation's **transcontinental railroad** in 1869 contributed greatly to the nation's economic and industrial growth. Some examples of the benefits of using the railroads include raw materials being shipped quickly by the mining companies and finished products being sent to all parts of the country. Many wealthy industrialists and railroad owners saw tremendous profits steadily increasing due to this improved method of mass transportation. The railroads are responsible for America's "last frontier" because of the ability for transportation settlers then had.

As business grew, methods of sales and promotion were developed. Salespersons went to all parts of the country promoting the various products. Large department stores in the growing cities began offering the varied products at affordable prices. People who lived far from the cities still had the advantage of using a mail-order service for what they needed. The developments in communication, such as the **telephone and telegraph,** increased the efficiency and prosperity of big business.
The Rise of Monopolies

Investments in corporate stocks and bonds resulted from business prosperity. Individuals began investing heavily with an eager desire to share in the profits. Their investments made available the needed capital for companies to expand their operations. From this, banks increased in number throughout the country, making loans to businesses and significant contributions to economic growth. At the same time, during the 1880s, government made little effort to regulate businesses. This gave rise to monopolies where larger businesses eliminated their smaller competitors and assumed complete control of their industries.

Some owners in the same business would join or merge to form one company. Others formed what were called **trusts,** a type of monopoly in which rival businesses were controlled but not formally owned. Monopolies had some good effects on the economy.

Out of them grew the large, efficient corporations that made important contributions to the growth of the nation's economy. Also, the monopolies enabled businesses to keep their sales steady and avoid sharp fluctuations in price and production. At the same time, the downside of monopolies was the unfair business practices of the business leaders. Some acquired so much power that they took unfair advantage of others. Those who had little or no competition would require their suppliers to supply goods at a low cost, sell the finished products at high prices, and reduce the quality of the product to save money.

The Dawn of the Progressive Era

The late 1800s and early 1900s was a period of reform. There were efforts of many to make significant changes in the areas of politics, society, and the economy to reduce the levels of poverty and improve the living conditions of those affected by it.

Regulating big business and eliminating governmental corruption while making it more responsive to the needs of the people were on the list of reforms to be accomplished. Until 1890, there was very little success, but from 1890 on, the reformers gained increased public support and were able to achieve some influence in government. Historians refer to the years between 1890 and 1917 as the **Progressive Era** (for more information, see Skill 9.2).

Skilled laborers were organized into a labor union called the **American Federation of Labor,** in an effort to gain better working conditions and wages for its members.

Farmers were producing more food than people could afford to buy. This was the result of new farmlands rapidly sprouting on the plains and prairies, development and availability of new farm machinery, and newer and better methods of farming. Farmers tried selling their surplus abroad but faced stiff competition from other nations selling the same farm products. Other problems contributed significantly to their situation. Items they needed for daily life were priced exorbitantly high. Having to borrow money to carry on farming activities kept the farmers constantly in debt. Higher interest rates, shortage of money, falling farm prices, dealing with the so-called middlemen, and the increasingly high charges of the railroads for hauling farm products to large markets all contributed to the desperate need for reform to relieve the plight of American farmers.

SKILL 4.5   **Demonstrate knowledge of the impact of totalitarianism in the twentieth century (e.g., fascist Italy, Nazi Germany, Soviet Union).**

In a **totalitarian** state the political authority that has authority over society is the state. In this type of political system, the state attempts to control public and private life. The concept was first discussed in the 1920s but became relevant to the Western world during the Cold War era after the end of World War II and the tensions between the free world and the communist world were evident.

Fascist Italy

Fascism became popular in some areas of Europe in the 1920s. Although there were differences in the fascist movements, they all encompassed the ideas of nationalism, a belief in a social hierarchy, a rule of the elites, and the belief that individual interests are of less importance than the welfare of the nation.

Benito Mussolini was Italy's and Europe's first fascist ruler. As a young man, Mussolini was a socialist. However, he fought in World War I and realized opportunities of leadership were possible. After the war he criticized the role Italy's government had taken in the peace talks and blamed the government for the problems with the Treaty of Versailles. In 1919, he organized the Fascist Party and the **Black Shirts** who would be used to enforce the authority of the government. Three years later he took it upon himself declare that the Italian government needed reorganizing and that he was the person the people should look to for the restoration of order.

Mussolini declared himself dictator and became known as Il Duce, "the leader." Italy's fascist government organized youth groups, similar to the Nazi youth groups, which supported the government. Boys were expected to become soldiers and girls were expected to be mothers of sons and daughters who supported the fascists. Mussolini wanted to expand the Italian Fascist population and, as a result, instituted a tax savings for large families. His government reduced unemployment and instituted a public works program. Italy invaded Ethiopia in 1935 and the country became part of Italy's empire. Italy also supported the Spanish fascists during the Spanish Civil War in 1939.

Italy and Germany signed an alliance, and Mussolini began adopting discriminatory policies against the Jews. Italy joined World War II after Hitler invaded Poland. In 1942, President Roosevelt met with Prime Minister Winston Churchill in Casablanca, Morocco, and decided the fate of Italy by deciding to secure Sicily. As the Allied forces entered Italy, Mussolini resigned and was arrested. After the Allies liberated Italy, Mussolini attempted to escape into Switzerland. He was captured and executed.

Nazi Germany

Nazi Germany refers to the period in Germany from 1933 to 1945 when **Adolf Hitler** led the National Socialist German Workers' Party and controlled the government. Hitler's government was a totalitarian government that controlled most aspects of the peoples' lives.

President von Hindenburg of the Weimar Republic appointed Adolf Hitler as Chancellor in 1933. Hitler combined the presidency and the office of Chancellor when he became dictator after von Hindenburg's death in 1934. Germany, like many countries of the world, was affected by the Great Depression. Hitler undertook public works and increased military spending to eliminate unemployment and restore the country's economy. During this time, the autobahns were built and the peoples' car, the Volkswagen, came into being.

The Nazis were anti-Semitic and considered the Aryans to be the master race. Jews, intellectuals, religious leaders, and others who opposed the government or were viewed as inferior were persecuted. **Concentration camps** were forced labor camps for those the Nazis believed to be undesirable. Many Jews and others were exterminated in gas chambers at the camps. These policies of mass murders were termed the **Holocaust.**

Nazi leaders were tried for war crimes in Nuremberg after the war.

Soviet Union

The Soviet Union was in existence for nearly seventy years. Its beginnings can be traced to the 1917 Russian Revolution. After the czar had been removed from office, a second revolution led by **Vladimir Lenin** took place. Lenin's followers removed the provincial government and began a civil war between two parties, the Reds and the Whites. The Reds were pro-revolutionaries and communists. They enlisted the support of workers and peasants and were victorious. The Reds unified many of the republics and after Lenin died, **Joseph Stalin** became the party's leader.

Under Stalin, the Soviet Union adopted a planned economy and industrialized. The country also adopted the concept of **collectivism**. Stalin's government repressed those opposing him, whether communists or not. The Soviet Union signed a nonaggression pact with Germany but Germany disregarded the pact and invaded the country in 1941.

The Soviets joined the Allies, captured parts of Germany, and took part in the division of Berlin and the country of Germany. The Soviets occupied countries that were to become known as the **Eastern Bloc**.

Because of ideological and political differences, the Soviet Union and the United States entered into a period known as the **Cold War.**

The Soviets and Americans engaged in a race for outer space, and the Russians placed the first satellite into orbit. During the Cold War, the Soviet Union planned to assemble missiles in Cuba, and was confronted by the John F. Kennedy administration. The Cold War era continued as the Soviets invaded Afghanistan in 1979.

Mikhail Gorbachev introduced reforms to bring the Soviet Union closer to democracy. Because of deteriorating economic conditions in the Soviet Union, his policies were not successful. In 1991, the Communist Party was banned, Gorbachev resigned, and the Soviet Union (of twelve republics) was dissolved.

SKILL 4.6   Analyze the causes and effects of World War I and World War II.

World War I: 1914–1918

The causes of World War I included the surge of nationalism, the increasing strength of military capabilities, massive colonization for raw materials needed for industrialization and manufacturing, and military and diplomatic alliances. The initial spark, which started the conflagration, was the assassination of Austrian Archduke Francis Ferdinand and his wife in Sarajevo, Yugoslavia.

Twenty-eight nations were involved in the war, not including colonies and territories.

The war began July 28, 1914, and ended November 11, 1918. The Treaty of Versailles concluded the war.

The war cost a total of $337 billion, increased inflation and huge war debts, and caused a loss of markets, goods, jobs, and factories.

Politically, old empires collapsed. Many monarchies disappeared and smaller countries gained temporary independence. Communists seized power in Russia and, in some cases, nationalism increased.

Socially, total populations decreased because of war casualties and low birth rates. There were millions of displaced persons as villages and farms were destroyed. Cities grew. Women made significant gains in the work force and at the ballot box. There was less social distinction and fewer classes. Attitudes completely changed and old beliefs and values were questioned. The peace settlement established the League of Nations to ensure peace, but it failed to do so.

World War II: 1939–1945

The provisions of the Treaty of Versailles, the peace treaty that ended World War I, ultimately led to the Second World War. Countries that had fought in the first war were either dissatisfied over the "spoils" of war, or were punished so harshly that resentment continued building to an eruption twenty years later.

The economic problems of both winners and losers of World War I were never resolved, and the worldwide Great Depression of the 1930s dealt the final blow to any immediate rapid recovery. Democratic governments in Europe were severely strained and weakened, which in turn gave strength and encouragement to extreme political movements that promised to end the economic chaos in their countries.

Nationalism, which had been a major cause of World War I, grew even stronger and seemed to feed the feelings of discontent, which became increasingly rampant. Because of unstable economic conditions and political unrest, harsh dictatorships arose in several of the countries, especially where there had been no history of experience in democratic government. Countries such as

Germany, Japan, and Italy began to aggressively expand their borders and acquire additional territory.

In all, fifty-nine nations became embroiled in World War II, which began September 1, 1939, and ended September 2, 1945. These dates include both the European and Pacific theaters of war.

The horrible tragic results of this second global conflagration were more deaths and more destruction than in any other armed conflict. The war completely uprooted and displaced millions of people.

The end of the war brought renewed power struggles, especially in Europe and China, with many Eastern European nations as well as China coming under complete control and domination of the communists, supported and backed by the Soviet Union.

With the development of and deployment of two atomic bombs against two Japanese cities, the world found itself in the **Nuclear Age**.

The peace settlement established the United Nations.

SKILL 4.7   **Understand significant events related to the twentieth-century spread and fall of communism (e.g., Cold War, Korean War, Vietnam War) and the post-Cold War world (e.g., globalization, radical Islamic fundamentalism, terrorism).**

The Spread and Fall of Communism

The Cold War

In 1946, Joseph Stalin stated publicly that the presence of capitalism and its development of the world's economy made international peace impossible. This resulted in an American diplomat in Moscow named **George F. Kennan** proposing, as a response to Stalin and as a statement of U.S. foreign policy, that the goal of the United States was to contain or limit the extension or expansion of Soviet communist policies and activities.

After Soviet efforts in Iran, Greece, and Turkey, President **Harry Truman** stated what is known as the **Truman Doctrine**. This doctrine committed the United States to a policy of intervention in order to contain or stop the spread of communism throughout the world.

After 1945, social and economic chaos continued in Western Europe, especially in Germany. Secretary of State **George C. Marshall** came to realize that Europe had serious challenges, and to assist in the recovery, he proposed a program known as the European Recovery Program, which came to be known as **the Marshall Plan**.

Although the Soviet Union withdrew from any participation, the United States continued the work of assisting Europe in regaining economic stability. In Germany, the situation was critical, with the American Army shouldering much of the staggering burden of relieving the serious problems in the environment and economy. In February 1948, Britain and the United States combined their two military occupation zones, with France joining them in June.

The major thrust of U.S. foreign policy from the end of World War II to 1990 was the post-war struggle between noncommunist nations, led by the United States, and the Soviet Union and the communist nations who were its allies. It was referred to as a **Cold War** because its conflicts did not lead to a major war of fighting, or a "hot war." Both the Soviet Union and the United States embarked on an arsenal buildup of atomic and bombs as well as other nuclear weapons. Both nations had the capability of destroying each other, but because of the continuous threat of nuclear war and accidents, extreme caution was practiced on both sides.

The efforts of both sides to serve and protect their political philosophies and to support and assist their allies resulted in a number of events during this forty-five-year period.

Economics were a main concern as well as political factors. A concern in both countries was that resources such as oil and food from other like-minded countries would not be allowed to flow to "the other side."

The Soviet Union kept a tight leash on its supporting countries, including all of Eastern Europe. The **Warsaw Pact** was a military treaty that bound the signatories to come to the aid of one another. The Western nations responded by creating a military organization of their own, the **North American Treaty Organization (NATO).**

The main symbol of the Cold War was the **arms race**, a continual buildup of missiles, tanks, and other weapons that became ever more technologically advanced and increasingly more deadly.

The ultimate weapon, which both sides had in abundance, was the **nuclear bomb**. Spending on weapons and defensive systems eventually occupied great percentages of the budgets of the United States and the Soviet Union. The war was a cultural struggle as well. Cold War tensions spilled over into many parts of life in countries around the world. The ways of life in countries on either side of the divide were so different that they seemed entirely foreign to outside observers.

The Cold War continued in varying degrees from 1947 to 1991, when the Soviet Union collapsed. Other Eastern European countries had seen their communist governments overthrown by this time as well, marking the shredding of the "Iron Curtain." The **Iron Curtain** referred to the ideological, symbolic and physical separation of Europe between East and West.

Mikhail Gorbachev was elected General Secretary by the Politburo in 1984, bringing with him a program of reform intended to bolster the flagging Soviet economy. As part of his plan, Gorbachev instituted a policy of economic freedoms called ***perestroika***, which allowed private ownership of some businesses, and relaxed the government's control over the media in a policy of openness, called ***glasnost***. Gorbachev also instituted free, multiparty elections.

Gorbachev thought these new policies would apply pressure on the more conservative members of the government, thereby increasing his support. The media seized upon their new freedom, however, and began reporting on the corruption and economic problems of the Soviet Union, which had been largely hidden from the public by the previous state-controlled news services. Meanwhile, the United States, under President **Ronald Reagan**, had rapidly increased its military spending, outpacing the Soviet Union and increasing economic pressure.

Faced with growing independence movements in many of the Eastern Bloc countries, the government under Gorbachev reversed the former leader Leonid Brezhnev's policies of tight control via the Communist Party. As the countries of Eastern Europe and Soviet states began pulling away from Russia, all these factors came together to cause the dissolution of the Soviet Union.

Korean War and Vietnam War

Asia was a prime battleground. The Soviet Union had allies in China, North Korea, and North Vietnam, and the United States had allies in Japan, South Korea, Taiwan, and South Vietnam. The Korean War and Vietnam War were major conflicts in which both protagonists played big roles but did not directly fight each other.

Japan annexed **Korea** and ruled it from 1910 until the end of World War II. At the conclusion of the war, the country was divided at the 38th parallel. U.S. military forces occupied the southern part of the country and the Soviets occupied the north. The 38th parallel became a line of division when free elections were not held after the war and the country was unified as expected.

Full-scale war broke out in 1950 when North Koreans crossed the border into South Korea. Soldiers from countries belonging to the United Nations were sent to South Korea as a peacekeeping force and to assist the South Korean forces. The North Koreans were driven back but China entered the war on the side of the North. The Soviets supplied aid to the North and to the Chinese. The Korean War ended when an armistice was signed in 1953 and the 38th parallel became the border that divided the country. A buffer zone, called the **demilitarized zone,** was established between the two areas.

The **Vietnam War** began in 1956 and took place in Vietnam, Laos, and Cambodia. Vietnam was divided into North and South. The North was communist and the South was anticommunist. The South Vietnamese Communists were known as the Viet Cong, and they used guerrilla warfare as a tactic against the anticommunists. The United States supported the South Vietnamese with air and ground forces to prevent the spread of communism. The North Vietnamese had the goal of unifying the country under communist rule. The United States continued to increase its military presence until 1968 when it was determined there might not be a U.S. victory. The South Vietnamese continued fighting as American troops were withdrawn. The Paris Peace Accords ended the war in January 1973.

Post-Cold War World

Globalization

The concept of **globalization** attempts to bring businesses and people of the world into closer contact. The efforts of globalism were apparent before World War I during the Age of Imperialism. After World War II, the movement began again when countries made agreements, such as the **Bretton Woods Agreement**, to facilitate trade and monetary policy. It slowed during the Korean War era and continued to slow until after the Cold War and the time when the Eastern bloc countries gave up communism for free market economies.

Today the concept of globalization encompasses the areas of international business, trade, construction, tourism, health, transportation, the environment, and economics. It is an interchange of products and ideas that has grown because of electronic communications such as the Internet and cellular phones. Improved air transportation has also linked economies and cultures. Today there are multinational corporations, joint ventures, and free trade areas that lessen or eliminate tariffs.

Nongovernmental organizations and international charities and philanthropic organizations are also important to the concept of globalization as are international organizations such as the World Health Organization, the International Monetary Fund, and international sporting events such as the Olympics and the soccer World Cup.

Globalization and greater connectivity between nations have negatively impacted nations, also. **Outsourcing** has affected the availability of jobs in countries that are outsourcing and the environment has been affected by air pollution and climate change. **Offshore tax havens** have developed to shelter income from taxation, organized crime has international links, and the drug trade and **human trafficking** have become international problems.

Terrorism

Terrorism, which has become a serious international problem, is the use of violence to frighten, coerce, or intimidate people and achieve political goals of those using violence. Terrorists try to right political and social injustices, and they believe violence will be successful in bringing about the needed changes.

There are different types of terrorism.

- Some political states, such as Nazi Germany, have used terrorism to carry out foreign policy.
- Bioterrorism releases toxic weapons, such as viruses and bacteria, into the environment.
- Cyberterrorism involves the use of computers and technology to disable communications networks.
- Ecoterrorism is the use of violence against industries that are perceived as a threat to animals and wildlife.

- Nuclear terrorism involves attacks on nuclear facilities and building nuclear weapons for acts of destruction.

Terrorism affects a country in various ways. It can disrupt an economy, lessen tourism, and cause deaths. It can also strengthen the resolve of governments to combat and defeat the violent acts.

International groups such as the United Nations and NATO and governments of countries throughout the world attempt to fight terrorism in various ways.

In 1979, the country of Syria was classified as a sponsor of terrorism. Today, the Syrian government disputes the classification but Westerners believe the Syrian government continues to support terrorist groups.

Two bombs were detonated by terrorists near the finish line of the Boston Marathon in 2013. The homemade bombs killed three people. The suspects were not linked to any specific terrorist group, but the suspects were Muslims who held extreme Islamic beliefs.

Radical Islamic Fundamentalism

Radical Islamic fundamentalists have been linked to terrorist activities since the 1990s and are a threat to international stability. **Radical Islamic fundamentalism** is a militant ideology that promotes the resentment of the West. The radical Islamic fundamentalists believe that Islam provides solutions to the world's problems and that their views promote the goal of an Islamic state. They view the West as a source of the world's problems because the West is focused on human will rather than on the holy law of Islam. They consider the West as infidels and terrorism as the best way to fight the infidels.

SKILL 4.8   **Analyze the influence of significant individuals of the nineteenth and twentieth centuries (e.g., Charles Darwin, Mohandas Gandhi, Adolf Hitler, Nelson Mandela, Mao Zedong, Mother Teresa).**

Charles Darwin

Charles Darwin was a nineteenth-century English naturalist whose theory of natural selection is the basis of evolutionary science. In the 1830s, Darwin spent five years examining and gathering fossils and specimens from around the world, contributing greatly to the natural scientific knowledge of his day. Based on his observations, Darwin arrived at the theory that different species of animals develop from a common source over many generations.

Darwin's theory was controversial when he published *The Origin of Species* in 1860 because it conflicts with Creationism, which states that all living things are created by God. Although Darwin did not include any speculation about human origins or evolution, the implications of his theory were clear, and he was confronted by the religious and scientific community at the time. Darwin's theory revolutionized the studies of natural science and biology as well as other fields of science.

Mohandas Gandhi

Mohandas Gandhi was a leading political and spiritual figure of the twentieth century and is best known as the leader of India's drive for independence from Great Britain. He became known by the honorific **Mahatma** (a Sanskrit word meaning "great-souled" or "venerable").

Born in Gujarat, India, in 1869, Gandhi studied law in London and spent several years in South Africa, where he experienced racial discrimination. He became a pioneer of *satyagraha* (loosely translated as "insistence on truth"), resistance through mass nonviolent civil disobedience. He developed this concept to implement and teach methods of passive resistance and nonviolent civil disobedience, including hunger strikes and boycotts, to influence British leaders. He also wrote several books including his autobiography, *The Story of My Experiments with Truth.* Gandhi was assassinated by a fanatic in 1948, shortly after India won its independence.

Nelson Mandela

Nelson Mandela was a major figure and leader in the struggle against apartheid in South Africa. In the 1960s he was sentenced to life imprisonment for sabotage and conspiracy by the South African white government. In 1990, he was released from prison as part of an effort to reach a compromise with South African blacks. He was a leading spokesperson for the anti-apartheid movement and the dismantling of racist policies in South Africa. He died in 2013 at his home in Johannesburg.

Mao Zedong

Mao Zedong was the founder of the People's Republic of China. He was born into a Chinese peasant farming family in 1893. When the 1911 revolution against the monarchy began, Mao joined the army. After the overthrow, in 1918, he became a member of the Chinese Communist Party and eventually began a small Soviet republic in the Chinese mountains. Mao was a skillful orator and many joined his cause. After Japan was defeated in World War II, China became embroiled in a civil war. In 1949, Mao established the People's Republic of China. As the party's leader, Mao instituted land reform by making land communal. His plans for a better economy failed and others who believed they could better lead the country took command. Mao returned to power in 1966 when he launched the **Cultural Revolution** which destroyed much of China's cultural heritage. Mao died in 1975.

Mother Teresa

Mother Teresa was a Roman Catholic missionary and sister who worked in India with people who had contracted AIDS and tuberculosis. Born about 1910 to Albanian parents in what is now Macedonia, she was baptized Agnes Gonxha Bojaxhiu. The religious order she belonged to required vows of poverty and free service to the poor. She received the 1979 Nobel Peace Prize.

Mother Teresa was a controversial figure. People admired her for her charitable work but also criticized her for not helping to create cleaner conditions in the hospices that she organized, and for her endorsement of some of the Catholic Church's more controversial doctrines, such as opposition to contraception and abortion. She died in 1997.

Adolf Hitler

Adolf Hitler, an Austrian, was a Nazi whose charismatic leadership helped him gain followers but led to the deaths of millions during the Holocaust. Hitler became Chancellor of Germany in 1933. He became the German leader after the president's death and was at the country's helm during World War II. He committed suicide in Berlin in 1945 as the Russian army moved into the German capital.

Other Significant Individuals

Other significant individuals in the nineteenth century offering art, literature, music, nursing and science, civil rights efforts, business acumen, western exploration, and leadership include, but are not limited to:

Hans Christian Andersen
Susan B. Anthony
Jane Austen
Clara Barton
Napoleon Bonaparte
Emily and Charlotte Bronte
Johannes Brahms
Louis Braille
Andrew Carnegie
Kit Carson
Mary Cassatt
Anton Chekhov
Frederic Chopin
Davy Crockett
Cochise
Frederick Douglass
Wyatt Earp
Ralph Waldo Emerson
Thomas Edison

William Lloyd Garrison
Paul Gauguin
Wild Bill Hickok
Chief Joseph
Jenny Lind
Abraham Lincoln
Gustav Mahler
Andrew Mellon
J. P. Morgan
Friedrich Nietzsche
Florence Nightingale
Louis Pasteur
John D. Rockefeller
Sitting Bull
Harriet Beecher Stowe
Levi Strauss
Nicola Tesla
Harriet Tubman
Vincent van Gogh

DOMAIN II   U.S. HISTORY

COMPETENCY 5: EXPLORATION AND COLONIZATION

THE TEACHER UNDERSTANDS SIGNIFICANT HISTORICAL EVENTS AND DEVELOPMENTS IN THE EXPLORATION AND COLONIZATION OF NORTH AMERICA AND THE DEVELOPMENT OF COLONIAL SOCIETY.

SKILL 5.1   Understand the causes and effects of European exploration and colonization of North America, including interactions with Native American populations.

Northern European countries laid claim to vast areas of North America. **Spain's** influence was in Florida, the Gulf Coast from Texas all the way west to California and south to the tip of South America, and some of the islands of the West Indies. **France**'s control centered from New Orleans north to what is now northern Canada including the entire Mississippi Valley, the St. Lawrence Valley, the Great Lakes, and the land that was part of the Louisiana Territory. A few West Indies islands were also part of France's empire. **England** settled the eastern seaboard of North America from Maine to Georgia, and some parts of Canada. Some West Indies islands also came under British control. New York originally was the **Dutch** New Amsterdam.

One interesting aspect of this was how each of the three major Western European powers, especially England, claimed lands that extended partly or all the way across the continent regardless of the fact that the others claimed the same land. The wars for dominance and control of power and influence in Europe would eventually extend to the Americas, especially North America.

New France

The part of North America claimed by France was called New France and consisted of the land west of the Appalachian Mountains. This area of claims and settlement included the St. Lawrence Valley, the Great Lakes, the Mississippi Valley, and the entire region of land westward to the Rocky Mountains. The French established permanent settlements at what is present-day Montreal and New Orleans, thus giving them control of the two major gateways into the vast, rich interior of North America. The St. Lawrence River, the Great Lakes, and the Mississippi River along with its tributaries made it possible for the French explorers and traders to roam at will, virtually unhindered in exploring, trapping, trading, and furthering the interests of France.

Most of the French settlements were in Canada along the St. Lawrence River. Only scattered forts and trading posts were found in the upper Mississippi Valley and Great Lakes region. The rulers of France originally intended New France to have vast estates owned by nobles and worked by peasants who would live on the estates in compact farming villages—the New World version of the Old World's medieval system of feudalism.

However, it did not work out that way. Each of the nobles wanted his estate to be on the river for ease of transportation. New France's settled areas were eventually established as a string of farmhouses stretching from Quebec to Montreal along the St. Lawrence and Richelieu Rivers.

French fur traders occupied the unsettled areas of the interior. They established contact with the friendly tribes, spending the winters with them, getting the furs needed for trade. In the spring, they returned to Montreal in time to trade their furs for the products brought by the cargo ships from France, which usually arrived at about the same time.

Most of the wealth of New France was from the fur trade that provided a livelihood for many people. Manufacturers and workmen in France, ship owners and merchants, as well as the fur traders and their Native American allies, all benefited. However, the freedom of roaming and trapping in the interior was a strong enticement for younger, stronger men without families and resulted in slow growth and relative weakness in the areas settled along the St. Lawrence.

During the eighteenth century, the rivalry with the British grew stronger and stronger. New France was united under a single government and enjoyed the support of many Native American allies. The French traders were very diligent in not destroying the forests and driving away game upon which the Native Americans depended for life. It was difficult for the French to defend all of their settlements as they were scattered over half of the continent.

By the early 1750s, France was the most powerful nation in Western Europe. Its armies were superior to all others, and its navy was giving the British stiff competition for control of the seas. The stage was set for confrontation in both Europe and America.

Spanish Settlements

Spanish settlement had its beginnings in the Caribbean with the establishment of colonies on Hispaniola (at Santo Domingo, which became the capital of the West Indies), Puerto Rico, and Cuba. There were a number of reasons for Spanish involvement in the Americas:

- The spirit of adventure
- The desire for land
- Expansion of power, influence, and empire
- The desire for great wealth
- Expansion of Roman Catholic influence and conversion of native peoples

The first permanent Spanish settlement in what is now the United States was in 1565 at St. Augustine, Florida. Later, in 1609, they established a permanent settlement in the southwestern United States at Santa Fe, New Mexico. At the peak of their power, the area in the United States claimed, settled, and controlled by Spain included Florida and all land west of the Mississippi River. Of course, France and England also lay claim to the same areas. Nonetheless, the Spanish built ranches and missions, and the Native Americans who came in contact with the Spaniards were introduced to animals, plants, and seeds from the Old World that they had never seen before. The animals included horses, cattle, donkeys, pigs, sheep, goats, and poultry.

Spain's control over its New World colonies lasted more than three hundred years, longer than England's or France's did. To this day, Spanish influence remains in names of places, art, architecture, music, literature, law, and cuisine.

The Spanish settlements in North America were not commercial enterprises but were for protection and defense of the trading and wealth from their colonies in Mexico and South America. Russian seal hunters came down the Pacific coast, the English moved into Florida and west into and beyond the Appalachians, and the French traders and trappers made their way from Louisiana and other parts of New France into Spanish territory. The Spanish failed to develop the colonial trade that was so important to self-sustaining colonial economic development. Consequently, the Spanish settlements in the present-day United States never really prospered.

British Colonies

Before 1763, when England was rapidly on the way to becoming the most powerful of the three major Western European powers, its Thirteen Colonies, located between the Atlantic and the Appalachians, physically occupied the least amount of land. As the colonists moved west and settled the lands of the Mississippi and Ohio river valleys, they cleared land for farming and settlements that the Native Americans and French had used for hunting and trapping activities.

Nonetheless, the thirteen English colonies were successful in developing settlements beyond the eastern seaboard, and by the time they had gained their independence from Britain, the colonies were able to govern themselves. They had a rich historical heritage of law, tradition, and documents leading the way to constitutional government conducted according to laws and customs. The settlers in the British colonies highly valued individual freedom, democratic government, and getting ahead through hard work.

SKILL 5.2   **Demonstrate knowledge of individuals, events, and issues that shaped the development of colonial society, including interactions among Europeans, Africans, and Native Americans.**

European Interaction with Native Americans

The people who lived in the Americas before Columbus arrived had a thriving, connected society. The civilizations in North America tended to spread out more and were in occasional conflict but maintained their sovereignty for the most part

Native Americans in North America had a spiritual and personal relationship with the various spirits of nature and a keen appreciation of weaving, woodworking, and metalworking. Various tribes dotted the landscape of what is now the United States. They struggled against one another for control of resources such as food and water but had no concept of ownership of land, since they believed that they were living on the land with the permission of the spirits.

The Native Americans mastered the art of growing many crops and were willing to share that knowledge with the various Europeans who arrived. Artwork made of hides, beads, and jewels was popular.

During the American Revolution, there was competition with the British for the allegiance of Native Americans east of the Mississippi River. Many Native Americans sided with the British in the hope of stopping the expansion of the American colonies into the lands they occupied.

By the terms of the **Treaty of Paris**, which ended the Revolutionary War, a large amount of land occupied and claimed by Native Americans was ceded to the United States. The British, however, did not inform the native people of the change. The government of the new nation first tried to treat the tribes who had fought with the British as conquered people and claimed their land. This policy was later abandoned because it could not be enforced.

European Interactions with Africans

Europeans benefited from the slave trade that brought Africans to North America and the West Indies. The Africans were sold as slaves to plantation owners to work in the fields of tobacco, cotton, and rice crops in the South.

Although most Africans in the South were laborers, each plantation home had slaves who worked at domestic tasks. The slaves usually lived in family units in areas on the plantations. They worked during daylight hours and if they worked on Sundays they were often given lighter workloads. In the South, the slaves who worked on plantations retained many of their heritage and religious traditions.

In the North, most Africans worked as house servants. Most household servants were female, but the men were used as gardeners and tradesmen who worked in shops. In New England, the Puritans made attempts to Christianize the Africans. They usually lived in areas over kitchens and stables and worked each day of the week. The slaves who worked on Sundays were often given fewer tasks to complete. Urban slaves had more opportunities to communicate with others through trips to the marketplace. They also were usually better dressed and better fed than Southern slaves.

SKILL 5.3   **Analyze political, economic, and cultural reasons for establishment of the Thirteen Colonies.**

The thirteen English colonies, with only a few exceptions, were considered **commercial ventures** to make a profit for the crown or the company or whoever financed the colony's beginnings. One colony was established as a **philanthropic enterprise** and three others were primarily established for **religious reasons**. The other nine colonies were started for **economic reasons**. Settlers in these unique colonies came for different reasons:

- Religious freedom
- Political freedom
- Economic prosperity

- Land ownership

The colonies were divided generally into three regions—New England, Middle, and Southern. The culture of each was distinct and affected attitudes, ideas toward politics, religion, and economic activities. The geography of each region also contributed to its unique characteristics.

New England Colonies

The **New England colonies** consisted of Massachusetts, Rhode Island, Connecticut, and New Hampshire. Life in these colonies was centered on the towns. Each family farmed its own plot of land, but the short summer growing season and limited amount of good soil gave rise to other economic activities such as manufacturing, fishing, shipbuilding, and trade.

The vast majority of the settlers shared similar origins, coming from England and Scotland. Towns were carefully planned and laid out the same way. The form of government was the town meeting where all adult males met to make the laws. The legislative body, called the General Court, consisted of an Upper and Lower House.

Middle Colonies

The **Middle colonies** (also called **Middle Atlantic colonies**) included New York, New Jersey, Pennsylvania, Delaware, and Maryland. New York and New Jersey were once the Dutch colony of New Netherlands, and Delaware was at one time New Sweden. These five colonies from their beginnings were considered "melting pots," with settlers from many different nations and backgrounds. The main economic activity was farming with the settlers scattered over the countryside cultivating rather large farms.

The local tribes of Native Americans in the region were not as much of a threat as they were in New England, so settlers did not have to settle in small farming villages. The soil was very fertile, and a milder climate provided a longer growing season.

The farms in the Middle colonies produced a large surplus of food not only for the colonists themselves but also for sale. This colonial region became known as the "breadbasket" of the New World, and the New York and Philadelphia seaports were constantly filled with ships being loaded with meat, flour, and other foodstuffs for the West Indies and England.

There were also other economic activities such as shipbuilding, iron mines, and factories producing paper, glass, and textiles. The legislative body in Pennsylvania was unicameral, consisting of one house. In the other four colonies, the legislative body had two houses. Units of local government were in counties and towns.

Southern Colonies

The **Southern colonies** were Virginia, North Carolina, South Carolina, and Georgia. Virginia was the first permanent successful English colony, and Georgia was the last. The year 1619 was a very important year in the history of Virginia and the United States for three very significant reasons.

- Sixty women were sent to Virginia to marry and establish families.
- Twenty Africans (the first of thousands) arrived.
- Virginia colonists were granted the right to self-government. They began by electing representatives to the House of Burgesses, their own legislative body.

The major economic activity in this region was farming. Here the soil was very fertile and the climate mild with a long growing season. The large plantations were located largely in the coastal or tidewater areas and eventually required large numbers of slaves. Although the wealthy slave-owning planters set the pattern of life in this region, most of the people lived inland away from coastal areas. They were small farmers and few owned slaves.

The settlers in these four colonies came from diverse backgrounds and cultures. Virginia was colonized mostly by people from England while Georgia was started as a haven for debtors from English prisons. Pioneers from Virginia settled in North Carolina while South Carolina welcomed people from England and Scotland, French Protestants, Germans, and emigrants from islands in the West Indies. Products from farms and plantations included rice, tobacco, indigo, cotton, and some corn and wheat.

Other economic activities included lumber from the pine forests and fur trade on the frontier. Cities such as Savannah and Charleston were important seaports and trading centers.

The Southern planters and the people living in the coastal cities and towns had a way of life similar to lifestyles in towns in England. The influence was seen and heard in how people dressed and talked. The architectural styles of houses and public buildings and the social divisions or levels of society mimicked that of England. Both the planters and city dwellers enjoyed an active social life and had strong emotional ties to England.

On the other hand, life inland on the frontier had marked differences. All facets of daily living—clothing, food, housing, economic and social activities—were all connected to what was needed to sustain life and survive in the wilderness. The frontier settlers were self-sufficient and extremely individualistic and independent. There were few levels of society or class distinctions as they considered themselves to be the equal of all others, regardless of station in life. The roots of equality, independence, individual rights, and freedoms were strong and well-developed. Frontier people were not likely to be admired for their fancy dress, expensive house, eloquent language, or titles following their names.

SKILL 5.4   **Demonstrate knowledge of the foundations of representative government in the United States (e.g., ways in which the Mayflower Compact, the Iroquois Confederacy, the Fundamental Orders of Connecticut, and the Virginia House of Burgesses contributed to the growth of representative government).**

The most familiar form of government to most Westerners is the **representative government**, commonly called a **republic** or **democracy**. The idea behind this form of government is that the people in a society are ultimately responsible for their government and the laws that it passes, enforces, and interprets in that they, the people, elect many of the members of that government.

The representative government began, in Western tradition, in Greece, with democracy. It then progressed to the republic in Rome and from there to other democracies and republics, including the United States and many other countries around the world.

Mayflower Compact

The Mayflower Compact is considered the earliest American governmental document. Signed in 1620 by forty-one passengers of the *Mayflower,* the Compact pledged loyalty to King James and affirmed an agreement among the settlers at Plymouth to form a political body with the power to pass its own laws and ordinances. While simple in its structure, the Mayflower Compact expressed an ideal of self-government that was to flourish in America.

Iroquois Confederacy

The confederacy of Iroquois tribes was known as the **Haudenosaunee,** the League of Peace and Power. The Iroquois are often called "the people of the longhouse." Their original homeland was in upstate New York between the Adirondack Mountains and Niagara Falls. As a result of migration and conquest, they controlled most of the northeastern United States and eastern Canada by the time of the first European contact. The confederacy consisted of five nations in the beginning and then a sixth nation was added. It had a constitution known as the Gayanashagowa ("Great Law of Peace") that was created prior to the arrival of Europeans. This document was recorded in memory by using a device in the form of special beads called wampum. There is no consensus among historians about the date of the origin of this constitution, but it is believed to have been created sometime between 1142 and the early 1600s.

Fundamental Orders of Connecticut

Connecticut's Fundamental Orders are considered, by some, to be the first written constitution in the colonies. In 1638, three Connecticut communities joined together to describe in a written document the structure of powers of their government. In 1639, the document was adopted. It had provisions that were similar to those included in the U.S. Constitution that was adopted in 1789.

Virginia House of Burgesses

The House of Burgesses was established in Virginia in 1619 and was the first legislative assembly in the colonies that had as its members, elected representatives. The burgesses, elected representatives, met with the governor of Virginia and his council during. Beginning in 1643, the burgesses met separately and became the "lower house" of the assembly.

The legislature passed several important laws that King Charles II later repealed. England tried to liit the power of the House of Burgesses but it continued to play an important role in government. Patrick Henry led the opposition to the Stamp Act, and the legislature adopted a resolution against the Act. After the burgesses voted their support of the Boston residents who had objected to the tax on tea, the Virginia governor dissolved the legislature. The burgesses reconvened and met to discuss events that would lead to the creation of the First Continental Congress. In June 1776, the burgesses adopted a new constitution for Virginia.

The House of Burgesses was officially dissolved after the new constitution was written because the constituion created a new assembly. Many of the burgesses became statesmen and colonial leaders. George Washington, Thomas Jefferson, Patrick Henry, and Richard Henry Lee were members of the House of Burgesses.

SKILL 5.5   **Analyze the influence of various factors on the development of colonial society (e.g., geography, slavery, processes of spatial exchange [diffusion]).**

Geography

New England Colonies

New England had rocky soil, short growing season, a long seacoast, rivers, and large supplies of timber. Residents of the New England colonies were primarily small farmers, boat builders, or fishermen.

Each family had its own subsistence farm with supporting livestock. Women were expected to care for the children and take care of the household, and men to tend to the farming and livestock. Families encouraged their sons to continue to farm and provided them with land and livestock to establish them. Women were expected to marry. Blacksmiths and millers and other associated tradesmen found a living in inland towns, and in towns along the seacoast, trading and fishing were the dominant occupations.

Middle Colonies

The Middle colonies had a more diverse population than New England, with immigrants from the Netherlands, Scotland, Ireland and Germany making up the largest groups. These people were also largely farmers, each group bringing its own methods and techniques. Family structure was similar to that in New England, but unlike their Puritan counterparts, German and Dutch women were allowed to own property and could often be found working in the fields. Middle-colony seaport towns became major centers of trade, and laborers could find work on the docks and as sailors. Many of these workers were African descendants. As these towns grew, so did the merchant class, and some colonists began to build real fortunes.

Southern Colonies

Social and economic organizations were different in the Southern colonies. Instead of several small farms, large tracts of agricultural land were collected into plantations centered by large, palatial houses. Wealthy families, who took their social cues from Britain, owned these plantations.

Labor on the plantations was accomplished by slaves. Poor whites in the Southern colonies might also find work on plantations or sharecrop on borrowed farmland.

Slavery

Slavery influenced the economic development of the Chesapeake area and the Southern colonies. As the settlers realized the agricultural potential of these areas, they developed large plantations. The large plantations needed a work force, and the Atlantic slave trade supplied the needed labor.

Slaves became commodities that were required for the economic survival of the plantations and for the luxury of plantation life. Slaves were owned and considered property of their owners. After the colonies became independent, the issue of whether or how to count slaves for determining representation in Congress was one that the framers of the Constitution was required to decide.

Spatial Exchange (Diffusion)

The way people are distributed in an area is called **spatial diffusion.** It is also known as spatial exchange. Because spatial diffusion concerns the population distribution, it is important to determine *why* people migrated to an area and why they are located in specific geographical spaces.

The settlement of New England is an example. The Pilgrims, who were given permission to settle the New World, wanted religious freedom and freedom from persecution. They had been given a charter to settle in what is present-day Virginia. However, the *Mayflower* was blown off course—approximately five hundred miles off course—and instead of landing in the Southern colony of Virginia, they landed on the shores of what later became known as Massachusetts. Religion was also the basis of migration to the Middle colonies. Good agriculture and land ownership brought people to Virginia.

Spatial diffusion was important in the settlement of inland areas during colonial times. Individuals who wanted to own land, escape from the strict religious atmosphere of New England colonies, and an opportunity to explore the wilderness moved into the western river valleys in what is today the Midwest.

COMPETENCY 6: THE REVOLUTIONARY ERA AND THE EARLY YEARS OF THE REPUBLIC

THE TEACHER UNDERSTANDS SIGNIFICANT HISTORICAL EVENTS AND DEVELOPMENTS OF THE REVOLUTIONARY ERA AND THE EARLY YEARS OF THE REPUBLIC, INCLUDING THE FOUNDATIONS OF REPRESENTATIVE GOVERNMENT IN THE UNITED STATES.

SKILL 6.1   **Demonstrate knowledge of individuals, events, and issues that shaped the development of U.S. society during the Revolutionary Era and early years of the Republic.**

French and Indian Wars

By the 1750s in Europe, Spain was no longer the most powerful nation in the world. Rivalry remained between Britain and France. Between 1689 and 1763, France and England had engaged in a series of armed conflicts. Those conflicts ended up being fought mostly in North America and are known in America as the **French and Indian Wars.**

- The War of the League of Augsburg in Europe, 1689 to 1697, also called King William's War and the Nine Years War, took place mostly in Flanders but became the first French and Indian War.
- The War of the Spanish Succession, 1702 to 1713, also called Queen Anne's War, became the second French and Indian War.
- The War of the Austrian Succession, 1740 to 1748, also called King George's War, was the third French and Indian War.
- The final conflict, 1754 to 1763 was the fourth French and Indian War. In Europe where it began, it is known as the Seven Years' War, and in Canada it is known as the War of the Conquest.

Britain and France fought for possession of colonies—especially in Asia, the Caribbean, and North America—and for control of the seas. But none of these conflicts was decisive.

The fourth French and Indian War caused more than a million deaths, and in the twentieth century Winston Churchill called it a world war since it took place in Europe, Asia, and North America. The result was the end of France's being a major colonial power in North America—and the beginning of Great Britain's becoming the dominant power in the world.

In America, both sides had advantages and disadvantages. The British colonies were well-established and consolidated in a smaller area than the French. British colonists outnumbered French colonists 23 to 1. Except for a small area in Canada, French settlements were scattered over a much larger area (roughly half of the continent) and were smaller.

However, the French settlements were united under one government and were quick to act and cooperate when necessary. In addition, the French had many more Indian allies than the British. The British colonies had separate, individual governments and very seldom cooperated, even when necessary. In Europe, at that time, France was the more powerful of the two nations.

Both sides enjoyed victories and suffered defeats. **William Pitt** was one individual who can be given the credit for British victory. Pitt was a strong leader, enormously energetic, supremely self-confident, and determined to achieve a complete British victory. Despite the advantages and military victories of the French, Pitt succeeded. He sent more troops to America, strengthened the British Navy, and gave officers of the colonial militias ranks equal to the British officers. He saw to it that Britain took the offensive and kept it.

Of all the British victories, perhaps the most crucial and important was winning Canada. The French depended on the St. Lawrence River for transporting supplies, soldiers, and messages, and it was the link between New France and France. Tied into this waterway system were the connecting links of the Great Lakes and the Mississippi River and its tributaries, along which were scattered French forts, trading posts, and small settlements.

When, in 1758, the British captured Louisburg on Cape Breton Island, New France was doomed. Louisburg gave the British Navy a base of operations preventing French reinforcements and supplies getting to their troops. Other forts that fell to the British included Frontenac, Duquesne, Crown Point, Ticonderoga, Niagara, those in the upper Ohio Valley, and, most importantly,

Quebec—and finally Montreal. Spain entered the war in 1762 to aid France but it was too late. British victories occurred all around the world—in India, in the Mediterranean, and in Europe.

In 1763 in Paris, Spain, France, and Britain met to draw up the **Treaty of Paris** (also known as the **Treaty of 1763,** different from the Treaty of Paris of 1783). Great Britain received most of India and all of North America east of the Mississippi River, except for New Orleans. Britain received from Spain the control of Florida and returned Cuba and the islands of the Philippines to Spain. France lost nearly all its possessions in America and India but was allowed to keep an island fishing colony off Canada and a few Caribbean islands. France gave Spain New Orleans and the vast territory of Louisiana west of the Mississippi River.

Events in the British Colonies

Britain was now the most powerful nation. The colonial militias and their officers gained much experience in fighting which was very valuable later. The Thirteen Colonies began to realize that cooperating with each other was the only way to defend themselves. The years before the outbreak of fighting were a time of revolutionary ideas and a time of building a new nation.

After the French and Indian Wars, England had a large war debt. Parliament imposed taxes on the colonies to recoup needed funds. Parliament passed the **Sugar Act** and the **Stamp Act**, and the colonists resisted. Parliament repealed the Stamp Act, but colonists formed groups such as the Sons of Liberty. They met, they discussed, and they hung British officials in effigy. Parliament passed the **Townshend Acts** that imposed a tax on glass and tea, among other products and sent troops to help the customs officers enforce the new acts. (For further discussion of these acts, see Skills 6.2 and 6.3.)

Tensions continued to rise and in 1770, the **Boston Massacre** took place. A system of "networking" was initiated when committees of correspondence were organized as a way to keep abreast of news throughout the colonies. When Parliament gave the East India Company a monopoly over the sale of tea, the colonists reacted—by not purchasing the tea, by refusing to drink the tea, and by dumping the cargos of tea overboard in what is known as the **Boston Tea Party.**

Outbreak of the Revolutionary War

The colonists became more organized to decide how to respond to the coercive acts of Parliament. Colonial representatives held the First Continental Congress and the British sent soldiers to keep the colonists under control. In April 1775, the British were advancing to capture ammunition stored outside of Boston. Shots were fired at Lexington and Concord, and the Revolutionary War began. The colonists also took steps to decide their future course of action in relation to their status with England.

Approximately one-third of the colonists did not want to break with England. They were the **Loyalists**. Most of them lived in the Southern colonies but those in the North belonged to the wealthy merchant class, were government officials, or clergy. As problems with England escalated, many Northern Loyalists fled to Canada and the Caribbean islands. Loyalists in the Southern colonies joined the British army.

Many of the Native Americans joined forces with the British because they feared colonial expansion on to their lands in the frontier. The slaves, in general, supported the British because they believed they would be free. Many of the colonists neither supported independence nor continued alignment with Britain and wanted to watch the developments without taking sides.

Early in 1776, **Thomas Paine** wrote the essay *Common Sense* and gathered support against the British from the colonists. Paine's document appealed to the masses because it supported the belief that the people had the common sense to rule themselves.

The Second Continental Congress met in June 1776 and appointed a committee to draft a document declaring independence. The **Declaration of Independence** was approved the next month.

SKILL 6.2   **Analyze causes of the American Revolution (e.g., mercantilism, British policies following the French and Indian War).**

British Policies

The earliest signs of the American Revolution became evident over the issue of trade and taxation. In 1765, the British Parliament passed the **Stamp Act**, which directly taxed trade in the American colonies.

As primary colonial harbors, New York City and Boston would have felt the sting from this tax most severely. In 1765, New York was the site of the Stamp Act Congress, a collection of representatives from the colonies united in opposition to the Stamp Act, claiming that only colonial governments had the right to pass taxes on the colonial trade. New York merchants led a boycott on British goods in protest and were later joined by Boston merchants. On the date when the Stamp Act was to have gone into effect, violence erupted in New York City and an effigy of the colonial governor was burned. The New York assembly also refused a direct request from the British military to enforce the **Quartering Act**, which required colonists to house and feed British troops.

Fearing revolution, King George III repealed the Stamp Act in 1766. At the same time, however, Parliament passed a series of acts designed to give Britain even more power over colonial affairs. New York continued to refuse to enforce the Quartering Act as tensions grew and revolution sparked.

Mercantilism

Mercantilism was a trade policy system in which the American colonists provided raw materials to Britain and Britain used the materials to manufacture products which they sold to the colonists and to other nations. The system benefited the British because if the colonists sold their raw materials to their mother country, they could not sell to nations that competed with Britain.

Britain passed a series of regulations, called the Navigation Acts. These acts required British ships to carry goods, that colonial goods could not be shipped to countries without first going through England or Scotland, and that the America colonies could not compete with British manufacturing. These acts benefited Britain but restricted colonial trade and lowered the price of colonial products, such as tobacco. Britain enforced the rules by revoking the Massachusetts Bay Colony's charter when it learned of the colonists' attempt to bypass the laws by smuggling goods. However, Britain mainly followed the policy of **salutary neglect** and did not enforce the rules in the hope that the colonists would remain loyal.

SKILL 6.3   **Understand significant political and economic issues of the Revolutionary Era (e.g., taxation without representation, enforcement of the Navigation Acts, Lexington, Concord, winter at Valley Forge, Treaty of Paris of 1783).**

Taxation Without Representation

The colonists' protest of **"no taxation without representation"** was meaningless to the English. Parliament represented the entire nation, was completely unlimited in legislation, and had become supreme. The colonists considered their colonial legislative assemblies equal to Parliament, which was totally unacceptable in England. New ideas and traditions grew extremely fast, pushing aside what was left of the old ideas and old traditions. By 1763, Britain considered its American colonies as being a "territorial" empire. The stage was set and the conditions were right for a showdown.

It all began in 1763 when Parliament decided to have a standing army in North America to reinforce British control. In 1765, the **Quartering Act** was passed and required the colonists to provide supplies and living quarters for the British troops. In addition, efforts by the British were made to keep the peace by establishing good relations with the Native Americans. Consequently, a proclamation was issued that prohibited American colonists from making any settlements west of the Appalachians until treaties were signed with the Native Americans.

The **Sugar Act** of 1764 required efficient collection of taxes on molasses brought into the colonies and gave British officials free license to conduct searches of the premises of anyone suspected of violating the law. The colonists were taxed on newspapers, legal documents, and other printed matter under the **Stamp Act of 1765**. Although a stamp tax was already in use in England, the colonists would have none of it. After an ensuing uproar of rioting and mob violence, Parliament repealed the tax.

Great exultation, jubilance, and wild joy resulted when news of the repeal reached America. Attached to the repeal, however, was the **Declaratory Act** that plainly stated Parliament still had the right to make all laws for their colonies. The law included the right to tax, which the colonists believe could only be required if approved by their own colonial legislatures.

Other acts leading up to armed conflict included the **Townshend Acts** that were passed in 1767 taxing lead, paint, paper, and tea brought into the colonies. This increased anger and tension, resulting in the British sending troops to New York City and Boston.

In Boston, mob violence provoked retaliation by British troops, bringing about the deaths of five people and the wounding of eight others. The **Boston Massacre** shocked Americans and British alike. Subsequently, in 1770, Parliament voted to repeal all the provisions of the Townshend Acts with the exception of the tea tax. Although the tax on tea sold by the British East India Company was substantially reduced in 1773, the colonists' anger was fueled once more because Parliament had given the company an unfair trade advantage and forcibly reminded the colonists of the British right to tax them. Merchants refused to sell the tea, colonists refused to buy and drink the tea, and a shipload of it was dumped into Boston Harbor—in an event remembered as the Boston Tea Party.

Navigation Acts

Parliament passed the Navigation Acts to maintain Britain's economic supremacy in the area of trade. The acts provided that only British ships could transport goods to and from its colonies. The acts also required that certain products, such as tobacco, sugar, and cotton that were grown or produced in the colonies, could only be exported to foreign countries through British ports.

Lexington and Concord

The sites of Lexington and Concord marked the outbreak of the American Revolution. Early in 1775, the British declared that the colony of Massachusetts was in a state of rebellion. British troops were sent to capture weapons and military stores they believed were stored in Concord. Paul Revere and John Dawes were notified of the British plan, and they rode to Lexington and Concord to warn the colonists. The first shots were fired at Lexington, and the British proceeded to Concord. The minutemen inflicted heavy damage on the British soldiers in Concord and they retreated to Boston. These two battles were the first battles of the American Revolution, and the shots fired at Concord were said to be the **"shot heard around the world."**

Winter at Valley Forge

Valley Forge is located about twenty miles northwest of Philadelphia, Pennsylvania. The Continental army, under the command of George Washington, had suffered many defeats during 1777, and among them was the British capture of Philadelphia. Washington moved his troops to Valley Forge to regroup during the winter and to watch the British as they controlled Philadelphia.

Washington's troops were cold, hungry, sick, and poorly clothed. During the winter some soldiers deserted. Others died from disease. Washington's leadership of the troops was questioned. The Continental Congress had not supported the troops with funding or supplies until some of its members visited Valley Forge. During the winter months the troops were trained by a Prussian soldier, Baron von Steuben, who improved the soldiers' military skills. Martha Washington and other women visited Valley Forge and attended to injured soldiers, sewed clothes, and knit socks for the soldiers.

After the long winter, troops learned that France had become an ally. The British evacuated Philadelphia and the Continental army retook the city. The winter at Valley Forge had been one of endurance and resolve and one where the soldiers became disciplined and more skilled militarily.

Treaty of Paris of 1783

The Treaty of Paris of 1783 ended the American Revolution. The British had surrendered at Yorktown but the signing of the treaty Britain's recognition of the colonies' independence. England gave up its territory in North America, with the exception of Canada. The Americans were given fishing rights in Canadian waters.

SKILL 6.4   **Demonstrate knowledge of the foundations of representative government in the United States (e.g., the Articles of Confederation and issues of the Philadelphia Convention of 1787, such as major compromises and arguments for and against ratification).**

Articles of Confederation

The first political system under which the newly independent colonies tried to organize themselves was called the Articles of Confederation. It was drafted after the Declaration of Independence in 1776, passed by the Continental Congress in 1777, ratified by the thirteen states, and became effective in 1781.

The newly independent states were unwilling to give too much power to a national government. They were already fighting Great Britain and did not want to replace one harsh ruler with another. After many debates, the form of the Articles was accepted. Each state agreed to send delegates to the Congress. Each state had one vote in the Congress. The central government of the new United States of America consisted of a Congress of two to seven delegates from each state with each state having just one vote. The government under the Articles solved some of the postwar problems but had serious weaknesses.

The Articles gave Congress the power to declare war, make peace, and appoint military officers but limited the powers of Congress by giving the states final authority. Although Congress could pass laws, at least nine of the thirteen states had to approve a law before it went into effect. Congress could not pass any laws regarding taxes. To get money, Congress had to ask each state for it—but no state could be forced to pay. Some of its other powers included: borrowing and coining money, directing foreign affairs, building and equipping a navy, regulating weights and measures, and asking the states to supply men and money for an army. The delegates to Congress had no real authority since each state carefully and jealously guarded its own interests and limited powers under the Articles. Also, the delegates to Congress were paid by their states and had to vote as directed by their state legislatures.

The serious weaknesses were:

- Lack of power to regulate finances over interstate trade
- Lack of power to regulated finances over foreign trade
- Lack of power to enforce treaties
- Lack of power to maintain the military

Thus, the Articles created a loose alliance among the thirteen states. The national government was weak, in part because it did not have a strong chief executive to carry out laws passed by the legislature. This weak national government might have worked if the states had been able to get along with each other. However, many different disputes arose, and there was no way of settling them.

The Philadelphia Convention

In May 1787, delegates from all states except Rhode Island met in Philadelphia. At first, they met to revise the Articles of Confederation as instructed by Congress, but they soon realized that much more was needed. Abandoning the instructions, they set out to write a new **Constitution**, a new document, the foundation of all government in the United States and a model for representative government throughout the world.

The first order of business was the agreement among all the delegates that the convention would be kept secret. No discussion of the convention outside of the meeting room would be allowed. They wanted to be able to discuss, argue, and agree among themselves before presenting the completed document to the American people.

The delegates were afraid that if the people were aware of what was taking place before it was completed, the entire country would be plunged into argument and dissension and it would be extremely difficult, if not impossible, to settle differences and come to an agreement.

The reason Rhode Island did not send delegates helps to explain the conflict. **Patrick Henry** was one well-known person on that side who was concerned that creation of a powerful central government would subvert the authority of the state legislatures. Between the official notes kept and the complete notes of future President **James Madison**, an accurate picture of the events of the convention is part of the historical record. The delegates went to Philadelphia representing different areas and different interests. They all agreed on a strong central government but not one with unlimited powers. They also agreed that no one branch of government could control the branches.

It would be a republican form of government (sometimes referred to as **representative democracy**) in which the supreme power was in the hands of the voters who would elect the men who would govern for them. The separation of powers into three branches of government was a built-in system of checks and balances to keep power balanced and provided for the individuals and the states as well as an organized central authority to keep a new, inexperienced, young nation on track. The system of government was flexible enough that it has continued in its basic form to this day—through civil war, foreign wars, economic depression, and social revolution for over two hundred years.

The Great Compromise

One of the first serious controversies involved the small states versus the large states over representation in Congress. Virginia's Governor **Edmund Randolph** proposed that state population determine the number of representatives sent to Congress. The plan was known as the

Virginia Plan. New Jersey delegate William Paterson countered with what is known as the **New Jersey Plan** giving each state equal representation.

After much argument and debate, the **Great Compromise** or **Connecticut Compromise** was proposed by **Roger Sherman**. It was agreed that Congress would have two houses. The Senate would have two Senators from each state, giving equal powers to the states in the Senate. The House of Representatives would have its members elected based on each state's population. Both houses could draft bills to debate and vote on—with the exception of bills pertaining to money, which were required to originate in the House of Representatives.

The Three-Fifths Compromise

Another controversy involved the economic differences between North and South and concerned the counting of the African slaves for determining representation in the House of Representatives. The Southern delegates wanted this but did not want the number to determine the amount of taxes to be paid. The Northern delegates argued that the slaves for should be counted for tax purposes but not for representation. The resulting agreement was known as the **three-fifths compromise**. Three-fifths of the slaves would be counted for both taxes and determining representation in the House.

The Commerce Compromise

The last major compromise, also between the North and South, was the **Commerce Compromise**. The economic interests of the North were ones of industry and business whereas the South's economic interests were primarily in farming. The Northern merchants wanted government to regulate and control commerce with foreign nations and with the states. Southern planters opposed this idea because their point of view was that any tariff laws passed would be unfavorable to them. The acceptable compromise to this dispute was that Congress was given the power to regulate commerce with other nations and the states, including levying tariffs on imports. However, Congress did not have the power to levy tariffs on any exports. This increased Southern concern about the effect it would have on the slave trade.

The delegates finally agreed that the importation of slaves would continue for 20 more years with no interference from Congress. Any import tax could not exceed ten dollars per person. After 1808, Congress would be able to decide whether to prohibit or regulate any further importation of slaves.

Federalist Papers

When work was completed and the document was presented, nine states needed to approve for it to go into effect. There was plenty of discussion, argument, and debate. The opposition had three major objections:

- The states were being asked to surrender too much power to the national government.
- The voters did not have enough control and influence over the men who would be elected to run the government.
- There was no "bill of rights" guaranteeing hard-won individual freedoms and liberties.

To encourage the states to ratify the Constitution, a series of articles were written by **Alexander Hamilton** and others explaining the advantages of the new form of government. These articles were called the **Federalist Papers.** Eleven states finally ratified the document, and the new national government went into effect. In 1789, the Electoral College unanimously elected George Washington as the first president, and the new nation was on its way.

SKILL 6.5   **Understand the origin and development of American political parties (e.g., Federalists, Democratic-Republicans, Jacksonian democracy, Whigs, Democrats).**

Federalists and Democratic-Republicans

The **Federalists** favored the ratification of the Constitution and favored a strong central government, tariffs, and a good relationship with Britain. Formed by **Alexander Hamilton,** The Federalists were the first political party in the United States. George Washington supported Federalist views but John Adams was the first, and only, president who is considered a Federalist president. Chief Justice of the U.S. Supreme Court, John Marshall, was a Federalist.

The **Democratic-Republicans** believed in states' rights and represented more rural areas whereas the Federalists had more members in the cities. James Madison and Thomas Jefferson were Democratic-Republicans.

John Adams's administration was marked by the new nation's first entanglement in international affairs. Britain and France were at war. President Adams's Federalist Party supported the British, and Vice President **Thomas Jefferson's Republican Party** supported the French.

The nation was brought nearly to the brink of war with France, but Adams managed to negotiate a treaty that avoided full conflict. In the process, however, he lost the support of his party and was defeated after one term by Thomas Jefferson.

Through the early 1790s, Jefferson as Secretary of State and Alexander Hamilton as Secretary of the Treasury had led the two political parties. Jefferson and Hamilton were different in many ways. Not least were their views on what should be the proper form of government of the United States. This difference helped to shape the parties that formed around them.

Hamilton wanted the federal government to be stronger than the state governments. Jefferson believed that the state governments should be stronger. Hamilton supported the creation of the first Bank of the United States. Jefferson opposed it because he felt that it gave too much power to wealthy investors who would help run it.

Jefferson interpreted the Constitution strictly. He argued that nowhere did the Constitution give the federal government the power to create a national bank. Hamilton interpreted the Constitution loosely. He pointed out that the Constitution gave Congress the power to make all laws "necessary and proper" to carry out its duties. He reasoned that since Congress had the right to collect taxes, then Congress had the right to create the bank.

Hamilton wanted the government to encourage economic growth. He favored the growth of trade, manufacturing, and the rise of cities as the necessary parts of economic growth. He favored the business leaders and mistrusted the common people. Jefferson believed that the common people, especially the farmers, were the backbone of the nation. He thought that the rise of big cities and manufacturing would corrupt American life.

When Congress began to pass many of Hamilton's ideas and programs, Jefferson and James Madison decided to organize support for their own views. They met with several important New York politicians, including its governor, **George Clinton,** and **Aaron Burr**, a strong critic of Hamilton. Jefferson asked Clinton and Burr to help defeat Hamilton's program by getting New Yorkers to vote for Jefferson's supporters in the next election. Before long, leaders in other states began to organize support for either Jefferson or Hamilton.

Democrats

Two parties were formed from the Democratic-Republican Party after the election of 1824. In that election, **Andrew Jackson** had more electoral votes and more popular votes than the other candidates. However, because Jackson did not have a majority of the electoral votes, it was necessary for the House of Representatives to select a new president. The Speaker of the House was **Henry Clay**, from Kentucky. Votes for Clay for president placed him fourth in Electoral College votes. Clay's personal feelings against Jackson caused him to form a coalition in the House that provided enough votes to place **John Quincy Adams** in the office of president. After Adams became president, he named Henry Clay Secretary of State. In 1828, the Democrat Party was formed, and Andrew Jackson was elected as the first Democrat president the same year.

Jacksonian Democracy

Andrew Jackson represented himself as the president of the common man. Many of the ideas of the Jacksonian Democrats were adopted from Jefferson's Democratic-Republican Party. Jackson and his followers represented a democratic spirit. They opposed big business, favored the common man, and wanted more participation by the average person in government. Jackson's followers wanted elected officials rather than appointed officials, and favored westward expansion and Manifest Destiny. The period of Jacksonian democracy lasted until slavery became an issue in the 1850s.

Whigs

The Whig Party also developed upon the dissolution of the Democratic-Republican Party but was formed to oppose Andrew Jackson's policies. The Whigs favored high tariffs to protect American products and believed a strong Congress was more important than a strong president.

William Henry Harrison and **Zachary Taylor** were both Whig presidents. Both of these presidents died in office and their vice presidents were Whigs. **Millard Fillmore** became president upon the death of Zachary Taylor and was the last Whig president.

The issue of slavery eventually divided the party and many in the North joined the Republic Party in the mid-1850s.

SKILL 6.6 **Analyze the challenges confronted by the government and its leaders in the early years of Republic and the Age of Jackson (e.g., economic programs and tariffs, court system, expansion of slavery, foreign relations, removal of Native Americans).**

Economic Programs

During the presidencies of George Washington and John Adams, Alexander Hamilton and other Federalists encouraged a strong national government and a sound fiscal policy. One of the aspects of that policy was the **creation of a national bank.** The Federalists also wanted to establish a good rapport with England and favored foreign trade to establish a business economy.

The Democratic-Republicans opposed the creation of a national bank. The bank was created but its charter was allowed to expire in 1811. After the War of 1812, Congress reconsidered the issue and charted a second national bank in 1816. The term of its life was twenty years. By the time Jackson became president many people believed the national bank was necessary because they believed it had maintained stability during periods of economic panic and crisis.

President Jackson, however, opposed the bank as unconstitutional and as something that would harm individual liberties. Congress voted to recharter the bank, and Jackson vetoed the bill. Congress did not override the veto but the issue became one in later elections.

During the Age of Jackson, most economic programs were focused on domestic issues. The age of "canal building" and internal improvements was a primary focus of the government during this time. Economic programs focused on ways to improve getting goods to market and helping the common man rather than bankers and businessmen in large cities.

Tariffs

The U.S. Constitution provided for tariffs. Alexander Hamilton, the first Secretary of the Treasury, encouraged the imposition of tariffs to provide a source of revenue without eliminating or harming foreign trade with the new country. Tariffs provided income for the United States but the rates were not high. Later the issue became one of whether the United States should impose a protective tariff to protect domestic products. Before and during the War of 1812, the issue of tariffs was raised again. During the election of 1824, Andrew Jackson had favored a protective tariff to pay for roads and canals and other internal improvements.

Court System

The first Supreme Court Chief Justice **John Marshall** made extremely significant contributions to the American judiciary. He established three basic principles of law, which became the foundation of the judicial system and the federal government. He established the doctrine of judicial review which gave the Supreme Court the power to determine the constitutionality of laws passed by Congress. During his tenure, the high court ruled that only the Supreme Court has the power to set aside laws passed by state legislatures when they contradict the U.S. Constitution. The early court also established the right of the Supreme Court to reverse decisions of state courts.

Expansion of Slavery

The Constitution addressed the issue of slavery in relation to the return of fugitive slaves, the importation of slaves, and the method of counting slaves for determining the number of representatives as state would have in the House of Representatives.

When the Northwest Territory was created, slavery was prohibited in the area. This prohibition essential created states that would be "free" as opposed to "slave" as they entered the Union. As territories outside the Northwest Territory applied for statehood, the issue of whether the territory would come into the Union as a "slave" or "free" state was important. Economic and social interests between North and South were often competing and Congress attempted to maintain a balance as territories applied to become new states.

President Jackson accepted the practice of slavery. He had used slave labor on his plantation but he also recognized that the issue of slavery's expansion could divide geographic sections of the country and divide the political parties. As a result, the Democrats avoided the issue during Jackson's tenure in office.

Foreign Relations

As a young nation, the United States wanted to be independent economically and not have any foreign nation direct its foreign policy. The Federalists wanted to be friendly with England after the American Revolution but others wanted to side with France in the disputes between the two countries.

Events leading up to the War of 1812 involved the **impressment of American sailors** and whether or not America could stay neutral. Britain felt threatened by the increasing strength and success of the U.S. merchant fleet, which was becoming a major competitor with the ship owners and merchants in Britain. The British issued the **Orders in Council**, which was a series of measures prohibiting American ships from trading with France. The orders prohibited American ships from entering any French ports, whether in Europe, India, or the West Indies. At the same time, Napoleon began efforts for a coastal blockade of the British Isles. He issued a series of Orders prohibiting all nations, including the United States, from trading with the British and threatened seizure of every ship entering French ports after they had stopped at any British port or colony.

America went to war against the British, and after defeating the British at the New Orleans, secured its position of neutrality.

During Andrew Jackson's presidency, foreign affirms were less of a concern than domestic issues. His administration had a serious conflict with France over the payment of a debt. The issue was resolved without war. He did not sanction the annexation of Texas without approval of Congress.

Removal of Native Americans

In the early years of the republic, Native Americans were removed from their homelands as the result of westward expansion. As settlers moved into the Northwest Territory and inhabited areas that had been hunting grounds for the Native Americans, the Native Americans moved to other lands. Skirmishes and fighting occurred throughout the new territory, and **William Henry Harrison** was the American soldier who defeated the Native Americans. His victory at the battle of Tippecanoe made him famous and provided his campaign slogan **"Tippecanoe and Tyler, too"** for the election of 1840 in which he and John Tyler were victorious.

Andrew Jackson had a definite plan to remove the Native Americans to west of the Mississippi River and eliminate their land claims east of the Mississippi. Most of the Native Americans living in northern parts of the United States had moved, or been removed. Therefore, it was those living in southeastern United States that Jackson wanted to remove. He did not consider them as a foreign nation but as subject to government control. Congress passed legislation during Jackson's administration that would permit the Native Americans to retain their tribal governments if they relocated to west of the Mississippi River to lands set aside by the federal government. Some of the Creeks refused and the government forcibly removed them from where they were living in Alabama.

The Cherokees who lived in Georgia also resisted removal. They filed suit in federal court and asked the Supreme Court to issue an injunction to prevent the state of Georgia from taking their land. Chief Justice Marshall's court ruled that the Supreme Court did not have jurisdiction over the Cherokees because they were not a "foreign nation" as intended by the framers. Although the Supreme Court found in favor of the Cherokees, eventually some of them entered into a treaty. Those who did not were forcibly removed by the military. This removal is known as the **"Trail of Tears."**

COMPETENCY 7: WESTWARD EXPANSION, THE CIVIL WAR, AND RECONSTRUCTION

THE TEACHER UNDERSTANDS SIGNIFICANT HISTORICAL EVENTS AND DEVELOPMENTS RELATED TO WESTWARD EXPANSION, THE CIVIL WAR, AND RECONSTRUCTION.

SKILL 7.1   **Demonstrate knowledge of westward expansion and its effects on the political, economic, cultural, and social development of the nation.**

Between the growing economy, expansion westward of the population, and improvements in travel and mass communication, the federal government faced periodic financial depressions. Contributing to these downward spirals were land speculations, availability and soundness of money and currency, failed banks, failing businesses, and unemployment. Sometimes conditions outside the nation would help trigger it but at other times, domestic politics and presidential elections affected it.

Westward expansion occurred for a number of reasons, the most important being economic. Cotton was highly important to the Southern states. The effects of the Industrial Revolution, which began in England, were now being felt in the United States. With the invention of power-driven machines, the demand for cotton fiber greatly increased the amount of yarn needed for spinning and weaving. Eli Whitney's cotton gin made the separation of the seeds from the cotton much more efficient and faster. This, in turn, increased the demand and more farmers became involved in the raising and selling of cotton.

The innovations and developments of better methods of long-distance transportation moved the cotton in greater quantities to textile mills in England as well as to mills in New England and the Middle Atlantic states. As prices increased along with increased demand, Southern farmers began expanding by clearing more land to grow more cotton. Movement, settlement, and farming headed west to utilize the fertile soils. This, in turn, increased the need for a large supply of cheap labor. The system of slavery expanded, both in numbers and in the movement to lands "west" of the South.

Many people in other fields of economic endeavor began to migrate. Trappers, miners, merchants, ranchers, and others were all seeking their fortunes. The **Lewis and Clark expedition** stimulated the westward push. Fur companies hired men, known as "Mountain Men" to go westward, searching for the animal pelts to supply the market and meet the demands of the East and Europe. These men explored and discovered the many passes and trails that would eventually be used by settlers in their treks west.

The **California Gold Rush** drew gold-seekers to the west. Missionaries who traveled west with the fur traders encouraged increased settlement and sent word back east for more settlers. The results were tremendous. By the 1840s, population increases in the Oregon country alone were at a rate of about a thousand people a year.

This mass migration westward put the U.S. government on a collision course with the Native Americans and with Great Britain, Spain, and Mexico.

The fur traders and missionaries ran up against the Native Americans in the Northwest as well as the claims of Great Britain for the **Oregon country**. The United States and Britain had shared the Oregon country but by the 1840s, with the increases in the free and slave populations and the demand of the settlers for control and government by the United States, the conflict had to be resolved. In a treaty signed in 1846 by England and the United States, the countries reached a peaceful resolution, with Britain giving up its claims south of the 49th parallel.

In the **American Southwest**, the results were exactly the opposite. Spain had claimed this area since the 1540s, had spread northward from Mexico City, and, in the 1700s, had established missions, forts, villages, towns, and very large ranches. After the purchase of the Louisiana Territory in 1803 (known as the **Louisiana Purchase**), Americans began moving into Spanish territory. A few hundred American families in what is now Texas were allowed to live there but had to agree to become loyal subjects of Spain.

In 1821, Mexico successfully revolted against Spanish rule, won independence, and chose to be more tolerant toward the American settlers and traders. The Mexican government encouraged and allowed extensive trade and settlement, especially in Texas. Many of the new settlers were Southerners who had brought with them their slaves. Slavery was outlawed in Mexico and was technically illegal in Texas although the Mexican government looked the other way.

With the influx of so many Americans and the liberal policies of the Mexican government, concerns grew over the possible growth and development of an American state within Mexico. Settlement restrictions, cancellation of land grants, outlawing slavery, and increased military activity brought everything to a head. The order of events included the fight for Texas independence, the brief **Republic of Texas**, eventual annexation of Texas, statehood, and finally war with Mexico.

The Texas controversy was not the sole reason for war. Since American settlers had begun pouring into the Southwest, cultural differences played a prominent part. Language, religion, law, customs, and government were different between the two groups. A clash was bound to occur. The impact of the entire westward movement resulted in the final borders of the present-day contiguous United States, a war with Mexico, the ever-growing controversy over slave versus free states, and finally the Civil War.

SKILL 7.2   **Understand the political, economic, and social roots of Manifest Destiny and the relationship between the concept of Manifest Destiny and the westward growth of the nation.**

Westward expansion seemed natural when the Northwest Territory was opened for settlement in the 1780s. Once settlers inhabited the Mississippi and Ohio river valleys, they believed they were destined to settle and rule the North American continent—from the Atlantic Ocean to the Pacific. One newspaper editor called this belief a **Manifest Destiny**. Early settlers believed that they were destined by God to rule the land.

After Lewis and Clark explored the Louisiana Territory, the brave and strong began settling the area. During the Jacksonian era, the idea of the frontier and equality of man spurred westward expansion. The Second Great Awakening also encouraged westward expansion. The Native Americans were thought of as needing to be Christianized, and missionaries began moving west to save souls and spread Christianity.

Economics played a role in Manifest Destiny because the land of the trappers and traders became open to settlement. Wagon trains and groups wanting to establish communities in fertile river valleys took up the call to venture west. The California Gold Rush beckoned. Planters who needed more, and better, land moved west, taking slaves with them. The westward movement required that the federal government address the issue of slave-holding states versus free states.

The movement west also involved control of land that was being claimed by foreign powers. Russia and Britain both claimed parts of what is today Oregon. Because people saw it as their destiny to settle all of North America, then it was their destiny to see that other powers did not rule it. Manifest Destiny became a national goal but with it developed issues that led to sectionalism and regionalism.

SKILL 7.3   Identify the territorial acquisitions that form the United States and explain the factors that influenced these acquisitions.

Because the nation extended its borders into the lands west of the Mississippi, thousands of settlers streamed into the unsettled areas. Equality for everyone, as stated in the Declaration of Independence, did not yet apply to minority groups, African Americans, or Native Americans. Voting rights and the right to hold public office were restricted in varying degrees in each state. All of these factors decidedly affected the political, economic, and social life of the country and all three were apparent in the attitudes of the three sections of the country on slavery.

European events had profoundly shaped U.S. policies, especially foreign policies. After 1815, the United States became much more independent from European influence and began to be treated with growing respect by European nations that were impressed that the young United States showed no hesitancy in going to war with the world's greatest naval power.

The United States purchased the **Louisiana Territory** from France to give the country access to the port of New Orleans and control of the Mississippi River trade. The purchase also doubled the size of the United States. After the purchase, President Jefferson appointed Captains Meriwether Lewis and William Clark to explore it, to find out exactly what had been bought. Their expedition went all the way to the Pacific Ocean, and they returned two years later with maps, journals, and artifacts. This led the way for future explorers to make available more knowledge about the territory and resulted in the westward movement and the belief in the doctrine of Manifest Destiny.

The **Red River Cession** was the next acquisition of land and came about as part of a treaty with Great Britain in 1818. It included parts of what later became North and South Dakota and Minnesota. In 1819, Florida, both east and west, was ceded to the United States by Spain along with parts of Alabama, Mississippi, and Louisiana.

The **Republic of Texas** was annexed in 1845, and after the war with Mexico in 1848, the U.S. government paid $15 million for what would become the states of California, Utah, and Nevada, and parts of four other states.

In 1846, the **Oregon country** was ceded to the United States. The acquisition extended the country's western border to the Pacific Ocean. The northern U.S. boundary was established at the 49th parallel. The states of Idaho, Oregon, and Washington were formed from this territory.

In 1853, the **Gadsden Purchase** rounded out the present boundary of the forty-eight contiguous states when payment was made to Mexico in the amount of $10 million for land that makes up the present-day states of New Mexico and Arizona.

SKILL 7.4   **Understand major issues and events of the United States-Mexican War and their impact on the United States.**

The slavery issue in Texas grew into a crisis. By 1836, Texas was an independent republic with its own constitution. During its fight for independence, Americans were sympathetic to and supportive of the Texans, and some recruited volunteers who crossed into Texas to help the struggle.

Problems arose when the Texas petitioned Congress for statehood. Texas wanted to allow slavery, but Northerners in Congress opposed admission to the Union because it would disrupt the balance between free and slave states and give Southerners in Congress increased influence. There were others who believed that granting statehood to Texas would lead to a war with Mexico, which had refused to recognize Texas independence. For the time being, statehood was put on hold.

Friction increased between land-hungry Americans swarming into western lands and the Mexican government, which controlled these lands. The clash was not only political but also cultural and economic. The Spanish influence permeated all parts of southwestern life—law, language, architecture, and customs. By this time, the doctrine of Manifest Destiny was in the hearts and on the lips of those seeking new areas of settlement and a new life. Americans were demanding the United States control the Mexican Territory and Oregon. Peaceful negotiations with Great Britain secured Oregon, but it took two years of war to gain control of the southwest for the United States.

In addition, the Mexican government owed debts to U.S. citizens whose property was damaged or destroyed during its struggle for independence from Spain. By the time war broke out in 1845, Mexico had not paid its war debts. The Mexican government was weak, corrupt, torn by revolutions, and insolvent. It was also bitter over American expansion into Texas and the 1836 Revolution which had resulted in Texas independence. In the 1844 presidential election, the Democrats pushed for annexation of Texas and Oregon, and after **James Polk** won the election, they started the procedure to admit Texas to the Union.

When Texas statehood occurred, diplomatic relations between the United States and Mexico were ended. President Polk wanted the United States to control the entire southwest, from Texas to the Pacific Ocean. He sent a diplomatic mission with an offer to purchase New Mexico and Upper California, but the Mexican government refused to even receive the diplomat. Consequently, in 1846, each nation claimed aggression on the part of the other and war was declared. The treaty was signed in 1848, and a subsequent treaty in 1853 completed the southwestern boundary of the United States, reaching to the Pacific Ocean.

SKILL 7.5   **Analyze ways in which slavery and other political, economic, and social factors led to the growth of sectionalism and to the Civil War.**

The Growth of Sectionalism

By 1860, the country was made up of three major regions, and the people in all three regions had a number of beliefs and institutions in common. Each, however, region had its own unique characteristics.

The **North** had a great deal of agriculture, but it was also industrial with towns and factories growing at a very fast rate. The **South** was largely agricultural, and it was becoming increasingly dependent on one crop, cotton. In the **West**, restless pioneers moved into new frontiers seeking land, wealth, and opportunity. Many were from the South and were slave owners, bringing their slaves with them. In different parts of the country, the views on tariffs, public lands, internal improvements at federal expense, banking and currency, and the issue of slavery were decidedly different.

The drafting, ratification, and implementation of the Constitution united thirteen independent states into a Union under one central government. The two crucial compromises that had been made concerning slaves had pacified Southerners, especially the slave owners, but the issue of slavery was not settled, and from then on, **sectionalism** became stronger and more apparent each year, putting the entire country on a collision course.

The Issue of Slavery

Slavery in the English colonies began in 1619 when twenty Africans arrived at the colony of Jamestown in Virginia. From then on, slavery had a foothold, especially in the agricultural **South**, where a large amount of labor was needed for the extensive plantations. Free men refused to work for wages on the plantations when land was available for settling on the frontier.

Therefore, slave labor was the only recourse plantation owners perceived. If it had been profitable to use slaves in New England and the Middle colonies, then perhaps slavery would have been more widespread. Slavery was profitable in the South, but not in the other two colonial regions.

The **Compromise of 1850** addressed the issue of slavery in the southwestern part of the United States in relation to admission to statehood and the number of free/slave states in Congress. As a result, sectionalism became more intense. Two years later, Congress passed a new Fugitive Slave Act that permitted runaway slaves to be returned to their owners. Northerners opposed the law. When the Kansas-Nebraska Act was passed and allowed popular sovereignty as to whether the state would be slave or free, violence increased and Kansas was referred to as "Bleeding Kansas." Sectionalism became more intense, and the country headed toward a civil war.

The Issue of Tariffs

This period of U.S. history was one of compromises, breakdowns of the compromises, desperate attempts to restore and retain harmony among the three sections, short-lived intervals of the uneasy balance of interests, and ever-increasing conflict. The issue of tariffs was divisive, especially between 1829 and 1833. The Embargo Act of 1807 and the War of 1812 had completely cut off the source of manufactured goods for Americans. Thus, it was necessary to build factories to produce what was needed.

After 1815, when the war had ended, Great Britain's strategy was to be ahead of its industrial rivals by supplying its goods in America. To protect and encourage the U.S.'s own industries and their products, Congress passed the **Tariff of 1816,** which required high duties to be levied on manufactured goods coming into the United States. Southern leaders, such as **John C. Calhoun** of South Carolina, supported the tariff with the assumption that the South would develop its own industries.

For a brief period after 1815, the nation enjoyed the **Era of Good Feelings.** People were moving into the West, industry and agriculture were growing, and a feeling of national pride united Americans in their efforts and determination to strengthen the country. However, over-speculation in stocks and lands for quick profits backfired. Cotton prices were rising, and many Southerners bought land for cultivation at inflated prices. Manufacturers in the industrial North purchased land to build more plants and factories as an attempt to have a part of this prosperity. Settlers in the West rushed to buy land to reap the benefits of the increasing prices of meat and grain. To have the money for all of these economic activities, all of these groups were borrowing heavily from the banks, and the banks themselves encouraged this by giving loans on insubstantial security.

In late 1818, the Bank of the United States and its branches stopped the renewal of personal mortgages and required state banks to immediately pay their bank notes in gold, silver, or in national bank notes. The state banks were unable to do this so they closed their doors and were unable to do any business at all. Since mortgages could not be renewed, people lost properties, and foreclosures were rampant throughout the country.

At the same time, cotton prices collapsed in the English market. Its high price had caused the British manufacturers to seek cheaper cotton from India for their textile mills. With the fall of cotton prices, the demand for American manufactured goods declined, revealing how fragile the economic prosperity had been.

In 1824, Congress, favoring the financial interests of the manufacturers in New England and the Middle Atlantic States, passed a higher tariff. This was proposed by **Henry Clay** and was called the American System. Money received from the tariffs was to be used for road-building and other infrastructure as well as creating a national bank. In addition, the 1824 tariff was closely tied to the presidential election of that year. Before the bill became law, Calhoun had proposed the very high tariffs in an effort to get Eastern business interests to vote with the agricultural interests in the South that were opposed to it. Supporters of candidate Andrew Jackson sided with whichever side best served their interests. The bill became law, to Calhoun's surprise, due mainly to the political maneuvering of **Martin van Buren** and **Daniel Webster.** By the time the higher 1828 tariff was passed, feelings were extremely bitter in the South, where many believed that the New England manufacturers greatly benefited from it. Vice President Calhoun, speaking for his home state of South Carolina, promptly declared that if any state felt that a federal law was unconstitutional, that state could nullify it.

In 1832, Congress lowered the tariffs to a degree but not enough to please South Carolina, which promptly declared the tariff null and void, threatening to secede from the Union.

In 1833, Congress lowered the tariffs again, this time at a level acceptable to South Carolina. Although President Jackson believed in states' rights, he also firmly believed in, and was determined to keep, the preservation of the Union. A constitutional crisis had been averted, but **sectional divisions** were getting deeper and more pronounced. Meanwhile, the **abolition movement** was growing rapidly, becoming an important issue in the North.

SKILL 7.6   **Demonstrate knowledge of individuals, events, and issues of the Civil War (e.g., Abraham Lincoln, Jefferson Davis, the Emancipation Proclamation, Lee's surrender at Appomattox Court House).**

Abraham Lincoln

In 1858, **Abraham Lincoln** and **Stephen A. Douglas** ran against each other for the office of U.S. Senator from Illinois and participated in a series of debates, which directly affected the outcome of the 1860 presidential election. Douglas, a Democrat, was up for reelection and believed that if he won the race, he had a good chance of becoming president in 1860. Lincoln, a Republican, was not an abolitionist who believed that slavery was wrong morally. He firmly supported the Republican Party principle that slavery must not be allowed to extend any further.

Douglas, on the other hand, had originated the doctrine of **"popular sovereignty"** and was responsible for supporting and getting through Congress the inflammatory **Kansas-Nebraska Act**. In the course of the debates, Lincoln challenged Douglas to show that popular sovereignty reconciled with the **Dred Scott decision**. Either way he answered Lincoln, Douglas realized he would lose crucial support from one group or another. If he supported the Dred Scott decision, Southerners would support him, but he would lose Northern support. If he stayed with popular sovereignty, Northern support would be his, but Southern support would be lost. His reply to Lincoln was that territorial legislatures could exclude slavery by refusing to pass laws supporting it, and that gave him enough support and approval to be reelected to the Senate. But it cost him the Democratic nomination for president in 1860.

Southerners came to the realization that Douglas supported popular sovereignty but not necessarily the expansion of slavery. Two years later, Lincoln received the nomination of the Republican Party for president.

In 1859, abolitionist **John Brown** and his followers seized the federal arsenal at Harper's Ferry in what is now West Virginia. His purpose was to take the guns stored in the arsenal, give them to slaves nearby, and lead them in a widespread rebellion. Colonel **Robert E. Lee** of the United States Army captured him and his men and, after being found guilty at trial, Brown was hanged. Southerners supposed that the majority of Northerners approved of Brown's actions, but in actuality, most of them were stunned and shocked. Southern newspapers took great pains to quote a small but well-known minority of abolitionists who applauded and supported Brown's actions. This merely served to widen the gap between the two sections.

The final straw came with the election of Lincoln to the presidency the next year. Due to a split in the Democratic Party, there were four candidates from four political parties. With Lincoln receiving a minority of the popular vote and a majority of electoral votes, the Southern states, one by one, voted to secede from the Union as they had promised they would do if Lincoln and the Republicans were victorious.

As 1860 began, the nation had extended its borders north, south, and west. Industry and agriculture were flourishing. Although the United States did not involve itself actively in European affairs, the relationship with Great Britain was much improved and Britain and other nations that dealt with the young United States accorded it more respect and admiration. Nevertheless, war was on the horizon. The country was deeply divided along political lines concerning slavery and the election of Abraham Lincoln.

Civil War

South Carolina was the first state to **secede** from the Union, and the first shots of the war were fired on Fort Sumter in Charleston Harbor. Both sides quickly prepared for war.

The North had a larger population; superiority in finances and transportation facilities; and manufacturing, agricultural, and natural resources. The North possessed most of the nation's gold, had about 92% of all industries, and almost all of the known supplies of copper, coal, iron, and various other minerals. Since most of the nation's railroads were in the North and Midwest, men and supplies could be moved wherever needed. Food could be transported from the farms of the Midwest to workers in the East and to soldiers on the battlefields. Trade with nations overseas could go on as usual due to control of the navy and the merchant fleet. The Northern states numbered twenty-four and included the western states of California and Oregon and the border states of Maryland, Delaware, Kentucky, Missouri, and West Virginia.

The Southern states numbered eleven and included South Carolina, Georgia, Florida, Alabama, Mississippi, Louisiana, Texas, Virginia, North Carolina, Tennessee, and Arkansas. These states made up the Confederacy. Although outnumbered in population, the South was completely confident of victory. They knew that all they had to do was fight a defensive war, protecting their own territory until the North, which had to invade and defeat an area almost the size of Western Europe, tired of the struggle and gave up.

Men from the South were conditioned to living outdoors and were more familiar with horses and firearms than many men from northeastern cities. Since cotton was such an important crop, Southerners felt that British and French textile mills were so dependent on raw cotton that they would be forced to help the Confederacy in the war. The South had specific reasons and goals for fighting the war, more so than the North. The major aim of the Confederacy never wavered—to win independence, the right to govern themselves as they wished, and to preserve slavery.

The Northerners were not as clear in their reasons for conducting war. At the beginning, most believed, along with Lincoln, that preservation of the Union was paramount. Only a few abolitionists looked on the war as a way to end slavery. However, by war's end, more and more Northerners had come to believe that freeing the slaves was just as important as restoring the Union.

Jefferson Davis

Another advantage of the South was that a number of its best officers had graduated from the U.S. Military Academy at West Point and had long years of army experience, exercising varying degrees of command in the wars with Native Americans and Mexicans. Jefferson Davis was one of the Southerners who had graduated from West Point. Davis had fought in the Mexican War and served as a U.S. Senator and Secretary of War. He became president of the Confederate States of America, but many did not consider him an effective leader. He paid more attention to military matters than to matters relating to the economy or financial affairs of the confederate states. He resisted public opinion and was unable to get along with those who disagreed with him. Although he was involved in the war plans for the South, he was unable to find a winning strategy.

War Issues

The war strategies for both sides were relatively clear and simple. The South planned a defensive war, wearing down the North until it agreed to peace on Southern terms. The exception was to gain control of Washington, D.C., go north through the Shenandoah Valley into Maryland and Pennsylvania in order to drive a wedge between the Northeast and Midwest, interrupt the lines of communication, and end the war quickly. The North had three basic strategies:

- Blockade the Confederate coastline in order to cripple the South.
- Seize control of the Mississippi River and interior railroad lines to split the Confederacy in two.
- Seize the Confederate capital of Richmond, Virginia, driving southward and joining up with Union forces coming east from the Mississippi Valley.

Emancipation Proclamation and Gettysburg

On January 1, 1863, President Lincoln issued an executive order that proclaimed the freedom of slaves in the Confederate states that were considered to be in rebellion. It did not apply to slaves in Union-held areas or states that were not in rebellion. Freedom for those slaves would be handled differently. The proclamation only freed the slaves. It did not make them citizens or declare slavery illegal. Nor did the proclamation compensate slave owners.

As the war progressed, the South was winning many battles. However, the battle at Gettysburg in July 1863 was a turning point. Until Gettysburg, Lincoln's commanders, **McDowell, McClellan, Burnside, and Hooker,** had only limited success. **Lee**, on the other hand, had many able officers including **Jackson and J.E.B. Stuart** upon whom he depended heavily.

Jackson died at Chancellorsville and was replaced by **James Longstreet.** When Lee decided to invade the North he depended on **J. E. B. Stuart** and his cavalry to keep him informed of the location of Union troops and their strengths.

Four things worked against Lee at Gettysburg:

- The Union troops gained the best positions and the best ground first, making it easier to make a stand there.
- Lee's move into Northern territory put him and his army a long way from food and supply lines.
- Lee thought that his Army of Northern Virginia was invincible and could fight and win under any conditions or circumstances.
- Stuart and his men did not arrive at Gettysburg until the end of the second day of fighting, and by then, it was too little too late. He and the men had had to detour around Union soldiers, and he was delayed in getting the information Lee needed.

Lee was convinced the army would be victorious. Longstreet was concerned about the Union troops occupying the best positions and felt that regrouping to a better position would be an advantage. He was also very concerned about the distance from supply lines. Consequently, Lee made the mistake of failing to listen to Longstreet and following the strategy of regrouping back into Southern territory toward the supply lines. Lee thought that regrouping was retreating and was almost an admission of defeat.

It was not the intention of either side to fight at Gettysburg but the fighting began when a Confederate brigade stumbled into a unit of Union cavalry while looking for shoes. The third and last day Lee launched the final attempt to break Union lines. **General George Pickett** sent his division of three brigades under Generals Garnet, Kemper, and Armistead against Union troops on **Cemetery Ridge** under the command of General Winfield Scott Hancock. Union lines held, and Lee and the defeated Army of Northern Virginia made their way back to Virginia. Although Lincoln's commander George Meade successfully turned back a Confederate charge, he and the Union troops failed to pursue Lee and the Confederates. Nonetheless, this battle was the turning point for the North. After this, Lee never again had the troop strength to launch a major offensive.

The day after the battle of Gettysburg, July 4, **Vicksburg,** Mississippi, a city on the Mississippi River, surrendered to Union **General Ulysses Grant**, thus severing the western Confederacy from the eastern part.

In September 1863, the Confederacy won its last important victory at **Chickamauga.** In November, the Union victory at Chattanooga made it possible for Union troops to go into Alabama and Georgia, splitting the eastern Confederacy in two.

Lincoln gave Grant command of all Northern armies in March 1864. Grant led his armies into battles in Virginia while Sheridan and his cavalry did as much damage as possible. In a skirmish at a place called Yellow Tavern, Virginia, Sheridan's and Stuart's forces met, with Stuart being fatally wounded. The Union won the battle of Mobile Bay and in May 1864, William Tecumseh Sherman began his march to the sea and successfully demolished Atlanta, Georgia. He then moved on to Savannah. He and his troops turned northward through the Carolinas toward Grant and his troops in Virginia.

Lee's Surrender at Appomattox Courthouse

The battle at Appomattox Courthouse was one of the last battles of the Civil War. Robert E. Lee had moved north from Richmond, the Confederate capital, to meet other Confederate troops in

North Carolina. The Union cut off his path at Appomattox Courthouse, Virginia. On the morning of April 9, 1865, Robert E. Lee formally surrendered to General Grant. The terms of surrender were signed in the afternoon, and three days later, Lee's army was disbanded.

Effects of the Civil War

The Civil War took more American lives than any other war in history. The South lost one-third of its soldiers in battle compared to about one-sixth for the North. More than half of the total deaths were caused by disease and the horrendous conditions of field hospitals. Both sections paid a tremendous economic price but the South suffered more severely from direct damages.

Destruction was pervasive with towns, farms, trade, industry, lives, and homes of men, women, and children all destroyed. The entire Southern way of life was lost. The deep resentment, bitterness, and hatred that remained for generations gradually lessened as the years went by, but legacies of it surface and remain to this day.

After the war, the South had no voice in the political, social, and cultural affairs of the nation, almost eliminating the influence of the traditional Southern ideals. The Northern Yankee Protestant ideals of hard work, education, and economic freedom became the standard of the United States and helped influence the development of the nation into a modern, industrial power.

The effects of the Civil War were tremendous. The Civil War was called the first modern war. It changed the methods of waging war. It introduced weapons and tactics that, when improved later, were used extensively in wars of the late 1800s and 1900s. Civil War soldiers were the first to fight in trenches, fight under a unified command, and the first to wage a defense called "major cordon defense," a strategy of advance on all fronts. They were also the first to use repeating and breech-loading weapons. Observation balloons were first used during the war along with submarines, ironclad ships, and mines. Telegraphy and railroads were put to use first in the Civil War. It was considered a modern war because of the vast destruction and was "total war" involving the use of all resources of the opposing sides. There was probably no way it could have ended other than with the total defeat and unconditional surrender of one side or the other.

By executive proclamation and constitutional amendment, slavery was officially and finally ended although there remained deep prejudice and racism, still raising its ugly head today. The Union was preserved and the states were finally truly united. **Sectionalism**, especially in the area of politics, remained strong for another one hundred years, but not to the degree nor with the violence that existed before 1861. The Civil War may have been American democracy's greatest failure because from 1861 to 1865, calm reason that is basic to democracy fell to human passion. Yet, democracy did survive.

The victory of the North established that no state has the right to end or leave the Union. Because of unity, the United States became a major global power. Lincoln had never proposed to punish the South. He was most concerned with restoring the South to the Union in a program that was flexible and practical rather than rigid and unbending. In fact, he never really felt that the states had succeeded in leaving the Union but that they had left the "family circle" for a short time. His plans for reconstruction consisted of two major steps. First, all Southerners who took an oath of allegiance to the Union and promised to accept all federal laws and proclamations dealing with slavery would receive a full pardon. The only people excluded from this would be men who had resigned from civil and military positions in the federal government to serve in the Confederacy, those who were part of the Confederate government, those in the Confederate army above the rank of lieutenant, and Confederates who were guilty of mistreating prisoners of war and blacks.

The second prong of Lincoln's plan was that states would be able to write new constitutions, elect new officials, and return to the Union fully equal to all other states on certain conditions, among them that a minimum number of persons (at least 10 percent of those who were qualified voters in their states before secession from the Union who had voted in the 1860 election) must take an oath of allegiance.

SKILL 7.7   **Analyze the effects of Reconstruction on the political, economic, and social life of the nation.**

As the war dragged on to its bloody, destructive conclusion, Lincoln was concerned and anxious to get the states restored to the Union. Lincoln showed flexibility in his thinking as he made changes to his **Reconstruction** program to make it as easy and painless as possible. Unfortunately, Lincoln was assassinated before Congress could approve many of his proposed changes. After Andrew Johnson became president and the **Radical Republicans** gained control of Congress, harsh measures of Reconstruction were implemented. Before being allowed to rejoin the Union, the Confederate states were required to agree to all federal laws. Between 1866 and 1870, all of the states had returned to the Union, but by that time Northern interest in Reconstruction was fading.

The economic and social chaos in the South after the war was severe, with starvation and disease rampant—especially in the cities. The U.S. army provided some relief of food and clothing for both whites and blacks, but the major responsibility fell to the **Freedmen's Bureau.** Though the bureau agents helped Southern whites to a certain extent, their main responsibility was to the freed slaves. They were to assist the freedmen to become self-supporting and protect them from being taken advantage of by others. Northerners looked on it as a real and honest effort to help the South out of the chaos it was in. Most white Southerners charged the bureau with causing racial friction, deliberately encouraging the freedmen to consider former owners as enemies. As a result, as Southern leaders began to be able to restore life as it had once been, they adopted a set of laws known as **"black codes"** that contained many of the provisions of the prewar "slave codes." There were certain improvements in the lives of freedmen, but the codes denied the freedmen their basic civil rights. In short, except for the condition of freedom and a few civil rights, white Southerners made efforts to keep the freedmen's lives subordinate to theirs.

Radicals in Congress pointed out these illegal actions by white Southerners as evidence that Southerners were unwilling to recognize, accept, and support the complete freedom of African Americans and could not be trusted. Congress drafted its own program of Reconstruction, including laws that would protect and further the rights of blacks. Three amendments were added to the Constitution. The **Thirteenth Amendment** of 1865 that outlawed slavery throughout the entire United States. The **Fourteenth Amendment** of 1868 made African Americans citizens. The

Fifteenth Amendment of 1870 gave African Americans the right to vote and made it illegal to deny anyone the right to vote based on race.

Federal troops were stationed throughout the South during Reconstruction and protected Republicans who had taken control of Southern governments. Bitterly resentful, many white Southerners fought the new political system by joining a secret society called the **Ku Klux Klan**, using violence to keep African Americans from benefiting in society after the Civil War.

Reconstruction officially ended when the last federal troops left the South in 1877.

Reconstruction had a limited success since it set up public school systems and expanded legal rights of black Americans. Nevertheless, white "redeemer governments" rapidly worked to undo much of the changes resulting from Reconstruction.

Lincoln and President Johnson had considered the conflict of Civil War as a "rebellion of individuals" but Congressional Radical Republicans, such as Senator **Charles Sumner**, considered the Southern states as complete political organizations that were now in the same position as any unorganized territory and should be treated as such. Radical House leader **Thaddeus Stevens** considered the Confederate states not as territories, but as conquered provinces and felt they should be treated that way. President Johnson refused to work with Congressional moderates, insisting on having his own way. As a result the Radicals gained control of both houses of Congress, and when Johnson opposed their harsh measures, they came within one vote of impeaching him

General Grant was elected president in 1868 and served two scandal-ridden terms. He was an honest, upright person but lacked political experience. His greatest weakness was a blind loyalty to his friends. He absolutely refused to believe that his friends were dishonest and stubbornly would not admit to their using him to further their own interests. One of the sad results of the war was the rapid growth of business and industry with large corporations controlled by unscrupulous men. However, after 1877, some degree of normalcy returned and there was time for rebuilding, expansion, and growth of the United States.

COMPETENCY 8: THE UNITED STATES AS A WORLD POWER

THE TEACHER UNDERSTANDS SIGNIFICANT HISTORICAL EVENTS AND DEVELOPMENTS RELATED
TO THE EMERGENCE AND ROLE OF THE UNITED STATES AS A WORLD POWER AND THE EFFECTS
OF MAJOR DECISIONS AND CONFLICTS ON THE UNITED STATES.

SKILL 8.1 Understand factors and events that contributed to the emergence of the
United States as a world power between 1898 and 1920 (e.g., imperialism,
Panic of 1893, acquisition of Hawaii, Spanish-American War, U.S.
involvement in and effects of World War I).

Imperialism

Imperialism is a country's expanding its authority and influence over other countries and areas.
During the late 1800s and early 1900s, the United States extended its influence to other areas of
the world. Once the American West was subdued and firmly under United States control, the
United States started looking beyond its shores. Overseas markets were becoming important as
American industry produced goods more efficiently and manufacturing capacity grew. Out of
concern for the protection of shipping, the United States modernized and built up the Navy, which
by 1900 ranked third in the world, giving it the means to become an imperial power. The first
overseas possessions acquired by the United States were **Midway Island** and **Alaska**. Alaska had
been purchased in 1867 from the Russians. Midway Island was also acquired in 1867.

By the 1880s, Secretary of State James G. Blaine pushed for expanding U.S. trade and influence
to Central and South America, and in the 1890s, President Grover Cleveland invoked the **Monroe
Doctrine** to intercede in Latin American affairs when it looked as though Great Britain was going
to exert its influence and power in the Western Hemisphere.

This success enlarged and expanded the role of the United States in foreign affairs. Under the
administration of **Theodore Roosevelt**, the U.S. armed forces were built up, greatly increasing
military strength. Roosevelt's foreign policy was summed up in the slogan of "Speak softly and
carry a big stick," backing up the efforts in diplomacy with a strong military. During the years
before the outbreak of World War I, evidence of the emergence of the United States as a world
power could be seen in a number of actions.

Using the Monroe Doctrine of non-involvement of Europe in the affairs of the Western
Hemisphere, President Roosevelt forced Italy, Germany, and Great Britain to remove their
blockade of Venezuela. He gained the rights to construct the **Panama Canal** by threatening force,
and he assumed the finances of the Dominican Republic to stabilize its economy and prevent any
intervention by Europeans. In 1916 under President **Woodrow Wilson**, U.S. troops were sent to
the Dominican Republic to keep order.

Panic of 1893

The Panic of 1893 was a sharp decline in the United States economy that resulted in several bank
failures, widespread unemployment, and a drop in farm crop prices. The panic resulted partly from

a run on the gold supply when people began exchanging U.S. silver notes for gold. The federal reserve of gold soon reached its minimum level and no more notes could be redeemed. The price of silver fell and thousands of companies went bankrupt, including several major railroads.

High unemployment continued for over five years following the panic. The economy and the practice of using silver and gold to back U.S. Treasury notes became central issues in the 1896 presidential election. **William McKinley** won the election and restored the confidence of the people. The economy began to recover before McKinley was assassinated.

Acquisition of Hawaii

In the Pacific, the United States lent its support to American sugar planters who overthrew the Kingdom of Hawaii and eventually annexed it as U.S. territory in 1898. During the 1830s and 1840s Hawaii traded with England and France, and the United States became concerned that Hawaii might eventually be colonized by one of the European countries. In 1849, the United States and Hawaii signed a friendship treaty, and the islands became a port where whaling ships stopped for provisions, a place where missionaries found converts to Christianity, and a place whose pineapple industry provided economic benefits to U.S. financial interests.

In 1893, the Americans deposed the Hawaiian queen and planters urged that the United States annex the islands. President Grover Cleveland opposed annexation and attempted to restore the monarchy. However, America became involved in the Spanish-American War, and Hawaii was annexed in 1898.

Spanish-American War

During the 1890s, Spain controlled such overseas possessions as Puerto Rico, the Philippines, and Cuba. Cubans rebelled against Spanish rule, and the U.S. government found itself besieged by demands from Americans to assist the Cubans in their revolt. The event that proved a turning point for the **Spanish-American War** in 1898 was the explosion of the *USS Maine.* Congress declared war on Spain, and the United States quickly defeated Spain. The war with Spain also triggered the dispatch of the fleet under Admiral **George Dewey** to the Philippines, followed by American military troops. Victory over the Spanish proved fruitful for American territorial ambitions. The peace treaty gave the U.S. possession of **Puerto Rico, the Philippines, Guam, and Hawaii**.

Although Congress passed legislation renouncing claims to annex Cuba, in a rare moment of idealism, the United States gained control of the island of **Puerto Rico**; a permanent deep-water naval harbor at Guantanamo Bay, Cuba; the Philippines; and various other Pacific islands formerly possessed by Spain. The decision to occupy the Philippines rather than grant it immediate independence, led to a guerrilla war. The **Philippines Insurrection** lasted until 1902 and U.S. rule over the Philippines lasted until 1942.

U.S. Involvement in and Effects of World War I

President Woodrow Wilson kept America out of World War I during his first term in office. However, Americans became enraged at the actions of the Germans when they sank the British passenger liner, the *Lusitania*, and more than one hundred Americans lost their lives. After the Germans approached the Mexican government about becoming allied, Congress voted, in 1917, to enter the war against Germany.

There were many effects of the war—for the countries participating and for areas of the world that would be carved up for the victors and realigned the economic purposes. The Paris peace talks and resulting Treaty of Versailles were humiliating for the Germans. Lands were taken away, borders were redesigned, and war reparations were ordered to be paid. The economic interests of England and France were considered when dividing up the Middle East with its vast oil resources. New countries were formed and the League of Nations was established. The U.S. Congress, however, did not vote for the United States to become a member, despite the fact that the League had been the idea and a goal of President Wilson.

SKILL 8.2   **Analyze how national and international decisions and conflicts between World War I and World War II affected the United States (e.g., the Fourteen Points, isolationism, reasons for U.S. involvement in World War II).**

The Fourteen Points

Some ten months before World War I ended, President Wilson proposed a program called the **Fourteen Points** as a method of bringing the war to an end with an equitable peace settlement. Five points set out general ideals; eight pertained to immediately working to resolve territorial and political problems; and the fourteenth point counseled establishing an organization of nations to help keep world peace.

When Germany agreed in 1918 to an armistice, it assumed that the peace settlement would be drawn up on the basis of these Fourteen Points. However, the peace conference in Paris ignored the points, and Wilson had to be content with efforts at establishing the **League of Nations**. Italy, France, and Great Britain wanted retribution. Their treaties severely punished the Central Powers—taking away arms and territories and requiring payment of reparations. Germany was punished the most, and had to assume the responsibility for causing the war. The League of Nations was created but U.S. membership was not approved by the U.S. Congress.

Isolationism

After World War I, America tended to be less involved in world affairs and be more isolationist. Several factors led the Americans to this result—the large death toll from the war, the decision not to become a member of the League of Nations, decisions to limit immigration, and the decision to raise tariff duties to protect American goods. Perhaps the most important reason was the Great Depression. America had serious problems to resolve within its borders to bring about a rebound in the economy.

The influence of the automobile, the entertainment industry, and the rejection of the morals and values of pre-World War I life resulted in the fast-paced **Roaring Twenties** and had significant effects on events leading to the Depression-era 1930s and another world war. Many Americans greatly desired the pre-war life and supported political policies and candidates in favor of the return to what was considered normal. It was desired to end government's strong role and adopt a policy of isolating the country from world affairs, a result of the war.

The decade of the 1920s saw tremendous changes in the United States, signifying the beginning of its development into its modern society. The shift from farm to city life was occurring in tremendous numbers. Social changes and problems were occurring at such a fast pace that it was extremely difficult and perplexing for many Americans to adjust to them.

The **Eighteenth Amendment** to the Constitution—the Prohibition Amendment—prohibited the manufacture or sale of alcoholic beverages throughout the United States and, politically, resulted in problems affecting society. Prohibition of the sale of alcohol had caused the increased activities of **bootlegging** and the rise of underworld **gangs** and the illegal **speakeasies**, the **jazz** music and dances they promoted. The customers of these clubs were considered "modern," reflected by extremes in clothing, hairstyles, and attitudes toward authority and life.

Movies and, to a certain degree, other types of entertainment, along with increased interest in sports figures and the accomplishments of national heroes, such as **Charles Lindbergh**, influenced Americans to admire, emulate, and support individual accomplishments.

The passage of the **Nineteenth Amendment** gave women their right to vote in all elections. The decade of the 1920s also showed a marked change in roles and opportunities for women with more and more of them seeking and finding careers outside the home.

The U.S. economy experienced a tremendous period of boom in the 1920s. Restrictions on business because of war no longer existed, and the conservatives in control adopted policies that helped and encouraged big business. To keep foreign goods from competing with American goods, tariffs were raised to the highest level. American manufacturers developed new products, and many different items, including refrigerators, radios, washing machines, and, most importantly, the automobile, became available to the American consumers.

Americans in the 1920s heavily invested in corporation stocks, providing companies a large amount of capital. The more money investors put into the stock market, the more the value of the stocks increased. This, in turn, led to widespread speculation that increased stock value to a point beyond the level that was justified by earnings and dividends.

Although many Americans demanded law and order, the administration of President **Warren G. Harding** was marked by widespread corruption and scandal, not unlike the administration of **Ulysses S. Grant**. The decade of the 1920s also saw the resurgence of such racist organizations as the Ku Klux Klan. As wild and uninhibited modern behavior became prevalent, this decade witnessed an increase in a religious tradition known as "**revivalism**" or emotional preaching.

Much of the stock speculation involved paying a small part of the cost and borrowing the rest, and this eventually led to the stock market crash and the Great Depression.

Europe was affected even more deeply. The 1930s saw the rise of Adolf Hitler and his **Nationalist Socialist Party** and the beginning of World War II.

International Tensions

World War I had seriously damaged the **economies of the European countries**, both the victors and the defeated, leaving them deeply in debt. There was difficulty on both sides paying off war debts and loans. It was difficult to find jobs, and some countries such as Japan and Italy found themselves without enough resources but more than enough people. Solving these problems by expanding the territory merely set up conditions for war.

Germany suffered horribly with runaway inflation ruining the value of its money and wiping out the savings of German citizens. Even though the United States made loans to Germany, which helped the government to restore some order and which provided a short existence of some economic stability in Europe, the Great Depression only served to undo any good that had been done. Mass unemployment, poverty, and despair greatly weakened the democratic governments that had been formed and greatly strengthened the increasing power and influence of extreme political movements, such as communism, fascism, and national-socialism, ideologies that promised to put an end to the economic problems.

The extreme form of patriotism called **nationalism** that had been the chief cause of World War I grew even stronger after the war ended in 1918. The political, social, and economic unrest fueled nationalism and it became an effective tool enabling dictators to gain and maintain power from the 1930s to the end of World War II in 1945. In the Soviet Union, **Joseph Stalin** succeeded in gaining political control and establishing a strong harsh dictatorship.

Benito Mussolini and the Fascist party, promising prosperity and order in Italy, gained national support and set up a strong government. In Japan, although **Emperor Hirohito** was considered ruler, actual control and administration of government was held by military officers. In Germany, the results of war, harsh treaty terms, loss of territory, and great economic chaos enabled Adolf Hitler and his Nazi Party to gain complete power and control in Germany.

Germany, Italy, and Japan initiated a policy of aggressive territorial expansion with Japan being the first to conquer. In 1931, the Japanese forces seized control of Manchuria, a part of China containing rich natural resources, and in 1937 began an attack on China, occupying most of its eastern part by 1938. Italy invaded Ethiopia in Africa in 1935, having it totally under its control by 1936. The Soviet Union did not invade or take over any territory but along with Italy and Germany, actively participated in the Spanish Civil War, using it as a proving ground to test tactics and weapons setting the stage for World War II.

In Germany, almost immediately after taking power and in direct violation of the World War I peace treaty, Hitler began the buildup of the armed forces. He sent troops into the Rhineland in 1936, invaded Austria in 1938 and united it with Germany, and in 1938 seized control of the Sudetenland which was part of western Czechoslovakia where mostly German lived. He moved into the rest of Czechoslovakia in March 1939, and, on September 1, 1939, began World War II in

Europe by invading Poland. In 1940, Germany invaded and controlled Norway, Denmark, Belgium, Luxembourg, the Netherlands, and France.

In Asia, the United States had opposed Japan's invasion of Southeast Asia, which was seen as an effort to gain Japanese control of that region's rich resources. Consequently, the United States stopped all important exports to Japan, whose industries depended heavily on petroleum, scrap metal, and other raw materials. Later, President Roosevelt refused to allow the Japanese to withdraw its funds from American banks. General Tojo became the Japanese premier in October 1941 and quickly realized that the U.S. Navy was powerful enough to block Japanese expansion into Asia.

U.S. Involvement in World War II

The United States avoided involvement in the war in Europe until the Japanese launched a surprise attack on the American naval base in the Hawaiian islands. The attack crippled the Pacific Fleet that was at anchor in **Pearl Harbor**. Temporarily the attack was a success. It destroyed many aircraft and disabled much of the U.S. Pacific fleet. In the end, it was a costly mistake as it quickly motivated the Americans to prepare for and wage war. After the attack that killed more than two thousand people, Congress declared war on Japan. Three days later, war was declared on Germany and Italy.

Military strategy in the European theater of war was developed by **Roosevelt, Churchill, and Stalin** with the plan of concentrating on Germany's defeat first, then Japan's. The start was made in North Africa, pushing Germans and Italians off the continent, beginning in the summer of 1942 and ending successfully in May, 1943. Before the war, Hitler and Stalin had signed a non-aggression pact in 1939, which Hitler violated in 1941 by invading the Soviet Union. The German defeat at Stalingrad, marked a turning point in the war and was brought about by a combination of entrapment by Soviet troops and death of German troops by starvation and freezing due to the horrendous winter conditions in Russia. All of this occurred at the same time the Allies were driving the Germans out of North Africa.

Preliminary work began in 1943 to create an organization that would prevent war from occurring again. The United States, Great Britain, the Soviet Union, and China sent representatives to Moscow where they agreed to set up an international organization that would work to promote peace around the earth. In 1944, the four Allied powers met again and made the decision to name the organization the **United Nations**. In 1945, a charter for the United Nations was drawn up and signed, taking effect in October of that year.

The liberation of Italy began in July 1943 and ended May 2, 1945. The third part of the strategy was **D-Day, June 6, 1944,** with the Allied invasion of France at Normandy. At the same time, starting in January 1943, the Soviets began pushing the German troops back into Europe, and they were greatly assisted by supplies from Britain and the United States.

The **Yalta Conference** took place in Yalta in February 1945, between the Allied leaders Winston Churchill, Franklin Roosevelt, and Joseph Stalin. With the defeat of Nazi Germany within sight, the three allies met to determine the shape of post-war Europe. Germany was to be divided into four zones of occupation, as was the capital city of Berlin. Great Britain, France, the Soviet Union, and the United States would each occupy a zone, and the four powers would administer Berlin which would be divided into four separate areas. Germany was also to undergo demilitarization and to make reparations for the war. Poland was to remain under control of Soviet Russia. Roosevelt also received a promise from Stalin that the Soviet Union would join the new United Nations. Following the surrender of Germany in May 1945, the Allies called the **Potsdam Conference** in July where Clement Attlee, Harry Truman, and Josef Stalin met outside of Berlin. The Potsdam Conference addressed the administration of post-war Germany and provided for the forced migration of millions of Germans from previously occupied regions.

By April 1945, Allies occupied positions beyond the Rhine, and the Soviets moved on to Berlin, surrounding it by April 25. Before war in Europe had ended, the Allies had agreed on a military occupation of Germany, with its being divided into four zones. After the war, the Allies agreed that Germany's armed forces would be abolished, the Nazi Party outlawed, and the territory east of the Oder and Neisse rivers taken away from German control. Nazi leaders were accused of war crimes and brought to trial. When Germany surrendered May 7, 1945, the war in Europe was finally over.

Meanwhile, in the Pacific, in the six months after the attack on Pearl Harbor, Japanese forces moved across Southeast Asia and the western Pacific Ocean. By August 1942, the Japanese Empire was at its largest size and stretched northeast to Alaska's Aleutian Islands, west to Burma, and south to what is now Indonesia. Invaded and controlled areas included Hong Kong, Guam, Wake Island, Thailand, part of Malaysia, Singapore, the Philippines, and Darwin on the north coast of Australia.

The raid of **General Doolittle**'s bombers on Japanese cities and the American naval victory at Midway along with the fighting in the battle of the Coral Sea helped turn the tide against Japan. Island hopping by U.S. Seabees and Marines and the grueling bloody battles fought resulted in gradually pushing the Japanese back toward Japan.

America's involvement in the war had resulted from the Japanese attack on Pearl Harbor. The country's involvement continued until Japan and Germany were defeated.

SKILL 8.3   **Analyze how national and international decisions and conflicts from World War II to the present have affected the United States (e.g., decision to use the atomic bomb, Cold War).**

Decision to Use the Atomic Bomb

After victory was attained in Europe, concentrated efforts were made to secure Japan's surrender. The United States dropped two **atomic bombs** on the cities of Hiroshima and Nagasaki. Japan formally surrendered on September 2, 1945, aboard the U.S. battleship *Missouri,* anchored in Tokyo Bay.

The development of the atomic bomb was probably the most profound military development of the war years. This invention made it possible for a single plane to carry a single bomb that was powerful enough to destroy an entire city. It was believed that possession of the bomb would serve as a deterrent to any nation because it would make aggression against a nation with a bomb a decision for mass suicide. The two nuclear bombs dropped in 1945 in Japan caused the immediate deaths of one hundred to two hundred thousand people, and far more deaths over time. The dropping of the bombs was (and still is) a controversial decision. Those who opposed the use of the atom bomb argued that was an unnecessary act of mass killing, particularly of noncombatants. Proponents argued that it ended the war sooner, thus resulting in fewer casualties on both sides.

After Japan's defeat, the Allies began a military occupation directed by American General Douglas MacArthur, who introduced a number of reforms that eventually rid Japan of its military institutions and transformed it into a democracy. A constitution was drawn up in 1947, transferring all political rights from the emperor to the people, granting women the right to vote, and denying Japan the right to declare war. Trials for war crimes of twenty-five war leaders and government officials were also conducted. The United States did not sign a peace treaty until 1951. The treaty permitted Japan to re-arm but took away its overseas empire.

The Cold War

The development and use of nuclear weapons marked the beginning of a new age in warfare that created greater distance from the act of killing and eliminated the ability to minimize the effect of war on noncombatants.

The introduction and possession of nuclear weapons by the United States quickly led to the development of similar weapons by other nations, proliferation of the most destructive weapons ever created, and massive fear of the effects of the use of these weapons, including radiation poisoning and acid rain. This led to the nuclear age and the Cold War. (For more discussion of the Cold War, see Skill 4.7.)

SKILL 8.4   **Demonstrate knowledge of significant individuals who shaped U.S. foreign policy from 1898 to the present (e.g., Alfred Thayer Mahan, Theodore Roosevelt, Woodrow Wilson, Franklin D. Roosevelt, Henry Kissinger).**

Alfred Thayer Mahan

A graduate of the U.S. Naval Academy in Annapolis, Alfred Mahan believed that the strength of a nation's navy was the answer to a strong foreign policy. His book, *The Influence of Sea Power upon History, 1660–1783,* was published in 1890. He was a strategist, and his theories were respected by leaders in European countries and Japan. Although he believed that countries that exhibited military strength could avoid war, other countries began increasing their military strength. The United States began increasing its naval power and by 1900 had the third most powerful navy in the world.

Theodore Roosevelt

Theodore Roosevelt believed in a strong U.S. foreign policy. He had fought in the Spanish-American War as a Rough Rider and had served as an Assistant Secretary of Navy and urged that the Americans not let Spain control Cuba in the 1890s.

When he became president, he encouraged the construction of a canal across Central America. The area was owned by Colombia and after negotiations were terminated, Roosevelt was quietly in favor of the revolution that took place. The revolutionaries won, the area was named **Panama,** and the new country agreed to a lease with the United States for construction of a canal.
Roosevelt took the position that the United States would intervene in any Western Hemisphere nation in which European powers were rightfully present and needed assistance. The **Roosevelt Corollary** was an extension of the Monroe Doctrine issued years before. However, the Monroe Doctrine had told the European countries they should stay out of Latin America. The Roosevelt Corollary, however, allowed the United States to intervene where it believed the Latin American countries needed assistence and protection from the European powers.

Theodore Roosevelt believed it was necessary to **"Speak softly and carry a big stick."** His foreign policies toward Asia also followed the saying. His administration agreed to Japan's annexation of Korea if Japan would not expand into China, the Philippines, or Hawaii. He also was involved in the negotiations between Germany and France over the control of Morocco.

Woodrow Wilson

President Wilson promoted the goal of neutrality in his first term of office. He believed that Latin American nations should be democratic and resolve their own problems and that American should not enter World War I. When insurgencies arose in Haiti and the Dominican Republic, Wilson sent troops to ensure a democratic form of government. He also supported a regime in Mexico that was attempting to oust a leader Wilson believed to be corrupt. In 1916, his administration purchased the **Virgin Islands** from Denmark.

The U.S. involvement in World War I came during his second term and resulted from the sinking by the Germans of the British passenger ship *Lusitania* that carried Americans. In January 1918, Wilson proposed his **"Fourteen Points"** to Congress as a program for self-rule of nations, disarmament of the defeated nations, and a dismantling of colonies owned by the defeated nations. The proposal also included the formation of a **League of Nations** to promote world peace.

Wilson led the American delegation at the Paris peace conference and promoted the idea of the League of Nations and other items he had earlier identified in the Fourteen Points. Wilson, a Democrat, had not included any Republicans in the American delegation. When the approval was needed for U.S. membership in the League, the Republican-controlled Senate did not vote in favor.

Franklin D. Roosevelt

Franklin Roosevelt became president when the concerns of the United States involved recovery from the stock market crash and the Great Depression. Congressional policy favored the isolations and passed laws to maintain America's neutrality. The **Neutrality Act of 1935** is an example. European events and the attack at Pearl Harbor resulted in America's entry into World War II. Before and during the war President Roosevelt was instrumental in making policy that would take place during and after the war. Some of the provisions included the goals of returning self-government to nations, global cooperation, freedom of the seas, and freedom of the seas.

The two leaders met again in 1943 in the North African city of Casablanca, Morocco. They decided the course of action against the Axis powers, especially Germany, and then on policies relating to the invasion of Sicily and Italy and opening up supply lines in the Pacific Ocean. The leaders also agreed that unconditional surrender was necessary to defeat the ideologies and philosophies of the Axis countries.

Later in the year, Roosevelt and Churchill met with China's leader Chiang Kai-shek in Cairo, Egypt to decide about post-war Asia. A few days later, Churchill, Roosevelt, and Joseph Stalin met in Tehran where they formulated a plan to open a second front against the Germans. They also recognized the independence of Iran.

In February 1945, Roosevelt, Churchill, and Stalin met in Yalta in the Crimea. The main discussion focused on Russia's entering the war in the Pacific theater and the lands Russia would receive in that area once Japan surrendered. They also discussed the future of Germany and the issue of reparations, Eastern Europe, and the United Nations.

Henry Kissinger

In 1968, Henry Kissinger was appointed National Security Advisor by President Richard Nixon. Kissinger is credited with creating a change of thinking in foreign policy during the Cold War, a change that moved Russia and the United States into some areas of cooperation. The policy was referred to as **"détente."**

Many of Kissinger's negotiations were done without the general public's knowledge. He negotiated changes of policy with China and he negotiated an end to the Vietnam War. In 1973, he became President Nixon's Secretary of State. He remained in that position during the administration of Gerald Ford and continued to pursue détente. During his last years as Secretary of State, he saw the policy of détente become unsuccessful and the fall of South Vietnam to the communists.

SKILL 8.5   **Demonstrate knowledge of significant events and issues that shaped U.S. foreign policy from 1898 to the present (e.g., Berlin airlift, Korean War, Sputnik I, Vietnam War, Marshall Plan, North Atlantic Treaty Organization, McCarthyism, Cuban Missile Crisis, the Gulf War).**

Marshall Plan

After World War II, the United States perceived the expansion of Communism in the world as its greatest threat. To that end, the country devoted a larger share of its foreign policy, diplomacy, and economic and military might to combating it. With the Soviet Union having emerged from the war as the *second* strongest power, the United States embarked on a policy known as **Containment.** This involved what came to be known as the **Marshall Plan** and the **Truman Doctrine.**

The Marshall Plan involved economic aid that was sent to Europe in the aftermath of the Second World War aimed at rebuilding European economies and preventing the spread of communism. The program was implemented in 1948 and was the idea of Secretary of State George Marshall.

Berlin Airlift

Berlin had been divided into four spheres of government at the conclusion of World War II. In the summer of 1948, the Soviets ordered Americans out of the Soviet sector and shut off all transportation, land access, and water access to West Berlin. Electricity was also cut off because the city's power plant was located in the Soviet sector. The United States decided to airlift supplies to the people and used the airports located in the American and British sectors to provide food and supplies to the people. President Truman authorized additional planes for the airlift, and the efforts of the British and Americans kept supplies provided to the Berliners and showed an adaptation to solve a problem caused by the Soviets.

North Atlantic Treaty Organization

The North Atlantic Treaty Organization (NATO) was established in 1949. The United States and Western European nations joined together to provide a system of defenses against communist aggression. NATO troops have served in Bosnia and Afghanistan, and they enforced a "no-fly" zone over Libya in 2011. NATO has its headquarters in Brussels, Belgium.

Korean War

The first "hot war" in the post-World War II era was the Korean War. It began in 1950 and ended in 1953. Elections that were scheduled to be held after the end of World War II did not take place. The country became divided when troops from Communist North Korea invaded democratic South Korea in an effort to unite both sections under communist control. The United Nations asked its member nations to furnish troops to help restore peace. Many nations responded and President Truman sent American troops to help the South Koreans. The war dragged on for three years and ended with a truce, not a peace treaty. Korea was divided and remains so to this day.

McCarthyism

McCarthyism was the hunt for communist infiltrators in America during the 1940s and 1950s. People were concerned about the threat of communism after World War II. Senator **Joseph A. McCarthy** made false accusations that communists had infiltrated the government of the United States. As a result of the accusations, searches were made for these communists, and artists and people in the film and entertainment industry were scrutinized with intensity for their communist beliefs. The anticommunist fervor and movements for communists continued until 1954.

Sputnik I

Sputnik was the first satellite to orbit the earth. It was launched in 1957 by the Soviets from Kazakhstan, then part of the Soviet Union. The launch triggered the **space race** and intensified the Cold War. Educational policy in the United States began to focus on science and technology to pass the Soviets in the space race and maintain a superior position over communism. It was in orbit approximately three month before it burned up and reentered the earth's atmosphere.

Cuban Missile Crisis

During the administration of President **John F. Kennedy**, Premier **Nikita Khrushchev** and the Soviets decided, as a protective measure for Cuba against an American invasion, to install nuclear missiles on the island. In October 1962, American U-2 spy planes took photographs over Cuba and identified sites as missile bases that were under construction. President Kennedy announced that the United States would quarantine Soviet ships heading to Cuba. The word "blockade" was not used because a "blockade" would have resulted in war. A week of incredible tension and anxiety gripped the entire world until Khrushchev capitulated. Soviet ships carrying missiles for the Cuban bases turned back and the crisis eased. After the crisis, a telephone "hot line" was set up between Moscow and Washington to make it possible for the two heads of government to have instant contact with each other.

Vietnam War

In 1954, the French were forced to give up their colonial claims in Indochina, the present-day countries of **Vietnam, Laos,** and **Cambodia.** Afterward, the communist northern part of Vietnam began battling with the democratic southern part over control of the entire country. In the late 1950s and early 1960s, U.S. presidents **Eisenhower and Kennedy** sent several military advisers and military aid to South Vietnam to assist and support South Vietnam's noncommunist government. During **Lyndon Johnson**'s presidency, the war escalated and thousands of American troops were sent to participate in combat alongside the South Vietnamese.

Many Americans refer to the Vietnam War as the "lost" war. The war was extremely unpopular in America and caused serious divisiveness among its citizens. In 1973, during President **Richard Nixon**'s second term in office, the United States signed an agreement ending war in Vietnam and restoring peace. The last of the American combat troops and prisoners of war remaining in Vietnam returned to America the same year. The communists unified the north and south and established a government.

Gulf War

After Iraq invaded and annexed Kuwait, the United States led coalition forces from more than thirty nations in an invasion against Iraq. The war began in August 1990 and had the code name of **Operation Desert Storm.** The war, also known as the Persian Gulf War and the First Iraq War, ended approximately seven months later. The formal cease-fire terms were decided upon by the United Nations. Subsequent events and controversies over the enforcement of terms led to the 2003 Iraq War.

SKILL 8.6   Understand the origins of major foreign policy issues currently facing the United States and the challenges of changing relationships among nations.

In 1971, President Nixon sent Henry Kissinger on a secret trip to Beijing to investigate whether or not it would be possible for America to give **diplomatic recognition to China**. In 1972, agreements were made for cultural and scientific exchanges, eventual resumption of trade, and future unification of the mainland with Taiwan. In 1979, formal recognition was achieved.

In the administration of President **Jimmy Carter**, Egyptian President **Anwar el-Sadat** and Israeli Prime Minister **Menachem Begin** met at presidential retreat **Camp David** and agreed, after a series of meetings, to sign a formal treaty of peace between the two countries. In 1979, Carter and his advisers perceived the Soviet invasion of Afghanistan as a threat to the rich oil fields in the Persian Gulf but at the time, U.S. military capability to prevent further Soviet aggression in the Middle East was weak. The last year of Carter's presidential term focused on the fifty-three American **hostages held in Iran**. When the shah was deposed, control of the government and the country was in the hands of the **Ayatollah Ruhollah Khomeini**.

President Carter froze all Iranian assets in the U.S., set up trade restrictions, and approved a risky rescue attempt, which failed. He had appealed to the United Nations for aid in gaining release for the hostages and to European allies to join the trade embargo on Iran. Khomeini ignored United Nations' requests for releasing the Americans and the Europeans refused to support the embargo because they feared losing access to Iran's oil. The hostages were released on the day of **Ronald Reagan**'s inauguration as president in 1981 when Carter released Iranian assets as ransom.

The foreign policy of President Reagan was, in his first term, focused primarily on the Western Hemisphere, particularly in Central America and the West Indies. U.S. involvement in the domestic revolutions of El Salvador and Nicaragua continued into Reagan's second term when Congress held televised hearings on what came to be known as the **Iran-Contra Affair**. A cover-up was exposed, showing that profits from secretly sold military hardware to Iran had been used to provide support to rebels, called Contras, who were fighting in Nicaragua. Nicaragua's neighbor, Costa Rica, constitutionally abolished its army after its civil war, favoring education and cultural development.

More than two hundred U.S. Marines were killed in 1983 in **Lebanon** when an Islamic suicide bomber drove an explosive-laden truck into U.S. Marines headquarters located at the airport in Beirut. This tragic event was the result of the unrest and violence between the Israelis and the Palestinian Liberation Organization (**PLO**) forces in southern Lebanon.

In the same month, U.S. Marines landed on the island of **Grenada** to rescue a small group of American medical students at the medical school and depose of the leftist government.

President Reagan reached an **arms-reduction agreement** with Soviet General Secretary **Mikhail Gorbachev**. Gorbachev began easing East-West tensions by stressing the importance of cooperation with the West. He also began easing the harsh and restrictive life of the people in the Soviet Union.

During President **George Bush**'s administration the Berlin Wall came down, resulting in the unification of Germany, the loss of power of the communists in other Eastern European countries, and the eventual **fall of communism in the Soviet Union** along with the breakup of its republics into independent nations. The countries of Poland, Hungary, Romania, Czechoslovakia, Albania, and Bulgaria replaced communism with democracy.

During the 1980s the former **Yugoslavia** began breaking apart into individual countries. A period of **ethnic cleansing** between Orthodox and Muslims was prevalent in the late 1980s and the 1990s. In Russia, as in the other former republics and satellites, democratic governments were put into operation and the difficult task of changing communist economies into ones of capitalistic free enterprise began. For all practical purposes, it appeared that the tensions and dangers of the post-World War II Cold War between the United States and Soviet-led Communism were over.

In 1989, President Bush sent U.S. troops to invade Panama and arrest the Panamanian dictator **Manuel Noriega.** Although Noriega had periodically assisted CIA operations with intelligence information, he had laundered money from drug smuggling and gunrunning through Panama's banks. When a political associate tried unsuccessfully to depose him and an off-duty U.S. Marine was shot and killed at a roadblock, Noriega was brought to the United States where he stood trial on charges of drug distribution and racketeering.

After **Saddam Hussein** invaded and occupied Kuwait, the United States and other nations successfully carried out Operation Desert Storm to liberate Kuwait.

President **Bill Clinton** sent U.S. troops to Haiti to protect the efforts of **Jean-Bertrand Aristide** to gain democratic power. He also sent troops to Bosnia to assist UN peacekeeping forces. Clinton withdrew American troops from Somalia where efforts were unsuccessful in ending starvation and restoring peace.

In 2003 the United States and Great Britain invaded Iraq because of the belief that Iraq had weapons of mass destruction and became involved in the **2003 Iraq War.** After the defeat of the Iraqi military, the United States occupied the country until the decline of violence. In 2007, the United States began withdrawing its military from Iraq. The final troops were withdrawn in 2011.

COMPETENCY 9: POLITICAL, ECONOMIC, AND SOCIAL DEVELOPMENTS FROM 1877 TO THE PRESENT

THE TEACHER UNDERSTANDS SIGNIFICANT POLITICAL, ECONOMIC AND SOCIAL DEVELOPMENTS IN THE UNITED STATES FROM 1877 TO THE PRESENT.

SKILL 9.1   **Understand political, economic, and social changes in the United States from 1877 to the present (e.g., in relation to political parties, transportation, labor unions, agriculture, business, race, gender).**

Political Parties

After the Civil War, the antislavery group of the Republican Party no longer existed. The newly freed slaves became Republicans, and the Southerners were mainly Democrats. The Republicans became interested in regulating big business, high tariffs, and direct elections of senators at the end of the nineteenth century. Democrats argued that the Republicans caused the Great Depression, and the Republicans begin to lose power during the 1930s. Moderates and conservatives wanted control of the Republican Party and the moderates gained momentum until the 1960s. The Moral Majority became important in the Republican Party during the 1980s. Democrats have been thought to be more liberal than the Republicans and have directed the Democratic Party since the era of the New Deal.

The **Watergate** scandal of the 1970s resulted in the first-ever resignation of a sitting American president. While the scandal involved the integrity of high government leaders, including the president, obtaining information held by the political party not in office was the original reason for the break-in at the Watergate complex.

Transportation

With the completion of the first **transcontinental railroad** in 1869, goods could be carried more quickly to market and products from one area of the country could be made available to people who lived in remote regions. Sleeper cars were added and passenger service became popular.

In the early 1900s, two transportation developments changed ways that people would travel in present times. Starting the first development, **Wilbur and Orville Wright** invented, constructed, and flew the first successful airplane. In 1927 **Charles Lindbergh** made the first solo flight across the Atlantic Ocean, flying from the U.S. East Coast to Paris, France, a distance of approximately 3,500 miles, in a little more than thirty-three hours. Planes were used to transport troops to the Normandy D-Day invasion beaches and have been used for troop transport since. Passenger planes were subsequently designed to provide more comfort and efficiency. First class, business class, and the flights of the Concorde are examples of increased speed and luxury of air travel.

The second development of the early 1900s that affect transportation was the development of the automobile and the assembly line. **Henry Ford**'s use of the assembly line for automobile production made the automobile available to the average person.

Labor Unions

Labor unions were first organized after the Civil War. The Knights of Labor was one of the first unions. In the 1880s, Samuel Gompers founded the **American Federation of Labor (AFL).**

During President Franklin D. Roosevelt's administration, in the 1930s, the **Congress of Industrial Organizations (CIO)** was formed. In 1935, Congress passed the Wagner Act, which protected the right of labor unions to organize, and **National Labor Relations Board** was created to regulate the private-sector unions. State laws and labor boards govern public-sector unions.

Union membership reached high levels in the 1950s. Since that time private-sector union membership has declined while public-sector union membership has increased. In 1955, the two large unions merged to form the **AFL-CIO.** Unions have shown much power throughout the years. However, legislation has defined several limits on the power of unions. For example, the **Taft-Hartley Act of 1947** prohibited unions from contributing to political candidates. Also, unions may not call for strikes if the national security will be threatened.

Agriculture

Inventions such as the Oliver plow, the improvement of farm wagons, the reaper-binders, and commercial combines revolutionized farming and agriculture in the late 1800s. Mechanization made farming easier and gave farmers the ability to produce more crops. In the early 1900s, tractors replaced draft animals on larger farms. The **Dust Bowl** was created by bad farming practices, and many families were forced to move from the lower Midwestern states due to a lack of good topsoil for farming.

Advances such as hydroponics and gene manipulation have increased yields and better crops since the 1950s. Many grains and crops are producing higher yields, and irrigation systems are providing needed moisture during period of drought.

Business

Business developed at a more rapid pace after the Civil War because rail lines provided transportation networks throughout the country. Industries such as the steel industry and Standard Oil expanded production and became major developers of the economy. As a result of the growth of big business the people who owned these businesses became wealthy. Many of the big businesses created monopolies and forced small business out of the arena.

As the result of monopolization and the formation of trusts, the federal government passed legislation making it an offense to monopolize. The first major antitrust legislation was the **Sherman Antitrust Act** that was passed in 1890. Other legislation, such as the **Robinson Patman Act** and the **Federal Trade Commission Act,** were passed to eliminate price fixing and unfair trade practices.

Entry into World War I created wartime industries. Business suffered during the Great Depression and Congress passed New Deal legislation to jump start the economy. When the country entered into World War II, factories were turned from domestic production to the needs of war—weapons, clothing, ships, aircraft, and military vehicles. The post-war peacetime economy turned toward consumer needs and housing. Houses were constructed and assembled on lots. Prefabricated housing became popular and new industries began constructing homes to meet the needs of society.

The global environment today meets the needs of many businesses. Companies can have their products exposed to the entire world. Manufacturing, sales, and distribution can take place in a global economy. The Internet and the World Wide Web make it possible to enter into business transactions nearly any place in the world.

Race

The **Fifteenth Amendment** prohibited the government from denying people the right to vote because of race. After the Civil War many former slaves tried to vote. However, some states imposed poll taxes on voters and others required the voter pass a literacy test. These were methods to eliminate or lessen the number of black voters.

"Jim Crow" laws were present in Southern states after the Civil War. The laws required blacks to use separate facilities, such as restrooms and drinking fountains, and some of the laws prohibited whites from conducting business with blacks. For example, white barbers were not permitted to cut a black person's hair in one state.

The **Ku Klux Klan** was an organized group that caused blacks problems after the Civil War but became less active in the 1870s. It gained more members after World War I and again after World War II. It has opposed the civil rights movement.

In 1896, the U.S Supreme Court decided the case of *Plessey* v. *Ferguson.* The case involved a Louisiana law that required blacks and whites to ride in separate train cars. Plessey challenged the law and the case found its way to the high court. The court's decision was that separate facilities were equal facilities. The **"separate but equal" doctrine** continued in force until the case of *Brown* v. *Board of Education.* In *Brown*, the U.S. Supreme Court held that separate facilities were inherently unequal. The *Brown* decision paved the way for integration of schools and other facilities.

The civil rights movement picked up momentum in the 1960s. Sit-ins, freedom rides, and the 1963 march on Washington took place before the passage of the 1964 Civil Rights Act that outlawed discrimination based on race, color, sex, religion, or national origin. This legislation was followed by the Civil Rights Act of 1968 that provided equal housing opportunities. **Martin Luther King, Jr.,** one of the leaders in the civil rights movement, preached about nonviolence.

Gender

The women's suffrage issue began in the mid-1800s when the Liberty Party included a plank in its platform that promoted women's voting rights. Leaders in the movement such as **Susan B. Anthony** and **Elizabeth Cady Stanton** brought the issue to the attention of Americans later in the nineteenth century.

The campaign for equal voting rights continued for many years. Women's active participation in the war efforts helped to bring more attention to the issue of women's suffrage and women's status in general. In 1920, after the **Nineteenth Amendment** to the U.S. Constitution granted women the right to vote.

Other gender issues have included problems relating to employment and equal opportunities. The Civil Rights Act of 1964 prohibited gender discrimination in hiring, promoting, or firing of employees. However, many issues relating to equal rights have persisted. The legal implications of sexual orientation and gender identity are issues today that are being debated and addressed by courts and legislatures throughout the United States. Some of the issues being addressed are marriages/unions, adoptions, and custody issues.

SKILL 9.2   **Demonstrate knowledge of the effects of reform and third party movements and their leaders on U.S. society (e.g., Populism, Progressive Era reforms, New Deal legislation, Susan B. Anthony, W. E. B. Du Bois, George Wallace).**

Populism

Populism is a philosophy concerned with the commonsense needs of average people. It often finds expression as a reaction against perceived oppression of the average people by the wealthy elite in society. The prevalent claim of populist movements is that they will put the people first. Populism is often connected with religious fundamentalism, racism, or nationalism. Populist movements claim to represent the majority of the people and call them to stand up to institutions or practices that seem detrimental to their well-being.

Populism flourished in the late nineteenth and early twentieth centuries. Several political parties, including the Greenback Party, the Populist Party, the Farmer-Labor Party, the Single Tax movement of Henry George, the Share Our Wealth movement of Huey Long, the Progressive Party, and the Union Party, were formed out of this philosophy.

In the 1890s, the People's Party won the support of millions of farmers and other working people. This party challenged the social ills of the monopolists of the "Gilded Age."

The tremendous change that resulted from the Industrial Revolution led to a demand for reform that would control the power wielded by big corporations. The gap between the industrial moguls and the working people was growing. This disparity between rich and poor resulted in a public outcry for reform at the same time that there was an outcry for governmental reform that would end the political corruption and elitism of the day.

Progressive Era

The period from 1890 to 1917 came to be known as the Progressive Era. This movement was fueled by the writings on investigative journalists—the **"muckrakers"**—who published scathing exposés of political and business wrongdoing and corruption. The result was the rise of a group of politicians and reformers who supported a wide array of populist causes. Although the leaders of this movement came from many different backgrounds and were driven by different ideologies, they shared a common fundamental belief that government should be eradicating social ills and promoting the common good and the equality guaranteed by the Constitution.

The reforms initiated by these leaders and the spirit of **Progressivism** were far-reaching. Politically, many states enacted the **initiative** and the **referendum**. The adoption of the **recall** was approved in many states. Several states enacted legislation that would undermine the power of political machines. On a national level, the two most significant political changes were (1) the ratification of the **Seventeenth Amendment**, which required that all U.S. Senators be chosen by popular election, and (2) the ratification of the **Nineteenth Amendment**, which granted women the right to vote.

Major economic reforms of the period included aggressive enforcement of the **Sherman Antitrust Act** and the passage of the **Elkins Act** and the **Hepburn Act** that gave the Interstate Commerce Commission greater power to regulate the railroads. The **Pure Food and Drug Act** prohibited the use of harmful chemicals in food, and the **Meat Inspection Act** regulated the meat industry to protect the public against tainted meat. Over two-thirds of the states passed laws prohibiting child labor. **Worker's compensation** was mandated, and the **Department of Commerce and Labor** was created.

President Theodore Roosevelt responded to **concerns over the environmental effects of the timber, ranching, and mining industries,** and as a result the government set aside 238 million acres of federal lands to protect those areas from development. Wildlife preserves were established, the national park system was expanded, and the National Conservation Commission was created. The Newlands Reclamation Act provided federal funding for the construction of irrigation projects and dams in semi-arid areas of the country.

Finally, the **Sixteenth Amendment** was ratified, establishing an income tax. This measure was designed to relieve the poor of a disproportionate burden in funding the federal government and make the wealthy pay a greater share of the nation's tax burden. **The Federal Trade Commission (FTC)** was established in 1915 to investigate business activities and assure fair and free competition among businesses.

New Deal Legislation

The 1929 stock market crash was the powerful event that is generally interpreted as the beginning of the Great Depression in America. Although the crash of the stock market was unexpected, it was not without identifiable causes. The 1920s had been a decade of social and economic growth and hope but the attitudes and actions of the 1920s regarding wealth, production, and investment created several trends that quietly set the stage for the 1929 disaster.

Franklin D. Roosevelt won the White House on his promise to the American people of a "new deal." Upon assuming the office, Roosevelt and his advisers immediately launched a massive program of innovation and experimentation to try to bring the Depression to an end and get the nation back on track. Congress gave the president unprecedented power to act to save the nation.

During the next eight years, the most extensive and broadly based legislation in the nation's history was enacted. The legislation was intended to accomplish three goals—relief, recovery, and reform.

Step One: Relief

The first step in the **New Deal** was to relieve suffering. This was accomplished through a number of job-creation projects.

Step Two: Relief

The second step of the New Deal, the recovery aspect, was to stimulate the economy. **The National Recovery Administration** attempted to accomplish several goals:

- Restore employment
- Increase general purchasing power
- Provide character-building activity for unemployed youth
- Encourage decentralization of industry and divert population from crowded cities to rural or semirural communities
- Develop river resources in the interest of navigation and provide cheap power and light
- Complete flood control on a permanent basis
- Enlarge the national program of forest protection and to develop forest resources
- Control farm production and improve farm prices
- Assist home builders and homeowners
- Restore public faith in banking and trust operations
- Recapture the value of physical assets, whether in real property, securities, or other investments

These objectives and their accomplishment implied a restoration of public confidence and courage.

Step Three: Reform

The third step of the New Deal was to create social and economic change through innovative legislation. Among the "alphabet organizations" set up to work out the details of the recovery plan, the most prominent were:

- **Agricultural Adjustment Administration** (AAA), designed to boost farm income by readjusting agricultural production and prices
- **Civilian Conservation Corps** (CCC), designed to give wholesome, useful activity in the forestry service to unemployed young men
- **Civil Works Administration** (CWA) and the **Public Works Administration** (PWA), designed to give employment in the construction and repair of public buildings, parks, and highways
- **Works Progress Administration** (WPA), whose task was to move individuals from relief rolls to work projects or private employment

To provide economic stability and prevent another crash, Congress passed the **Glass-Steagall Act** that separated banking and investing. The **Securities and Exchange Commission** was created to regulate dangerous speculative practices on Wall Street. The **Wagner Act** (National Labor Relations Act) guaranteed a number of rights to workers and unions in an effort to improve worker-employer relations. The **Social Security Act of 1935** established pensions for the aged and infirm as well as a system of unemployment insurance.

Susan B. Anthony

The issue of women's rights was a priority for Susan B. Anthony, a lecturer and writer who devoted her life to social reform. Her dedication to the issue of women's suffrage helped propel the country in the direction of granting women the right to vote. She also supported the temperance movement and the abolition of slavery. She and Elizabeth Cady Stanton formed many organizations in support of women's suffrage. Anthony endured accusations and ridicule and was arrested for voting in New York, but by the end of her life she had gained considerable public recognition for her tireless work. She was instrumental in obtaining Congressional support of the **Nineteenth Amendment,** which gave women the right to vote. She died in 1906, fourteen years before the amendment was passed.

W. E. B. Du Bois

William Edward Burghardt Du Bois was a professor of sociology, history, and economics who became an influential civil rights activist. He protested racism, discrimination in education and employment, and the Jim Crow laws. He was also a prolific author and a proponent of Pan-Africanism. In 1909, he became a co-founder of the **National Association for the Advancement of Colored People (NAACP).** W. E. B. Du Bois died one year before the Civil Rights Act of 1964 was enacted.

George Wallace

George Wallace was a two-time Democratic governor of Alabama in the 1960s through the 1980s. He ran for the presidency but was not nominated by his party. In the 1960s he attempted to stop the integration of the Alabama public schools but was unable to do so. After an attempt was made on his life in 1972, he was paralyzed and used a wheelchair the rest of his life. In addition to his views on race, he was considered a populist.

SKILL 9.3   **Analyze the causes and effects of industrialization in the United States.**

There was a marked degree of industrialization before and during the Civil War, but at the war's end, industry in America was small. After the war, dramatic changes took place. Machines replaced hand labor, extensive nationwide railroad service began making possible the wider distribution of goods, the invention of new products were made available in large quantities, and large amounts of money from bankers and investors became available for the expansion of business operations. American life was definitely affected by this phenomenal industrial growth.

Cities became the centers of this new business activity, resulting in mass population movements to and tremendous growth in urban areas. This new boom in business resulted in huge fortunes for some Americans and extreme poverty for many others. The discontent this caused resulted in a number of new reform movements from which came measures controlling the power and size of big business and measures to help the poor.

Industry before, during, and after the Civil War was centered mainly in the North. The late 1800s and early 1900s saw the increasing buildup of military strength and the United States becoming a world power.

The use of machines in industry enabled workers to produce a large quantity of goods much faster than they did by hand. With the increase in business, hundreds of workers were hired, assigned to perform a certain job in the production process. This was a method of organization called **division of labor** and by increasing the rate of production, it allowed businesses to lower prices for their products to make them affordable for more people. As a result, sales and businesses were increasingly successful and profitable.

A great variety of **new products and inventions** became available. The typewriter, telephone, barbed wire, the electric light, the phonograph, and the gasoline automobile are examples. From this list, the one that had the greatest effect on America's economy was the automobile.

The increase in business and industry was greatly affected by the many rich natural resources that were found throughout the nation. The industrial machines were powered by the abundant water supply of the Northeast. The construction industry needed wood and other materials and depended heavily on lumber from the forests. Large quantities of coal and iron ore were needed for the steel industry and the construction of skyscrapers, automobiles, bridges, railroad tracks, machines, and other products. Other minerals such as silver, copper, and petroleum played a large role in industrial growth. Petroleum was especially important because gasoline was refined from petroleum and was used as fuel for the increasingly popular automobile.

SKILL 9.4 **Demonstrate knowledge of significant individuals who shaped political, economic, and social developments in the United States from 1877 to the present (e.g., Jane Addams, Henry Ford, Franklin D. Roosevelt, Martin Luther King, Jr., Cesar Chavez, Betty Friedan, Malcolm X).**

Jane Addams

Jane Addams was a social worker and reformer in the late nineteenth and early twentieth centuries. She is recognized as the founder of the **social work** profession. Her efforts and activities during the Progressive Era focused on improving communities. She founded Hull House, a settlement house in Chicago. She worked for women's rights and for peace. Addams was awarded the Nobel Peace Prize in 1931, becoming the first American woman to be awarded the prize.

Henry Ford

Henry Ford was an inventor and an expert businessman. He manufactured the first automobile that middle-class consumers could purchase. The reason for his success was his development and use of the assembly line. The **Ford Model T** that he created in 1908 became a popular automobile, and within ten years approximately one-half the cars sold were Model Ts. Henry Ford was also a pacifist, opposed World War I, and published anti-Semitic writings.

Franklin D. Roosevelt

The U.S. economy was in the Great Depression when Franklin D. Roosevelt was elected president in 1932. Roosevelt guided the country back to economic help through programs in his "New Deal." He was president during World War II and met with leaders throughout the war to develop policies for the post-war world. He died in office before World War II concluded. Harry Truman, his vice president, became president in 1945.

Eleanor Roosevelt

Eleanor Roosevelt was the wife of President Franklin D. Roosevelt. She was well known and respected throughout the world for her humanitarian and diplomatic activities. During her husband's presidency, she gave press conferences and wrote a newspaper column. After his death, she continued her work to improve human rights and represented the United States in the United Nations General Assembly from 1949 to 1952.

Martin Luther King, Jr.

Martin Luther King, Jr., was an African American clergyman and leader of the American civil rights movement. He advocated nonviolent opposition to segregation and wanted people to notice injustice. His April 1963 "Letter from Birmingham Jail" explained the purpose of nonviolent action as a way to make people notice injustice. In August of that year, he led the march on Washington, at which he delivered the "I Have a Dream" speech. In 1964, at the age of thirty-five, he became the youngest man to receive the Nobel Peace Prize. King was assassinated in 1968.

Cesar Chavez

Cesar Chavez was an American labor leader who, in the 1960s, organized food harvesters in California into the United Farm Workers. Many of the members were Mexican Americans, like Chavez. The union led nationwide boycotts against the table grape industry and the lettuce industry. He is known for his commitment to nonviolence.

Betty Friedan

Betty Friedan was an author and founder of the National Organization for Women (NOW). Her goal was to have women equal to men in American society. She was a feminist and helped to expand the feminist movement in the United States. She supported the Equal Rights Amendment that was passed by Congress but not ratified by the states.

Malcolm X

Malcolm X was a human rights activist and a Muslim minister. He became a member of the Nation of Islam and advocated black supremacy. He challenged Martin Luther King's nonviolence approach to integration and believed the challenge should be made in whatever way was necessary to accomplish the purpose. He was assassinated in 1965, and his autobiography was published a short time later.

Frederick Douglass

Frederick Douglass was a nineteenth-century African American writer, orator, social reformer, and abolitionist. Born a slave in Maryland in 1910, Douglass escaped slavery. He gained recognition as an intellectual and an orator who challenged many people's views of African Americans. In his later years, he was active in efforts to overturn Jim Crow laws. He wrote an autobiography, *Narrative of the Life of Frederick Douglass,* relating the violence that was turned upon him because of his beliefs

Margaret Sanger

Margaret Sanger was a nurse who founded of the birth control movement in the 1910s and 1920s. She also fought for the repeal of laws that existed in most states that prohibited contraception. In 1916, she opened the first birth control clinic in the United States. Later, she founded organizations that evolved into the Planned Parenthood Federation. Although she was criticized for supporting eugenics, she gained widespread recognition for her contributions to reproductive rights. She died in 1966.

SKILL 9.5 **Demonstrate knowledge of events and issues that shaped political, economic, and social developments in the United States from 1877 to the present (e.g., ratification of the Nineteenth Amendment, Great Depression, passage of the G.I. Bill, passage of the Civil Rights Act of 1964, urbanization, antitrust legislation, immigration restriction, globalization, terrorism).**

Ratification of the Nineteenth Amendment

The Nineteenth Amendment gave women in the United States the right to vote. Women's suffrage had been a significant movement in the United States and throughout the world from the mid-1800s. Susan B. Anthony and Elizabeth Cady Stanton were two American leaders in the suffrage movement, though they did not live to see the amendment passed. In 1918, the amendment passed the House of Representatives with the necessary two-thirds majority vote. In June 1919, it was approved by the Senate and sent to the states for ratification. Suffragists campaigned nationwide to secure ratification, and in August 1920 the amendment received the two-thirds majority of state ratification required to make it the law.

Great Depression

The Great Depression was a result of the stock market crash in 1929. The effects of the Depression were felt around the world.

The Great Depression hit the United States tremendously hard, resulting in bank failures, loss of jobs due to cutbacks in production and a lack of money leading to a sharp decline in spending which, in turn, affected businesses, factories and stores, and higher unemployment. Farm products were not affordable so the farmers suffered even more. Foreign trade sharply decreased, and in the early 1930s, the U.S. economy was effectively paralyzed. President Franklin Roosevelt instituted a series of programs called the "New Deal" to assist the economy and get people back to work.

Passage of the G.I. Bill

The **Servicemen's Readjustment Act** of 1944 is the formal name for the G.I. Bill. This law was passed by Congress to provide benefits such as low-cost mortgages, unemployment allowances, home and business loans, and payments for education to returning World War II veterans, who were called G.I.s.

Passage of the Civil Rights Act of 1964

In the 1960s, the civil rights movement under the leadership of **Martin Luther King, Jr.,** gained momentum. During President **Lyndon B. Johnson**'s administration, the **Civil Rights Act of 1964** became a law. The law prohibited discrimination on the basis of race, sex, gender, color, and national origin.

Urbanization

Urbanization refers to geographic areas becoming more urban than rural. During the Industrial Revolution, people moved from farms and rural areas to cities to work in the factories. Urbanization continued as rail lines connected cities with rural and outlying areas. City populations increased until the 1950s. The trend away from urbanization was evidenced in the move from the city to the suburb when transportation facilities allowed people to live farther from work. Later, many cities experienced a revitalization effort in which young people were moving back into cities and cities began to benefit from urbanization.

Antitrust Legislation

The first major antitrust legislation was the Sherman Antitrust Act of 1890. The act prevented combinations in restraint of trade. The act was designed to eliminate the abuses of trusts such as the Standard Oil Trust and of other big businesses that were creating monopolies. Other antitrust legislation has made price discrimination and types of typing arrangements illegal. The FTC Act of 1914 established the Federal Trade Commission and has addressed deceptive trade practices.

Immigration Restriction

Immigrants arriving from Europe before the Industrial Revolution were primarily from Western Europe. After industrial growth spurred the American economy in the late 1800s, more people were emigrating from southern and eastern European countries.

Asians came to the United States during the California Gold Rush to work in mines. Later they worked on the transcontinental railroad. Many lived in large cities along the West Coast. Japanese and other Asians moved to the United States after the Civil War. In the 1880s, Chinese immigration was no longer permitted and in 1924, quotas were established for the number of immigrants who could enter the United States, and Japanese immigrants were excluded from the United States.

President Truman introduced the **Displaced Persons Act in 1948** to facilitate the admission of more than four hundred thousand persons from Europe. During the 1950s, the immigration policy became very restrictive. Refugees from communist Europe were admitted under the president's Escapee Program of 1952 and the Refugee Relief Act of 1953. In 1965, quotas based on national origin were abolished.

Globalization

Today's society is a global society in many ways. Business, communications, transportation, and tourism are all aspects of a global society.

The length of time it took in the past to do business or become connected in some way with another part of the world has changed, and globalization is part of daily operations. Contracts can be entered into by parties anywhere in the world. Since the invention of the Internet and the World Wide Web, communications can take place instantaneously throughout the world. Transportation has developed to the point where a person can be in another area of the world within a matter of hours. The expansion of tourism and interest in other cultures has made globalization possible.

For more discussion of globalization, see Skill 4.7.

Terrorism

Terrorism is a feared threat to a country's security. Terrorism has occurred throughout the world for many years, but the first large-scale attack of terrorism on the United States occurred on September 11, 2001. After that date, the United States created government departments, chiefly the Department of Homeland Security, to deal with terrorism. Terrorism has not been limited to the United States and is a world problem.

For more discussion of terrorism, see Skill 4.7.

SKILL 9.6   **Analyze the impact of civil rights movements in the United States, including the African American, Hispanic, Native American, and women's rights movements.**

African American Civil Rights Movement

The phrase "the civil rights movement" often refers to the nationwide effort made by black people and those who supported them to gain rights equal to whites and to eliminate segregation. This movement is generally understood in terms of the period of the 1950s and 1960s.

Some of the important people in the civil rights movement have been:

- **Rosa Parks,** an African American seamstress from Montgomery, Alabama who, in 1955, refused to give up her seat on the bus to a white man. Her actions are generally understood as the spark that lit the fire of the Civil Rights movement, and she has been generally regarded as the "mother of the Civil Rights movement."
- **Martin Luther King, Jr.,** the most prominent member of the civil rights movement. King promoted nonviolent methods of opposition to segregation.
- **James Meredith**, the first African American to enroll at the University of Mississippi.
- **Ralph Abernathy**, a major figure in the civil rights movement who succeeded Martin Luther King, Jr., as head of the Southern Christian Leadership Conference.
- **Stokeley Carmichael**, one of the leaders of the Black Power movement who called for independent development of political and social institutions for blacks. Carmichael called for black pride and maintenance of black culture. He was head of the Student Nonviolent Coordinating Committee.

As a result of the civil rights movement, national legislation was passed that prohibits discrimination on the basis of race in many areas, including housing, employment, voting rights, public accommodations, and education.

Hispanic Civil Rights Movement

The Hispanic civil rights movement has been focused on the social and economic integration of Hispanics into American society and achieving the same benefits of American life as others. The movement includes Hispanics who have come to America from many Latin countries. This is an ethnic, not a racial, movement.

Native American Civil Rights Movement

The 1960s saw an expansion of the movement for Native American rights. It also was the time period that the American Indian Movement was created. This movement has focused on inferior housing conditions of the Native Americans and the necessity of the government honoring treaty obligations. In 1972, activists protested the government's failure to honor treaty obligations. They also encouraged Congress to pass the Indian Civil Rights Act of 1968, which guaranteed them civil rights and equal protection.

Women's Rights Movement

The women's rights movement is concerned with the equal rights and freedoms of women as differentiated from broader ideas of human rights. These issues are generally different from those that affect men because of biological conditions or social constructs. The rights the movement has sought throughout history include:

- The right to vote
- The right to work
- The right to fair wages
- The right to bodily integrity and autonomy
- The right to own property
- The right to an education
- The right to hold public office
- Marital rights
- Parental rights
- Religious rights
- The right to serve in the military
- The right to enter into legal contracts

The movement for women's rights has resulted in many social and political changes. Many of the ideas that seemed radical one hundred years ago are now common.

Legislation such as Title IX of the Education Act that prohibits discrimination against women in education has led to the expansion of women's sports programs and teams in colleges and universities. Other legislation has been passed in the areas such as workplace, pay, family leave, and consumer credit protection.

DOMAIN III TEXAS HISTORY

COMPETENCY 10: EXPLORATION AND COLONIZATION

THE TEACHER UNDERSTANDS SIGNIFICANT HISTORICAL DEVELOPMENTS AND EVENTS IN TEXAS THROUGH THE BEGINNING OF THE MEXICAN NATIONAL ERA IN 1821.

SKILL 10.1   **Understand the important similarities and differences among Native American groups in Texas including the Gulf, Plains, Pueblo, and Southeastern groups.**

Texas has a rich and diverse cultural background as shown by the various Native American groups who lived in Texas before the arrival of Spanish settlers in the 1500s. Each of these groups had unique characteristics but also shared some lifestyle developments.

Southeastern Groups

The **Caddoes,** in Northern Texas, were the most culturally advanced group in the region. They had a matrilineal society, tracing their lineage through the maternal instead of the paternal line. The Caddoes were successful agriculturists who grew maize, beans, watermelons, figs, tobacco, and squash. They were mentioned by the Spanish explorers as *Tejas,* which means "friend" in the native language. This is where the name of Texas originated.

The **Coahuiltecans** lived near the Rio Grande. The Coahuiltecans survived on roots, herbs, and cactus plants. Due to their relatively remote location, decimation from disease, and intertribal warfare, this tribe became extinct at an early date.

There were also a number of different tribes that migrated west in the early nineteenth century into Texas from east of the Mississippi. These tribes included **Cherokee, Choctaw, Chickasaw, Kickapoo,** and **Shawnee.**

Gulf

The **Karankawas** lived on the gulf between the current sites of Galveston and Corpus Christi. They were nomadic hunter-gatherers who relied on small game and fish for sustenance. They were known for being tall and muscular, wearing very little clothing. The Karankawas were also famous for practicing ceremonial cannibalism in which they would consume parts of conquered enemies.

Plains

The **Wichitas** separated from other Caddo peoples and migrated into the southern plains. The tribe gained horses during the 1700s and used the animal as a tool to more efficiently hunt buffalo and support their nomadic lifestyle. One unusual aspect of the Wichitas' lifestyle was that they had a mixed economy in which they not only hunted for food but also had a vast agricultural system in which they grew corn, beans, squash, and tobacco.

The **Comanches** migrated to Texas from Wyoming during the 1600s. By the late 1600s, the Comanches acquired horses by raiding Pueblo villages. They were the most skilled tribe in terms of horse breeding and training. The Comanches were feared and respected for their great mobility, horsemanship, and ferocity during warfare.

The **Lipans** were one of the most important subgroups of the **Apaches** in Texas. Initially, they had made serious trouble by raiding tribes for food and plunder. The Lipan was mainly a nomadic group subsisting on hunting-gathering and raiding other tribes. They gained horses after raiding Spanish and Pueblo settlements, which made them even more formidable.

The **Kiowas,** or the "main people," migrated from western Montana to the Black Hills during the early 1700s. At this time, they obtained horses, which drastically improved their mobility and led to a lifestyle that was rather typical of the other Plains groups who hunted buffalo and lived in tepees. In contrast, the Kiowas had several characteristics similar to the Aztecs such as drawing pictographic calendars to record tribal events and worshiping a similar stone idol. By the 1790s, they had migrated to present-day southern Kansas and Oklahoma, becoming powerful allies of their Comanche and Apache neighbors.

Pueblo

The **Tonkawas,** in Central Texas, were a mobile tribe much like the Comanches and hunted bison, deer, and an assortment of smaller game. The Tonkawas had early contact with the Spanish resulting in the tribe obtaining horses by the mid-1500s. The Tonkawa were the traditional enemy of the Apaches, often siding with whoever fought against them.

SKILL 10.2   Demonstrate knowledge of the traditional historical points of reference in the history of Texas during the Spanish colonial period.

The Spanish colonial period, from 1519 to 1821, can be viewed as three historical eras: exploration, cultural assimilation, and protective occupation.

Exploration

The exploration era of Texas' Spanish colonial period involved a rudimentary evaluation of the land and its resources. In 1519, Spanish adventurer **Alonso Álvarez de Pineda** was the first European to explore and map what is now the coastline of Texas. He was sent on a mission by the Spanish governor of Jamaica in search of resources (see also Skill 10.4).

From 1540 to 1542, Spanish explorer Francisco de Coronado led an expedition through what is now the southwestern United States including Northern Texas. He was determined to find the mythical Seven Cities of Cibola.

Cultural Assimilation

The cultural assimilation era of the Spanish colonial period occurred when Native Americans began to adapt to the Hispanic culture in Texas. This assimilation initially happened through intermediaries, but eventually from the Spanish themselves.

While Texas was part of New Spain, widespread permanent settlement did not occur until 1716, when several missions were established. The missions led to the conversion of many Native American tribes as well as the establishment of towns such as San Antonio, Goliad, and Nacogdoches. Because of Native American attacks, the population was very small until 1785 when a peace agreement with the Comanches was drawn up.

Protective Occupation

In the era of protective occupation, the Spanish presence in Texas was consumed by international events more than the purpose of growing an empire. In 1762, France formally withdrew its claim of Texas when the entirety of Louisiana became part of New Spain. This withdrawal reduced the importance of Texas as a buffer state, resulting in a mass relocation of settlers from east Texas to San Antonio. However, Spain returned Louisiana back to France in 1799 due to the huge costs of governing the entirety of the region.

In 1803, as part of the Louisiana Purchase, France sold Louisiana to the United States, which led to a dispute with Spain over the boundary between Texas and the new American territory. This dispute was resolved in 1819, when it was agreed that the Sabine River would be the geographic boundary between the two nations.

The Mexican War of Independence was fought from 1810 to 1821. The Spanish colonial period ended in 1821 when Spain formally gave up its claim of New Spain, resulting in Texas becoming a province of the new nation of Mexico.

SKILL 10.3   **Understand the major causes and effects of European exploration and colonization of Texas.**

Widespread colonization of the American continents began after the voyages of **Christopher Columbus** in 1492. The European nations that became global powers as a result of colonization of the New World were Portugal, Spain, Holland, France, and England.

Three key factors behind the large-scale European exploration of the New World included searching for new trade routes to Asia, improvements in technology, and the enhancement of political and economic power.

New Trade Routes to Asia

Before the Age of Exploration, European traders used overland routes to access lucrative Asian spices; however, the Ottoman Empire cut off these trade routes. This action led to state-funded expeditions to discover an alternate sea route to Asia.

Portugal was the first nation that sought a new route. Under the leadership of Prince Henry the Navigator, the Portuguese embarked on finding a route to Asia going around Africa. Bartolomeu Dias was the first European to reach the bottom of the continent in 1488, and Vasco da Gama went around the Cape of Good Hope in 1497. Because of these discoveries, Portugal became the first European nation to benefit from the riches of Asian trade.

In order to compete with Portugal, the Spanish crown hired young navigator Christopher Columbus to find Asian trade routes in the West. The voyages of Columbus introduced an unknown continent of resources and wealth, though he believed that he had landed in India. By 1519, Spanish explorer Alonso Álvarez de Pineda explored the coast of Texas (see Skill 10.2).

Improvements in Technology

European exploration was facilitated by several innovations, such as the creation of smaller, quicker ships like the **caravel** and **galleon**. These ships were ideal for long-range travel because they were inexpensive to build, quick, and maneuverable.

Key inventions that aided the rise of European exploration included the **astrolabe, magnetic compass,** and **traverse board**. The astrolabe was a tool used to determine latitude first used at sea in 1481. The magnetic compass showed explorers what direction they were travelling. The traverse board helped explorers track the speed and direction of the ship.

Enhancement of Political and Economic Power

European nations sought to strengthen their political and economic power through territorial expansion. **Spain** controlled a massive empire that included Florida, most of the American southwest, California, Mexico, much of the Caribbean, and most of South America. **France's** influence was the Louisiana territory and Canada. **England** controlled thirteen colonies in the eastern portion of North America and some parts of Canada. **The Netherlands** ruled over New Amsterdam, which became New York in 1664 after the British gained control. **Portugal** influenced the Brazilian region of South America.

Effects of European Exploration and Colonization

As a result of these massive empires, European conflicts were fought on a global scale, often putting the native occupants in the middle. In essence, the era of exploration and colonial expansion led to European dominance and influence throughout the world.

Atlantic Slave Trade and Columbian Exchange

One of the biggest effects of European expansion into the New World was the establishment of the Atlantic slave trade, which began in the 1300s. European colonists wanted to exploit the natural resources of their new homes, but there was labor shortage in the Americas.

The solution was to use Africans as slaves. These slaves were typically purchased by European slave traders from African tribal leaders. Although more slaves were transported to South America than North America, the long-term effects were racism in the Americas, economic stagnation in Africa, and political division in the United States.

The Columbian Exchange also resulted from European expansion. This was an exchange of plants, diseases, animals, and technology that occurred after the voyages of Christopher Columbus in 1492.

For further discussion of the Atlantic slave trade and the Columbian Exchange, see Skill 3.4.

Genocide of Native Americans

Another effect of European colonization was the decline of the Native American populations. Many deaths were caused by violent actions of European settlers. However, most Native American deaths can be attributed to the spread of communicable diseases.

One of the results of the Columbian Exchange was the transfer of communicable diseases from Europeans to Native Americans. These diseases included smallpox, measles, and influenza. Because Native Americans had absolutely no contact with these diseases before the arrival of Europeans, they were not immune to them. Approximately 85 to 90 percent of the Native American population was annihilated by these diseases. In some regions, native populations were completely wiped out.

SKILL 10.4   **Understand how significant individuals, events, and issues shaped the early history of Texas from the Spanish Colonial Era to the Mexican National Era (e.g., Álvar Núñez Cabeza de Vaca, José de Escandón, Fray Damián Massanet, Francisco Hidalgo, Alonso Álvarez de Pineda, Moses Austin).**

From the time Spanish explorers first explored the coasts of Texas in 1519 through the Mexican War of Independence until American colonization into Texas in the 1820s, many important individuals and events shaped the history of Texas.

Alonso Álvarez de Pineda was a Spanish explorer who was the first European to explore and map the Gulf Coast of present-day Texas in 1519. His expedition established that Florida was a peninsula, established the boundaries of the Gulf of Mexico, and disproved a sea passage to Asia.

Álvar Núñez Cabeza de Vaca was a Spanish explorer who explored most of the region that would eventually be known as Texas. He wrote detailed accounts of his dealings with many Native American tribes in the region in *La Relacíon*.

José de Escandón was the first Spanish governor of *Nuevo Santander,* which extended from the Pánuco River to the Guadalupe River in present-day Texas. He was known as the Exterminator of the Pames of Querétaro for his barbaric behavior toward Native Americans.

Fray Damián Massanet was a Spanish Franciscan priest who co-founded the first mission in New Spain in 1683 with **Francisco Hidalgo**, the *College of Santa Cruz de Querétaro.* For over a decade, the priests tried to establish missions in east Texas, but could not obtain proper support from New Spain. Since he was not able to procure the assistance New Spain, Hidalgo sent a letter the French governor of Louisiana for assistance in 1711. In response, French missionary **Louis Juchereau de St. Denis** was sent to east Texas to help. They were the driving forces behind establishing missions in eastern Texas like *Mission San Francisco de los Tejas* and *Mission Santísimo Nombre de Maria* in 1689. These missions were abandoned in 1693 due to hostilities with Native Americans who blamed the Spanish for a smallpox outbreak. These missions were paramount because they led to the permanence of the European occupation of Texas.

The Mexican War of Independence was fought from 1810 to 1821. For a review of its significant events and individuals, see Skill 11.1.

Moses Austin was a leader in the American lead industry and the first American to obtain permission to settle in Texas in 1820. After his death, his son, **Stephen F. Austin**, took his place as the leader of the enterprise. On January 3, 1823, Stephen Austin received a grant to colonize near the Brazos River.

SKILL 10.5   **Understand the impact of major geographic features of Texas on Native Americans and settlers, and how various groups altered the natural environment through the beginning of the Mexican National Era.**

The geographic regions of Texas can be divided into four distinct geographic regions. These regions are the Gulf Coast, Interior Lowlands, Great Plains, and Basin and Range Province.

The **Gulf Coast** reaches from the Gulf of Mexico to the Balconies Fault and Eastern Cross Timbers inland. The **Interior Lowlands** stretch from Caprock Escarpment in the west, the Edwards Plateau in the south, and the Eastern Cross Timbers to the east. The **Great Plains** include the Texas panhandle, Llano Estacado, Edwards Plateau, Toyah Basin, and Llano Uplift. The **Basin and Range Province** includes the Sand Hills, Stockton Plateau, desert valleys, wooded mountain slopes, and desert grasslands.

Irrigation

Irrigation was one of the most important ways that both Native Americans and Spanish settlers altered the geographic landscape of Texas.

Spanish explorers like Coronado documented that Native Americans were growing crops using a primitive form of irrigation by gathering and diverting run-off water to fields. Some Spanish explorers noted that Native American groups near present-day El Paso and Pecos developed irrigation systems that ran off from the Rio Grande and Pecos rivers.

The first Spaniards to practice irrigation were the **Franciscans** from 1716 to 1744 who supervised the creation of *acequias,* which supplied water to seven missions near San Antonio. The first crop that was grown using irrigation was corn, but soon other crops were successfully grown.

In the Gulf Coast region, irrigation led to the successful growth of citrus fruits and cotton while the Great Plains provided grains, alfalfa, and cotton.

Ranching

Another important way that the Spanish settlers altered the physical environment was the introduction of domesticated farm animals like cattle, pigs, and chickens. Before the arrival of Europeans, there were no large domestic animals in New Spain. The introduction of domestic animals was an important part of the Columbian Exchange (see Skill 10.4).

SKILL 10.6   Demonstrate knowledge of significant cultural and economic developments in Texas history through the beginning of the Mexican National Era.

The primary economic and cultural lifestyle in early Texas consisted of a Native American hunting and gathering economy. After the arrival of European settlers, the region shifted to an almost exclusively agriculture-based economy.

Although most Native American groups of Texas were hunter-gatherers, there were a few tribes that practiced small-scale agriculture. The Caddoes (see Skill 10.1) lived a relative stationary lifestyle in which they grew crops like corn, squash, and beans. They also hunted game to supplement their diet. The Pueblos also relied heavily on these crops but also practiced early forms of irrigation. On the Plains, the Wichitas practiced a form of mixed economy where they relied on both agriculture and hunting. This was unusual for Native American groups living on the Plains.

When the Spanish arrived in the region, they introduced livestock such as pigs, sheep, goats, and cattle. Spanish agriculture was limited to a few Catholic missions near San Antonio and El Paso. Spaniards introduced crops like wheat, oats, barley, onions, peas, and watermelons in addition to domesticated farm animals. The spread of agriculture was slow to develop in the region due to the dominance of nomadic Native American groups like the Comanches and Apaches. Spanish settlers also began irrigating the land in 1716 (see Skill 10.5).

Due to the efforts of Spanish missions throughout the state and several humiliating defeats, most Native American groups were Christianized by the end of the eighteenth century.

After gaining independence from Spain in 1821, Mexico encouraged individuals to settle in Texas in order to act as defense forces against unruly Native American groups and foreign powers. As a result, Moses Austin obtained the first colonial grant to settle in the region. His son Stephen F. Austin led three hundred families from the United States to central Texas in a settlement named *San Felipe de Austin*. The Americans introduced the slave-based cotton-plantation system, expanded commercial livestock production, and established many small non-slave family farms.

The **General Colonization Law** of 1824 permitted any head of household to claim land in Mexico regardless of race or immigration status.

The Constitution of 1824 established a republican government for Mexico. Despite the best of intentions, it failed to define the rights of Mexican states within the republic including Texas. In addition, it was incredibly vague on slavery, which was active mainly in Texas.

COMPETENCY 11: INDEPENDENCE, STATEHOOD, CIVIL WAR RECONSTRUCTION AND
                AFTERMATH

THE TEACHER UNDERSTANDS SIGNIFICANT HISTORICAL DEVELOPMENTS AND EVENTS IN TEXAS
FROM 1821 TO 1900.

SKILL 11.1   **Demonstrate knowledge of the individuals, issues, and events related to
              Mexico becoming an independent nation and the impacts of this event on
              Texas.**

The Mexican War of Independence (1810–21) was not a continuous war but a series of uprisings
over political turmoil in Spain and New Spain culminating in the creation of the nation of Mexico.

Political Turmoil in Spain

Due to an enormous amount of war debt caused by the Napoleonic Wars in the early nineteenth
century, Spain decided to obtain tax revenues from their existing North American colonies. In
1804 a royal decree ordered the confiscation of some lands owned by the Catholic church, and
gave them to the crown. Once these resources began to run out, a financial crisis in New Spain
began.

Napoleon invaded Spain in 1808, forcing Ferdinand VII to abdicate the throne in favor of Joseph,
an action that was unpopular in New Spain. The ***criollos,*** those born in New Spain who had longed
for a greater say in local government, promoted a provisional government that supported deposed
King Ferdinand while the ***peninsulars,*** the ruling class born in Spain, supported the current viceroy
government. **Viceroy Jose de Iturrigaray** supported the *criollo* but was removed from office in a
coup by the *peninsulars*. After arresting many *criollo* leaders and shipping Iturrigaray back to
Spain, **Pedro Garibay** was made the new viceroy.

Revolts in New Spain

In 1810 New Spain was still suffering through a horrific economic downturn due to changes in
overseas trade, poor crop harvests, drought, and famine. In Querétaro, a mining region hit hard by
economic uncertainty, the revolution began when priest and chief conspirator **Father Miguel
Hidalgo y Costilla** formally denounced the ruling class on September 16, 1810.

The battles between the *criollos* and *pensinsulars* were at a stalemate until new viceroy Francisco
Javier Venegas and **General Félix María Calleja** had Hidalgo's army on retreat toward northern
provinces.

In Texas, the **Casas Revolt** swung the revolution back in favor of the rebels when
Governor **Manuel Antonio Cordero y Bustamante** had 700 troops defect in January 1811 after
being confronted by 7,000 rebel troops in Coahila. Governor Manuel Salcedoe of Texas was
unseated in January 22, 1811 by **Juan Bautista de las Casas**. The victory was short-lived as Casas
was forcefully removed from office by **General Juan Manuel Zambrano**.

On March 21, 1811, **Ignacio Elizondo** ambushed the insurgents, capturing many of their important leaders including Father Hidalgo.

On August 1813, **General Joaquín de Arredondo** defeated the rebels at the **Battle of Medina,** which secured Texas for the royal crown. **José María Morelos y Pavón** took over the revolution. He was more organized and politically savvy, and had a clearer plan for the future of Mexico. After the execution of Hidalgo, Morelos took control of the insurgents. Under his detailed leadership, the rebels formally declared their independence and drafted a constitution. However, he was unable to gain broad support for the movement and was captured and subsequently executed in November 1815. At this point, the revolution was at a stage of stagnation until 1820 when events in Spain provided the final motivation for independence.

Creation of the Nation of Mexico

In January 1820, an army revolt in Argentina sparked revolution throughout the Spanish empire. Ferdinand VII had been reinstated as king in 1813. Tired of King Ferdinand's despotic behavior, rebels in Spain forced him to reinstate the Constitution of 1812. However, once the reformed constitutional Cortes (sovereign assembly) regained power, they refused to acknowledge colonial grievances. Tensions between colonial authorities and Mexican citizens became incredibly hostile.

Spanish official **Agustín de Iturbide** negotiated with the Mexican revolutionary leader **Vincente R. Guerrero** for independence in the **Plan de Iguala** on February 24, 1821. This plan called for a constitutional monarchy, maintaining the rights and lands of the Catholic church, and equality between the *criollos* and *peninsulars*. After arriving from Spain to rule colonial Mexico, **Juan O'Donoju** saw that this plan would not work. He signed a treaty granting Mexico its independence on August 24, 1821.

SKILL 11.2   **Demonstrate knowledge of important individuals, events, and issues related to the Texas Revolution (e.g., the Law of April 6, 1830, Fredonian Rebellion, Battle of Gonzales, Surrender at Goliad, Battle of the Alamo, Battle of San Jacinto, George Childress, Juan N. Seguin, Antonio López de Santa Anna, William B. Travis, James Fannin).**

The Texas Revolution officially started with the **Battle of Gonzales** in October 1835 and ended on May 14, 1836 with the **Two Treaties of Velasco.** However, many events and minor skirmishes resulting from social and political differences between American settlers and the Mexican government set the stage for the revolution.

Americans first began to settle in Texas at the end of 1821 when Stephen F. Austin and several families settled in Central Texas (see Skill 10.6). Mexico enacted the **State Colonization Law of March 24, 1825,** an attempt to bring people to the states of Coahuila and Texas, encourage agriculture, and assist commerce. Although Americans were allowed to settle in these states, Mexicans would receive first choice of lands. Americans were given a temporary pass of taxation but had to agree to take an oath to obey federal and state constitutions, practice the Christian faith, and behave with high morals. In exchange for these vows, these settlers would become citizens of Mexico.

By the mid-1820s, Mexico began to reconsider its immigration leniency because Americans often squatted on Mexican lands rather than formally apply for them. In addition, Americans would often ignore local customs and colonial statutes while imposing their own customs in the region.

In 1826 **Haden Edwards** declared that the Nacogdoches area was an independent nation called the Republic of Fredonia. The **Fredonian Rebellion** was minor, but cemented fears that continued immigration into Texas would cause even more secessionist support. As a result of troubles in Texas, the centrist government in Mexico implemented the **Law of April 6, 1830,** which voided the *empresario* contracts that did not comply with Mexican law. The law further curtailed immigration from the United States and the bringing of slaves into Mexico, and provided military forts to police the borders. This law was unpopular among not only American settlers but also Mexican political leaders who believed that American immigration into Texas only strengthened their economic viability.

On September 15, 1829 Mexican president Vincente R. Guerrero issued the **Guerrero Decree,** which prohibited slavery in Mexico. Inhabitants of Texas vehemently denounced this law, and Guerrero quickly succumbed to pressure excluding Texas from the decree.

In early 1833, **Antonio López de Santa Anna** deposed the centrist government in Mexico City and eliminated provisions in the Law of April 6, 1830 that restricted immigration into Texas. However, Santa Anna quickly reverted back into a centrist government violating the rights of the clergy and privileged classes. The return of a centrist government caused many small uprisings throughout the nation, and many feared that Texas would soon follow.

When Texas found out that Mexican troops were being sent north, Texan militants, led by **William B. Travis**, captured Anahuac on June 30, 1835. The first armed conflict between Mexico and the Texans occurred at the **Battle of Gonzales** in October 1835. The Texans defeated Mexican forces during the **Goliad Campaign of 1835**. This victory not only provided the rebel Texans with valuable weapons but cut off the Mexican army from the gulf, which prevented them from rearming.

In early 1836, Santa Anna crossed the Rio Grande determined to crush the Texas rebellion, and was highly successful at first. Despite some setbacks, Texas formally declared its independence and named **Sam Houston** major general of the Texas army at the **Convention of 1836**. The Texas Declaration of Independence, written by Texan attorney **George Childress**, was modeled after the United States Declaration of Independence.

At this time, Santa Anna was marching toward San Antonio, and on February 23, 1836, the Mexican army laid siege on a small San Antonio mission named The Alamo for thirteen days. **The Battle of the Alamo** occurred on March 6, 1836 when the Mexican army defeated the Texas army decisively. Although this was a victory for Mexico, the cost was incredibly high as Santa Anna lost nearly 600, or one-third, of his troops. Survivor **Juan N. Seguin** spread the message, "Remember the Alamo," which became a rallying cry for Texas independence.

On March 9, 1836, Mexican general **José de Urrea** was heading toward Goliad. After many victories, he captured General James Fannin and the Goliad army. At the **Surrender at Goliad,**

Fannin surrendered, hoping the army would be treated as honorable prisoners of war. However, Santa Anna had the entire Goliad army executed on March 27, 1836 despite reassurances of eventual release.

At this point, Santa Anna had believed that the war was over despite pleas from his generals that there was much work to be completed. The only one who prevented Mexican victory was General Sam Houston. He had been on the retreat for months since learning of the Alamo and Goliad. However, he intercepted Mexican couriers who revealed the size and location of Santa Anna's army. At the **Battle of San Jacinto,** Texas forces either killed or captured the entire Mexican army including Santa Anna in eighteen minutes. Santa Anna ordered his second-in-command, General Vincente Filisola, to remove his army from Texas.

The war ended on May 14, 1836 when the **Two Treaties of Velasco** were agreed upon, in which Mexico would recognize Texas as an independent nation.

SKILL 11.3   **Demonstrate knowledge of important individuals, events, and issues related to the history of the Republic of Texas and early Texas statehood (e.g., Stephen F. Austin, Lorenzo de Zavala, Sam Houston, Joshua Houston, Mary Maverick, Mirabeau Lamar, the Córdova Rebellion, the Council House Fight, the Santa Fe Expedition, United States-Mexican War).**

Early Texas Republic

The first challenge of the new republic was setting up a viable government. Interim president **Isaac Burnet** called for an election in order to accomplish four things: approve the constitution, authorize the amendment of the constitution, and elect a president, and consider annexation to the United States. The three candidates for president were **Stephen F. Austin, Henry Smith,** and **Sam Houston.**

In the fall of 1836, the Constitution of the Republic of Texas was written by **Lorenzo de Zavala**. The constitution was essentially a carbon copy of the United States Constitution.

On September 5, 1836 Houston was elected first president of the Republic of Texas. He was elected by a populace that believed that Houston would bring stability to the nation, obtain recognition from world powers and early annexation to the United States, and pursue state recognition from Mexico. The election also resulted in the acceptance of the constitution and the refusal to allow Congress to amend the constitution. As president, Houston advocated for vigilance in dealing with Mexico, annexation into the United States, and peace treaties with Native Americans.
While serving as the first president of Texas, Sam Houston always had his personal servant and friend **Joshua Houston** by his side. An educated slave, Joshua met some of the most influential men in Texas. In 1862, Houston freed Joshua even though it was technically illegal.

Mirabeau Lamar was the first vice president and second president of the Republic of Texas. Nominated by opponents of Sam Houston (who was not permitted to serve consecutive terms), Lamar was elected president in November 1838. As president, he faced many serious problems such as Mexican invasion, gaining national recognition, poor relations with Native Americans, currency inflation, bankrupt government, and no commercial treaties. First, he drove the Cherokees and Comanches from Texas. Second, he pursued recognition from nations like Great Britain and France, but he vehemently opposed annexation into the United States. Third, he established the **Texas State Library.** Finally, he sought a long-term peace treaty with Mexico, but was unsuccessful despite obtaining recognition from France, Great Britain, and Belgium.

The Córdova Rebellion was a rebellion plot against the Republic of Texas in the summer of 1838. Main conspirator Alcade Vicente Córdova supported the Texas Revolution against Mexico until independence was declared. With support from the Cherokee tribe, Córdova sought to bring down the Texas government. On March 29, 1839, **General Thomas J. Rusk** defeated the rebellion with Córdova escaping to Mexico.

The Council House Fight was a quarrel between Texas peace delegates and the Comanches. On March 19, 1840, these two groups met in order to establish peace after two years of conflict. The Comanches wanted Texas to officially recognize their homeland Comancheria whereas Texans wanted prisoners of war to be released. The meeting ended in violence when shots were fired killing twelve Comanches. Any chance of peace between these groups ended, resulting in years of warfare and turmoil.

The Santa Fe Expedition was a military and commercial venture purposed with establishing the northern boundaries of Texas by claiming parts of New Mexico. President Lamar also sought to obtain control over the Santa Fe Trail in order to procure trade with New Mexico. The expedition was deemed a failure since the group was captured by Mexican forces and held captive for over a year. The failure of the Santa Fe Expedition was deemed a huge blemish on Lamar's record as president.

Mary Maverick was an early Texas pioneer whose memoirs served as a critical source of daily life in San Antonio during the Republic of Texas and early statehood.

Annexation of Texas

After several years of debate in Texas and the United States regarding the viability of annexation, the United States and Texas both signed the **Treaty of Annexation** on April 12, 1844, and Congress ratified the treaty on March 1, 1845.

The annexation of Texas caused relations between the United States and Mexico to be strained. The primary cause of tensions was a dispute regarding the Texas-Mexico border and a disputed stretch of land in New Mexico and Colorado. In response, President James K. Polk attempted to negotiate the purchase of these lands, but was refuted. In response, Polk used a series of minor skirmishes between Mexican troops and **General Zachary Taylor** to convince Congress to declare war on Mexico on May 13, 1846.

United States-Mexican War

The **United States-Mexican War** lasted from May 13, 1846 until March 10, 1848. Once war was declared, American forces quickly took control of New Mexico, California, and eventually Mexico City. After the conquest of the Mexican capital, the United States and Mexico signed the Treaty of Guadalupe Hidalgo on February 2, 1848. It was ratified by Congress on March 10.

As a result of the treaty, Mexico ceded 525,000 square miles of territory (New Mexico and California) in exchange of $15 million and the assumption of Mexico's debts to American citizens. In addition, Mexico agreed to recognize the loss of Texas and established the Rio Grande as the border.

SKILL 11.4   **Demonstrate knowledge of important individuals, issues, and events of the Civil War and Reconstruction in Texas (e.g., Jack Coffee Hays, John Bell Hood, John B. Magruder, Battle of Galveston, Battle of Palmito Ranch).**

The issues that divided the North and South during the Civil War troubled most Texans. Most Texans were incredibly loyal to the Union; however, they had fundamental problems with Northern attacks on slavery despite the fact that only one of four families in Texas owned slaves.

When South Carolina seceded from the Union in December 1860, Texans decided that they should hold a secessionist convention on February 23, 1861, when they voted to leave the United States and joined the Southern Confederate States of America. As many as 90,000 Texans enlisted to fight in the Civil War.

One of General Robert E. Lee's best regiments was **John Bell Hood**'s Texas Brigade. After being promoted to major general on October 10, 1862, he commanded regiments at Second Bull Run, Antietam, Fredericksburg, and Gettysburg. On July 18, 1864, Hood was given command of the Army of Tennessee with which he led disastrous defeats in Franklin and Nashville. While retreating into Mississippi, Hood's men sang "The Yellow Rose of Texas."

John B. Magruder arrived in Texas on October 10, 1862 after being reassigned by General Lee. His greatest success was a victory at the **Battle of Galveston** where the Confederate army recaptured Galveston Island It remained under Confederate control throughout the remainder of the war despite a war-long Union blockade of the Gulf Coast.

Despite news of General Lee's surrender in April 1865, **John Salmon ("Rip") Ford** defeated Union forces during the **Battle of Palmito Ranch** on May 13, 1865. This would be the final battle of the American Civil War. On June 2, 1865, Generals Magruder and **Edmund Kirby Smith** surrendered their command to Union forces.

Some men, like Tennessee-born **John ("Jack") Coffee Hays,** a military officer in the Republic of Texas, remained neutral during the Civil War. Hayes had repelled a Mexican Invasion of Texas in 1842 and successfully thwarted numerous Native American attacks during that period. He was also instrumental in developing training techniques unique in frontier warfare. Jack Coffee Hayes is also remembered as a prominent Texas Ranger (see Skill 11.6).

SKILL 11.5   Understand the major effects of Reconstruction on the political, economic, and social life of Texas.

In the years of **Reconstruction** following the Civil War, Texas was in turmoil because of economic, social, and political issues caused by the war. Under President Andrew Johnson's Reconstruction plan, each Southern state would be given a provisional governor who had to call a convention in which each state would nullify secession, abolish slavery, and repudiate the state's Civil War debt. Once this work was completed, the convention would elect a new governor, legislature, and other state officials.

The Constitutional Convention of 1866

In Texas, **Andrew J. Hamilton** was appointed interim governor by President Johnson. Hamilton was the choice to lead Texas during Reconstruction because he had supporters from the pre-war **antebellum elite** and Unionists alike. In order to participate in the convention, a delegate had to plead an oath of amnesty which was designed to empower the Unionists while minimizing the power of the antebellum elite.

After the election of 1866, the pre-war power structure was reaffirmed. Although the antebellum elite lost political power after the war, they remained economically viable. Despite attempts at excluding them from the political processes of Reconstruction, they participated in the convention. In fact, many moderate Unionists were willing to compromise with the old guard. Moderate **James W. Throckmorton** was named president of the convention.

During the convention, Texans were only willing to accept the bare minimum of the president's demands. The delegates denounced secession, deeming it null and void. They accepted the abolition of slavery providing former slaves basic rights but refused to grant black suffrage. In a controversial move, they declared that all laws enacted during the Civil War that did not conflict with federal laws would remain on the books. In the final act of the convention, conservative Throckmorton was elected governor of Texas.

Legislation during Reconstruction

The **Bureau of Refugees** was formed in September 1865 in order to help freed slaves transition from slavery to freedom. Despite white fears, this act accomplished very little to advance freed blacks economically. In fact, freed slaves were encouraged to stay where they were and accept contract jobs that tied them to plantations creating a new form of slavery.

The **Eleventh Legislature** met on August 6, 1866, and did everything in their power to return Texas back to the antebellum status quo. The legislature appointed prominent secessionists to the U.S. Senate and refused to ratify the Thirteenth and Fourteenth Amendments. They also passed a series of "black laws" as a way of limiting black labor to apprenticeships, contract labor, and vagrancy laws. Unionists argued that the regime of governor Throckmorton did all that it could to usurp Reconstruction; in fact, the two men elected to the U.S. Senate were not allowed to take office.

In response to the actions of Southern states like Texas, the **First Reconstruction Act** was enacted on March 2, 1867. The act broke up the Southern states into military districts. Texas was placed in the Fifth Military District. As a result, Governor Throckmorton was forcefully removed from office for impeding the progress of Reconstruction. Because of countless complaints of corruption against Texas officials, **Commander Charles Griffin,** military commander of Texas, removed numerous officials throughout the state.

A second convention met at Austin from June 1868 to February 1869. Because conservatives decided to not participate in the convention, a new state constitution was written and ratified in January 1870. They accepted the Fourteenth and Fifteenth Amendments and named two more senators, thus complying with the requirements for readmission into the Union. On March 30, 1870, **President Ulysses Grant** readmitted Texas to the Union, ending Reconstruction.

SKILL 11.6   Understand the major causes and effects of the expansion of settlement along the frontier in Texas and of the conflicts between some settlers and Native American groups (e.g., Quanah Parker, Texas Rangers, Buffalo Soldiers).

The expansion of settlement along the frontier in Texas was due to several factors such as the arrival of the railroads, new homestead laws, and removal of Native American groups from the Plains.

In order to increase its economic development, Texas began offering tax incentives to railroad companies to build railroads. Subsidies to the International Railroad Company, Southern Trans-Continental, and Southern Pacific were huge indicators of the potential of Texas.

In 1872, the legislature passed two important homestead laws. First, families that did not currently own land would be sold 160 acres for one dollar an acre, but had to live on the land for three years and pay all processing fees. Second, an exemption was made that restricted homesteaders who lived on less than 200 acres of land from a forced sell.

Conflicts between Settlers and Native Americans

In order to guarantee the safety of new settlers, Texans wanted to move Native Americans out of the Plains, but these groups were not inclined to voluntarily leave. Many years of vicious battles followed, and all Native Americans in Texas were moved to reservations.

Quanah Parker was the last chief of the Quahada Comanches and an important figure in Native American resistance and reservation life. In the 1860s, the Quahada were considered the most troublesome group of Comanches for white settlers, and essentially controlled the plains of Texas. As more and more American hunters gathered on the Plains, the buffalo population dwindled to an unsustainable level. Since buffalo was a staple of the Quahada diet, Parker pursued a multi-tribe alliance in order to drive hunters away from their lands. On June 27, 1864, a group of 700 Cheyennes, Arapahoes, Kiowas, and Comanches attacked a group of 28 hunters. The Native Americans were handily defeated by the better armed hunters. Due to growing pressure from the army and severe starvation, the Quahada agreed to move to the Kiowa-Comanche Reservation. Once on the reservation, Parker was named chief of the Comanches by the American government due to his seamless transition to reservation life. He was a pragmatic leader who encouraged his people to adopt self-sufficiency and self-reliance through agriculture and education.

Texas Rangers

The Texas Rangers unofficially formed in 1823 when Stephen F. Austin hired ten frontiersmen to engage in an expedition to exact revenge against Native Americans. On November 24, 1835, the Texas Rangers were made official by Texas lawmakers. They were considered the more efficient way to defend the frontier from attacks by disgruntled Native Americans and the borders with Mexico. Jack Coffee Hays was a prominent Texas Ranger (see Skill 11.4). Today, the **Texas Ranger Division** is a law enforcement agency based in Austin.

When the Democrats came to power in 1874, the legislature created two new regiments to handle growing violence on the frontier. First, a special force of rangers led by Captain Leander H. McNelly regained order in the lawless Dewitt County and Nueces Strip. Second, the Frontier Battalion, led by Major John B. Jones, fought the Comanches and Kiowas, severely deflating the morale of these tribes.

Buffalo Soldiers

In September 1866 Congress commissioned the Buffalo Soldiers, a military regiment whose members originally came from the U.S. Army, as the first completely African American brigade during peacetime. The Buffalo Soldiers mainly served in the Southwest and Plains regions in order to fight Native American groups.

SKILL 11.7   Demonstrate knowledge of the impact of major economic and technological developments in Texas in the period 1821 to 1900.

From 1821 to 1900, the economy of Texas expanded exponentially due to the rise and expansion of the railroad industry. During the late nineteenth century, the railroad industry boosted not only agriculture, but manufacturing as well. The main industries that grew during this period were flour mills, lumbering, meat packing, and cottonseed oil.

Up until the Civil War, the plantation system dominated the landscape of the Texas economy. After the war, the plantation system continued with contracted tenant farmers instead of slaves.

The economy of Texas continued to expand during the late nineteenth century in addition to serious problems and many cultural changes. The primary component of the Texas economy was agriculture, which expanded dramatically during this period. Despite the growth of farms, prices were on the decline, which led to greater debt and more mortgaged farms. These issues led to farmers joining the **Farmer's Alliance,** which sought to pursue farmers to practice cooperative farming using credit rather than cash.

At the end of the nineteenth century, the cottonseed industry was on the rise in Texas. In fact, Texas was the largest producer of cottonseed in the nation.

After the establishment of the railroad industry, removal of Native Americans on the Plains, and the decimation of the buffalo population (see Skill 11.6), the ranching industry expanded between 1875 and 1885. However, prices declined because cattle populations were greater than demand. The **Texas and Southwestern Cattle Raisers Association** was formed in 1877 to deal with problems facing the cattle industry.

SKILL 11.8   **Understand the impact of major geographic features of Texas on migration, settlement patterns, and economic development and how various groups altered the natural environment.**

During the nineteenth century, many changes to the natural environment occurred at the hands of farmers, immigrants, and hunters. Many of these changes, such as irrigation and migration, were driven by the diverse geography of Texas. However, settlers and hunters also changed the biological diversity of the state.

Migration and Irrigation

The population of Texas expanded significantly with migration coming mainly from the American South. The growing population primarily settled on the frontier of the state in the panhandle and the southern Plains, and near the Pecos River.

Large-scale irrigation in Texas began in Del Rio in 1868 and expanded into the Pecos River area, Rio Grande area, and Fort Stockton area. By the 1890s, modern irrigation systems had been established near the Coastal Plains and the El Paso region.

Changes in the Natural Environment

Settlers severely impeded Texas' natural environment in the latter half of the nineteenth century. Wildlife suffered from overhunting and overfishing throughout the state. Cattle replaced buffalo in the Plains while hunters and fishermen decimated many species of animal life. In response to these changes, the **Office of State Fish Commissioner** was created in 1879.

In addition, the lumber industry changed the landscape of the eastern Texas forests. Lumbering significantly reduced the forests of east Texas. As a result, the state legislature created the **Forestry Association** in 1890.

SKILL 11.9   **Demonstrate knowledge of major cultural developments in Texas in the period 1821 to 1900.**

Education and Literacy

One of the greatest cultural achievements of nineteenth-century Texas was the development of an education system. The various churches greatly encouraged education in the state, resulting in the founding of several denominational colleges. The state founded the **Agricultural and Mechanical College** (now Texas A & M) in 1876 and the **University of Texas** in 1873.

The new colleges and universities drew students from the public education system. Enrollment increased from 176,245 students in 1880 to 515,544 students in 1900. As a result, the overall literacy in Texas grew from 70 percent to 86 percent during that same time period of just twenty years. In 1884, the **Office of State Superintendent of Instruction** and school districts were founded. They used tax dollars to fund education, which was hugely instrumental in the rise of literacy rates.

Racially Segregated Lifestyles

Because of Anglo-American racism, African Americans and Hispanic Americans lived rather segregated lifestyles during the late nineteenth century in Texas. They developed separate social communities.

To help address a lack of economic opportunities, African Americans formed **Colored Farmers Alliance** in the 1880s. Despite segregation in the schools with lower budgets than white schools, African American schools' literacy rates improved. Segregated African American churches formed several important colleges, including **Prairie View A & M College**.

Hispanic Americans were often day laborers working in agricultural jobs, although some did own small businesses. One of the great accomplishments of Hispanic Americans in Texas was their ability to maintain their culture through Spanish newspapers.

Development of Recreation

At the end of the nineteenth century, recreation became increasingly important in urban areas where football and baseball games, circuses, and theaters began to become popular. The **Texas Professional Baseball League** was formed in 1888.

College football teams also began to compete during this period. In 1894, Texas A & M and University of Texas played the first college football game in the state.

COMPETENCY 12: TEXAS IN THE TWENTIETH AND TWENTY-FIRST CENTURIES

THE TEACHER UNDERSTANDS SIGNIFICANT HISTORICAL DEVELOPMENTS AND EVENTS IN TEXAS FROM 1900 TO THE PRESENT.

SKILL 12.1   **Understand the impact of individuals and reform movements such as the Progressive movement and the Civil Rights movement on Texas in the late nineteenth and twentieth centuries (e.g., Jane McCallum, Lulu Belle Madison White, Manuel C. Gonzales, Oveta Culp Hobby, James Hogg, Hector Garcia).**

Like most of the United States during the first two decades of the twentieth century, Texas possessed an optimism that would reflect the Progressive movement. During this period, Texas underwent many social movements including women's suffrage, Prohibition, corporate regulation, and civil rights movements for African Americans and Mexican Americans.

Jane McCallum was a suffragist leader who fought for women's suffrage and Prohibition during the early twentieth century. In 1915 she was named president of the Austin Women's Suffrage Association. She often worked with **Minnie Fisher Cunningham** of the **Texas Equal Suffrage Association** in order to promote women's suffrage statewide. She was also adamant in obtaining a state and federal amendment that would establish universal suffrage.

Lulu Belle Madison White was a civil rights leader during the 1940s and 1950s who also campaigned for suffrage, equal pay for all, and desegregation of public institutions. She joined the **National Association for the Advancement of Colored People (NAACP)** in 1937. In 1943, she became the executive director of the Houston branch of the NAACP. White was the first woman in the South to hold such a position. In 1946, she became the state director of the NAACP where she fronted the important case of *Sweatt* v. *Painter* (1950), which ended segregation on the University of Texas campus. *Sweatt* served as a precedent for the landmark case of *Brown* v. *Board of Education* (1954).

Manuel C. Gonzales was Mexican American civil rights leader who played an important role in the founding of organizations like the **Mexican Protective League** in 1917, the **Asociacón Juridica Mexicana** in 1921, the **Sons of Texas** in 1922, and the **League of United Latin Citizens** in 1929. He was an active supporter of the **Good Neighbor Commission,** which was an agency formed in 1943 to solve social, cultural, and economic difficulties of Mexican Americans.

Oveta Culp Hobby was an attorney and journalist who became the first secretary of the **U.S. Department of Health, Education, and Welfare.** She was also the first commanding officer of the **Women's Army Corp** and chairperson of the board of the *Houston Post.*

James Hogg became the first native Texan to serve as its governor, in 1890. His term was based on five principles. These included upholding the state constitution, establishing the Railroad Commission, creating railroad stock and bond law that reduced watered-down stock, regulating state and municipal bonds, and regulating alien land ownership.

Hector Garcia was a Mexican American doctor and civil rights leader who founded the **American G.I. Forum (AGIF)** in 1948. This organization was initially formed to help Mexican American veterans obtain medical services denied by the U.S. Department of Veteran Affairs. Eventually, the AGIF expanded to assist Mexican Americans with voting rights, segregation, and civil right violations. The AGIF was a plaintiff for *Hernandez* v. *Texas* (1954), which established that

Mexican Americans along with all other racial groups all possessed the right to equal protection under the law.

SKILL 12.2   Understand the political, economic, cultural, and social impacts of major events in the twentieth century, including World War I, the Great Depression, World War II, and the Cold War on the history of Texas.

Impact of World War I on Texas

The events leading to World War I captivated Texans from the beginning to the sinking of the *Maine* in May 1915. The Texas legislature introduced a resolution demanding that relations between the United States and Germany be severed. In addition, Texans were upset that Germany was provoking trouble on the Mexican border. Germany was attempting to start a war between Mexico and the United States in order to prevent American intervention in Europe.

President Woodrow Wilson was adamant that he would avoid war in Europe until the **Zimmermann Letter** was captured. This letter uncovered a secret plot in which Germany offered Mexico all of its lost territory to the United States in Texas, New Mexico, Arizona, and California in exchange for Mexico declaring war on the United States and encourage Japan to join as well. The United States declared war on Germany on April 2, 1917.

Not only did more than 198,000 Texans fight during the war, but millions of Texas participated in massive domestic campaigns. These included Liberty and Victory bonds, war stamps, and food conservation programs called "Hoovering."

Impact of the Great Depression

The Great Depression severely affected the world's economy. Before 1929 Texans were in a great state of confidence due to a growing populations and economy. However, on "Black Tuesday," October 29, 1929 that optimism quickly faded.

President Herbert Hoover's response aimed at correcting the weaknesses of the stock market. Through 1930 Hoover often argued that the Depression would soon be over. Many Texans viewed the Depression as nonexistent. Most believed that since the heart of the Depression was all the way in New York, they were safe because of their resilient, self-sufficient agricultural-based economy.

Since the Depression worsened throughout the nation in 1930, Texans had to recognize that there was a problem. Because the Hoover administration was unable to unburden the hardships caused by the Depression to families, private charities and churches exhausted their resources until local governments intervened.

Like in most of the nation, Texans blamed President Hoover for not doing enough to curtail the effects of the Great Depression. During the election of 1932, most Texans supported Democratic candidate **Franklin D. Roosevelt** and his **"New Deal"** with 88.7 percent of the vote.

Texas native **John Nance (Cactus Jack) Garner** was Roosevelt's vice president, and was considered one of the most influential vice president s in history. Texan **Jesse H. Jones** was the head of **Reconstruction Finance Corporation (RFC),** which disbursed ten billion dollars to banks, agriculture, railroads, and public works. All of the money would be paid back in full. Most Texans supported the New Deal as they believed that a fair portion of the benefits would only help Texas.

Governor **James Allred** was considered the New Deal governor of Texas. He was incredibly popular because he did not hesitate to funnel New Deal money into the state. During his term, he focused on the Civilian Conservation Corps, Works Projects Administration, National Youth Administration, and Public Works Association.

Another aid to the state's economy was the **Texas Centennial** celebration of 1936. The state pumped twenty-five million dollars into the state's economy by creating a world's fair. The celebration included the building of monuments, markers, museums, and restorations. Once Congress passed the **National Social Security Act** in 1935, he set in motion complementary legislation dealing with old-age pensions, unemployment compensation, teacher pensions, and help for children and the disabled. Governor Allred established the **Texas Department of Public Safety,** which combined the Texas Rangers and the State Patrol into one department.

In 1937, many Texans began to become wary of the New Deal mainly because of the growing power of the president. In the **"court packing" plan,** Roosevelt wanted to add several justices each time a justice turned seventy but did not retire (see Skill 17.6). During his 1938 campaign for reelection, Roosevelt attempted to purge the Democratic Party of members who criticized his plans. These events led to the formation of a Texas political group known as the **Jeffersonian Democrats,** who vehemently opposed Roosevelt's presidency. They presented the first serious, organized effort among disenchanted Democrats and Republicans to oppose the New Deal. Some Jeffersonian Democrats were Houston attorney W. P. Hamblen, businessman John Henry Kirby, and former congressman Joseph W. Bailey, Jr.

Impact of World War II

As with most of the nation, one of Texas' greatest contributions during World War II was rationing of meat, sugar, gas, rubber, and auto parts. While Texas governor Coke R. Stephenson accepted rationing, he vehemently opposed the rationing of gasoline.

During the war, Texas farmers produced large amounts of food, which helped the United States become the granary of the war effort. Wartime industries in Texas included munitions factories, aircraft factories, steel mills, synthetic rubber factories, paper mills, and shipyards. Due to a shortage of labor, many people moved from rural areas into cities while many women worked "unconventional" jobs in factories. Because of these war demands, migration to Texas reached 450,000 within four years.

Impact of the Cold War

The United States and Soviet Union were allies during World War II, but soon became bitter enemies over competing ideologies and views on post-war Europe. This decades-long rivalry led many Texans to serve in both the military and on the home front.

In Texas, the Cold War led to citizens fearing the consequences of a possible armed conflict between the United States and the Soviet Union. These fears were reinforced during conflicts like the Korean War, the Vietnam War, and the Cuban Missile Crisis. In addition, Texans feared nuclear annihilation resulting in large-scale building of many underground bomb shelters in their backyards.

During the Cold War, Texas became the site for numerous military bases that trained young men and women in a desegregated military. Many of these bases are still operational.

SKILL 12.3 **Understand the political, economic, and social impact of major events and individuals in the latter half of the twentieth and early twenty-first centuries on the history of Texas (e.g., Kay Bailey Hutchison, Barbara Jordan, Eddie Bernice Johnson, Henry B. Gonzalez, Lyndon B. Johnson, James Farmer, George Walker Bush, Craig Anthony Washington, Immigration, Rust Belt to Sun Belt migration).**

Modern Texas Leaders and Issues

Texas has had a wonderful history of political leadership during the latter half of the twentieth and early twenty-first centuries. These leaders dealt with a number of issues such as racism, reform movements, and immigration.

Kay Bailey Hutchison became the first woman senator from Texas in 1993. She served in the U.S. Senate for twenty years. During her tenure, she maintained adamant support of NASA and term limits in Congress.

Barbara Jordan was the first African American congresswoman from the Deep South and the first woman elected into the Texas senate. In 1966 she was elected to the senate, where she championed for the state's first minimum wage law and the **Texas Fair Employment Practices Act**. In 1972, she was elected into the United States House of Representatives, where she demanded the impeachment of President Richard M. Nixon.

Eddie Bernice Johnson, an African American representative from Texas' 30th district, used her position of lawmaker to create a forum for fighting discrimination. Johnson advocated for legislation meant to curb housing discrimination and investigations into unfair government contracts.

James Farmer, a civil rights leader, founded the **1961 Freedom Ride,** which led to the desegregation of interstate transportation in the United States. He also founded the **Congress of Racial Equality (CORE),** whose goal was to end segregation through nonviolence.

Craig Anthony Washington, a representative from Texas, opposed bills related to the North American Free Trade Agreement (NAFTA) and NASA. This was because he believed that these resources should be applied to assist low-income families. He has long advocated for women and minorities to be more active in local politics.

Over the last several years, the issue of **immigration** has become a hot button among Texas citizens. Ever since Texas was a republic, Mexican immigrants would often migrate into the state to seek agricultural jobs. Due to the expansion of agriculture in the American South, many Mexicans viewed this region as a logical way to escape the poverty of their homeland. In fact, 700,000 Mexicans were living in Texas by 1930. Up to this time, most Mexican Americans faced the challenges of having their voices ignored due to the racist views of the time. After World War II, Mexican Americans began to enjoy more political opportunities due to a new wave of leadership.

Henry B. Gonzalez was the first Mexican American representative elected from Texas in 1961. He chaired the Committee on Assassinations of President John F. Kennedy and Martin Luther King, Jr., and called for the impeachments of President Ronald Reagan and George W. Bush.

The issue of undocumented workers (sometimes called illegal immigrants) continues to be a huge debate among Texans. One argument would be that illegal immigrants are not only breaking the law but costing the state billions of dollars due to public programs like welfare and food stamps. However, the other side argues that Mexican immigrants are refugees seeking a better life in America.

The **Rust Belt to Sun Belt migration** was the largest intra-American movement since the 1950s. As manufacturing in the South was expanding, American steel and coal industries in the North were on the decline. This led to the mass exodus beginning in the 1970s from the American North (Pennsylvania, Ohio, Michigan, Illinois, etc.). People from that region moved to states like California, Nevada, Florida, and Texas.

U.S. Presidents from Texas

In the latter half of the twentieth and early twenty-first centuries, Texas provided the nation with two U.S. presidents, **Lyndon B. Johnson** and **George W. Bush**. Both presidents were polarizing figures that began their tenures with enormous optimism and support but became hugely unpopular over a number of issues.

Lyndon B. Johnson became the first Texas-born president after the Kennedy assassination in Dallas in November 1963. His presidency brought many changes such as the Civil Rights Act of 1964, the Voting Rights Act of 1965, and the Great Society program. In foreign policy, Johnson made the choice to honor Kennedy's commitment in Vietnam. The escalation of the war turned both Democrats and Republicans against Johnson. In addition, Texans had grown weary of

Johnson because of antiwar protests, growing social programs, and racial unrest. With his political support nonexistent, he announced that he would not seek another term as president.

George W. Bush was the 46th governor of Texas and the 43rd president of the United States. He began his career as an oil mogul in Texas and co-owner of the Texas Rangers baseball team. In 1994 Bush was elected governor of Texas over the popular incumbent **Ann Richards**. His campaign focused on four principles: welfare reform, tort reform, crime reduction, and educational improvement. In 2000 Bush was elected president of the United States in a highly contested and controversial election against vice president **Albert Gore, Jr.** The two-term Bush presidency began with heavy approval, especially after his administration's poise and leadership after the **9/11 attack,** but after long wars in Afghanistan and Iraq and prolonged recession, his approval ratings were incredibly low.

SKILL 12.4 **Understand the impact of major developments in manufacturing, the petroleum and gas industry (e.g., Spindletop), commercial agriculture (e.g., cotton, citrus, beef, and dairy production), and suburbanization and how various groups altered the natural environment from 1900 to the present.**

Manufacturing and the Petroleum and Gas Industry

The early 1900s served as a transition period for the development of manufacturing in Texas. In 1901 the discovery of the **Spindletop Oilfield,** Texas's first oil reservoir, was the main catalyst for change. It was the first of a long line of petroleum discoveries that would expand the Texas economy like never before. During the next decade, manufacturing expanded in a variety of products until the Great Depression.

The period between 1900 until World War I was defined by the growth of the petroleum industry. The petroleum industry transformed Texas from a primarily agricultural state with few major cities into a largely industrialized state with several large cities. This boom lasted until the 1940s when production peaked.

Because of an energy crisis caused by production peaks and political instability in some countries, the world's supply of petroleum was tightened. This caused oil prices to increase which greatly benefited Texas oil companies. By the 1980s and 1990s, the oil industry in Texas was on the decline.

Commercial Agriculture and Suburbanization

At the beginning of the 1900s, Texas farmers were experiencing an economic revival. With the combination of technological, scientific, economic, and political factors, large commercial farms came to dominate Texas agriculture. These farms would acquire sophisticated machinery that allowed for greater efficiency by using less labor for more crops. In addition, stock farmers developed better breeding techniques to improve results. These innovations drove many of the small farms out of business but actually resulted in more food being produced on less acreage.

Because of rapid urbanization and the advent of World War I, the demand for agricultural goods was on the rise. Because of this high demand, prices of the commodities also increased. These positive conditions led to further growth of the agricultural industry.

The high demand caused Southern Texas land promoters to advertise the lower Rio Grande delta as a place for agricultural innovation. In 1908 **Charles Volz** and **John H. Shary** launched the **citrus industry** in Willow, Cameron, and Hidalgo counties. By 1929, roughly 85 percent of the citrus trees grown were grapefruit trees. In addition, these same counties became leaders in the commercial truck farming industry growing vegetables like onions, cabbage, lettuce, carrots, beets, and spinach.

During this period, **cotton** production increased from 3.4 million bales to 4.3 million bales per year. The cotton industry expanded because of innovations like the development of cotton species that grow better on the Plains by scientists from the **Texas Agricultural Experiment Station** in Lubbock and the widespread use of the tractor.

Throughout most of the state, crop land was scattered with grazing land, meaning that stock farming was the most prevalent. **Beef production** was the most lucrative agricultural enterprise in Texas. Another aspect of the cattle industry, **dairy production,** grew substantially as **suburbanization** spread throughout the state.

By the end of the twentieth century, Texas agriculture remained a critically important industry to both the state and nation. Agriculture brings roughly fifty-two billion dollars annually to the state's economy, making Texas one of the leading farm states.

SKILL 12.5   **Understand the effect of major developments in computer technology, transportation (including aerospace), and medical research on the contemporary economic and social history of Texas.**

Computer Technology

Texas is one of the hot spots in the United States for the development of computer technology. The computer technology industry positively influences the state economy by providing citizens with thousands of jobs. Austin and Dallas are major centers for this industry. Austin is often referred to as "Silicon Hills" because it is where the major players in semiconductor design like Silicon Laboratories and AMD are located. Google, Electronic Arts, Facebook, and Apple all have offices in Austin. In addition, Dell is located in the suburb of Round Rock.

Dallas is often cited as the home of the integrated circuit and microprocessor. North Dallas is often called "Silicon Prairie" due to companies like Texas Instruments, Perot Systems, and EDS all having offices in the area.

Transportation Industry

Transportation in Texas includes a vast network of airports, railroads, mass public transportation, seaports, and space stations. Each of these forms of transportation has assisted in the growth of the Texas economy.

Dallas/Fort Worth International Airport, known as DFW, is the largest airport in Texas and second largest in the United States. Only Denver International Airport is larger. DFW is the largest hub of American Airlines. In recent years, DFW and Houston's George Bush Intercontinental Airport have ranked among the ten busiest airports in the nation.

The Lyndon B. Johnson Space Center in Houston is NASA's center for astronaut training, research, and flight control. Often referred to as Mission Control, the Johnson Center is used to train American and foreign astronauts. The facility was built in 1963 on lands donated by Rice University and named for the first Texan to be elected president.

During the late nineteenth century, the railroads were the most important means of transportation in Texas. Although the state has the longest railway mileage, that number continues to dwindle.

There are currently several mass public transportation systems in Texas. Dallas Area Rapid Transit (DART) became the first public transportation system to use light rail carts in the American Southwest in 1996. In Houston, the Metropolitan Transit Authority of Harris County, Texas (METRO) operates bus and light rails. San Antonio, Fort Worth, Austin, Arlington all have their own versions of public transportation.

Sea ports provide an important means of transportation in Texas with its more than one thousand miles of coastline. The Port of Houston is the largest and most important port in Texas. It is the busiest U.S. port in terms of foreign tonnage. The Port of Galveston is also paramount to the Texas economy; it was the largest port in Texas until a massive hurricane in 1900 devastated it.

Medical Research

The Texas Medical Center is the largest medical center in the world. Located in Houston, it is composed of fifty-four health-related nonprofit buildings. The center was founded in 1945 by businessman Monroe Dunaway Anderson. He funded the project with an initial donation of $300,000 and provided for an additional $19,000,000 after his death.

Many academic institutions have established a variety of medical research centers. The University of Texas Medical Branch (UTMB) established a Marine Biomedical Institute in 1969, an Institute for Medical Humanities in 1973, the Center for Molecular Science in 1991, and a Center for Biomedical Engineering in 1991. Baylor College of Medicine created the AIDs Research Center in 1991.

A number of Texans revolutionized medical care. Some examples were cardiac surgeons Michael E. DeBakey and Denton A. Cooley, cell T. C. Hsu, and oncologist R. Lee Clark.

DOMAIN IV GEOGRAPHY, CULTURE, AND THE BEHAVIORAL AND SOCIAL SCIENCES

COMPETENCY 13: PHYSICAL GEOGRAPHY CONCEPTS, NATURAL PROCESSES, AND EARTH'S PHYSICAL FEATURES

THE TEACHER UNDERSTANDS BASIC GEOGRAPHIC CONCEPTS, NATURAL PROCESSES INVOLVING THE PHYSICAL ENVIRONMENT, AND EARTH'S PHYSICAL FEATURES.

SKILL 13.1 **Understand the concept of physical region as an area of Earth's surface with unifying physical characteristics (e.g., soils, climate, vegetation, river systems).**

The earth's surface is made up of 70 percent water and 30 percent land. Physical features of the land surface include mountains, hills, plateaus, valleys, canyons, plains, deserts, deltas, and other minor landforms. Earth's water features include oceans, seas, lakes, rivers, and canals.

Physical Regions

Landforms

Mountains are landforms with steep slopes at least 2,000 feet or more above sea level. Mountains are found in groups called mountain chains or mountain ranges. At least one range can be found on six of the earth's seven continents. North America has the Appalachian and Rocky Mountains. South America has the Andes. The Himalayas are in Asia, and Australia has the Great Dividing Range. The Alps are in Europe and the Atlas, Ahaggar, and Drakensburg Mountains are in Africa.

Hills are elevated landforms rising to an elevation of about 500 to 2000 feet. They are found on all continents including Antarctica, where they are covered by ice.

Plateaus are elevated landforms that are usually level on top. Depending on location, they range from being very cold to cool and healthful. Some plateaus are dry because they are surrounded by mountains that keep out any moisture. One example is the Kenya Plateau in East Africa, which is very cool. The plateau extending north from the Himalayas is extremely dry, whereas plateaus in Antarctica and Greenland are covered with ice and snow.

Plains are areas of flat or slightly rolling land, usually lower than the landforms next to them. Sometimes they are called lowlands, and some are located along seacoasts. Plains support the majority of the world's people. Some are found inland. Many have been formed by large rivers resulting in extremely fertile soil for successful cultivation of crops and numerous large settlements of people. In North America, vast plains areas extend from the Gulf of Mexico north to the Arctic Ocean and between the Appalachian and Rocky Mountains. In Europe, rich plains extend east from Great Britain into central Europe and on into the Siberian region of Russia. Plains in river valleys are found in China (the Yangtze River valley), India (the Ganges River valley), and Southeast Asia (the Mekong River valley).

Valleys are land areas that are found between hills and mountains. Some have gentle slopes containing trees and plants. Other valleys have very steep walls and are referred to as **canyons.** One notable example is Arizona's Grand Canyon of the Colorado River.

Deserts are large dry areas of land receiving ten inches or less of rainfall each year. Among the larger deserts of the world are Africa's Sahara Desert, the Arabian Desert on the Arabian Peninsula, and the desert Outback that covers roughly one-third of Australia.

Deltas are areas of lowlands formed by soil and sediment deposited at the mouths of rivers. The soil is generally very fertile and most fertile river deltas are important crop-growing areas. One example is the Nile delta in Egypt that is known for its production of cotton.

Other minor landforms include mesas, basins, foothills, marshes, and swamps. **Mesas** are the flat tops of hills or mountains. The mountains or hills usually have steep sides. Sometimes plateaus are also called mesas. **Basins** are considered to be low areas drained by rivers or low spots in mountains. **Foothills** are generally considered a low series of hills found between a plain and a mountain range. **Marshes** and **swamps** are wet lowlands providing growth of such plants as rushes and reeds.

Water Features

Oceans are the largest bodies of water on the planet. The four oceans of the earth are the Atlantic Ocean, one-half the size of the Pacific and separating North and South America from Africa and Europe; the Pacific Ocean, covering almost one-third of the entire surface of the earth and separating North and South America from Asia and Australia; the Indian Ocean, touching Africa, Asia, and Australia; and the ice-filled Arctic Ocean, extending from North America and Europe to the North Pole. The waters of the Atlantic, Pacific, and Indian Oceans also touch the shores of Antarctica.

Seas are smaller than oceans and are surrounded by land. Some examples include the Mediterranean Sea found between Europe, Asia, and Africa and the Caribbean Sea, touching the West Indies and South and Central America. A lake is a body of water surrounded by land. The Great Lakes in North America are good examples.

Rivers, considered a nation's lifeblood, usually begin as very small streams, formed by melting snow and rainfall, flowing from higher to lower land, emptying into a larger body of water, usually a sea or an ocean. Examples of important rivers of the world include the Nile, Niger, and Zaire rivers in Africa; the Rhine, Danube, and Thames rivers in Europe; the Yangtze, Ganges, Mekong, Hwang He, and Irrawaddy rivers in Asia; the Murray-Darling in Australia; and the Orinoco in South America.

Canals are water passages constructed to connect two larger bodies of water. Famous examples include the Panama Canal across Panama's isthmus that connects the Atlantic and Pacific oceans and the Suez Canal that connects the Red and Mediterranean seas in the Middle East between Africa and the Arabian Peninsula.

Unifying Physical Characteristics

Soils

Soil is composed of a mixture of materials and it supports plant life. It is also the result of the influences of climate, weathering, the earth's particles, and erosion. There are different types of soil.

Saline soil is found in dry reasons and has a high content of salt. The salt prevents plants from taking water from the soil and can slow plant germination and growth. The saline content also prevents good irrigation of the soil.

Sandy soil causes water to drain rapidly and makes the soil dry to touch. Sandy soil warms more quickly than other soils. They are easy to work with because its particles have large spaces between them.

Clay is a type of heavy soil that has tiny particles. This soil can store large quantities of water and becomes sticky when it is wet. Its tiny particles cause it to be dense, but it is good for growing plants because water drains slowly from it.

Silt is a soil that is finer than sandy soil. It is very smooth to touch and retains water very well. However, it drains slowly and feels cold to touch.

Peat is dark brown or black and is compressed. This type of soil has high water content and a lot of organic matter. Peat holds water and is used for growing plants. This type of soil began forming more than nine thousand years ago when glaciers melted and caused plants to decay. When the plants decayed under the water left by the rapidly melting glaciers, there was an accumulation of organic matter. That matter became peat.

Loam is made up of a combination of silt, clay, and sand. Humus is also part of this type of soil. Loam is a dark soil that crumbles when held or touched. Loam is used in gardening because it holds nutrients but drains well and permits air to move freely between particles.

Climate

Climate is the average weather or daily weather conditions for a specific region or location over an extended period of time. Studying the climate of an area includes gathering information on the area's monthly and yearly temperatures and its monthly and yearly amounts of precipitation. Another characteristic of an area's climate is the length of its growing season.

In northern and central United States, northern China, south-central and southeastern Canada, and the western and southeastern parts of the former Soviet Union is found the climate of four seasons, the **humid continental climate**—spring, summer, fall, and winter. Cold winters, hot summers, and enough rainfall to grow a variety of crops are the major characteristics of this climate. Some of the world's best farmlands and important activities such as trading and mining are found in humid continental climates. Differences in temperatures throughout the year are determined by the distance a place is inland, away from the coasts.

The **steppe,** or prairie climate, is located in the interiors of the large continents of Asia and North America. Steppes are dry flatlands that are far from ocean breezes and are called prairies or the Great Plains in Canada and the United States and steppes in Asia. Although the summers are hot and the winters are cold, the big difference is rainfall. In the steppe climate, rainfall is light and uncertain and ranges between ten and twenty inches a year. Where rain is more plentiful, grass grows. In areas of less rainfall, the steppes or prairies gradually become deserts. Examples are the Gobi Desert of Asia; deserts of central and Western Australia, the southwestern United States, and in the smaller deserts found in Pakistan, Argentina, and Africa south of the Equator.

The two major climates found in the high latitudes are tundra and taiga. **Tundra** means "marshy plain" and is a Russian word that aptly describes the climatic conditions in the northern areas of Russia, Europe, and Canada where winters are extremely cold and very long. Surprisingly, less snow falls in the area of the tundra than in the eastern part of the United States. However, due to the harshness of the extreme cold, very few people live there and no crops can be raised.

The **taiga** is the northern forest region and is located south of the tundra. The world's largest forestlands are found here along with vast mineral wealth and fur bearing animals. Very few people live here because of an extremely short crop-growing season. The winter temperatures are colder and the summer temperatures are hotter than those in the tundra because the taiga climate region is farther from the waters of the Arctic Ocean. The taiga is found in the northern parts of Russia, Sweden, Norway, Finland, Canada, and Alaska where most of their lands are covered with marshes and swamps.

The humid **subtropical climate** is found north and south of the tropics and is very moist. The areas having this type of climate are found on the eastern side of continents and include Japan, mainland China, Australia, Africa, South America, and the United States where warm ocean currents are found. The winds that blow across these currents bring in warm moist air all year round. Long, warm summers and short, mild winters result in a long growing season that allows for different crops to be grown several times a year. All of these factors contribute to the productivity of this climate type, one that supports more people than any of the other climates.

The **marine climate** is found in Western Europe, the British Isles, the U.S. Pacific Northwest, the western coast of Canada and southern Chile, southern New Zealand and southeastern Australia. A common characteristic of these lands is that they are either near water or surrounded by it. The ocean winds are wet and warm, bringing a mild rainy climate to these areas. In the summer, the daily temperatures average at or below 70 degrees F. During the winter, because of the warming effect of the ocean waters, the temperatures rarely fall below freezing.

In certain areas of the earth there exists a type of climate unique to areas with high mountains, usually different from their surroundings. This type of climate is called a **vertical climate** because the temperatures, crops, vegetation, and human activities change and become different as one ascends the different levels of elevation. At the foot of the mountain, a hot and rainy climate is found and many lowland crops are cultivated. As one climbs higher, the air becomes cooler, and the climate changes sharply. Here, different economic activities take place, such as grazing sheep and growing corn. At the top of many mountains, snow is found throughout the year.

Vegetation

Vegetation is the plant life of a certain area. Because of the numerous regions throughout the world, vegetation is varied.

The main plants of the steppe are grasses. However, in higher altitudes some thorny bushes and shrubs can be found.

In the tundra some vegetation grows on rocks and is formed from fungus and algae. This vegetation is called lichen. Mosses and grasses also grow in the tundra.

The taiga is a forested area. Spruce, evergreens, firs, and pine trees live in these areas. Although coniferous forests predominate, some broadleaf trees such as aspens and willows can survive in the taiga. Where the soil is damp, mosses and lichen will grow on the ground or in damp areas. Grasses thrive wherever there are areas of sunshine.

Subtropical climates have hot summers and mild-to-cool winters. These climates have enough precipitation for agriculture and are home to various types of vegetation. Evergreen forests are dominant in subtropical areas. The needle-leaf evergreens include pines and cypress. Broadleaf evergreens include ferns, shrubs, and small palms.

Tropical climates vary. Some receive rain throughout the year but others have long dry seasons. As a result, tropical vegetation varies and is dependent upon the geographic location. Puerto Rico's El Yunque National Forest is an example of a tropical rainforest.

Marine vegetation includes all plants that live seas or oceans. The specific type of vegetation depends upon the location of the body of water. Polar zones have limited vegetation. Bodies of water in the temperate and tropical zones have large quantities of algae and grasses. Algae are the most common types of marine vegetation and they produce organic matter. Plankton is an example of marine vegetation. Grasses that grow in marine climates grow under the water in depths up to approximately three hundred feet. Algae are used in medicines and by food, petroleum, and textile industries.

Vegetation in desert areas is sparse. The plants must adapt to extremely hot and dry climates. Many desert plants appear to be spiny. Desert plants often have very few, or no, leaves and long roots that provide them water from deep within the earth. The cacti are examples because of their appearance and ability to store water.

Woodlands are characterized by sunlight, limited shade, and soils that have a lot of organic matter. Deciduous and coniferous trees grow well in woodlands as do grasses and shrubs.

River Systems

River systems are made up of large rivers and numerous smaller rivers or tributaries that flow into them. Examples include the vast Amazon River system in South America and the Mississippi River system in the United States.

SKILL 13.2 **Analyze ways in which physical processes shape patterns in the physical environment (e.g., lithosphere, atmosphere, hydrosphere, biosphere).**

Environmental Spheres

The **biosphere** includes the places on earth, its waters, and its atmosphere that support life. The **atmosphere** is the air or the gaseous area that surrounds the earth. The **hydrosphere** includes the waters on the earth and in the area that surrounds the earth. **Lithosphere** is the thick crust and upper mantle of the earth.

Although the hydrosphere, lithosphere, and atmosphere can be described and considered separately, they are actually constantly interacting with one another. Energy and matter flows freely between these different spheres. For instance, in the water cycle, water beneath the earth's surface and in rocks in the lithosphere is exchanged with vapor in the atmosphere and liquid water in lakes and the ocean the hydrosphere. Similarly, significant events in one sphere almost always have effects in the other spheres. The recent increase in **greenhouse gases** provides an example of this ripple effect.

Additional greenhouse gases produced by human activities are released into the atmosphere where they build up and cause widening holes in certain areas of the atmosphere and global warming. Examples of the effects that increasing temperatures have had on the hydrosphere include rising sea levels, increasing water temperature, and climate changes. These lead to even more changes in the lithosphere, such as glacier retreat and alterations in the patterns of water-rock interaction such as run-off and erosion.

Plate Tectonics

Data obtained from many sources led scientists to develop the theory of **plate tectonics.** This theory is the most current model that explains not only the movement of the continents but also the changes in the earth's crust caused by internal forces.

Plates are rigid blocks of earth's crust and upper mantle. These rigid solid blocks make up the lithosphere. The earth's lithosphere is broken into nine large sections and several small ones. These moving slabs are called plates. The major plates are named after the continents they are "transporting." The plates float on and move with a layer of hot rock in the upper mantle resembling plastic. Geologists believe that the heat currents circulating within the mantle cause this plastic-like zone of rock to slowly flow, carrying along the overlying crustal plates.

Movement of these crustal plates creates areas where the plates diverge and areas where the plates converge. A major area of **divergence** is located in the mid-Atlantic. Currents of hot mantle rock rise and separate at this point of divergence, creating new oceanic crust at the rate of two to ten centimeters per year. **Convergence** is when the oceanic crust collides with either another oceanic plate or a continental plate.

The oceanic crust sinks, forming an enormous trench and generating volcanic activity. Convergence also includes continent-to-continent plate collisions. When two plates slide past one another, a **transform fault** is created.

These movements produce many major features of the earth's surface, such as mountain ranges, volcanoes, and earthquake zones. Most of these features are located at plate boundaries where the plates interact by spreading apart, pressing together, or sliding past each other. These movements are very slow, averaging only a few centimeters a year.

Boundaries form between spreading plates where the crust is forced apart in a process called **rifting.** Rifting generally occurs at mid-ocean ridges. Rifting can also take place within a continent, splitting the continent into smaller landmasses that drift away from each other, thereby forming an ocean basin between them. The **Red Sea** is a product of rifting. As the sea floor spreading takes place, new material is added to the inner edges of the separating plates. In this way the plates grow larger, and the ocean basin widens. This is the process that broke up the super continent **Pangaea** and created the **Atlantic Ocean**.

Boundaries between plates that are colliding are zones of intense crustal activity. When a plate of ocean crust collides with a plate of continental crust, the more-dense oceanic plate slides under the lighter continental plate and plunges into the mantle. This process is called **subduction**, and the site where it takes place is called a subduction zone. A subduction zone is usually seen on the sea floor as a deep depression called a trench.

Crustal movement where plates slide sideways past each other produces a plate boundary characterized by major faults capable of unleashing powerful earthquakes. The San Andreas Fault forms such a boundary between the Pacific Plate and the North American Plate. **Orogeny** is the term given to natural mountain building.

A mountain is terrain that has been raised high above the surrounding landscape by volcanic action, or some form of tectonic plate collisions. The plate collisions could be intercontinental or ocean floor collisions with a continental crust (subduction). The physical composition of mountains includes *igneous, metamorphic,* or *sedimentary* rocks. Some mountains may have rock layers that are tilted or distorted by plate collision forces.

Glaciers and the Ice Age

A **glacier** is a large mass of ice that moves or flows over the land in response to gravity. Glaciers form among high mountains and in other cold regions.

There are two main types of glaciers: valley glaciers and continental glaciers. Erosion by **valley glaciers** is a U-shaped erosion that produces sharp-peaked mountains such as the Matterhorn in Switzerland. Erosion by **continental glaciers** often rides over mountains and leaves smooth rounded mountains and ridges.

A time period in which glaciers advance over a large portion of a continent is called an **ice age**. Remains of plants and animals found in warm climates help to support the theory of periods of warmth during the past ice ages.

The most recent ice age began between two and three million years ago. This age saw the advancement and retreat of glacial ice over millions of years. Theories relating to the origin of glacial activity include plate tectonics, where it can be demonstrated that some continental masses, now in temperate climates, were at one time blanketed by ice and snow. A theory for cause involves changes in the earth's orbit around the sun, changes in the angle of the earth's axis, and the wobbling of the earth's axis. Support for the validity of this theory has come from deep ocean research that indicates a correlation between climatic sensitive microorganisms and the changes in the earth's orbital status.

A continental glacier covered a large part of North America during the most recent ice age. Evidence of this glacial coverage remains as abrasive grooves, large boulders from northern environments dropped in southerly locations, glacial troughs created by the rounding out of steep valleys by glacial scouring, and the remains of glacial sources called **cirques** that were created by frost wedging the rock at the bottom of the glacier.

About twelve thousand years ago, a vast sheet of ice covered a large part of the northern United States. This huge, frozen mass had moved southward from the northern regions of Canada as several glaciers.

SKILL 13.3   Demonstrate knowledge of how Earth-Sun relationships affect physical processes and patterns on Earth's surface.

Earth is the third planet away from the sun in our solar system. Earth's numerous types of motion and states of orientation greatly affect global conditions, such as seasons, tides, and lunar phases. The earth orbits the sun with a period of 365 days. During this orbit, the average distance between Earth and Sun is ninety-three million miles. The shape of Earth's orbit around the sun deviates from the shape of a circle only slightly. This deviation, known as the **earth's eccentricity**, has a very small effect on Earth's climate. Earth is closest to the sun at **perihelion,** occurring around January 2 of each year, and it is farthest from the sun at **aphelion,** occurring around July 2. Because Earth is closest to the sun in January, the northern winter is slightly warmer than the southern winter.

Earth also rotates on its own axis, which is tilted relative to the plane of Earth's orbit. This tilt results in the light from the sun striking more directly on different parts of Earth as Earth travels around the sun in the course of a year.

This causes the seasons of the year and is the most obvious effect of the **Earth-Sun relationship**. Summertime in the Northern Hemisphere is when Earth is tilted toward the sun and the sun's rays strike it more directly, raising the surface temperature. At the same time, the Southern Hemisphere is tilted away from the sun and the sun's rays strike the surface at more of an angle, making it cooler. This is winter. Each hemisphere passes through spring and fall in the cycle between the two extremes.

This cycle has a direct effect on the earth's weather. As different parts of the planet warm and cool, air currents develop that gather and distribute moisture over the surface of the planet. Hurricanes, for instance, develop in the warm waters near the equator and spin northward or southward into cooler regions, often bringing destruction where they cross land.

The water cycle is also dependent on the Earth-Sun relationship. Evaporation and weather cycles carry water from the ocean into the atmosphere and distribute it in higher land, such as mountain ranges. Here the water is stored as snow or ice until some of it begins to melt as the seasons grow warmer. Water then flows downward toward the sea again, forming streams and rivers that carry sediment and cause erosion, altering the surface of the earth. Rivers and lakes also provide important resources for humans, who often choose nearby sites to establish towns and cities. Earth's tilt relative to the sun creates extremes at the earth's poles, where there is darkness for six months and daylight for six months, with the sun never striking the surface directly. This results in permanently cold conditions where vast amounts of water are frozen as ice and snow.

Tides

The orientation of and gravitational interaction between the earth and the moon are responsible for the ocean tides that occur on earth. The term **tide** refers to the cyclic rise and fall of large bodies of water. Gravitational attraction is defined as the force of attraction between all bodies in the universe. At the location on earth closest to the moon, the gravitational attraction of the moon draws seawater toward the moon in the form of a **tidal bulge.** On the opposite side of the earth, another tidal bulge forms in the direction away from the moon because at this point, the moon's gravitational pull is the weakest.

Spring tides are especially strong tides that occur when the earth, sun, and moon are in line, allowing both the sun and the moon to exert gravitational force on the earth and increase tidal bulge height. These tides occur during the full moon and the new moon.

Neap tides are especially weak tides occurring when the gravitational forces of the moon and the sun are perpendicular to one another. These tides occur during quarter moons.

SKILL 13.4   Analyze relationships among climate, vegetation, soil, and geology to explain the distribution of plants and animals in different regions of the world.

Climate, vegetation, soil, and geology can affect which plants and animals live in various regions of the world. The temperature, type of soil, and physical aspects of the terrain determine the types of life that can be sustained in the area. Plant life and animal life are interdependent and form the basis of each type of living environment.

When plants and animals interact with the physical environment, an **ecosystem** is formed. The earth has several ecosystems, and they can vary in size and shape. Ecosystems can vary according to complexity. Larger ecosystems can consist of wide areas, such as the steppe or tundra. The soil, climate, and geology of the ecosystems determine which vegetation can survive and maintain life because the physical environment keeps plants and animals alive.

The ecosystems provide water for plant growth, and plants provide nourishment for animals. Soil is an important part of the process because when either dies, its decay enters the earth and new plants use the nutrients. The decay, root systems of plants, and chemicals of water flowing into the soil from bedrock make new layers of soil. Ecologically, the elements are interdependent and create the atmosphere for life that exists in a particular ecosystem.

Ecosystems may have similar environments but they may contain different types of plant and animal life, depending upon the part of the world where the ecosystems are located.

SKILL 13.5 **Demonstrate knowledge of the patterns and characteristics of major landforms, climates, and ecosystems of Earth and the processes that produce these patterns and characteristics (e.g., factors that influence physical regions such as elevation, latitude, ocean currents, mountain barriers, tectonic processes).**

Patterns and Characteristics

Landforms

Landforms are categorized by characteristics such **as elevation, slope, orientation, stratification, rock exposure,** and **soil type.** Landforms by name include mounds, hills, cliffs, valleys, and others. Oceans and continents exemplify highest-order landforms. Landform elements are parts of a landform that can be further identified. The generic landform elements include **pits, peaks, channels, ridges, passes, pools,** and **planes** and can be often extracted from a digital elevation model using some automated or semi-automated techniques.

Elementary landforms (segments, facets, relief units) are the smallest homogeneous divisions of the land surface, at the given scale/resolution. A plateau or a hill can be observed at various scales ranging from few hundred meters to hundreds of kilometers. Hence, the spatial distribution of landforms is often fuzzy and scale-dependent as is the case for soils and geological strata.

A number of factors, ranging from plate tectonics to erosion and deposition, can generate and affect landforms. Biological factors can also influence landforms—for example, the role of plants in the development of dune systems and salt marshes, and the work of corals and algae in the formation of coral reefs.

Climates

Weather is the condition of the air that surrounds the day-to-day atmospheric conditions including temperature, air pressure, wind, and moisture or precipitation which includes rain, snow, hail, or sleet. Examples are the tornadoes that occur in various parts of the country in spring and fall. **Climates,** the average weather conditions over a long period of time, result from a pattern of reoccurring characteristics and may result from long-term occurrences, such as the glacial age. Climates can be classified by regions or areas and take into account weather patterns, the atmosphere, oceans, and the land's topography. Climate can also be classified by causes and by effects. The factors that cause a climate constitute one form of classification, and the effects that result from factors—such as vegetation grown—form another classification.

The **Köppen system** classifies climates and was developed in the early 1900s. This system uses vegetation, temperature, and precipitation to classify climate. The system uses a letter classification method and was named for the person who developed it. Other systems of classification are based on soil water conditions and moisture.

Ecosystems

An ecosystem functions as a community of plants, animals, and other organisms that interact with one another and are interdependent elements of the environment. An ecosystem may be microscopic or encompass larges areas of the earth and each system is different.

Although different, all ecosystems have some common characteristics. Plants are part of the food chain of an ecosystem because they consumed by animals and other organisms and provide nutrients for those who benefit from their decay. Water, energy from the sun, and carbon dioxide are also important elements of all ecosystems.

Factors That Influence Physical Regions

Elevation

Elevation, the distance above or below sea level, has an effect on climate. Air density is less as the elevation increases. Temperatures are cooler at higher elevations because the air is less dense. The snow falls at higher elevations are heavier, also, because the air is less dense and does not hold heat. Elevations below sea level are hot and dry. Death Valley is an example of an area that has no rain and is below sea level.

Latitude

Latitude is the distance north or south of the equator and it is an important factor in establishing climate conditions of physical regions of the earth. Regions that are closer to the equator will receive more direct sun and those regions farther away will have less sun exposure and the rays will be less direct. Latitude also affects precipitation and the amount of evaporation.

Ocean Currents

Ocean currents move constantly and are driven by wind. The currents move warm or cold water and affect physical regions because they redistribute heat. Warm currents transport the heat of the tropics to cooler areas to make the lands warmer. Cool currents move from high latitudes to low and make the land cooler. An example of an ocean current that provides warmer air to regions is the **Gulf Stream.** Hurricanes and their storm systems follow ocean currents and may propel currents of water. Because water has a greater heat capacity than air, the currents can chill or heat the air and be a source of precipitation by serving as a source of vapor that turns into clouds.

Mountain Barriers

Mountains can cause climate change because they can cut off rain to lands on the other side of the barrier. When an area receives less rain, the plant and animal life is altered. Also, the wind and precipitation patterns become changed when a barrier lessens rainfall. Mountain barriers can create winds and cause the winds to move up and over their slopes. Barriers can also increase wind speed in the high pass areas. When mountains act as barriers, one side of the mountain will usually be drier and have less rainfall and snow.

Tectonic Processes

The earth's outer shell is composed of a series of places that move. The plates' movement is called the **tectonic process,** and this process affects the amount of volcanic activity in an area and alters ocean currents. It also changes the distribution of continents. When plates crash during the tectonic process, new sea floors can be created and the distribution and elevation of continents can be affected.

COMPETENCY 14: GLOBAL AND REGIONAL PATTERNS OF CULTURE AND HUMAN GEOGRAPHY

THE TEACHER UNDERSTANDS GLOBAL AND REGIONAL PATTERNS OF CULTURE AND CHARACTERISTICS AND PROCESSES ASSOCIATED WITH DIFFERENT CULTURAL REGIONS.

SKILL 14.1   **Understand the concept of cultural region as an area of Earth's surface with unifying cultural characteristics (e.g., language, religion, economy, political system).**

Social scientists use the term **culture** to describe the way of life of a group of people. This would include not only art, music, and literature but also beliefs, customs, languages, traditions, and inventions—in short, any way of life, whether complex or simple.

Language

The purpose of language is to create and explain ideas and information. Most, if not all, countries have a national language. However, in some countries there is great linguistic diversity. Multiple languages and dialects of a national language account for some of the diversity. It is important for people to preserve their heritage and share their past, whether it is family history or folktales from their geographic area. People who live in a rural area of a country and speak a dialect of the national language are as interested in sharing ideas and preserving heritage as are city dwellers who speak the national language without accent or dialect because language is a way of preserving culture and passing it to future generations. As a result, it is an important characteristic of culture.

Religion

Belief systems, like other cultural elements or institutions, are spread through human interaction. It is thus natural that religions and belief systems may have regional or cultural markers that are transmitted across regions. Religions and belief systems generally originate in a particular region, with elements that are culturally or regionally defined or influenced. As belief systems are introduced to new groups or societies, some of those regional and cultural markers will also penetrate the new society.

By the same token, as interaction between the originating society and the new society continues and the belief system finds new expression, some regional or cultural elements introduced by the new society will be carried back to the originating culture.

Belief systems are introduced to new societies in a variety of ways. One method is military and political conquest. As the originating society conquers a new territory and incorporates it into the political entity, belief systems are frequently either peaceably spread to the conquered people or forced upon them in the name of cultural unity. This has occurred frequently in human history. The rise and spread of the Islamic empire both converted and forced the conversion of conquered peoples to Islam. Another example may be seen in the conversion of the Emperor Constantine to Christianity and his imposition of Christianity upon Rome as the national religion or the Spanish imposition of Catholicism on Native Americans.

Belief systems are also introduced through other types of human interaction. This occurs through commercial interaction, the identification of common or similar primitive mythologies (for example, similar stories of creation and Great Flood). Educational interaction and cultural sharing between cultures also frequently carry religious belief systems, as well.

Economy

Economy is an important characteristic of culture. Natural resources, labor supplies, and capital will affect the type of money-making activities that take place in a region or country and the income levels of its people. In an area that lacks these characteristics, the possibilities for manufacturing and large-scale production will be limited. Some economies are directed by individual entrepreneurship and others are planned economies where the government is involved in the economic objectives of the country. The United States economy is based on capitalism, ownership of private property, and a free-market economy with limited government involvement.

Political Culture

A political culture defines the relationship between a culture's government and its people. Democracies, socialist states, and communistic states are examples of different political systems. Some political cultures encourage participation and debate that can lead to positive change. Other political cultures focus on the goals and directions of the leaders and expect the citizens to obey without dissent.

Geography

The term geography is defined as the study of earth's features and living things as to their location, relationship with each other, how they came to be there, and why it is so important.

Cultural geography studies the location, characteristics, and influence of the physical environment on different cultures around the earth. Also included in these studies are comparisons and influences of the many varied cultures. Ease of travel and up-to-the-minute, state-of-the-art communication techniques ease the problems of understanding cultural differences and make it easier to come in contact with them.

Physical geography is concerned with the locations of such earth features as climate, water, and land; how these relate to and affect each other and human activities; and what forces shaped and changed them. All three of these earth features affect the lives of all humans having a direct influence on what is made and produced, where it occurs, how it occurs, and what makes it possible. The combination of the different climate conditions and types of landforms and other surface features work together all around the earth to give the many varied cultures their unique characteristics and distinctions.

Physical and political locations are precisely determined in two ways. First, surveying is done to determine boundary lines and distance from other features. Second, exact locations are precisely determined by imaginary lines of latitude (parallels) and longitude (meridians). The intersection of these lines at right angles forms a grid, making it possible to pinpoint an exact location of any place using any two grid coordinates.

SKILL 14.2 Analyze ways in which cultural processes of innovation and diffusion shape patterns in the human environment.

Innovation is the introduction of new ways of performing work or organizing societies, and can spur drastic changes in a culture. Prior to the innovation of agriculture, for instance, human cultures were largely nomadic and survived by hunting and gathering their food. Agriculture led directly to the development of permanent settlements and a radical change in social organization. Likewise, technological innovations in the Industrial Revolution of the nineteenth century changed the way work was performed and transformed the economic institutions of western cultures. Recent innovations in communications are changing the way cultures interact today.

Cultural diffusion is the movement of cultural ideas or materials between populations independent of the movement of those populations. Cultural diffusion can take place when two populations are close to one another, through direct interaction, or across great distances, through mass media and other routes. American movies are popular all over the world, for instance.

Adaptation is the process that individuals and societies go through in changing their behavior and organization to cope with social, economic, and environmental pressures.

Acculturation is an exchange or adoption of cultural features when two cultures come into regular direct contact. An example of acculturation is the adoption of Christianity and Western dress by many Native Americans in the United States.

Assimilation is the process of a minority ethnic group largely adopting the culture of the larger group it exists within. These groups are typically immigrants moving to a new country, as with the European immigrants who traveled to the United States at the beginning of the twentieth century and assimilated into the American culture.

Extinction is the complete disappearance of a culture. Extinction can occur suddenly, from disease, famine or war when the people of a culture are completely destroyed, or slowly over time as a culture adapt, acculturate or assimilate to the point where its original features are lost.

SKILL 14.3   **Demonstrate knowledge of locations and cultural and environmental features of major world regions (e.g., East Asia, sub-Saharan Africa, Latin America, Europe, Southwest Asia, North Africa) and regions of the United States and Texas.**

Locations

Physical locations of the earth's surface features include the four major hemispheres and the parts of the earth's continents in them. **Political locations** are the political divisions within each continent. Both physical and political locations are precisely determined in two ways: (1) Surveying is done to determine boundary lines and distance from other features. (2) Exact locations are precisely determined by imaginary lines of latitude (parallels) and longitude (meridians). The intersection of these lines at right angles forms a grid, making it possible to pinpoint an exact location of any place using two grid coordinates.

The Eastern Hemisphere, located between the North and South Poles and between the Prime Meridian (0 degrees longitude) east to 180 degrees longitude, consists of most of Europe, all of Australia, most of Africa, and all of Asia, except for a tiny piece of the easternmost part of Russia that extends east of 180 degrees longitude.

The Western Hemisphere, located between the North and South Poles and between the Prime Meridian (0 degrees longitude) west to 180 degrees longitude, consists of all of North and South America, a tiny part of the easternmost part of Russia that extends east of 180 degrees longitude, and a part of Europe that extends west of the Prime Meridian (0 degrees longitude).

The Northern Hemisphere, located between the North Pole and the Equator, contains all of the continents of Europe and North America and parts of South America, Africa, and most of Asia.

The Southern Hemisphere, located between the South Pole and the Equator, contains all of Australia, a small part of Asia, about one-third of Africa, most of South America, and all of Antarctica.

Of the seven continents, only one contains just one entire country and that is the only island continent, **Australia** (the term Oceania is sometimes used to encompass Australia and smaller islands of the tropical Pacific Ocean). Australia's political divisions consist of six states and one territory: Western Australia, South Australia, Tasmania, Victoria, New South Wales, Queensland, and Northern Territory.

Cultural and Environmental Features

Asia

Asia consists of forty-nine separate countries, including China, Japan, India, Turkey, Israel, Iraq, Iran, Indonesia, Jordan, Vietnam, Thailand, and the Philippines.

The countries of **East Asia** include China, Korea, Taiwan, and Japan, all of which have been influenced by Chinese history and culture. Despite the common background the area has many nationalities and ethnic groups within its borders. Religion has played a major role in the culture, and Buddhism, Hinduism, Confucianism, and Taoism are major religions in the area. The region has great ethnic diversity.

Geography in East Asia is varied and includes mountains, plateaus, steppes, desserts, and plants. Water is important to the environment and borders parts, if not all, of the East Asian countries.

Oil pollution is a problem in the East Asian Sea. The 2011 earthquake and tsunami that struck Japan caused great devastation.

Southwest Asia includes the countries that make up the Middle East. Iraq, Iran, Lebanon, Jordan, and Syria are part of Southwest Asia as are Yemen, Saudi Arabia, and the Gulf States. The Anatolia peninsula of Turkey is also part of Southwest Asia.

The area that was once known as the "Cradle of Civilization" is known for its mountains, highlands, and plateaus. The Iranian and Anatolian plateaus are examples.

The environment of the area is linked oil, much of it being in reserves along the Persian Gulf and under the sea. More than half of the world's oil reserves are located in this part of Asia.
An increase in population has become a problem for the countries of Southwest Asia. This is because of the numbers of unskilled workers who moved to the area to work in the petroleum industry.

Africa

Africa is made up of more than fifty separate countries. Some of them are Egypt, Nigeria, South Africa, Zaire, Kenya, Algeria, Morocco, and the large island of Madagascar.

The **North African** countries of Algeria, Tunisia, Morocco, and Libya are called the Maghreb. Egypt, the Nile Valley, and Sudan are also part of North Africa. North Africa exhibits great ethnic diversity. Mountains, deserts, and uplands represent the geography of the area. The Atlas Mountains of Morocco and the Sahara and Arabian deserts are examples.

The environment has been impacted by oil discoveries and the lack of adequate water. Water shortages are present in more than half of the countries, and the dams built to provide electricity in Egypt have impacted the amount of natural silt that the Nile River is now able to leave on the land. Oil and water shape the environment of these very arid lands. In areas with Mediterranean climates, such as the Atlas Mountains and the Levant, deforestation and overgrazing are environmental concerns.

Culturally, **sub-Saharan Africa** is diverse. The literacy rate is low, although more young people are receiving educations today than in the past. One legacy of European-drawn borders is the ethnic diversity that characterizes almost every African state. Nigeria contains as many as one hundred sixty different groups. Even countries such as Swaziland that are occupied almost entirely by a single ethnic group are usually subdivided along lines of kinship and social affiliation. Swahili is a major language but the picture is complicated by the fact that the various African societies speak as many as two thousand different languages and have an array of religious beliefs. It is extremely difficult to obtain reliable census data broken down along tribal affiliation or ethnic group membership. Estimates of the number of indigenous Africans range from twenty-five million to three hundred fifty million.

The environment of sub-Sahara Africa is varied. The Sahara and Kalahari deserts dominate much of the landscape. The Cape Mountains border South Africa along the country's southern shores, and the Congo River that traverses Central Africa, the Nile River whose source is sub-Saharan Africa, and the Zambezi River are the main rivers in this area of Africa. The rivers' waterfalls have been used to harness electricity but also pose problems for transportation of goods through the network of rivers. The area is the world's fastest growing region but tropical disease remains a problem, resulting in shorter life spans. Soils are infertile and desertlike areas are increasing due to human actions. There is a need for wildlife conservation because some animals are becoming endangered and may become extinct. Deforestation is also a problem.

Latin America

Latin America consists of countries that speak Romance languages and covers three regions of the Western Hemisphere—South America, Middle America, and Caribbean islands. Thirteen separate nations together occupy the continent of South America, among them such nations as Brazil, Paraguay, Ecuador, and Suriname. Middle America is made up of Mexico; Central American countries such as Panama, Guatemala, and Honduras; and islands in the West Indies such as Cuba, Trinidad, and Jamaica. Catholicism is the predominant religion but African traditions are present in the culture. Spanish is the most-spoken language but Portuguese is spoken in Brazil, and French is the primary language on the islands of Martinique and Guadeloupe.

In South America more than 80 percent of the population lives in urban areas, causing urban pollution from the use of private vehicles. Deforestation is another environmental concern, and the major rivers, such as the Amazon and Orinoco, present environmental concerns due to overfishing.

Europe

Europe has more than forty separate nations and a variety of cultures. Each country has its own language, and regional dialects exist within each country. Germany has its own language while the people living in the German-speaking canton of Switzerland speak a different form of German. People who live in Bavaria in southern Germany speak a dialect very different from those who live in the Lubeck, Hamburg, and other areas in northern Germany. Although the people in each country have their own cultures, some general divisions can be drawn to identify different cultures based upon similar languages and historical, religious, and ethnic heritage.

Countries in **Northern Europe** include the Scandinavian countries of Sweden, Norway, and Denmark, the Baltic States of Lithuania, Estonia, and Latvia, and Finland. Scandinavian countries share a common language heritage. Finland is a Nordic country but not a Scandinavian country because it does not share the same Indo-European language heritage, ethnic, or historical heritage.

Central and **Eastern European countries** share a common history after World War II because they were under the rule of communism. Poland, Hungary, Slovakia, and the Czech Republic are Central European countries whereas countries such as Bulgaria and Romania are geographically more eastern. However, they are designated as Eastern Europe because of communist rule after World War II that separated the West from the East. The Catholic church and Orthodox churches are predominant in Eastern Europe and most languages have a Slavic origin.

Southern European countries include, among others, Spain, Portugal, Italy, Greece, and the southeastern Balkan states of the former Yugoslavia including, Serbia, Montenegro, Kosovo, Macedonia, Croatia, Bosnia and Herzegovina, and Albania. The countries have warm Mediterranean climates, but their cultures are very different. Catholicism is the dominant religion of Italy, Portugal, and Spain whereas the Balkan areas are predominantly Orthodox or Islamic. The Balkan languages include Slavic, Greek, Albanian, Romance, and Turkic-based languages. The Romance languages provide the basis for most of the other Mediterranean languages.

Western Europe has a variety of languages and religions. Some of the countries include France, Germany, Belgium, Austria, England, Scotland, Ireland, and Wales. Because of the many cultural heritages and historical backgrounds, it is easy to understand why there is so much cultural diversity.

The environment of Europe is as varied as its cultures. Resources include rich agricultural lands, and industrial facilities. The warm winds and ocean currents provide a maritime climate and keep cold Arctic air from the land. Northern Europe's main crops are wheat and potatoes. Sheep and cattle provide food and dairy products. Southern Europe, with its Mediterranean climate has hot summers and rainy, cold winters. Grapes and olives are grown in abundance. Forestry is an important industry for Europe because it employs more than three million people. The industry includes the manufacture of paper products and furniture as well as products used in the construction industry. Cork is a forestry product in southern Europe and supplies more than three-fourths of the world's needs. Fisheries play an important role in the economy of Europe. Most fishing takes place in the eastern Atlantic Ocean and the Mediterranean Sea. Overfishing has caused concerns that some fish, such as the Bluefin tuna, will become extinct.

Chromium mines are present in Turkey and silver mines are present in Poland. Chromium is mined to use in stainless steel. Titanium is mined in Norway and is used in aircraft, naval vessels, and the space industry. Norway has large oil deposits and is a primary exporter of natural gas. Offshore oil deposits in the North Sea can be beneficial to Europe's future energy sources.

Europe's business environment is becoming an important part of the global economy. Frankfurt, Germany, is a center for commerce and finance. It also is a transportation hub for international and European travel and hosts international trade shows. The judicial environment is present in The Hague in the Netherlands. The International Court of Justice and International Criminal Court are located in The Hague. Northern Europe's Estonia is home to many software developers and is becoming a technology-based environment nation.

Russia

Culturally, Russia is thought of as European although approximately three-fourths of its land is in Asia. The Russian language consists of the Cyrillic alphabet and has Slavic roots. After the country freed itself from communist rule, the Orthodox, Buddhist, Jewish, and Islamic religions were approved by the government. The cultural backgrounds of the Russian people are very different, depending upon the region of the country in which they live. Nomads began living in the steppes and domesticated horses. The Slavic Cossacks inhabited southern Russia along the Volga River and inhabited areas that because towns such as Kazan, Samara, and Volgograd (formerly Stalingrad).

Russia has approximately 20 percent of the world's forests and some significant wilderness areas in Siberia and the Russian Far East. Lake Baikal is one of the world's deepest lakes and contains approximately 20 percent of the world's freshwater. Many environmental concerns have arisen as a result of the upheavals in the past twenty years. In the 1990s, the country suffered an economic crisis that affected the environment when previously unused resources were tapped to extract large amounts of gas, oil, and mineral resources. Environmental problems of deforestation, pollution, and nuclear waste exist today because of government policy during the Soviet era that focused on industrialization.

United States

U.S. culture is varied because of the many ethnic groups that have settled the country. During the colonial era, most immigrants came for northern and western Europe. During the Industrial Revolution, the people who came to work in factors were mainly from southeastern Europe. Asians, Latin Americans, and Africans have also added to the cultural heritage of the country.
The United States has abundant natural resources. Even with a population that now tops three hundred million, the possibility for coaxing more natural resources from the land and the waters is good. It is not inexhaustible, however.

Some U.S. regions are known for certain things. Oil can be found in great abundance in Texas, Oklahoma, Alaska, and a handful of other states. Most of them make oil drilling and production a big business. Output reaches staggering numbers in some cases. The oil is used to power machinery and transportation devices the world over. The ideal is to achieve a balance between wringing as much oil out of the land as possible while preserving the land underneath the oil. This balance is not always, and sometimes never, achieved. Sometimes it is not even attempted.

Another natural resource in abundance is natural gas. This resource is found in Texas, Oklahoma, Wyoming, Utah, Colorado, Louisiana, Arkansas, Michigan, North Carolina, Pennsylvania, and New York. Natural gas is transported through pipes into homes and other buildings to provide energy. Like oil, natural gas comes from deep within the ground. Some deposits are easier to get than others, and some methods of extraction are simpler and more cost-effective. Natural gas is more "natural" in nature than oil and can be used in place of oil. For example, natural gas powers buses, trains, some cars, and other transportation devices.

Coal is another natural fuel resource found in great amounts in the United States. Coal can be found in thirty-eight of the fifty states. Among the top coal-producing states are Montana, Illinois, Wyoming, West Virginia, Kentucky, Pennsylvania, Ohio, Colorado, Texas, and Indiana. Twenty-four percent of the world's recoverable reserves of coal can be found within the borders of the United States. Coal can be mined on the surface or underground. Both methods have their associated costs and risks, including harmful effects on the land and air around coalmines.

A host of other minerals can be found and mined in the United States. Among them are chromium, copper, gypsum, iron oxide, phosphate, salt, selenium, silica, silicon, silver, sulfur, tin, tungsten, and zinc. These minerals are found to varying degrees in certain regions. The way they are extracted from the earth varies by type of mineral. Some are easier to extract than others. The mining of some leaves horrible scars, from which the land does not easily recover.

Texas

The varied geography of Texas has produced some vastly different settlement patterns, economic developments, and political conflicts over the hundreds of years that people have been migrating to the area. The vast plains of central and western Texas are perfect for agricultural and ranch land. Wheat, cotton, sorghum, and cattle are the top-producing industries. Ranches consist of two thousand or more acres, and mid-sized farms are between five hundred and two thousand acres. The recent trend has been to convert native rangelands and croplands to "improved pastures." The result is a significant loss of wildlife habitat. The division of large properties is called "fragmenting," and this often results in having insufficient quantities of land for farming.

There has been a conflict in Texas regarding **confined animal feeding operations (CAFO)**. Almost 80 percent of Texas farms are small farms under 500 acres that occupy 15 percent of the land. About 42 percent of farms have fewer than 100 acres, and they are largely in the eastern part of the state. The farms with between 100 and 5 hundred acres tend to be near the Piney Woods where there are 4 national forests; the Texas part is home to 17 state parks. Crops grown in East Texas include rice, watermelon and other fruits, vegetables, peanuts, alfalfa, and cotton.

The Gulf Coast is known for its oil and its ports. Nearly all of the state's varied products flow out through the state's Gulf Coast ports. Texas is known for its oil production and its oil exports.

The larger cities of Texas—Houston, Austin, Dallas, and Fort Worth, most noticeably—are known for their dedication to technology. Many Internet and computer companies make their homes in Texas, and the state is a leader in space and scientific development efforts.

Politics throughout the history of the state have been contentious. Early on, it was the Americans versus the Mexicans, as American settlers arrived. After Mexico gave up all claims to Texas, a reverse immigration took place. The question of legal vs. illegal immigrants continues to be a huge policy debate today. This is the case in other states, as well, but more so in Texas because it shares such a long border with Mexico.

Another source of contention is the struggle between the ranch politics of yesteryear and the high-tech politics of today. Farmers and ranchers have different interests than atomic scientists, and these different interests often clash in the halls of Austin policymakers.

In a sense, geography is driving all of this, since farmers and ranchers have their concerns largely because of their location and urban parties gain their perspectives from their environments, which are much more metropolitan. Oil companies and their lobbyists must be heard from as well. Oil continues to be a staggeringly large business in Texas, and oil interests often clash with those of other industries.

SKILL 14.4   **Understand how the components of culture (e.g., land use, systems of education, religion, language) affect the way people live and shape the characteristics of regions.**

Land Use

Far and away the largest factor influencing land use is **population**. A burgeoning population demands a lot from the land for food, living, and industrial use. The more people who want to live in a certain area, the more the land in that area will have to be transformed to meet that population need. In some cases, the land is simply appropriated. Naturally aerated land is perfect for farms and ranches, with an abundance of water and natural food for the crops and animals; in other cases, however, the land is transformed—agricultural land becoming industrial land, for example, or farmland being developed in favor of living space. In all cases, the land is being used to support the population, which is growing and expanding its needs and demands.

Geography is another influence on land use, sometimes as a limiter and sometimes as an invitation. Inhospitable lands are usually not highly populated because of the inherently harsh living conditions. Geography does not always have to be a limiter, however. Fertile land that is excellent for farming will, in most cases, be put to good agricultural use. The presence of a large body of water will routinely result in the human use of that water in some way, as a source of drinking water for people and animals or as a source of nourishment for crops. Rare indeed is the body of water that has not been appropriated in some form or fashion by humans.

Geography can also form natural boundaries for settlements and civilizations. Mountain ranges and large bodies of water make effective borders between states and countries. If a civilization that has a mountain range or a river or ocean as a boundary wants to grow, it might be forced to grow upward rather than outward, at least in those locations bordered by these landforms or bodies of water. Prime examples of this are New York City and San Francisco and Tokyo, all of which have limited land on which to build but which use that land to the fullest by building tall skyscrapers that house many people and businesses.

Disease and devastation can often influence land use as well. In general, areas of the world that have seen deadly outbreaks of viruses or deadly wars experience a population decrease that, in turn, creates a drop in land use. Especially if the disease is waterborne, the land cannot be used for some time after the devastation ends since cleanup can sometimes take a generation to be totally effective. The same is true of war zones, especially those contaminated by bombs and land mines.

Necessity is the most basic influence over land use. Growing populations need more land, geographically challenged civilizations need to get creative in using their land, and damaged land needs time to heal.

Systems of Education

Congress passed the **Land Ordinance of 1785** to establish the process for obtaining land in the Northwest Territory. One of the concerns relating to settlement of the area was that the inhabitants of the new territory would have access to education. The territory was divided into townships and the townships were divided into one-mile square sections. Each section was numbered, and one section in each township was set aside for publically funded schools. Today, many schools are still located in those designated sections.

The allotment of funds for land grant colleges also affected the system of education in the United States. Funding for colleges that would teach agriculture was allotted by the federal government in the mid-1800s. Michigan State University and Purdue University (in Indiana) are two such schools.

The Midwest is recognized for its good farmland. Many of the people who settled the area in the late 1700s and early 1800s remained in one of the states that was carved out of the original Northwest Territory, and many became farmers. These states include Indiana, Illinois, Ohio, Michigan, and part of Wisconsin. The provisions for establishing educational systems created by the Land Ordinance of 1785 and the **Morrill Act,** which funded land-grant colleges, were important for the area that has become one of the most significant agricultural regions of the United States.

Religion

Religion, as an element of culture, can shape the characteristics of a region. The **Quakers,** who are known as peace-loving people, settled the areas of southern Michigan and became farmers. Many were involved in helping slaves find their way to freedom before the Civil War and played important roles in the Underground Railroad. Where the lines of the transport system ended, many of the former slaves stayed and lived in the agricultural areas settled by the Quakers.

The **Studebaker brothers** developed the automobile industry in northern Indiana. They hired Eastern European laborers to work in their factory. Many of the people employed were Catholics who took with them their religion and architectural ideas for building new churches. As a result, many churches today in the northern Indiana area and South Bend, where the Studebaker brothers had their factory, have the appearance of classically designed European churches and cathedrals.

Language

Language shapes the characteristics of a region. As immigrants came to America and settled large cities, those with the same cultural heritage and language settled in neighborhoods where they could communicate with each other and carry on traditions that were important to them. The Irish, Polish, Puerto Ricans, Chinese, Greeks, and Italians, among others, established neighborhoods where they could live with people who had similar backgrounds and language skills and could share the challenges of a new country.

Language groups also dot the countryside in more rural areas. The German-speaking people who settled the Utopian Amana colonies in Iowa are an example. Although English is spoken in the colonies today, the German influence continues.

SKILL 14.5   **Demonstrate knowledge of the growth, distribution, movement, and characteristics of world populations (e.g., trends in past world population growth, push and pull factors affecting major national and international migrations, ways in which physical and cultural factors affect migration, how migration and immigration have affected societies), and understand the benefits and challenges of globalization.**

World Population Characteristics

A population is a group of people living within a certain geographic area. Populations are usually measured on a regular basis by census, which also measures age, economic, ethnic and other data. Populations change over time due to many factors, and these changes can have significant impact on cultures.

When a population grows, it must either expand its geographic boundaries to make room for new people or to increase its density. **Population density** is the number of people in a population divided by the geographic area in which they live. Cultures with a high population density are likely to have different ways of interacting with one another than those with low density.

As a population grows, its economic needs change. More basic needs are required, and more workers are needed to produce them. If a population's production or purchasing power does not keep pace with its growth, its economy can be adversely affected. The **age distribution** of a population can impact the economy, as well, if the number of young and old people who are not working is disproportionate to those who are employed.

Growth in some areas may spur migration to other parts of a population's geographic region that are less densely populated. This **redistribution of population** also places demands on the economy, as infrastructure is needed to connect these new areas to older population centers, and land is put to new use.

Populations can grow naturally when the rate of birth is higher than the rate of death or when new people are added from other populations through immigration. **Immigration** is often a source of societal change as people from other cultures bring their institutions and language to a new area. Immigration also impacts a population's educational and economic institutions as immigrants enter the workforce and place their children in schools.

Populations can also decline in number, when the death rate exceeds the birth rate or when people migrate to another area. War, famine, disease, and natural disasters can also dramatically reduce a population. The economic problems from population decline can be similar to those from over population because economic demands may be higher than can be met. In extreme cases, a population may decline to the point where it can no longer perpetuate itself and its members and their culture either disappear or are absorbed into another population.

Migrations of population occur for several reasons. Those who were seeking religious freedom came to America to found colonies in present-day New England. The potato famine in Europe during the mid-1800s resulted in a migration of Germans and Irish to the shores of America. People migrate to avoid hunger, starvation, and oppression. Inhabitants of African countries that are war-torn have left those areas to seek a life that is free from starvation and conflict.

Benefits and Challenges of Globalization

Today's society is a global society in many aspects, and with it comes challenges and benefits. Freedom of movement is more prevalent today than it was a decade ago. However, the economic challenges for people living in developing nations continues to be present. Disease, lack of sanitation, overuse of natural resources, and low levels of income plague many areas of the world. At the same time, tourism, business opportunities, and betters standards of living can result from globalization.

SKILL 14.6 **Analyze ways in which political, economic, and social processes shape cultural patterns and characteristics in various places and regions (e.g., analyzing political, economic, social, and demographic indicators to determine the level of development and standard of living in countries).**

Cultural Patterns of Race, Ethnicity, and Religion

Variations in race, ethnicity and religion—both real and perceived—are primary ways in which cultures and cultural groups are defined. They are useful in understanding cultures, but can also be the source of cultural biases and prejudices. Tension between groups can arise for various reasons, leading to longstanding conflict between some groups.

Groups that have minority status within a larger group are often disadvantaged in their societies owing to the dominant group favoring its own members in social and political policies and in daily interactions. These kinds of majority/minority relationships can be based on race, ethnic grouping, and religion.

Ethnic and religious tension can also arise from traditional historical relationships between groups. Ethnicity and religion are two frameworks by which social views can be passed from generation to generation, perpetuating tension and conflict between groups. Religion can also play an important role in relationships between groups. Some religious beliefs directly conflict with others, giving rise to disagreement.

Standard of Living

Standard of living refers to the comfort and wealth of a person or group. Necessities of life, income, and material goods are considered in determining various standards. **Political** indicators for standard of living include the stability of a government. Wars, internal conflicts, extreme or excess government involvement in life of citizens, and violent reactions of political dissent can cause a lack of political stability. Where countries or regions experience negative political indicators, one can expect that the standard of living will not be as high as in countries with political stability.

The poverty level of a region and the affluence of residents are **social** indicators of standards of living. Types of available housing and costs of housing in an area provide a glimpse of whether a region has a high standard of living. The availability of material goods also is a social indicator of standard of living. In some countries the idea of vehicle ownership is not even considered whereas in other parts of the world families own multiple vehicles.

Economic indicators include income levels, the cost of goods and services, and environmental quality. The availability of employment is important, as is the inflation rate. Basic necessities such as food, clothing, and shelter are resources that are considered in determining the economic standard of living of an area. **Demographic** indicators include, among other things, the population within an area, the services and goods available with that specific area, educational facilities, recreational opportunities, and comparison costs of living.

SKILL 14.7 **Apply knowledge of the history and significance of major religious and philosophical traditions (e.g., Buddhism, Christianity, Confucianism, Hinduism, Islam, Judaism, Realism, Idealism).**

Religion can be closely tied to ethnicity, as it is frequently one of the common social institutions shared by an ethnic group. Like ethnicity, religion varies in practices and beliefs even within the large major religions.

Major Religious Traditions

Eight common religions are practiced today. Each of these has divisions or smaller sects within them. Not one of them is totally completely unified. Judaism, Christianity, and Islam are "Abrahamic" religions. About 3.8 billion people claim to be part of an Abrahamic religion.

Judaism is the oldest of the eight religions and was the first to teach and practice the belief in one God, Yahweh. The Torah comprises the first five books of the Hebrew Bible.

Christianity came from Judaism, grew, and spread in the first century throughout the Roman Empire despite the persecution of early Christians. A later schism resulted in Western (Roman Catholic) Christianity and Eastern (Orthodox) Christianity. Protestant sects developed as part of the Protestant Revolution. The name "Christian" means one who is a follower of Jesus Christ. Christians are expected to follow Jesus' teachings written in the New Testament and to live by the laws and principles of the Hebrew Bible, which Christians call the Old Testament.

Islam was founded in Arabia by Muhammad, who preached about God, Allah. Islam spread through trade, travel, and conquest and followers of it fought in the Crusades. In addition, they fought other wars against Christians and, later, against the Jewish nation of Israel. Followers of Islam, called Muslims, live by the teachings of their holy book called the Koran and their prophets who begin with Adam and conclude with Muhammad.

Hinduism was begun by people called Aryans around 1500 BCE and spread into India. The Aryans blended their culture with the culture of the Dravidians, the natives they conquered. Today Hinduism has many sects, promotes polytheistic worship, and espouses a belief in reincarnation. A prominent feature of Hinduism in the past was a rigid adherence to and practice of the caste system, which is forbidden today by law.

Buddhism began in India, was developed from the teachings of Prince Gautama, and spread to most of Asia. Its beliefs opposed the worship of deities, the Hindu caste system, and the supernatural. Buddhists believe that worshipers must be free of attachment to all things worldly and devote themselves to finding release from life's suffering.

Confucianism is a Chinese philosophy based on the teachings of the Chinese philosopher Confucius. There is no clergy and no belief in a deity or in life after death. It emphasizes political and moral ideas with respect for authority and ancestors. Rulers were expected to govern according to high moral standards.

Daoism is a native Chinese belief system with veneration for many deities and natural phenomena. It teaches all followers to make the effort to achieve the two goals of happiness and immortality. Practices and rituals include meditation, prayer, magic, reciting scriptures, special diets, breath control, beliefs in geomancy, fortune telling, astrology, and communicating with the spirits of the dead.

Shinto is the native religion of Japan and developed from native folk beliefs about worshiping spirits and demons in animals, trees, and mountains. According to its mythology, deities created

Japan and its people, which resulted in worshiping the emperor as a god. Shinto has no strong doctrines on salvation or life after death. A person may belong to any other religion at the same time.

Philosophical Traditions

Idealism is a philosophy grounded in the idea that reality is fundamentally mental and immaterial. Its focus is on the belief that human ideas shape society. The foundations for this philosophical concept were developed in India and Greece during the fourth century CE and were revived in Europe during the eighteenth century.

Realism is a philosophy that is contrasted with idealism. This philosophy is based on the concept of reality and not on ideas. Realism focuses on what happened in the past and what will happen in the future. Realists believe that present beliefs will bring people closer to the understanding of reality.

SKILL 14.8   Understand the importance of place for populations (e.g., Mecca, Jerusalem, Cuzco, Ganges River, Shrine of Guadalupe).

Places are distinguished from one another by the physical and human characteristics that make them unique. As a human population inhabits and interacts with its environment, a place may become symbolic of that population and become closely associated with it. Other social factors such as political and religious traditions can enhance the importance of a place in the esteem of a population.

Mecca, a city in Saudi Arabia, is an example of a place that is important to the worldwide Muslim population as a holy center. Tradition holds that Abraham, a figure in Judaism and Christianity as well as Islam, built a shrine in Mecca, which is now at the center of a large mosque. The founder of Islam, Muhammad, declared the shrine and Mecca to be holy places that all devout Muslims should visit. Millions of people travel to the mosque in Mecca every year as part of a large pilgrimage called the Haj.

Jerusalem holds a similar importance in the religious traditions of Judaism, Christianity, and Islam. According to these faiths, King Solomon built a temple in Jerusalem in the tenth century BCE that was the resting place of God. Two other temples followed on the same site until Romans destroyed the third temple in 70 CE. The ruins of one wall of this temple are still visited today by Jews, who stand at it and pray. The site of the temple is currently the site of one of Islam's holiest sites, the Dome of the Rock, which is believed to be the place where Mohammad ascended to Heaven. In the Christian faith, Jerusalem is significant as the place where Jesus was crucified.

In the Hindu tradition, the **Ganges River** in India is considered a goddess and its waters are believed to have purifying powers. Bathing in the Ganges is thought to remove impurity and sin, and followers frequently put the ashes of cremated bodies of family members in the river in the belief that this action will liberate their souls. Many Hindu festivals are held along the banks of the Ganges, and several temples are constructed nearby.

The **Shrine of Guadalupe**, in Mexico, commemorates the vision of the Virgin Mary that Catholics believe was experienced by a native peasant in the sixteenth century. Juan Diego Cuauhtlatoatzin was a native convert to Catholicism who claimed he had seen the vision on a hillside where Mary told him to build an abbey. He reported the vision to the church, and a shrine was built at the site. The story was used by the Spanish church to convert further Mexican natives and has become a central part of the Mexican national heritage and the shrine an important symbol of the church's importance in that heritage.

Cuzco, a city in modern Peru, was once the capital of the Inca civilization. The city was planned in four quarters, each corresponding to the four regions of the empire and had a road leading out to that region. In this fashion, the population of Cuzco emphasized the central importance the city had to the empire and created a microcosm of the Inca territory.

SKILL 14.9   Demonstrate knowledge of the impact of religion on the way of life in the United States.

The Pilgrims were among the first English settlers who build a colony in North America. These revolutionaries were **fleeing religious persecution** not only in their homeland but also in their adopted homeland. They wanted to worship their God in the way they wanted, and the state-run religion back home would not let them do that. The Pilgrims found complete freedom of religion in their new homeland and made the most of their opportunity. They also brought with them Christianity's "Golden Rule," a statement that tells one to treat others as you would wish to be treated. This concept also exists in all the major religions.

As more and more people settled on the eastern coast of what is now America, religious diversity grew. The picture was by no means always this rosy. **Puritans**, the largest group of Protestants to immigrate to America, practiced a rather stern policy of seeking out and targeting people who did not share their strict religious views and expelling them from the communities where the Puritans held sway. The most famous examples of such discrimination are probably **Anne Hutchison** and **Roger Williams,** both dynamic preachers who were forced to leave Massachusetts for having views different than the Puritan majority there even though they were both Puritans themselves. Williams founded the neighboring colony of Rhode Island, and Hutchinson followed him there before settling in New York.

Another religion to suffer at the hands of Puritans in America was the **Society of Friends**, or the Quakers. A religion also founded in England, the Quakers had sometimes vastly different views than the Puritans did, and this led to trouble in America. The most extreme case of Puritan persecution came in 1660, when the Massachusetts Puritans hanged Quaker leader Mary Dyer for refusing to convert to Puritanism. The Pennsylvania colony was later founded as a refuge for Quakers.

Maryland was founded in large part as a colony for **Catholics**, supporters of Mary Stuart, the embattled queen for whom the colony was named. The language of the colony's charter contained absolutely no reference to religion, a significant departure from the charter language of, for instance, Massachusetts.

The Church of England, or **Anglicanism**, was the church founded by King Henry VIII and preferred by his daughter Queen Elizabeth I. Anglicans found a haven in Virginia, which was more an economic powerhouse than anything else. The Virginia Anglicans, however, wanted all Virginians to be Anglicans and went out of their way to convince new settlers to embrace the old religion.

The Second Great Awakening was an **evangelical Protestant revival** that preached personal responsibility for one's actions both individually and socially. This movement was led by preachers such as **Charles Finney,** who traveled the country preaching the gospel of social responsibility. This point of view was taken up by the **mainline Protestant denominations** (Episcopal, Methodist, Presbyterian, Lutheran, and Congregational). Part of the social reform movement that led to an end to child labor, to better working conditions, and to other changes in social attitudes arose from this new recognition that the Christian faith should be expressed for the good of society.

Closely allied to the Second Great Awakening was the **temperance movement**. The temperance movement's desire to end the sale and consumption of alcohol arose from religious beliefs, the violence many women and children experienced from heavy drinkers, and from the effect alcohol consumption had on the work force.

Deists believed in the general idea of a supreme being but did not think this being took such an active part in human lives. Famous Deists included some of the country's most well-known names, including George Washington, James Madison, and Thomas Jefferson. Jefferson, framer of the Declaration of Independence; Madison, framer of the Bill of Rights; and Washington, a leader that everyone in America followed—did not profess a great love of religion and did not emphasize it in their writings or in their actions.

The government documents of the newly formed United States sanctioned no religion whatever. Rather, the First Amendment to the Constitution states that Congress will not sanction *any* religion. This was certainly a departure from the charters of states such as Massachusetts in the seventeenth and eighteenth centuries that demanded their citizens believe and behave in certain ways.

SKILL 14.10 Recognize relationships of the arts to the times in which they were created in the United States and world areas.

Until the Renaissance, the church was the only place where people could be educated. The Bible and other books were hand-copied by monks in the monasteries. Cathedrals were built and were decorated with art depicting religious subjects.

Coming into importance at this time was the era of knighthood and its code of chivalry as well as the tremendous influence of the Roman Catholic Church. With the increase in trade and travel, cities sprang up and began to grow. Craft workers in the cities developed their skills to a high degree, eventually organizing guilds to protect the quality of the work and to regulate the buying and selling of their products.

The **Renaissance** ushered in a time of curiosity, learning, and incredible energy that sparked the desire for trade to procure new, exotic products and to find better, faster, cheaper trade routes to get to them.

Renaissance artists pioneered a new method of painting and sculpture—that of portraying real events and real people as they really looked, not as the artists imagined them to be. One does not have to look further than Michelangelo's *David* to see this. For more information on the art, literature, music, and other contributions of the Renaissance, see Skill 3.3

The **classical symphony** grew out of the eighteenth century Italian overture, which usually had three separate movements and was played as a prelude to an operatic or vocal concert. Early symphonies were short and were included in musical programs with other works, mainly vocal. In the early years of the nineteenth century, **Ludwig van Beethoven** began to experiment with the form of the symphony, expanding it into an extended orchestral work that is usually the main piece in a program.

The novel, in its modern sense, emerged during this time period. Lengthy pieces of fiction had appeared before 1700, but they were extensions of romantic tales or were written in verse. *Pamela, or Virtue Rewarded* by Samuel Richardson was published in 1740, and was a full-length, realistic prose story in a contemporary setting. It is widely considered the first novel. The form grew popular, and by the 1840s was the prominent form of important fiction.

In art, the primary expression of the first part of the twentieth century was **modernism**. The avant-garde perspective encouraged all types of innovation and experimentation. Key elements of this movement have been abstraction, cubism, surrealism, realism, and abstract expressionism. Notable among the artists of this period for the birth or perfection of particular styles are Henri Matisse, Pablo Picasso, George Rouault, Gustav Klimt, George Braque, Salvador Dali, Hans Arp, Rene Magrite, and Marcel Duchamp.

In the United States, **realism** tended to find regional expressions including the Ashcan school and Robert Henri and Midwestern Regionalism and Grant Wood. Other particularly notable painters are Edward Hopper and Georgia O'Keeffe. The New York School came to be known for a style called **abstract expressionism** and included such artists as Jackson Pollock, Willem de Kooning, and Larry Rivers. Other painters of the period were Mark Rothko, Clement Greenberg, Ellsworth Kelly, and the artists of the Op Art Movement.

In **sculpture**, many of the same patterns and trends were applied. Innovations included the exploration of empty space (Henry Moore), the effort to incorporate cubism in three dimensions (Marcel Duchamp), and the use of welded metal to create kinetic sculpture (Alexander Calder).

Postmodernism has been defined as the expansion of forms and the valuing of innovation since 1950. This type of art has included Minimalism, Figurative Styles, Pop Art, Conceptual Art and Installation Art. **Photography** also developed as an art form during the twentieth century.

By the beginning of the twentieth century, **literature** was reflecting the struggle of the modern individual to find a place and a meaning in a new world that seemed like a jungle. Literature has reflected the observation that not only does the modern human not know how to find meaning but that he or she does not actually know what he or she is seeking. It is this crisis of identity that has been the subject of much modern literature. This can be seen in the writings of Joseph Conrad, Sigmund Freud, James Joyce, Eugene O'Neill, Luigi Pirandello, Samuel Beckett, George Bernard Shaw, T. S. Eliot, Franz Kafka, Albert Camus, Boris Pasternak, Graham Greene, Tennessee Williams, and a host of others.

Musical theater was an evolution from the operettas of the Romantic Period, the traditions of the European music hall, and American vaudeville. Most notable in this form are Leonard Bernstein and Steven Sondheim. **Film music** also developed during this century. The soundtracks for films were either adaptations of classical music or new compositions from composers such as Elmer Bernstein, Bernard Herrman, Max Steiner, and Dmitri Tiomkin.

American **popular music** evolved from folk music and emerged the first half of the century. It was characterized by a consistent structure of two verses, a chorus, and a repetition of the chorus. The songs were written to be sung by average persons, and the tunes were usually harmonized. Much of this music originated in New York's Tin Pan Alley. Particularly notable during this period were Irving Berlin, George and Ira Gershwin, and a host of others. After World War II, teen music began to dominate. New forms emerged from various ethnic and regional groups including the blues, rhythm and blues, and rap from the African American community. Country music from the south, including Texas, and folk music, jazz, rock 'n' roll, and a variety of rock music from cultures across the country also became popular.

COMPETENCY 15: INTERACTIONS BETWEEN HUMAN GROUPS AND THE PHYSICAL ENVIRONMENT

THE TEACHER UNDERSTANDS THE NATURE AND SIGNIFICANCE OF INTERACTIONS AMONG PEOPLES, PLACES, AND ENVIRONMENTS.

SKILL 15.1   **Analyze ways in which humans depend on, adapt to, and modify the physical environment in a variety of cultural and technological contexts.**

Food, clothing, and shelter are the three basic needs of human beings. As early humans increased in number and moved into new parts of the world, they had to adapt to their new environments by adopting new ways to obtain these needs.

Early humans hunted animals and gathered **food** from wild sources. Taking their basic support from nature required them to move with their food sources. Game animals might migrate, and seasonal food sources might require groups to travel to the regions where the food could be had. To take full advantage of varying areas where food could be found, portable methods of shelter such as the Native American tepee or the Mongolian yurt were developed. These shelters could be carried from place to place, allowing a greater range of mobility.

Clothing enabled humans to adapt to the wider range of climates they discovered as they moved from place to place, both in their annual circuit and as they moved into new wilderness areas with lower average temperatures. Clothing protects the body from cold, sun exposure, and the elements. In very hot climates, early humans wore little or no clothing. The advantages of having an extra layer of protection were soon realized, however, and basic coverings were fashioned from animal skin. Foot coverings were developed to protect the feet from rough ground and sharp rocks. In colder climates, clothing was crucial for survival. Animal pelts with the fur attached provided warmth. Foot coverings could also be fur-lined or stuffed with grass. Mittens or gloves kept vulnerable fingers warm and protected.

As humans moved away from hunting and gathering into agricultural pursuits, other materials for clothing became available. Wool-bearing animals were domesticated and plant fibers were woven into cloth. During the Industrial Revolution, cloth-weaving methods took a great stride forward, greatly expanding the use of woven cloth clothing.

Agriculture also expanded the types of food that were available. Grains and fruits could be grown in place, and meat could be obtained from domesticated animals. Not all climates are suitable for all crops, however, and humans have had to adapt varieties and methods to successfully produce food. Just as their environment shaped their needs, so did the environment provide the means to meet those needs. For thousands of years, food and **shelter** had to be obtained from local resources or from resources that could be grown locally. Human technology has reached a point now, however, that we are able to supply food to any location on the planet and adapt clothing and shelter to any environment, even outer space.

SKILL 15.2   **Understand and analyze how people, places, and environments change over time and are connected and interdependent (e.g., impact of different types of natural disasters).**

Changing Environments

Human communities subsisted initially as gatherers—collecting berries, leaves, and roots, exploiting many resources lightly rather than depending heavily on just a few. With the invention of tools it became possible to dig for roots, hunt small animals, and catch fish from rivers and oceans. Humans observed their environments and soon learned to plant seeds and harvest crops. As people migrated to areas in which game and fertile soil were abundant, communities began to develop.

Division of Labor

When people acquired the knowledge to grow crops and the skills to hunt game, they began to understand **division of labor**. Some members of the community tended to agricultural needs while others hunted game.

Settlements began in areas that offered natural resources to support life—food and water. With the ability to manage the environment, populations begin to concentrate. The ability to transport raw materials and finished products brings mobility. With increasing technology and the rise of industrial centers comes a migration of the workforce.

As habitats attracted larger numbers of people, environments became crowded, and there was competition. The concept of division of labor and sharing of food soon came in more heavily populated areas. Experience led to the development of skills and of knowledge that make the work easier. Farmers began to develop new plant species, and hunters began to protect animal species from other predators for their own use. This ability to manage the environment led people to settle down, guard their resources, and manage those resources.

Camps soon became villages. Villages became year-round settlements. Animals were domesticated and gathered into herds that met the needs of the village. With the settled life, it was no longer necessary to "travel light." Pottery was developed for storing and cooking food.

By 8000 BCE, culture was beginning to evolve in these villages. Agriculture was developed for the production of grain crops, which led to a decreased reliance on wild plants. Domesticating animals for various purposes decreased the need to hunt wild game. Life became more settled. It was then possible to turn attention to such matters as managing water supplies, producing tools, and making cloth. There was both social interaction and the opportunity to reflect upon existence. Mythologies arose as did various belief systems. Rituals arose that reenacted the mythologies that sought to explain the meaning of life.

As **farming and animal husbandry** skills increased, the dependence upon wild game and food gathering declined. With this change came the realization that a larger number of people could be supported on the produce of farming and animal husbandry.

Two things seem to have come together to produce cultures and civilizations—a society and culture based on agriculture and the development of centers of the community with literate social and religious structures. The members of these hierarchies then managed the water supply, irrigation, rituals, and religious life. They also exerted their own right to use a portion of the goods produced by the community for their own subsistence in return for their management.

Further division of labor and community development resulted from:

- Sharpened skills
- Development of more sophisticated tools
- Commerce with other communities and increasing knowledge of their environment
- Resources available to them
- Responses to the needs to share goods, order community life, and protect possessions from outsiders

As trade routes developed and travel between cities became easier, trade led to specialization. Trade enables people to obtain the goods they desire in exchange for the goods they are able to produce. This, in turn, leads to increased attention to refinements of technique and the sharing of ideas. The knowledge of a new discovery or invention provides knowledge and technology that increases the ability to produce goods for trade. As each community learns the value of the goods it produces and improves its ability to produce the goods in greater quantity, industry is born.

Urban Growth

Cities are the major hubs of human settlement. Almost half the population of the world now lives in cities. These percentages are much higher in developed regions. Established cities continue to grow. The fastest growth, however, is occurring in developing areas. In some regions there are **metropolitan areas** made up of urban and suburban areas. Some cities and urban areas have become interconnected into a **megalopolis.** The Tokyo-Kawasaki-Yokohama area is an example.

The concentrations of populations and the divisions of these areas among various groups that constitute the cities can differ significantly. North American cities are different from European cities in terms of shape, size, population density, and modes of transportation. While in North America, the wealthiest economic groups tend to live outside the cities, the opposite is true in Latin American cities.

Rural areas tend to be less densely populated due to the needs of agriculture. More land is needed to produce crops or for animal husbandry than is required for manufacturing. Rural areas, however, must be connected via communication and transportation in order to provide food and raw materials to urban areas. Social policy addresses basic human needs for the sustainability of the individual and the society. The concerns of social policy, then, include food, clean water, shelter, clothing, education, health, and social security.

We can examine the spatial organization of the places where people live. For example, in a city, where are the factories and buildings for heavy industry? Are they near airports or train stations? Are they on the edge of town, near major roads? What about housing developments? Are they near these industries, or are they far away? Where are the other industry buildings? Where are the schools, hospitals, and parks? What about the police and fire stations? How close are homes to each of these things? Towns and, especially, cities are routinely organized into neighborhoods, so that each house or home is near to most things that its residents might need on a regular basis. This means that large cities have multiple schools, hospitals, grocery stores, fire stations, and other services.

Related to this is the distance between cities, towns, villages, or settlements. In certain parts of the United States, and definitely in many countries in Europe, the population settlement patterns achieve megalopolis standards with no clear boundaries from one town to the next. Other, more sparsely populated areas have towns that are few and far between and have relatively few people in them. Some exceptions to this exist, of course, like oases in the deserts. For the most part, however, population centers tend to be relatively near one another with small towns nearby.

Environmental and geographic factors have affected the pattern of urban development in Texas and the rest of the United States. In turn, urban infrastructure and development patterns are interrelated factors, which affect one another.

The growth of urban areas is often linked to the advantages provided by its geographic location. Before the advent of efficient overland routes of commerce such as railroads and highways, water provided the primary means of transportation of commercial goods and, as a result, most large American cities are situated along bodies of water.

Connected and Interdependent Areas

As transportation technology advanced, the supporting infrastructure was built to connect cities with one another and to connect remote areas to larger communities. The railroad, for example, allowed for the quick transport of agricultural products from rural areas to urban centers. This newfound efficiency not only further fueled the growth of urban centers, but changed the economy of rural America. When farmers who had once practiced only subsistence farming began growing enough to support one's own family, a new infrastructure was developed—one that meant farmers could convert agricultural products into cash by selling them at market.

For urban dwellers, improvements in building technology and advances in transportation allowed for larger cities. Growth brought a new set of problems, unique to each location. The bodies of water that had made the development of cities possible in their early days also formed natural barriers to growth. Further infrastructure in the form of bridges, tunnels, and ferry routes were needed to connect central urban areas with outlying communities.

As cities grew in population, living conditions became more crowded. As roads and bridges became better, and transportation technology improved, many people began to look outside the city for living space. Along with the development of these new suburbs came the infrastructure to connect them to the city in the form of commuter railroads and highways. In the case of New York City, which is situated mainly on islands, a mass transit system became crucial early on to bring essential workers from outlying areas into the commercial centers.

The growth of suburbs had the effect in many cities of creating a type of economic segregation. Working-class people who could not afford new suburban homes or, perhaps, an automobile to carry them to and from work were relegated to closer, more densely populated areas. Frequently, these areas had to be passed through by those on their way to the suburbs, and rail lines and freeways sometimes bisected these urban communities.

In the modern age, advancements in telecommunications infrastructure may have an impact on urban growth patterns as information can pass instantly and freely between almost any two points on the globe, allowing those in remote areas access to some aspects of urban life. Flight has made possible global commerce and goods exchange on a level never before seen. Foods can be flown around the world, and, with the aid of refrigeration techniques, kept fresh enough to sell in markets nearly anywhere. The same is true of medicine and, unfortunately, weapons.

Impact of Natural Disasters

Natural disasters such as storms, volcanic eruptions, floods, typhoons, earthquakes, and tsunamis can cause devastation to communities. But, many times, people living in remote regions are equally or even impacted more greatly because they are not near a center or urban area where they can obtain assistance.

Populations can be displaced and be required to migrate to another geographic area that has been left unharmed by the disaster. With an influx of people into a new area, strain will be placed on services and existing facilities, ranging from schools to medical services to employment.

Numerous examples link natural disasters to migration and have long-term effects on communities and people throughout the world. After Hurricane Mitch hit Central America in 1998, many affected by the storm migrated to the United States. Rising sea levels in the Maldives will cause people to relocate before their islands disappear. Floods have had long-term effects on communities. One example was the 2007 flood that resulted in India being the recipient of Bangladeshis after a massive flood affected millions of households in Bangladesh.

SKILL 15.3   **Understand types and patterns of settlement, physical and human geographic factors that affect where people settle (e.g., transportation routes, availability of resources), and processes of the development of settlement over time.**

Humans are social animals and are almost always found to be living in groups. In the past, the choice of places where humans settled to was dictated largely by the location of the **resources** needed to survive. Agricultural communities arose in areas of farmable land, and fishing communities were located along coastlines and riverbanks. As trade and commerce grew, settlements were established to serve as market centers and to support the economic activity of the surrounding areas. These settlements were often centrally located, in places that allowed for easy **transportation.** Cities often developed at the confluence of two rivers or flat land where good roads could be built and the waters could be used for transportation.

Over time, many small communities grew into towns and cities. These central communities often outgrew their surrounding neighbors, incorporating them into larger and larger population centers. Before the Industrial Revolution, large towns still relied on trade and support of the smaller surrounding communities, and so they were spaced out across the earth's surface. Following the wave of industrialization in the nineteenth century, cities became production centers and transportation infrastructure improved, allowing for even faster urban growth that no longer required the economic support of nearby communities. In some areas where space is limited, for example along the east coast of the United States and on the island nation of Japan, large cities grew together into enormous networks of urban areas.

Patterns of present **human settlement** differ from population to population, based on **history, cultural tradition,** and **geography**. The United States has large areas of agricultural and undeveloped land, and has many people living in rural areas in small towns. The same is true in other countries with large land areas, such as China. Japan, on the other hand, is an island country with the ocean as a natural boundary. As a result, much of Japan is urban.

Cultural and historical differences also affect settlement patterns. The United States saw prosperous growth following World War II, allowing many people to purchase new homes and automobiles. The smaller communities and rural land surrounding urban centers were developed into suburban communities connected to urban centers by highways and railways. People with low income remained in the cities. This is the opposite pattern from how many Central and South American cities were settled. In large urban centers such as Mexico City, wealthier people live in the central areas, and poorer people inhabit the outskirts of the city, often in shantytowns or slums. **New urbanism** is the current alternative to the automobile-oriented lifestyle in the United States.

SKILL 15.4   **Analyze the influence of physical and human geographic factors on political, social, cultural, and economic developments in U.S. and world history (e.g., Dust Bowl, opening of the Panama and Suez canals).**

Dust Bowl

During the 1930s severe dust storms eroded agricultural lands in the southern plains of the United States. The poor condition of the soil was caused by prolonged droughts and plowing, planting, and agricultural methods that removed a top layer of soil that could no longer anchor the lower layers. Winds blew away the top soil and continued moving and removing soil for about a decade. Many families were forced to move from their homes in order to try to earn a living elsewhere. The Dust Bowl covered parts of Texas, Oklahoma, New Mexico, Colorado, and Kansas.

Opening of the Suez Canal

The Suez Canal connects the Mediterranean Sea and the Gulf of Suez. Napoleon Bonaparte had plans to construct a canal in the late 1700s but miscalculations of sea levels put a halt to the project. After the French convinced the Egyptians to let them build a canal, they began and completed construction of a canal in 1869. The canal moved goods more easily and more quickly but eventually conflicts arose over the use and control of the canal. In 1956, Egypt took control of the canal and used the income from the ships' passage for the construction of the Aswan High Dam. Israel invaded Egypt, and the invasions by France and England followed to secure free passage for their goods. Egypt sank numerous ships to block passage. The closing of the Suez Canal reached a crisis level and the United Nations intervened to negotiate a truce. The canal reopened a year later after Egypt removed the sunken ships. Since that time the canal has been closed several times because of Egypt's conflicts with Israel.

The Suez Canal has been reopened and is a significant way for companies to shorten the time needed to transport goods to the Indian subcontinent, Africa, and other parts of the world.

Opening of the Panama Canal

The opening of the Panama Canal sped the transportation of goods and people between the Atlantic Ocean and the Pacific. Before the opening of the canal, ships found it necessary to sail around Cape Horn at the tip of South America in order to reach one ocean from another. The need for quicker transit around South America was realized when gold was discovered in California in the late 1840s. Colombia owned the present-day Isthmus of Panama and in 1855 the United States constructed a railroad across the area. The French company that constructed the Suez Canal was awarded rights to build a canal across the Isthmus of Panama. The French company's financial problems and the spread of tropical diseases put a halt to construction. Another French company purchased assets of the defunct company.

The United States became interested in owning the canal after its victories in the Spanish-American War. In 1902, the U.S. Congress approved the purchase and the United States and Colombia signed a treaty to that effect. However, Colombia's government did not ratify the treaty. Political maneuvering and a movement for Panamanian independence culminated in the U.S.

recognition of the Republic of Panama and a treaty being signed with Panama that gave the United States exclusive possession of the Panama Canal Zone in exchange for annual payments of money to the Panamanian government by the United States.

American engineers began developing ideas for construction of the canal in 1906. Eight years later, the canal was completed. In 1977, Panama and the United States entered into a treaty that provided for the return of the canal to Panama in 1999.

SKILL 15.5   Analyze the impact of the Neolithic agricultural revolution on human life and on the development of the first civilizations.

The earliest human societies were centered on hunting animals and gathering wild food for survival. As the seasons of the year passed, the areas where food animals and plants could be found changed. To follow the food supply, humans were nomadic, living in temporary shelters that could be carried along or relying on natural shelters such as caves.

This all began to change in the Neolithic period starting around 10,000 years ago in the Middle East, when evidence suggests that humans began a transition to agriculture as a source for food. This transition took place at different times in different places. The **Fertile Crescent,** a large area in present-day Egypt and the Middle East, is one area where the transition is well-studied. The Fertile Crescent contains three major rivers and an excellent climate for growing annual plants such as wheat.

This is also the area that hosted the earliest human civilizations, and is sometimes called the Cradle of Civilization. Agriculture allowed human populations to remain in one place year round, rather than having to follow wild food sources. This sedentary way of living led to the development of permanent settlements for people who raised food. The river systems provided easy transportation between settlements, and people began to exchange ideas and trade with one another. Freed from the demands of constantly moving from place to place, humans began to develop into more complex societies and improve methods of communication by developing writing. Some of the earliest human writing known today is a tally of crop production.

As these societies became more complex, a hierarchical organization developed and settlements began thinking of themselves as belonging to a common group of people. This idea of a "state" of people sharing a common background and belonging to one organized society was the beginning of civilization. As writing and language progressed and the social hierarchy was established, a form of government was implemented and codes of laws were passed, marking the beginning of civilized culture.

SKILL 15.6   **Demonstrate knowledge of how population growth and modernization have affected the physical environment throughout history.**

Population Growth

A population is a group of people living within a certain geographic area. Populations are usually measured on a regular basis by a census, which also measures age, economic, ethnic, and other data. Populations change over time due to many factors, and these changes can have significant impact on the surrounding physical environment.

When a population grows in size, it becomes necessary for it to either expand its geographic boundaries to make room for new people or to increase its density. **Population density** is simply the number of people in a population divided by the geographic area in which they live. As density increases, the types of infrastructure needed to support a population change. Larger transportation systems and larger, denser dwellings such as apartment buildings are needed. These require additional resources to support them, impacting the surrounding environment.

Modernization

Forces of population growth have been accentuated in modern times as more efficient building techniques for modernization. Communications and transportation have allowed humans to occupy a wider area on the earth's surface. Resources such as oil and natural gas can be piped thousands of miles from where they are found to where they are used. Modern transportation allows people to live considerable distances from where they work. Moving these resources around the world has an impact on the environment in the form of fuel consumption and the reuse of land. The economic prosperity that is supported by this infrastructure can lead to further population growth, further strain on natural resources and the environment, and modernization to meet current needs.

SKILL 15.7   **Understand factors affecting the location of different types of economic activities and economic issues related to the location and management of key natural resources.**

Economic activities are closely tied to the availability of resources required to support them. These resources include the **raw materials** required to make a product, the **communication**s and **transportation infrastructure** needed to provide a service and a supply of people to work at the activity with the essential skills needed to do it efficiently.

Historically, many towns and cities grew up around a single economic activity. A mill town, for instance, was usually located along a river to harness its waterpower and was a central place for grain farmers from the surrounding regions to bring their products for processing. Mining towns and logging towns were organized in a similar way, with most of the economic survival of the community reliant on a local natural resource.

This kind of reliance could result in economic catastrophe if the central resource was depleted or not managed properly. Mines were abandoned after they failed to continue to produce enough ore. Over-logging in some areas led to the collapse of logging towns that could not find enough trees nearby to support their industry.

The failure of an economically active community places a strain on the entire economy, and many governments have taken action to manage key natural resources and prevent their depletion. Fishing is an example. Where populations of fish are monitored and regulations are passed that limit where and when commercial fishing can take place, a community has taken active steps to prevent or remove strains on the economy.

Modern transportation means that an economic activity is not as closely tied to location as it may have been in the past. Oil, for instance, is sometimes transported for thousands of miles to the refineries where it is processed. The technological improvements in transporting materials cheaply allows for production facilities to draw natural resources from a wider area, making production less reliant on location of resources. This presents new challenges in managing natural resources, however, as new sources must constantly be sought.

SKILL 15.8   **Understand relationships between physical and human geographic factors and political divisions, relationships, and policies (e.g., ways in which forces of conflict and cooperation influence control of Earth's surface, the influence of physical and human geographic factors on foreign policies of countries such as Iraq, Israel, Japan, and the United Kingdom).**

Physical geographic factors—features such as mountains, rivers, and deserts—are the natural characteristics of an area. **Human geographic factors** are the features created by human interaction with their environment such as canals and roads.

Political divisions are also human geographic characteristics. Political divisions are areas defined by actual political boundaries—country, city, county, or state.

Political boundaries can be the source of contention between adjacent countries. Following the end of World War II, the Allied forces redrew the southern boundaries of Iraq. In 1991, the former Iraqi leader Saddam Hussein declared that Iraq did not recognize the border and that the country intended to reclaim part of Kuwait, which contained rich oil fields. Iraq's invasion led to a military response from the United States and others in the First Gulf War.

The modern state of **Israel** was partitioned from Palestine and other countries in 1947, creating separate Jewish and Arab regions. These borders between Israel and Palestine have been a constant source of violent conflict between the two groups ever since. Border problems have also developed between Israel and its neighbors such as Egypt and Lebanon.

Both **Japan** and the **United Kingdom** are island nations. Surrounded by the sea and with limited natural resources, these countries developed policies of imperialism. Provided with the ocean as a natural defense against attack, they spread their regional control to provide them with economic, military, and natural resources.

Japan's influence extended through Southeast Asia into places like Korea.

England's imperial influence was much broader though, as the country engaged in a policy of colonialism. The British established colonies in North America, the Caribbean, and Australia in the seventeenth and eighteenth centuries. Britain's long association with the sea, as an island nation, provided it with the labor and expertise to make long sea journeys and transport its military to distant locations. As a primary world power, Britain extended its control over parts of the Middle East, Africa and India. Britain's geographic location—easily defended and allowing easy access to ocean transport—allowed it to exercise a global influence far beyond its own small area.

COMPETENCY 16: SOCIOLOGICAL, ANTHROPOLOGICAL, AND PSYCHOLOGICAL CONCEPTS AND PROCESSES

THE TEACHER APPLIES SOCIOLOGICAL, ANTHROPOLOGICAL, AND PSYCHOLOGICAL CONCEPTS AND PROCESSES TO UNDERSTAND CULTURAL FORMATION AND CHANGE, INTERGROUP RELATIONS, AND INDIVIDUAL DEVELOPMENT.

SKILL 16.1 Understand the role of culture as a foundation of individual and social behavior.

Beliefs are those things that are thought to be true. Beliefs are often associated with religion but beliefs can also be based on political or ideological philosophies. "All people are created equal" is an example of an ideological belief.

Cultural values are what a society thinks is right and wrong and are often based on and shaped by beliefs. The value that every member of the society has a right to participate in his or her government might be considered to be based on the belief that "All people are created equal." There are also personal values, and courage, integrity, and love can be personal values.

A culture's beliefs and values are reflected in the cultural products it produces, such as literature, the arts, media, and architecture. These products become part of a culture and last from generation to generation, becoming one way that culture is transmitted through time. A common language among all members of a culture makes this transmission possible.

Psychologists, sociologists, and anthropologists all study human social behavior, no matter that it is. Sociologists might study the social behavior of minorities. A psychologist might study the social behavior of the depressed, and an anthropologist might study the social behavior of family structures. Regardless of how social behavior is studied, each type of study shows that culture is the result of individual and societal beliefs and values.

SKILL 16.2   **Understand the evolving nature of race and gender relations in the United States, and know how people from various racial, ethnic, and religious groups have adapted to and modified life in the United States and contributed to a national identity.**

Definitions of Race and Ethnic Groups

Race is a term generally used to describe a population of people from a common geographic area that share certain common physical traits. Skin color and facial features have traditionally been used to categorize individuals by race. The meaning of the term "race" has generated some controversy among sociologists, anthropologists, and biologists. Biologically, a race of people shares a common genetic lineage. Socially, race can be more complicated to define, with many people identifying themselves as part of a group that others might not. This self-perception of race, and the perception of race by others, is perhaps more crucial than any genetic variation when trying to understand the social implications of variations in race.

An **ethnic group** is a group of people who identify themselves as having a common social background and set of behaviors, and who perpetuate their culture by traditions of marriage within their own group. Ethnic groups will often share a common language, religion, and ancestral background and frequently exist within larger populations with which they interact.

Ethnicity and race are sometimes interlinked, but they differ in that many ethnic groups can exist within a population of people thought to be of the same race. Ethnicity is based more on common cultural behaviors and institutions than common physical traits.

Race and Gender Relations in the United States

In the United States' early history, many diverse cultures were coming together in a steady stream of immigration to the New World. These cultures were mainly Western European. In theory, all the immigrants who came to the United States were allowed to maintain their languages and cultures. In practice, they usually assimilated into the American culture within two generations although their practices and traditions often survived in an Americanized form.

Usually tolerant of European immigrants and their cultural practices, some Americans have treated most nonwhite cultures as inferior. African Americans were enslaved for centuries, and even after the end of slavery were officially segregated from the European American society in some parts of the country.

Gender issues have historically included problems relating to employment and equal opportunities. The Civil Rights Act of 1964 prohibited gender discrimination in hiring, promoting, or firing of employees. However, sociologists argue that employers exercise subtle forms of both gender and racial discrimination in the workplace. These infractions are difficult to document and continue to challenge women and racial minority groups today.

Cultural Diversity and National Identity

The United States has always been a destination for people from other countries looking to improve their lives. Through most of its history, the majority of newcomers to the United States were whites from Europe, particularly in the period between 1890 and 1930, when there was a comparatively liberal immigration policy. Before the Civil War, African slaves who had been brought to the United States were taken primarily to the Southern states to live and work on plantations and farms. Following emancipation, many African Americans moved to urban areas where employment was more easily found.

Beginning around 1980, a shift in the nationality of new immigrants began, with an increase in the number of immigrants from Asian and Latin American countries. Political unrest and economic downturns led to surges in immigrants from troubled countries such as the Dominican Republic and Cambodia. The disparity between the economies of the United States and Mexico created a situation in which laborers from Mexico could find ample work in America.

In recent years, a respect for cultural diversity has grown worldwide and within the United States. The United States has sometimes been described as a **mixed salad bowl.** As with vegetables that retain their own identities in a salad, the various ethnic groups, races, and religious groups that have settled in America may have retained their own cultural identifies but, at the same time, adapted to life in the United States, modified their lives, and contributed to a national identity.

Texas, with its history of shifting dominant cultures and immigration, has been a leader within the United States in promoting cultural diversity. The Hispanic heritage of many Texas citizens is officially honored by the preservation of early settlements and artifacts such as the Ceremonial Cave, Espiritu Santo and Morhiss Mound, and ethnic and cultural concentrations of people who currently thrive in Texas.

SKILL 16.3 **Analyze ways in which cultures both change and maintain continuity (e.g., social movements, nationalization).**

People who have shared interests or who are connected by a common cause may be part of a social movement. **Social movement** can be formally or informally organized. Groups opposing alcohol formed a social movement, the temperance movement, and campaigned for the enactment of the Prohibition Amendment. Labor movements resulted in the formation of unions and organizations that promoted workers in industry.

Social movements have the effect of modifying society to meet current needs. However, social movements also maintain continuity by accomplishing changes that appear to be appropriate and timely and by focusing awareness of the continuing needs of society.

Nationalism is a feeling of spirit, devotion, pride, or patriotism that people have toward a country. Nationalism can have positive or negative effects on a country. For example, the sense of pride that Nazis had for Germany during World War II created effects that were extremely negative where the war effort was concerned, and deaths and war crimes occurred because of the Holocaust.

People who are seeking independence for their country exhibit a sense of nationalism and want this pride, and their actions, to result in the opportunity of self-rule. The French Revolution of the 1700s is an example of nationalism in Europe.

SKILL 16.4 **Demonstrate knowledge of the theoretical foundations of sociology and basic sociological principles and processes, including those related to group membership, roles, status, values, and stratification.**

Sociology is the study of human social behavior, especially the study of the origins, organization, institutions, and development of human society. The following is a brief review of some basic theoretical foundations and principles of sociology.

Theoretical Foundations of Sociology

The **social conflict theory** of sociology considers how social patterns result in some people in a society being dominant and others being oppressed. Karl Marx, W. E. B. Du Bois, and Jane Addams were advocates of this theory.

Theorists who believe that social interaction provides subjective meaning in human behavior follow the **interactionism** theory. They believe that peoples' everyday interactions result in features of society and that, as a result, society is always changing.

The **structural functionalism theory** presents the belief that society is made up of many component parts that that all of the parts work together to form stability. Auguste Comte was one of the followers of this theory.

Sociological Principles

Group membership is an example of collective association. A group consists of people who identify and interact with one another. The group may or may not be organized, and the group may have valued or hated objectives, but it facilitates social behavior. A group may be formed for a number of reasons and, as identified by sociologists, has a degree of cohesiveness that any other group may not have. Groups may include families, clubs, friends, and religious and fraternal associations.

Roles are patterns of behavior of a person in a society. Roles provide a basis for people dealing with situations and other people. Roles, for example, can include parent/child, teacher/student, attorney/client, and doctor/patient. Each person who has a role is expected to behave within the boundaries established for that role or position.

Status refers to a person's position in society. A person may have multiple statuses. For example, one person may be a father, a teacher, and a friend. Certain behaviors and obligations are expected for each status. If status is achieved because of merit, the status is called an **achieved status.** Status that has not been earned and is beyond one's control is referred to as an **ascribed status.** A teacher is an example of an achieved status, and a person of a certain race is an example of ascribed status.

Values are concepts, ethics, and conduct that people believe in. Some people believe that it is important to obtain as much education as possible. Other people may believe it is all right to steal for a living.

Stratification refers to levels. The different areas of society are divided into levels. Social stratification may be based on such things as economics, heritage, or religion—or a combination of those factors. Other stratification may be based on politics or position within a business or company. In some countries the stratification levels are rigid. In other countries, marriage, mobility, and economic factors can change one's level of stratification.

SKILL 16.5 Understand the role of social institutions (e.g., family, religion, educational system, science, mass media) in meeting basic societal needs.

Family, religion, education, science, and mass media mean have many levels of importance. As social institutions, each plays a role in meeting basic societal needs.

Family is a social institution that helps in meeting societal needs. Its overarching role is to develop good citizens and preserve society while promoting individuality and responsibility in the family's members.

Religion has multiple roles. Association with religion permits people to serve their beliefs by serving society and making society a better place. Religion also has the role of stabilizing peoples' lives and provides the basis for philanthropy.

An **educational system** provides information that becomes knowledge. It can help people to become more informed and better citizens. It can also present successes, failures, and mistakes of the past and focus on improving society in the future.

Science plays a pivotal role in society because it can produce a more informed, a healthier, and a more modern society. Inventions and discoveries maintain standards of living and health.

The **mass media** communicate events of importance to society. Whether the events are a government coup in a foreign country or the election of a new president in their own country, the media must keep society informed of current events. The media's role should be that of an unbiased observer that increases the knowledge of society and its citizens.

SKILL 16.6 Demonstrate knowledge of the roles of men, women, children, and families in historical and contemporary cultures.

The traditions and behaviors of a culture are based on the prevailing beliefs and values of that culture. Beliefs and values are similar and interrelated systems.

Family and Gender Roles in Colonial Times

During colonial times, residents of the New England colonies were primarily small farmers. Each family had its own subsistence farm with supporting livestock. Women were expected to do prepare all meals, make garments, care for the children, and take care of the household while men tended to the farming and livestock. Families encouraged their sons to continue to farm and provided them with land and livestock to establish them. Women were expected to marry instead of pursuing education or employment. New England settlers were primarily from England.

The Middle colonies had a more diverse population that New England, with immigrants from Holland, Scotland, Ireland, and Germany making up the largest groups. These peoples were also largely farmers, each group bringing its own methods and techniques. Family structure was similar to that in New England, but unlike their Puritan counterparts, German and Dutch women were allowed to hold property and could often be found working in the fields.

Southern culture during colonial times was more aristocratic than in other areas of the country. Plantation life afforded more luxury to the owners and more leisure time for families.

Changing Roles in American Culture

After the American Revolution, it was not uncommon for a woman to manage a large farm and plantation when her husband died or was away for war or business. Many women, especially but not only widows, owned businesses. Women worked as apothecaries, barbers, blacksmiths, sextons, printers, tavern keepers, and midwives.

During the Industrial Revolution, more women and children went to work outside the home as factory labor became common. Factory owners hired women and children when they could, because they could pay lower wages to women and children than to men. For some tasks, like sewing, women were preferred because they had training and experience. Federal reform of child labor was brought about by the Fair Labor Standards Act of 1938.

In contemporary American culture, there is a wide variety of family structures. In some families, men and women have similar economic roles and more of the household duties are shared than before. Families can be nontraditional in that the father may be a stay-at-home parent. Children are expected to become educated. Although most attend school, some are homeschooled.

In contemporary societies around the world, the roles of men, women, children, and families are based on values and beliefs that are important for that society. The roles have also evolved over time.

SKILL 16.7   **Understand ways in which socialization, cultural values, and norms vary across space and time and influence relationships within and among groups.**

Socialization

Socialization is the process by which humans learn the expectations their society has for their behavior, in order that they might successfully function within that society. Socialization takes place primarily in children as they are taught and learn the rules and norms of their culture. Children grow up eating the common foods of a culture and develop a "taste" for these foods, for example. By observing adults and older children, they learn about gender roles and appropriate ways to interact. The family is the primary influence in this kind of socialization and contributes directly to a person's sense of self-importance and personal identity.

Socialization varies according to the background of the groups. Some children, for example, may not be expected to participate in family discussions. Their relationship with adults, for example, will likely be different from the relationships of children who participate in discussions and the sharing of ideas.

Cultural Values

Cultural values influence relationships within and among groups. Immigrants to a country often attempt to maintain their cultural heritage. Some people retain language in addition to other features such as religion and foods. As children attend school and become "Americanized," their new cultural values may conflict with the old, and the new attitudes may have a negative influence on family members who want to cling to their heritage.

Norms

Sociologists have identified three main types of **norms,** or ways that cultures define behavioral expectations. These norms are called folkways, mores, and laws and each norm is associated with different consequences if the norms are violated. The folkways, mores, and laws of a society are based on the prevailing beliefs and values of a society.

Folkways are the informal rules of etiquette and behaviors that a society follows in day-to-day practice. Forming a line at a shop counter or holding a door open for an elderly person are examples of folkways in many societies. Someone who violates a folkway—by pushing to the front of a line, for instance—might be seen as rude but is not thought to have done anything immoral or illegal.

Mores are stronger than folkways in the consequences they carry for not observing them. Mores are customs derived from societal behavior. Cheating on a test or lying might violate a social more, and a person who does so may be considered immoral.

Laws are formal adoptions of norms by a society with formal punishment for their violation. Laws are usually based on the mores of a society. Killing is wrong, and society punished one who kills. The definition of and punishments for killing are codified as laws, for example. Laws are the most formal type of social norm, as their enforcement is specifically provided for. Folkways and mores, on the other hand, are primarily enforced informally by the fellow members of a society.

Norms help keep a society on a positive course. Where groups of people rebel, contradict, or disobey the established norms, there may be a breakdown of society. If the norms include not breaking laws, then juveniles, for example, who steal vehicles, vandalize property, and refuse to attend school affect society in a negative way. Their actions show a disregard for the norms established by the society and if left uncorrected their actions may affect the quality of a society.

SKILL 16.8   Demonstrate knowledge of the history and theoretical foundations of psychology.

Psychology is the study of human behavior and mental processes. It has its earliest roots in the growth of philosophy during the seventeenth and eighteenth centuries. Considered a part of philosophy until the late nineteenth century, psychology was often intertwined with religious thinking about human motivations and abilities.

In 1879, the German **Wilhelm Wundt** established a laboratory at Leipzig University to study psychology. This marked the beginnings of what would become the modern field of psychology. Wundt was a physiologist who introduced experimental observation into the study of human behavior by recording human reactions in controlled conditions.

In the United States, **William James** also established a laboratory for experimental psychology, at Harvard University. In 1890, James published an important early work in the field, *Principles of Psychology*, which posed many of the questions that frame psychological inquiry.

Austrian-born **Sigmund Freud** became active in the field at this time, as well, and developed a method on interpretive and introspective psychology called psychoanalysis. Freud's applied theories became popular partly because he openly discussed repression and sexuality as part of his analyses, topics that were considered taboo at that time.

Freud's subjective theories, which relied on introspection, were a departure from the experimental approach taken by Wundt and James. Partly in response to Freud, the field of behavioral psychology began to grow in the early twentieth century. **Behaviorism** held that psychology should be the study of human behavior and not rely on subjective introspection about mental processes.

Behaviorism was developed and championed by psychologists such as John B. Watson, Edward Thorndike, Ivan Pavlov, and B. F. Skinner, who showed that humans and other animals could be *conditioned* to exhibit certain behaviors in response to controlled conditions. This model dominated the field of psychology until the middle of the twentieth century, when research into language and neurology suggested that there might be an innate component to behavior and learning that the behaviorists had not included in their theories.

Modern psychology draws on all these fields and continues to grow across different fields of science. Neural psychology is closely linked to biology and physiology in its study of physical bases for behavior. **Cognitive psychology** studies the information processing abilities of the mind and has grown with the field of computer technology.

SKILL 16.9 **Demonstrate knowledge of behavioral, social, cognitive, and personality perspectives of human learning.**

Conditioning is a term used to describe a form of learning studied by behavioral psychologists. Conditioning is the pairing of a stimulus with a reaction so that the two become associated. In a famous experiment, the psychologist Ivan Pavlov used a bell to call dogs to food. After several times he found that the dogs would salivate whenever the bell rang, even when there was no food present. This is an example of **behavioral learning**.

Social learning is also called **modeling**, and is a theory of learning based on observation and replication. Social learning theory holds that humans learn by observing the behavior of others, especially in childhood.

The **cognitive approach** to learning focuses on the internal mental functions of the mind. Cognitive psychologists believe that the mind processes information in certain ways, which can be examined to determine how stimuli and behaviors are linked. Unlike behaviorism, cognitive theories of learning allow for individual choices and awareness of these processes.

Personality psychology is a field of study that examines the characteristics of individuals that make them similar and different from one another, and how these differences affect behavior and learning. Personality psychology recognizes different traits and types among human personality, and places importance on these differences in the learning environment.

SKILL 16.10 **Understand basic psychological principles and processes, including those related to motivation, sensation and perception, cognition, personality, relationships between biology and behavior, and relationships between the self and others.**

Psychological processes refer to the ways humans process information and perceptions and the behavior that is exhibited as a result. Language use, thinking, memory, problem solving, and communication are examples of psychological processes. These processes can be deliberate or take place without a person's conscious knowledge.

Motivation

Motivation is the strong desire toward a certain course of action. Seeking food and seeking freedom from harm are two elemental types of motivation. Motivation can involve other psychological processes as a person interacts within a social group to achieve the things toward which he or she is motivated, such as problem solving and communicating with language.

Sensation and Perception

Sensation refers to the stimuli we receive through our various senses, such as sight and hearing. This is the most basic biological process by which humans interact with their environment. Sensation provides the input for higher psychological processes such as communication. For example, we use sensation to hear the words of another person or to see words on a page but we use other psychological processes to make sense of these sights and sounds.

Perception is how we immediately interpret sensations. Perception is not the same as sensation, however, as it is common for the human mind to perceive things that it does not actually sense. An optical illusion that "fools" the eye into seeing something that is not actually present is an example of how perception can differ from actual sensation.

Cognition

Cognition is the use of mental processes to gain knowledge and understanding. Problem solving is one process. Remembering and thinking are other processes used in cognition. In order to use the processes, a person must use his or her brain, language, and perception. Cognition is an important goal of teaching because a student needs to pay attention, acquire new vocabulary for various subjects, and retain the information. Students will not have the same learning style but the goal of cognition must still be realized.

Relationships between Biology and Behavior

The relationship between biology and behavior encompasses many fields of psychology, including the study of such processes as motivation, sensation, and perception. Neural psychology studies the biology of brain functions at the level of the chemical reactions that take place and looks at how these functions are connected to higher processes.

Relationships between Self and Others

A branch of psychology called **social psychology** focuses primarily on how individuals behave and react in relation to others. This study involves asking questions about how individuals perceive themselves and how they view their role among the people they interact with. Psychological processes such as communication, learning, and perception are some of the areas that relate directly to this question.

DOMAIN V   GOVERNMENT AND CITIZENSHIP

COMPETENCY 17: DEMOCRATIC PRINCIPLES AND GOVERNMENT IN THE UNITED STATES

THE TEACHER UNDERSTANDS THE PRINCIPLES OF DEMOCRATIC GOVERNMENT AND THE STRUCTURE AND FUNCTIONING OF GOVERNMENT IN THE UNITED STATES.

SKILL 17.1   **Analyze the beliefs and principles reflected in the U.S. Constitution (e.g., republicanism, checks and balances, federalism, separation of powers, separation of church and state, popular sovereignty, individual rights) and other important historical documents (e.g., Declaration of Independence, Federalist Papers, English Bill of Rights).**

U.S. Constitution

The **Constitution of the United States** is the fundamental law of the republic. It is a precise, formal, written document the sets out the organization of government. It is the supreme law of the land and there is no national power superior to it. The debates conducted during the Constitutional Congress represent the issues and the arguments that led to the compromises in the final document. The foundations of government were stated to provide for the expansion of national life and to make it an instrument that would last for all time. To maintain its stability, the framers created an elaborate process for making any changes to it, and no amendment can become valid until it is ratified by three-fourths of the states.

Separation of Powers and Checks and Balances

The Constitution divides the government into three branches. Each branch has specific duties. The **legislative branch** makes the laws. The **executive branch** enforces the laws, and the **judicial branch** interprets the laws. The debates at the Constitutional Convention reflect the concerns of the Founding Fathers that the rights of the people needed to be protected from abrogation by the government itself and the determination that no branch of government should have enough power to override the others.

Republicanism

Republicanism is present in the Constitution because it provides for the election of representatives and senators by voters. A republican form of government is also called a representative democracy.

Federalism

The concept of federalism is present in the Constitution because the document refers to both the state and federal governments. The federal government is provided a list of powers. Those not expressly given to the federal government are reserved for the states.

Separation of Church and State

The First Amendment to the Constitution provides, among other things, the separation of church and state. One of the reasons this amendment, and the other nine amendments that are part of the Bill of Rights, was added to the Constitution was the promise to citizens that if the Constitution were ratified there would be provisions for individual rights. The framers did not want an entanglement between church and state and did not include reference to religion in the Constitution. However, in order to obtain enough votes for the document to be ratified, it was necessary to include amendments that protected individual rights from government interference.

Popular Sovereignty

The doctrine of popular sovereignty means that the rule and power of government lies with the people. The framers of the Constitution used the ideas of the Enlightenment in the document. Popular sovereignty expresses the idea of a social contract existing between government and the citizens and that the citizens should benefit from their government. The idea of popular sovereignty was expressed in the Declaration of Independence because if the government is not benefiting its citizens, it should be dissolved and new government instituted. The Declaration of Independence expressed this concept and the Constitution also expresses it in the Preamble. The Preamble to the Constitution states that the people are forming a government and explains why they are creating it—to form a perfect union, establish justice, and insure domestic tranquility, provide for the common defence, promote the general welfare, and secure the blessing of liberty to themselves and posterity.

Individual Rights

The Anti-Federalists opposed a strong central government. In order to secure the number of votes needed for ratification, the Federalists and framers agreed that individual liberties would be identified and included in amendments if the Constitution were ratified. The first ten amendments were passed, and they are called the **Bill of Rights.** The individual rights that are provided for include such rights as freedom of speech, freedom of the press, the right to bear arms, the right to be free from unreasonable searches and seizures, the right to confront witnesses and not incriminate oneself. The right to an attorney in criminal cases and the right to a public, speedy trial are also enumerated rights. Due process is a right guaranteed in the Bill of Rights as the right to be free from cruel and unusual punishment.

Declaration of Independence

The Declaration of Independence is an outgrowth of both ancient Greek ideas of democracy and individual rights and the ideas of the European Enlightenment and the Renaissance, especially the ideology of the political thinker John Locke. Thomas Jefferson was the principal author of the Declaration, and he borrowed much from Locke's theories and writings.

Essentially, Jefferson applied Locke's principles to the then-contemporary American situation. Jefferson argued that the reigning King George Ill had repeatedly violated the rights of the colonists as subjects of the British Crown.

The Declaration of Independence states that the king violated the reasons for which government had been instituted and that the colonists were left with no choice but to dissolve the bonds of government that were created and establish a new government. The Declaration expresses the belief that the colonists had tried all means to resolve the disputes peacefully but that the king had not listened to their grievances.

Federalist Papers

The Federalist Papers were written by Alexander Hamilton, John Jay, and James Madison to gain support for the states' ratification of the Constitution. The more than eighty articles were published using pseudonyms.

English Bill of Rights

The English Bill of Rights was an act of Parliament in 1689 that identified the rights of the Parliament and citizens and the obligations of the monarchy. It was the same as the Declaration of Rights that had been presented to King William III and Queen Mary II ("William and Mary") earlier that year when they had been asked to rule England.

SKILL 17.2   **Demonstrate knowledge of the structure and functions of the government created by the U.S. Constitution (e.g., bicameral structure of Congress, role of congressional committees, constitutional powers of the president, role of the cabinet and independent executive agencies, functions of the federal court system).**

Bicameral Structure of Congress

Congress is divided into two houses, the **House of Representatives** and the **Senate.** Seats in the House of Representative are apportioned to the states based on population, with every state having at least one. Each state has two senators serving in the Senate.

Before a law is passed, both houses of the Congress must approve it. A bill may be introduced in either house, and once it is passed by that house is sent to the other for consideration. If it passes both houses, it is sent to the president, who must sign the bill into law. Bills are very complex, and each house can make changes to the bill before it is put to a vote. Committees usually do this.

Role of Congressional Committees

Congress has several committees made up of representatives and senators that are designated to deal in certain areas such as judicial matters, defense, spending, and taxation. These committees consider proposed legislation, make amendments, and decide whether to release a bill to be voted on by the full body. The chair position of a congressional committee is usually held by a member of the majority party and is an important position.

Once a bill has passed both houses, a joint committee made up of members from both houses reviews it. Joint committees reconcile the two bills to arrive at one common proposal that can be voted on by both houses.

Constitutional Powers of the President

The president, who must be a native-born citizen, has the executive power to sign a bill into law. The Constitution grants the president the power to veto, or strike down, a law. A presidential veto can be overridden by a two-thirds vote of both houses of Congress. The president also has authority to negotiate treaties with other countries, and the president is the commander in chief of the military forces.

Role of the Cabinet and Independent Executive Agencies

The president appoints a **cabinet** (council of advisers) to lead the various departments of the executive branch of government. The Secretary of State oversees the State Department, which handles U.S. foreign relations. The Secretary of Defense is in charge of the Defense Department, which covers military and defense matters. The Defense Department is housed in the Pentagon. The U.S. Attorney General is the highest law enforcement official in the country and oversees the Justice Department. Other cabinet positions include the Departments of the Treasury, Interior, Agriculture, Commerce, Labor, Health and Human Services, Housing and Urban Development, Transportation, Energy, Education, Veterans Affairs, and Homeland Security.

Independent executive agencies oversee federal government functions. They operate outside the president's direct control because they are self-regulated. Their heads are appointed by the president but can only be removed for cause. The Environmental Protection Agency and Federal Trade Commission are examples of independent executive agencies.

Functions of the Federal Court System

The federal court system considers matters of federal law and cases between states. It consists of three primary divisions: the U.S. District Court, the U.S. Court of Appeals, and the U.S. Supreme Court. The District Court is the trial court in the federal system. The Circuit Courts of Appeals are divided into circuits based on geography. The final court to which a federal matter can be appealed is the U.S. Supreme Court.

The Supreme Court is made up of nine justices appointed by the president and approved by the Senate. The justices serve during "good behavior." The high court is headed by the Chief Justice, who is also appointed by the president. The Supreme Court does not consider every case that is appealed from the lower courts but chooses cases it wishes to review. Petitioners file a writ of certiorari with the court, asking the court to hear a case. The court has the discretion of accepting the case or denying review. Once the Supreme Court has decided a case, there is no higher court to which a party may appeal.

There are also specialized courts in the federal system. The bankruptcy court is an example.

SKILL 17.3   Analyze the processes by which the U.S. Constitution can be changed.

An amendment is a change or addition to the United States Constitution. An example is the Twenty-First Amendment, which cancels Prohibition. Prohibition was instituted when the Eighteenth Amendment was ratified in 1919. To date, twenty-seven Amendments to the Constitution have been ratified.

Amending the United States Constitution is extremely difficult. An amendment may start in Congress. One or more lawmakers propose the amendment, and then each House votes on it. The amendment must have the support of two-thirds of each House separately in order to progress on its path into law. An amendment may also be proposed by a national convention called by two-thirds of the state legislatures but this procedure has never been used.

The final and most difficult step for an amendment is the ratification by state legislatures. Three-fourths of the state legislatures must approve the amendment. Approvals need be only a simple majority in the state legislatures, but thirty-eight states must approve the amendment.

SKILL 17.4   Know procedures for enacting laws in the United States.

Federal laws are passed by the Congress and, with the exception of taxation legislation, can originate in either the House of Representatives or the Senate.

The first step in the passing of a law is for the proposed law to be **introduced in one of the houses of Congress.** A proposed law is called a **bill** while it is under consideration by Congress. A bill can be introduced, or sponsored, by a member of Congress by giving a copy to the clerk or by placing a copy in a special box called a hopper.

Once a bill is introduced, copies are printed, and the **bill is assigned to one of several standing committees** of the chamber in which it was introduced. The committee studies the bill and performs research on the issues it would cover. Committees may call experts to testify on the bill and gather public comments. The committee may revise the bill. Finally, the committee votes on whether to release the bill to be voted on by the full body. A committee may also lay aside a bill so that it cannot be voted on. Once a bill is released, it can be debated and amended by the full body before being voted on. If the bill passes by a simple majority vote, the bill is sent to the other chamber, where the process begins again.

Once a bill has passed both the House of Representatives and the Senate, it is **assigned to a conference committee made up of members of both houses.** The conference committee resolves differences between House and Senate versions of a bill, if any, and then sends it back to both chambers for final approval.

Once a bill receives final approval, it is **signed by the speaker of the house and the vice president,** who is also the president of the Senate. It is then **sent to the president** for consideration. The president may either sign the bill or veto it. If the president vetoes the bill, the veto may be overruled if two-thirds of both the Senate and the House vote to do so.

Once the president signs the bill, the bill becomes a law.

SKILL 17.5   **Analyze changes in the role of the U.S. government over time (e.g., civil rights, New Deal legislation, wartime policies).**

Since the ratification of the United States Constitution in 1789, the U.S. government has played an increasing role in the daily lives of American citizens and has gained in authority over the states.

The issue of this authority was one of the primary causes of the Civil War. Some states felt that the U.S. government exceeded its authority in attempting to ban slavery in new U.S. territories and, fearing that the federal government would try to ban slavery in existing states, seceded from the Union. This issue was visited again in the 1960s, when Congress passed the **Civil Rights Act of 1964** that declared state laws requiring racial segregation were illegal under federal law.

In the years leading up to the Great Depression, the prevailing view in the U.S. government was that government should not interfere in economic matters or provide social support to citizens who fell into poverty. As economic and social factors plunged the country into a depression, conditions worsened.

Upon taking office, President Franklin D. Roosevelt attempted to implement a series of "**New Deal**" policies that would use the power of the federal government to provide relief and work opportunities to those who had fallen into poverty. Many thought this was contrary to the intended role of government, and some of President Roosevelt's plans were struck down in the federal courts as unconstitutional.

Roosevelt's reforms put the United States back on the road to economic recovery, however, and he enjoyed immense popularity, largely because of this success. Since Roosevelt, Americans have, by and large, been more accepting of federal programs such as Social Security, which provides assistance from public funds. Roosevelt's New Deal changed the nature of the government's involvement in the daily lives of U.S. citizens.

The United States entered into **World War II** at the end of 1941, while Roosevelt was in office. During the war, the federal government instituted a series of ration programs that limited the availability of materials to consumers that were needed to support the military. American citizens mostly submitted willingly to these rations. Congress also cooperated with the president in the war effort, following a tradition of granting the executive branch extra leeway in exercising power during times of national war.

This would change in the years after World War II as the United States became involved in military conflicts in Korea and Vietnam where the effort did not have the same level of popular support.

SKILL 17.6   **Understand changing relationships among the three branches of the federal government (e.g., Franklin D. Roosevelt's attempt to increase the number of U.S. Supreme Court justices, War Powers Act, judicial review).**

The U.S. Constitution aims to balance power among the three branches of government and provide each with powers to check the authority of the other branches. Over the history of the United States, the branches have taken on powers not exclusively provided for in the Constitution but powers that have been honored by tradition and established practice. From time to time, one branch has made overt attempts to increase its power over another branch.

One such attempt was when **President Franklin D. Roosevelt** attempted to increase the number of justices in the Supreme Court. During the Great Depression, the U.S. federal judiciary had become unpopular, partly for striking down some of Roosevelt's New Deal policies as unconstitutional.

As popular sentiment grew against the courts, Roosevelt saw an opportunity to gain influence by introducing a plan that would increase the number of federal judges, including the number of Supreme Court justices, by allowing the appointment of a new judge for every judge who had reached the age of seventy years and had not resigned, up to fifteen members per court. Under the plan the president would have the appointees approved by the Senate, as with other appointments. Roosevelt claimed such measures were needed to reduce the workload on the federal court system, but many believed his real motives were to increase executive power over the judicial branch. His **"court packing" plan** backfired when prominent Democrats came out against it, and it was never implemented.

The Constitution states that the Congress has the authority to declare war and to raise money to support the military. The president is granted command of the military. In 1973, concerned over the military conflicts in Korea and Vietnam that had involved U.S. military forces without any declaration of war, Congress passed the **War Powers Act**, which required the president to seek approval from Congress within sixty days of committing U.S. troops to action. President Nixon vetoed the act, but Congress had enough votes to override the veto. The act increased congressional authority over the presidential role of commander in chief, and has been controversial as possibly being unconstitutional.

Judicial review is the concept that the federal courts, and in particular the U.S. Supreme Court, have the authority to declare an act of legislation unconstitutional, thereby nullifying it. This power is not specifically granted to the courts by the Constitution, but was established in 1803 in the case *Marbury* v. *Madison*. In this case, the court determined that a portion of the Judiciary Act of 1789 could not be allowed to stand because it sought to expand the jurisdiction of the Supreme Court beyond that specifically stated in the Constitution. From this ruling, it has been interpreted that the Congress does not have the power to pass a law that is contrary to the Constitution and that it is the responsibility of the federal courts to render decisions regarding the constitutionality of legislation.

SKILL 17.7   **Demonstrate knowledge of the impact of constitutional amendments on U.S. society (e.g., Thirteenth, Fourteenth, Fifteenth, Seventeenth, Nineteenth, Twenty-Fourth, and Twenty-Sixth Amendments).**

Amendments during Reconstruction

Three constitutional amendments were part of the Reconstruction effort to create stability and rule of law to provide, protect, and enforce the rights of former slaves throughout the nation.

Thirteenth Amendment

The **Thirteenth Amendment** abolished slavery and involuntary servitude, except as punishment for crime. The amendment was proposed on January 31, 1865. It ratified by the necessary number of states on December 18, 1865. The Emancipation Proclamation had freed slaves held in states that were considered to be in rebellion. This amendment freed slaves in states and territories controlled by the Union. The Supreme Court has ruled that this amendment does not bar mandatory military service.

Fourteenth Amendment

The **Fourteenth Amendment** provides for Due Process and Equal Protection under the law. It was proposed in 1866 and ratified in 1868. The drafters of the amendment took a broad view of national citizenship. The law requires that states provide equal protection under the law to all persons—not just all citizens.

This amendment was interpreted as overturning the *Dred Scott* case. The full impact of this amendment was not realized until the 1950s when it became the basis of ending school segregation in the Supreme Court case of *Brown* v. *Board of Education of Topeka, Kansas*. This amendment includes the stipulation that all children born on American soil, with very few exceptions, are U.S. citizens. There have been recommendations that this guarantee of citizenship be limited to exclude the children of illegal immigrants and tourists, but this has not yet occurred. There is no provision in this amendment for loss of citizenship.

The Fourteenth Amendment enabled the federal courts to intervene when necessary to guarantee due process and equal protection under the law. The amendment also enabled the courts reinforce due process and equal protection with other rights such as free speech, freedom of religion, protection from unreasonable search, and protection from cruel and unusual punishment.

Section II of the amendment established the "one man, one vote" apportionment of congressional representation. This ended the counting of blacks as three-fifths of a person. Section III of the amendment prevents the election to Congress or the Electoral College of anyone who has engaged in insurrection, rebellion, or treason. Section IV stipulated that the government would not pay "damages" for the loss of slaves nor for debts incurred by the Confederate government (e.g., with English or French banks).

Fifteenth Amendment

The **Fifteenth Amendment** prohibits the denial of the right to vote based on race, color, or previous condition of servitude. It was ratified in 1870.

Amendments Ratified during the Twentieth Century

The Sixteenth through Twenty-Seventh Amendments were ratified from 1913 and 1992.

The **Seventeenth Amendment** providing for direct election to the Senate was ratified in 1913. Previously, senators were appointed by state legislatures, not elected by the public at large.

The long battle for voting rights for women ended successfully in 1920 with the passage of the **Nineteenth Amendment,** which prohibits the denial of the right to vote based on gender.

The **Twenty-Fourth Amendment** prohibits the revocation of voting rights due to the nonpayment of poll taxes. It was ratified in 1964.

The **Twenty-Sixth Amendment,** lowering the legal voting age for Americans from the age of twenty-one to eighteen, was ratified in 1971.

SKILL 17.8   Analyze the impact of landmark Supreme Court decisions on U.S. society (e.g., *Marbury* v. *Madison, McCulloch* v. *Maryland, Cherokee Nation* v. *Georgia, Dred Scott* v. *Sanford, Plessy* v. *Ferguson, Schenck* v. *U.S., Brown* v. *Board of Education of Topeka, Engel* v. *Vitale, Miranda* v. *Arizona, Roe* v. *Wade, Regents of the University of California* v. *Bakke*).

Marbury v. *Madison*

The case of *Marbury v. Madison* established the doctrine of judicial review. President John Adams, a Federalist, ran for election in 1800, and was opposed by his vice president, Thomas Jefferson. Jefferson was elected in November 1800 but at that time, the new president did not take office until March of the following year. He wanted to appoint as many federalist judges as he could. He kept appointing judges long into the night before he left office the following day. The appointments are known as the **Midnight Judges.** One of these Midnight Judges was William Marbury, who was named to be justice of the peace for the District of Columbia.

The normal practice of making such appointments was to deliver a "commission," or notice, of appointment. This was normally done by the Secretary of State. Jefferson's Secretary of State at the time was James Madison. Jefferson did not want all those Federalist judges, so he told Madison not to deliver the commission.

Chief Justice Marshall and the other justices of the Supreme Court decided that since the power to deliver commissions to judges was part of the Judiciary Act of 1789 and *not* part of the Constitution itself, the provision of the legislation was in conflict with the Constitution and, therefore, illegal.

Furthermore, the court claimed, the *entire* Judiciary Act of 1789 was illegal because it gave to the judicial branch powers not granted to it by the Constitution.

The Supreme Court's decision gave the court a whole new power—the power to invalidate laws of Congress.

McCulloch v. *Maryland*

One of the chief political battles of the nineteenth century was between the federal government and state governments. The Supreme Court took this battle to heart and issued a series of decisions that, for the most part, made it clear that any dispute between governments at the state and federal levels would be settled in favor of the federal government. One of the main examples of this was *McCulloch* v. *Maryland*, which settled a dispute involving the Bank of the United States.

The United States at this time (1819) still had a federal bank, the Second Bank of the United States. The state of Maryland voted to tax all bank business not done with state banks. This was meant to be a tax on people who lived in Maryland but who did business with banks in other states.

However, the state of Maryland also sought to tax the federal bank. Andrew McCulloch, who worked in the Baltimore branch of the Bank of the United States, refused to pay the tax. The state of Maryland sued, and the Supreme Court accepted the case.

Writing for the court, Chief Justice John Marshall wrote that the federal government did indeed have the right and power to set up a federal bank. Further, he wrote, a state did *not* have the power to tax the federal government. "The right to tax is the right to destroy," he wrote, and states should not have that power over the federal government. The Bank of the United States did not survive, but the judicial review of the Supreme Court did.

Cherokee Nation v. *Georgia*

The Cherokee nation asked the U.S. Supreme Court to issue an injunction to prevent the Georgia legislature from taking land that they believed was theirs. The Cherokees filed the suit as a "foreign nation." The Cherokees argued that the Constitution permitted the Supreme Court to hear cases involving foreign nations. The court heard the case but did not decide the case on the merits. Instead, the court addressed the threshold issue of whether the court had jurisdiction over the Cherokees as a "foreign nation." The court decided it did not have jurisdiction because the Cherokees were using the term in a way that was not intended by the framers.

Dred Scott v. *Sanford*

Civil rights were addressed in the *Dred Scott* v. *Sanford* (1857) case, in which the Supreme Court declared that Dred Scott, a slave who had lived with his owner at various times in free states, had no legal standing to sue for his freedom. The Civil War changed public opinion, at least in the North, but the struggle for African Americans especially to achieve basic rights such as voting and owning property continued to varying degrees throughout the nineteenth and twentieth centuries.

Plessy v. *Ferguson*

In 1896, the Supreme Court heard the case of *Plessy v. Ferguson*. Howard Plessy was challenging a Louisiana law that required separate railroad cars for white and black passengers. Presiding over the lower court, Judge John Howard Ferguson had ruled that Louisiana had the right to regulate railroad companies as long as they operated within state boundaries. The Supreme Court declined to expand the equal protection clause and ruled that **"separate but equal"** railway cars were deemed appropriate and legal.

Schenck v. *United States*

Charles Schenck was a socialist who distributed pamphlets to American servicemen who had been drafted to serve in World War I. The flyers indicated the draft was a type of involuntary servitude and that the war was the result of capitalist greed. The flyers asked the servicemen to ask for a repeal of the draft. Schenck was arrested for violating the Espionage Act. He was found guilty of the offense and appealed the conviction. The conviction was based on a denial of his First Amendment right of free speech.

In 1919, the Supreme Court heard the case and ruled that First Amendments rights could be limited if the words created a "clear and present danger." In this case the flyers were handed out during the war and could be considered as insubordination. The court also indicated that in peacetime, the result may have been different because the flyers may have been considered harmless.

The **"clear and present danger"** standard remained the law for fifty years. In 1969, the Supreme Court began using the "imminent lawless action" test as the standard for determining First Amendment freedom of speech cases. The new standard protects more speech.

Brown v. *Board of Education*

The Supreme Court, ever mindful of public opinion, looked for an opportunity to try to reverse legalized segregation and found it in *Brown* v. *Board of Education of Topeka, Kansas* in 1954. It was a unanimous decision, and it overturned *Plessy* in ruling that "separate but equal facilities were inherently unequal." The case only applied only to public schools, but later cases involved other areas of society.

Engel v. *Vitale*

The New York State Board of Education approved a short prayer that was to be recited each morning in the public schools. The prayer was said to be nondenominational and participation was voluntary. Parents of some pupils objected and filed suit on First Amendment grounds that the prayer violated their children's beliefs, religions, and/or religious practices. The state court upheld the prayer because participation was voluntary.

The Supreme Court of the United States heard the case in 1962 and ruled that the prayer was unconstitutional because it was inconsistent with the establishment clause. The court held that its decision was based on the fact that there must be separation between church and state.

Miranda v. *Arizona*

In 1963, a man named Ernesto Miranda was arrested based on circumstantial evidence linking him to a kidnap and rape. After two hours of interrogation by police officers, Miranda signed a confession to the rape charge on forms that included the typed statement, "I do hereby swear that I make this statement voluntarily and of my own free will, with no threats, coercion, or promises of immunity, and with full knowledge of my legal rights, understanding any statement I make may be used against me." However, Miranda was not told of his right to counsel, and he was not advised of his right to remain silent or that his statements during the interrogation would be used against him before being presented with the form on which he was asked to write out the confession he had given orally.

In the resulting case of *Miranda* v. *Arizona* (1966), the Supreme Court identified information that arresting officers had to impart to those they were arresting, including language similar to the Bill of Rights, such as the right to an attorney, the right to avoid self-incrimination, and the right to a trial by jury. The **Miranda warning** ("Mirandizing" a suspect) is the formal warning that is required to be given by police to criminal suspects in police custody before they are interrogated. Its purpose is to ensure that the accused are aware of, and reminded of, these rights under the U.S. Constitution and know they can invoke them at any time during the interview.

Roe v. *Wade*

A Texas resident wanted to terminate her pregnancy by abortion. Texas law permitted abortions if they were necessary to save a woman's life but otherwise prohibited abortions. The issue before the U.S. Supreme Court was whether the Constitution embraced a woman's right to terminate a pregnancy by abortion. In *Roe* v. *Wade* (1973), the Supreme Court held that an abortion is a privacy right that the right to privacy is protected by the Fourteenth Amendment, and that during the first trimester of the pregnancy a woman has complete authority over the pregnancy.

Regents of the University of California v. *Bakke*

Regents of the University of California v. *Bakke* (1978) involved **affirmative action.** Allan Bakke, a white male, applied for medical school twice and his application was rejected both times. The school had reserved places for qualified minorities as part of an affirmative action plan. Bakke's test scores and credentials exceeded those of minority students accepted in the years his applications were rejected. He argued in court that he had been denied admission solely on the basis of race. The Supreme Court decided, in a five/four decision that Bakke should be admitted to medical school, that the rigid use of racial quotas violates the Fourteenth Amendment's equal protection clause, but that race could be used as one of several admission criteria.

SKILL 17.9   Understand the relationship between the states and the national government of the United States (i.e., federalism).

Federalism is a system of government where there is a central authority and political units. The Constitution is designed for the central authority to consist of the legislative, executive, and judicial branches of the federal government and the states representing the political units or the second part of the federalist structure. The Constitution provides that the federal government shall have certain powers, and it reserves certain powers for the states. There are **concurrent powers** whereby the states do not encroach upon powers of the federal government.

<u>Powers delegated to the federal government:</u>

1. Tax
2. Borrow and coin money
3. Establish postal service
4. Grant patents and copyrights
5. Regulate interstate & foreign commerce
6. Establish courts
7. Declare war
8. Raise and support the armed forces
9. Govern territories
10. Define and punish felonies and piracy on the high seas
11. Fix standards of weights and measures
12. Conduct foreign affairs

<u>Powers reserved for the states:</u>

1. Regulate intrastate trade
2. Establish local governments
3. Protect general welfare
4. Protect life and property
5. Ratify amendments
6. Conduct elections
7. Make state and local laws

<u>Concurrent powers:</u>

1. Tax
2. Borrow money
3. Charter banks and corporations
4. Establish courts
5. Make and enforce laws
6. Take property for public purposes
7. Spend money to provide for the public welfare

SKILL 17.10 **Demonstrate knowledge of the structure and functions of Texas state government and local governments.**

The American governmental system is a federal system: fifty individual states federated or forming or uniting as one nation. The national and state governments share the powers of government. Both national and state governments exist and govern by the will of the people who are the source of their authority. Local governmental systems operate under the same guidelines.

Texas State Government

State governments are mirror images of the federal government, with a few important exceptions. Governors are not technically commanders in chief of armed forces; state Supreme Court decisions can be appealed to federal courts; terms of state representatives and senators vary; judges, even of the state supreme courts, are usually elected by popular vote; governors and legislators have term limits that vary by state.

The government of Texas is like a miniature U.S. government. Texas has three branches of government—executive, legislative, and judicial. The governor heads up the executive branch, vetoes or signs bills into law, commands the state militia, and can call special sessions of the legislature.

The legislature has two houses (bicameral), a House of Representatives with one hundred fifty members and a Senate with thirty-one, which meet in regular session every two years. The judicial branch has many overlapping courts, of which the Supreme Court (civil cases) and the Texas Court of Criminal Appeals are the highest. Different from the U.S. government, judges are elected, as are many members of the executive branch.

Texas Local Government

The prevailing constitutional theory on the relationship of local governments to the state is the **unitary system.** This theory holds that local governments are the creations of the state. The powers, functions, and responsibilities that they exercise have been delegated or granted to them by the state government, and no local government has sovereign powers. This principle is referred to as the **Dillon rule.** The Dillon rule is applicable to local governments in Texas which are viewed as creations of the state with only those powers granted to them by the Texas Constitution and statutes.

Local governments vary widely across the country, although none of them has a judicial branch per se. Some local governments consist of a city council, of which the mayor is a member and has limited powers; in other cities, the mayor is the head of the government and the city council are the chief lawmakers. Local governments also have less strict requirements for people running for office than do the state and federal governments.

The authority of local government is granted by the state. Texas cities were granted home rule authority in 1912. Home rule means that the cities have discretion in determining policies that are within the limits set by state law.

General law cities are those with fewer than five thousand people. Cities with more than that number of people are **home rule cities** and may choose the form of government that satisfied the city's needs, so long as the form is not unconstitutional or conflict with state statutory law. Cities may have the form of **mayor/council, city commission, or council-manager**.

COMPETENCY 18: CITIZENSHIP AND POLITICAL PROCESSES IN THE UNITED STATES

THE TEACHER UNDERSTANDS POLITICAL PROCESSES IN THE UNITED STATES AND THE RIGHTS AND RESPONSIBILITIES OF U.S. CITIZENS.

SKILL 18.1   Understand the historical and contemporary roles played by political parties, interest groups, and the media in the U.S. political system.

Political Parties

It is important to realize that political parties are never mentioned in the United States Constitution. George Washington himself warned against the creation of "factions" in American politics that cause "jealousies and false alarms" because of the damage they could cause to the body politic. Thomas Jefferson echoed this warning, yet he would come to lead a party himself.

Americans had good reason to fear the emergence of political parties. They had witnessed how parties worked in Great Britain. Parties, called **factions** in Britain, were made up of people who schemed to win favors from the government. They were often more interested in their own personal profit and advantage than in the public good. Thus, the new American leaders were very interested in keeping factions from forming. It was, ironically, disagreements between two of Washington's chief advisors, Thomas Jefferson and Alexander Hamilton that spurred the formation of the first political parties in the newly formed United States of America.

Political parties have adopted different views throughout the history of the United States. Third parties have developed to promote certain issues. Although third parties have not usually maintained strong backing for long periods of times, they have been the cause of some of their ideas being infused into the two major political parties.

Interest Groups

A powerful source of political support is the **special interest group**. These groups, whose members want to effect political change—or make sure that such change does not take place—usually have a large number of dedicated individuals who do much more than vote: They organize themselves into political action committees, attend meetings and rallies, and work to make sure that their message gets out to a wide audience. Methods of spreading the word often include media advertising on behalf of the issue in question. Special interest groups also lobby political leaders by offering financial campaign support and the voting support of their members in exchange for a political leader's support for their particular issue.

Media

A free press is essential to maintaining responsibility and civic-mindedness in government and society. Broadcast, print, and electronic media in the United States serve as societal and governmental watchdogs.

First and foremost, the media report on the actions taken and encouraged by leaders of the government. In many cases, these actions are common knowledge. Policy debates, discussions on controversial issues, struggles against foreign powers in economic and wartime endeavors—all are topics of media reports. The First Amendment guarantees media in America the right to report on these issues, and the media reporters take full advantage of that right and privilege in striving not only to inform the American public but also to keep governmental leaders in check.

Public officials often hire public relations staff to manage their communications and public image. Public relations play an influential part in maintaining positive publicity for an official in order to gain and retain public support.

Traditional media outlets include newspapers, radio, and television. In recent years, the Internet and World Wide Web have introduced a wide range of new opportunities, including news websites as well as personal Websites and web logs, known as blogs.

William Randolph Hearst is known for his "yellow journalism." Edward W. Scripps set up the first chain of newspapers in the United States called the Scripps-McRae League and later set up the Scripps-Howard chain. Joseph Pulitzer established the *New York World* and *Evening World*, the first newspapers to include such modern features as comics, puzzles, columnists, illustrations, and sports.

SKILL 18.2   Demonstrate knowledge of processes for filling elective and appointive public offices.

Elective Offices

The process of filling an elective office usually involves a candidate making an official "filing." A filing is simply signing up for the office and completing the prescribed requirements. The purpose of filing is to be sure the candidate meets the requirements to be placed on a ballot. For example, if a primary election is held where candidates must designate their political party, then this is a requirement that must be met to be placed on the ballot. Deadlines for filing must be complied with. Campaigning follows the filing, and then voting takes place. Once a candidate wins an election, he or she is sworn into office.

Appointive Offices

Appointments are made by the president, governor, or head of city government. Appointees must go through a selection process. At the federal level, the Senate confirms the appointments. State and local governments have similar processes. The confirmation process may include hearings, such as when a federal judge is appointed by the president. Once the confirmation process is complete and the appointment has been confirmed, the person who has been appointed takes an oath of office.

SKILL 18.3   **Demonstrate knowledge of processes for making policy in the United States, the impact of technology on the political process, and ways in which different points of view influence decision making and the development of public policy at the local, state, and national levels.**

The Process of Policy Making

Policy making requires **interaction**. Public policies are based on law and deal with a problem or issue facing the country. The first step in policy making is to **recognize the problem**. If an area of the country suffers harm from extensive and severe tornadoes, for example, the government may decide it needs to help the victims to restore their communities. Once the problem is identified, then agencies, interest groups, administrators, and others must **decide the priorities** involved. If the policy is being made at the federal level, then the president may appoint task forces or research organizations to **formulate a policy**.

Government agencies and the legislature are often involved in policy-making decisions. Once the policy is formulated, it must be **adopted**. Perhaps the legislature or the president is the final authority. If funding is required for disaster relief, then Congress will pass legislation and the president will sign the bill or veto it.

Once the policy has been adopted, it can be **implemented**. Usually, at the federal level, administrative agencies implement the policy. For example, the Federal Emergency Management Agency (FEMA) is in charge of disaster relief. **Evaluating the policy** is the final step in policy making. The evaluation process covers the steps of policy making to determine whether the policy was beneficial, whether changes are needed, and whether it should be continued. Policies are made in similar ways at each level of government.

The Impact of Technology on the Political Process

The growth of technology has had a significant impact on the political process. Political candidates use technology in many ways.

Raising funds for campaigning is an important factor for all political candidates. The Internet, podcasts, Twitter, Facebook, and YouTube are powerful communication media platforms that can easily raise the ratings of political candidates with minimal costs. Through technology, politicians are able to access funds, impress political pundits, and spend less time and money on campaigning.

Technology also is a powerful influence for specific demographics. A proper presentation will gain ratings for candidates. Young, educated, and affluent voters will relate more to technological innovations than will older voters. Politicians and their campaign staffs use this differentiation to gain advantage in their political bids, utilizing technology to attract the youth while calling upon traditional methods to target older voters.

SKILL 18.4 **Understand rights guaranteed by the U.S. Constitution including each amendment in the Bill of Rights (e.g., due process, equal protection), and their role in protecting individual liberties.**

The **Bill of Rights** includes the first ten amendments to the United States Constitution. The first ten amendments were added after the ratification of the Constitution to provide for individual liberties. They address civil liberties and civil rights.

1. Freedom of speech, press, right to assembly, religion, separation of church and state, freedom
2. Right to bear arms
3. Security from the quartering of troops in homes
4. Freedom from unreasonable search and seizures
5. Right against self-incrimination, due process of law
6. Right to trial by jury, right to legal counsel
7. Right to jury trial for civil actions
8. Cruel or unusual punishment prohibited
9. These rights shall not deny other rights the people enjoy.
10. Powers not mentioned in the Constitution shall be retained by the states or the people.

The First Amendment

Freedom of Religion

Religious freedom has not been seriously threatened in the United States. The policy of the government has been guided by the premise that church and state should be separate. However, when religious practices have been at cross-purposes with attitudes prevailing in the nation at particular times, there have been restrictions placed on these practices. For example, there have been restrictions against the practice of polygamy that is supported by certain religious groups.

The idea of animal sacrifice that is promoted by some religious beliefs is generally prohibited. The use of mind-altering illegal substances that some groups use in religious rituals has been restricted. In the United States, all recognized religious institutions are tax-exempt in accordance with the idea of separation of church and state. All of these issues continue to occupy both political and legal considerations for some time to come.

Freedom of Speech, Press, and Assembly

Freedom of speech, press, and assembly historically have been given wide latitude in their practice, though there have been instances when they have been limited for various reasons. The classic limitation, for instance, in regards to freedom of speech, has been the precept that an individual is prohibited from yelling "Fire!" in a crowded theater. This prohibition is an example of the state saying that freedom of speech does not extend to speech that might endanger other people. There is also a prohibition against **slander,** or knowingly stating a deliberate falsehood against someone.

There are many regulations regarding freedom of the press. The most common examples are the various laws against **libel,** or the printing of a known falsehood. In times of national emergency, various restrictions have been placed on the rights of press, speech, and sometimes assembly.

Due Process

The **Fifth Amendment** provides for due process. Due process as pronounced in this amendment refers to due process at the federal level. The amendment states that people are entitled to due process but the amendment does not specify what due process is. The **Fourteenth Amendment** incorporated due process into the protections that state government must provide. Therefore, the due process of the Fifth Amendment is applicable to the states through the Fourteenth Amendment.

Equal Protection

The Fourteenth Amendment provides that people shall have equal protection under the law. The Fourteenth Amendment was added to the Constitution as one of the Civil War Amendments that was designed to give freed slaves liberties. Equal protection applies to cases involving issues of race, gender, religion, and national origin.

For more information on specific amendments, see Skill 17.7.

SKILL 18.5   **Demonstrate knowledge of efforts to expand the democratic process in the United States and understand the contributions of significant political and social leaders (e.g., George Washington, John Marshall, Frederick Douglass, Elizabeth Cady Stanton, Franklin D. Roosevelt, Martin Luther King, Jr.).**

The contributions of these significant political and social leaders have been discussed in other parts of this guide. The following paragraphs present highlights of the more detailed information presented earlier.

George Washington was commander in chief of the Continental army and became this country's first president. He shared the views of the Federalists, but he did not belong to the Federalist Party. During his tenure, the focus of the newly established country was to gain the respect of foreign nations and to avoid entanglements that could jeopardize the future of the new country.

John Marshall was the first Chief Justice of the United States Supreme Court. He wrote the opinion in *Marbury* v. *Madison* that established the doctrine of judicial review.

Frederick Douglass was a former slave and an abolitionist. He became a free man after supporters purchased his freedom. He published an autobiography and, after his freedom, published *The North Star*, a publication supporting the abolition movement.

Elizabeth Cady Stanton was an abolitionist and an activist for women's rights. She was one of the organizers of the Seneca Falls Convention in 1848. She and others, such as Susan B. Anthony, worked for women's suffrage.

Franklin D. Roosevelt became president during the Great Depression. His "New Deal" was a program that guided the United States out of the Depression and to a better economy. He was president during World War II but died before the war ended.

Martin Luther King, Jr. was an activist in the civil rights movement. He believed in peaceful resistance and nonviolence. He is remembered for, among other things, his "I Have a Dream" speech. He was awarded a Nobel Peace Prize before his death.

SKILL 18.6   **Demonstrate knowledge of the causes and effects of major reform movements in U.S. history (e.g., abolitionist movement, public education, temperance, women's rights, prison reform, civil rights movement).**

Abolitionist Movement

Perhaps the most intense and controversial movement was the abolitionists' efforts to end slavery. The abolitionist effort generally pitted Northern views against Southern views on the correctness of slavery. The slavery issue alienated and split the country, hardening Southern defense of slavery and contributing to four years of war. The movement had political fallout as well, affecting admittance of states into the Union and the government's continued efforts to keep a balance between total numbers of free and slave states. Congressional legislation after 1820, such as the Compromise of 1850 reflected this. "Bleeding Kansas" and John Brown's raid on a federal arsenal were also effects of the slavery issue and abolition movement.

Public Education

As the United States began expanding into the Northwest Territory, Congress realized the importance of education and identified a section of land in each township in the new territory that should be set aside for public schooling. Later, Congress set aside money for the establishment of colleges that would teach agriculture and related subjects. These schools were called land grant colleges and were the result of the Morrill Act.

Temperance

The temperance movement began to curb the abuses of drinking and drunkenness. Groups such as the Women's Christian Temperance Union were formed to sway public opinion and gain support for the evils of alcohol and the benefits of abstinence. In the late 1800s, the movement became more radical. Cary Nation was one of the leaders of this movement and she was known to attack bars with a hatchet. Partly as a result of the movement, Congress passed, and the states ratified the Eighteenth Amendment which was known as the Prohibition amendment. This amendment to the U.S Constitution prohibited the sale, manufacture, and importation of alcoholic beverages.

Women's Rights

The women's rights movement was a worldwide movement. It began in 1848 with the Seneca Fall Convention that was organized by Elizabeth Cady Stanton and others. The movement gained momentum in the United States largely through the efforts of Stanton and Susan B. Anthony and resulted in the passage of the Nineteenth Amendment in 1920, giving women the right to vote. Women's rights have made some progress since that time in areas of equality of pay, equality of education, and equality in the workplace. A related Equal Rights Amendment was passed by Congress but was not ratified within the permitted time.

Prison Reform

Overcrowded conditions, unsanitary conditions, and treatment of prisons caused Dorthea Dix to begin visiting prisons to determine whether the prisons should be reformed. Her efforts began in the early 1840s and drew the attention of other reformers. Her primary focus became the mentally ill and how they were treated. She gathered information and made the Massachusetts legislature aware of the horrible conditions. As the result of her efforts, public asylums were created for the mentally ill and debtors were no longer put into prison. The movement became a worldwide movement and the idea of rehabilitation was one of the results.

Civil Rights Movement

The civil rights movement gained momentum in the 1950s and 1960s. *Brown* v. *Board of Education* (1954) was an impetus for the movement. *Brown* involved a young African American student who lived in Topeka, Kansas, and wanted to attend a neighborhood school. The U.S. Supreme Court decided that separate schools were not equal. *Brown* signaled the beginning of desegregation of schools. The resistance and problems related from attempts to integrate propelled the civil rights movement. Demonstrations, freedom rides, marches, and sit-ins characterized types of activities that took place. The efforts resulted in the Civil Rights Act of 1964 which prohibited discrimination based on race.

SKILL 18.7   **Understand civic responsibilities (e.g., jury duty), the difference between personal and civic responsibilities, and the importance of voluntary individual participation in the U.S. political process.**

Citizenship in a democracy bestows on an individual certain rights, foremost being the right to participate in one's own government. Along with these rights come responsibilities, including the responsibility of a citizen to participate.

The most basic form of participation is the vote. Those who have reached the age of eighteen in the United States are eligible to vote in public elections. With this right comes the responsibility to be informed before voting, and not to sell or otherwise give away one's vote. Citizens are also eligible to run for public office. Along with the right to run for office comes the responsibility to represent the voters as fairly as possible and to perform the duties expected of a government representative.

Citizens should take responsibility to become informed of the issues and cast their votes as the result of information and a reasoned belief that their decision is best. Being informed of how one's government works and what the effects of new legislation is an essential part of being a good citizen.

In the United States, citizens are guaranteed the right to free speech: the right to express an opinion on public issues. In turn, citizens have the responsibility to allow others to speak freely. At the community level, this might mean speaking at a city council hearing while allowing others with different or opposing viewpoints to have their say without interruption or comment.

A good citizen also participates in the government by **serving on a jury** when called to do so. The U.S. Constitution provides that a defendant shall have a speedy public trial and a trial by jury. A jury is selected at random from various segments of society. The rule of law is an important part of democratic countries. By participating as a jury member, a citizen is helping to continue to permit the rule of law to exist and to provide the defendant in a criminal matter or both parties in a civil matter the rights to which they are entitled by law.

Almost all representative democracies in the world guarantee rights to their citizens and expect citizens to accept responsibilities as a member of that democracy. Rights and liberties can only continue if people take an active role in their government, render informed decisions, and participate in the judicial process.

COMPETENCY 19: TYPES OF POLITICAL SYSTEMS

THE TEACHER UNDERSTANDS THE DEVELOPMENT OF POLITICAL SYSTEMS AND THE SIMILARITIES AND DIFFERENCES AMONG MAJOR HISTORICAL AND CONTEMPORARY FORMS OF GOVERNMENT.

SKILL 19.1 **Understand major political ideas in history (e.g., the laws of nature and nature's God, divine right of monarchs, social contract theory, the rights of resistance to illegitimate governments) and analyze the historical development of significant legal and political concepts.**

Many of the significant legal and political concepts in American government came from earlier concepts that were expressed during periods such as the Enlightenment. **The laws of nature and nature's God** was a phrase that was used in the Declaration of Independence. The document states that it becomes necessary to dissolve the political bands and to be separate and have "equal station to which the Laws of Nature and of Nature's God entitle them" as a justification or reason why the colonists are stating they are independent.

The **divine right of monarchs** or divine theory of government was the expression of belief that rulers were appointed by God and, therefore, the people could not remove the ruler. The rulers of England and France propounded these theories in the 1600s and 1700s.

The **social contract theory** was the basis of the Mayflower Compact in which the Pilgrims pledged themselves to forming a government in the new world.

The rights of **resistance to illegitimate governments** developed from essays written by John Locke in the 1600s about his political philosophy. Locke expresses the view that people form governments for certain reasons and that when a ruler exhibits arbitrary power, then it is appropriate to resist because it is better for the public good. This idea is also expressed in the Declaration of Independence when the document identifies the king's unlawful acts and why resistance is necessary.

The philosophies expressed during the Enlightenment are extensions of earlier theories and present the idea that government is a social contract, that people have the right to alter governments and adopt new governments based on these principles. Many of these philosophies were adopted by the Founding Fathers when they wrote the Declaration of Independence and framed the new government by writing the Constitution.

SKILL 19.2   **Demonstrate knowledge of significant political documents in world history (e.g., Hammurabi's Code of Laws, Justinian's Code of Laws, Magna Carta, John Locke, Thomas Hobbes) and their impact on the development of political thought.**

Hammurabi's Code of Laws

The Babylonians of ancient Mesopotamia flourished for a time under their great contribution of organized law and code, called **Hammurabi's Code**. The code was name after the ruler Hammurabi and has been considered to be among the most important contributions of the Mesopotamian civilization.

Justinian's Code of Laws

The Byzantine emperor Justinian ruled in the 500s. The code of law is a reference work that contains a collection of laws and their interpretations. The laws include Roman laws and Byzantine laws. Laws had not been written down until this time. The Justinian Code has been used as a basis for laws in many countries.

Magna Carta

The charter known as Magna Carta (sometimes spelled Magna Charta) has been considered the basis of English constitutional liberties. It was granted to a representative group of English barons and nobles on 1215 by the British King John, after they had forced it on him. The English barons and nobles sought to limit what they had come to perceive as the overwhelming power of the monarchy in public affairs.

The Magna Carta is considered to be the first modern document that sought to try to limit the powers of the given state authority. It guaranteed feudal rights, regulated the justice system, and abolished many abuses of the king's power to tax and regulate trade. It said that the king could not raise new taxes without first consulting a Great Council that was made up of nobles, barons, and church people. Significantly, the Magna Carta only dealt with the rights of the upper classes and the nobility and all of its provisions excluded the rights of the common people. However, gradually the rights won by the nobles were given to other English people.

John Locke

John Locke, an English philosopher, was an important thinker on the nature of democracy during the mid- and late-1600s. He regarded the mind at birth as a *tabula rasa*, a blank slate upon which experience imprints knowledge and behavior. He did not believe in the idea of intuition or theories of innate knowledge. Locke also believed that all men are born good, independent, and equal. According to Locke, it is peoples' actions that will determine their fate. Locke's views, in his most important work, *Two Treatises of Government* (1690), attacked the theory of the divine right of kings and the nature of the state as conceived by Thomas Hobbes.

Locke argued that sovereignty did not reside in the state but with the people. He believed the state is supreme, but only if it is bound by civil and what he called **natural law.** Many of Locke's political ideas, such as those relating to natural rights, property rights, the duty of the government to protect these rights, and the rule of the majority were embodied in the Constitution of the United States. He further held that revolution was not only a right but also often an obligation, and Locke advocated a system of checks and balances in government, a government comprised of three branches—of which the legislative is more powerful than either the executive or the judicial. He also believed in the separation of the church and state. All of these ideas were to be incorporated in the Constitution of the United States. As such, Locke is considered in many ways the true founding father of our Constitution and government system. He remains one of history's most influential political thinkers to this day.

Thomas Hobbes

Thomas Hobbes, a slightly earlier English philosopher, was the author of *Leviathan.* He wrote this book in 1651 as a reaction to the disorders caused by the English civil wars that had culminated in the execution of King Charles I. The book was an early example of **social contract theory.**

Hobbes perceived people as rational beings, but unlike Locke, he had no faith in their abilities to live in harmony with one another without a government. The trouble was, as Hobbes saw it, people were selfish and the strong would take from the weak. However, the weak being rational would, in turn, band together against the strong. For Hobbes, the state of nature became a chaotic state in which every person would become the enemy of every other and became a war of all against all, with terrible consequences for all.

SKILL 19.3   **Analyze how governments have affected and reflected cultural values and provided for social control.**

A society's governmental institutions often embody its beliefs and values. **Laws,** for instance, reflect a society's values by enforcing its ideas of right and wrong. Laws are formal adoptions of norms by a society with formal punishment for their violation. Laws are usually based on the mores of a society. The moral that it is wrong to kill is codified in a law against murder, for example. Laws provide for social control by setting a standard for behavior and establishing punishment for deviating from that standard.

The structure of a society's **government** can reflect a society's ideals about the role of an individual in society. A democracy may emphasize that an individual's rights are more important than the needs of the larger society, whereas a socialist governmental institution may place the needs of the whole group first in importance.

These values are often reinforced in a culture's **educational institutions,** which are frequently established, funded, and regulated by its government. Education allows for the formal passing on of a culture's collected knowledge and also provides a common background for the members of a culture that contributes to social control.

In the case of the United States, many of the **core values** in the U.S. democratic system are reflected in the official structure and formation of the government. An example is found in the opening words of the Declaration of Independence, stating the belief in equality and the rights of citizens to "life, liberty and the pursuit of happiness."

The Declaration of Independence was a condemnation of the British king's tyrannical government, and these words emphasized the American colonists' belief that a government received its authority to rule from the people and that its function should not be to suppress the governed but to protect the rights of the governed, including protection from the government itself. These two ideals, **popular sovereignty** and the **rule of law,** are basic core values.

Central to the ideal of justice is an expectation that citizens will act in ways that promote the common good, that they will treat one another with honesty and respect, and will exercise self-discipline in their interactions with others. These are among the basic responsibilities of a citizen of a democracy.

SKILL 19.4   **Understand similarities and differences between the U.S. system of government and other political systems.**

The similarities and differences between the governments system of different nations can be understood by a review of the various political systems.

The **parliamentary system** of government has a legislature that usually includes a multiplicity of political parties and, often, coalition politics. There is division between the head of state and head of government. Head of government is usually known as a prime minister who is also usually the head of the largest party. The head of government and cabinet usually both participate and vote in the parliament. The head of state is most often an elected president, although in the case of a constitutional monarchy such as Great Britain, the sovereign may take the place of a president as head of state. A government may fall when a majority in parliament votes "no confidence" in the government.

Anarchism is a political movement that promotes the idea of elimination of all government and its replacement by a cooperative community of individuals. Sometimes it has involved political violence in its rule, such as when assassinations of important political or governmental figures take place. The historical banner of the movement is a black flag.

Communism is a belief as well as a political system. It is characterized by the ideology of class conflict and revolution, a one party state, strict police apparatus, and government ownership of the means of production and distribution of goods and services. It is a revolutionary ideology preaching the eventual overthrow of all other political orders and the establishment of one world with communist government. The historical banner of the communist movement is a red flag, and the flag has a variation of stars, hammer, and sickle, representing the various types of workers.

A **dictatorship** is the rule by an individual or small group of individuals that centralizes all political control in itself and often enforces its will with an aggressive police force.

Fascism is a belief as well as a political system, opposed ideologically to communism, although similar in basic structure. Characteristics of fascism include a one-party state, centralized political control, and a strict police system. Fascism tolerates private ownership of the means of production, though it maintains tight overall control. Central to fascist belief is the idolization of the leader and often an expansionist ideology. Examples are German Nazism and Italian Fascism.

The rule of a nation by a monarch is a **monarchy.** The nonelected, usually hereditary, leader is most often a king or queen. A monarchy may or may not be accompanied by some measure of democracy, open institutions, and elections at various levels. A modern example is Great Britain, which is a constitutional monarchy.

Socialism is a political belief and system in which the state takes a guiding role in the national economy and provides extensive social services to its population. It may or may not own outright means of production, but even where it does not, it exercises tight control. Socialism often promotes democracy. This is called democratic socialism. However, heavy state involvement produces excessive bureaucracy and, frequently, inefficiency. Taken to an extreme, socialism may lead to communism as government control increases and democratic practice decreases. Ideologically, the two movements of socialism and communism are very similar in both belief and practice.

Constitutionalism is a political system in which laws and traditions put limits on the powers of government.

Federalism is the idea of a strong, centralized national government to hold together the nation of states with each having powers.

SKILL 19.5   **Demonstrate knowledge of major forms of government in history (e.g., monarchy, authoritarian government, classical republic, liberal democracy, totalitarian government) and of the historical antecedents of major political systems.**

Historical Antecedents of Major Political Systems

In ancient times, early people developed primitive weapons and tools but were nomadic and mostly banded together in primitive hunting groups or "clans" in order to maximize their effectiveness in the hunt.

With the invention of the plow, farming was easier and people began to be able to remain in one place for a long time. Increases in farming production supplied sufficient food to enable the first large organized **city-states** to emerge. This occurred on a large scale first in the ancient

Mesopotamian region near the Tigris and Euphrates rivers in what is now modern Iraq. The first large, organized city-states were those in the land known as Sumer or Sumeria, later known as Babylonia.

Early primitive city-states began to unite and form bigger unions for greater protection and power, with each emerging new "nation" or "state" claiming control over a specific area of land and willing to fight for it. Thus, with the emergence of the first large nations, the first large organized armies also came into being and regular warfare emerged as a universal and historical fact of human existence. By the classical period of ancient history, the city-state had emerged as the dominant political form. City-states united at times into larger entities for greater protection against outside enemies. One example is the **Delian League** of ancient Greece, a union of several Greek city-states united against the power of ancient Persia.

With the division and collapse of the Roman Empire in the fourth century, the growth of large political entities in Europe was temporarily halted. Only very small units of political power survived the interim period of chaos and confusion after the break-up of the empire. The Germanic tribes that had originally fought the Romans now came to occupy the lands the Romans formerly controlled. Where the tribes had established themselves on the land, they became "united" out of sheer necessity against competing tribes. This in many cases extended little farther than appeals to a common kinship, language, and customs. In one sense, this was a burgeoning nationalism and it began to be expressed in the various interrelationships among them.

During the Middle Ages **feudalism** was the dominant form of political organization in Europe. Feudalism was the organization of people based on the ownership of land by a lord or other noble who allowed individuals known as peasants or serfs to farm the land and to keep a portion of it. The lord or noble, in return for the serfs' loyalty, offered them his protection. In practical effect, the serf was considered owned by his lord with little or no rights at all. The lord's sole obligation to the serfs was to protect them so they could continue to work for him. This system would last for many centuries. In Russia it lasted until the 1860s.

The final emergence of the **nation-state** is attributed to two principal causes. One major factor was the underlying fact of economic expansion that took place in the feudal system. This was mainly the result of a great expansion in trade and manufacturing which the creation of the Holy Roman Empire had helped to facilitate.

The feudal system had been dependent on small, isolated, units and these were unable to cope with the great trade expansion that was occurring. This gave rise to the system known as **mercantilism**, a system in which governments started to take an interest in the growing merchant trade and used their power in order to facilitate it. This led to groups of powerful merchants.

The various and independent feudal manors began to break up, leading to the growth of cities, expanded trade, and the growth of markets up through the period that came to be known as the Renaissance. At the same time, in the 1500s, the Protestant Reformation was beginning and eventually would lead to the waning influence of the massive power and control of Catholic church and allow the growth of various independent and powerful lords.

Major Forms of Government in History

The most familiar form of government throughout the history is the **monarchy**. We can include dictatorships or **totalitarian** and **authoritarian governments** in this description because the basic idea—that one person was in charge of the government—applies to all. In this kind of government, the head of state was responsible for governing his or her subjects. In earlier times, this meant laws that weren't exactly written down. However, with the passage of time written laws have increasingly become the standard.

Monarchies and one-person governments still exist today although they are rare. In these states, the emphasis is on keeping the monarch in power, and many laws are written with that purpose in mind. Authoritarian governments still exist today, and in this form of government, all the members of the government belong to one political party. Not all members of the government believe the same on small issues, but significant issues require party unity. Organization of alternative political parties is widely and strongly discouraged.

SKILL 19.6   **Analyze the process by which democratic-republican government evolved (e.g., beginnings in classical Greece and Rome, developments in England, impact of the Enlightenment).**

Classical Rome and Greece laid the foundations for our democracy. Direct participation in government and the indirect elections of representatives are examples that have been used in our government today.

During the **Enlightenment,** the idea of the **"social contract"** confirmed the belief that government existed because people wanted it to and that the people had an agreement with the government that they would submit to it as long as the government protected them and did not encroach on their basic human rights. This idea was first made famous by the Frenchman **Jean-Jacques Rousseau** but was also adopted by England's **Thomas Hobbes** and **John Locke** and America's **Thomas Jefferson.**

Jean-Jacques Rousseau lived in the 1700s and was one of the most influential political theorists before the French Revolution. His most important and most studied work is *The Social Contract.* He was concerned with what should be the proper form of society and government. However, unlike Hobbes, Rousseau did not view the state of nature as one of absolute chaos.

The problem, as Rousseau saw it, was that the natural harmony of the state of nature was due to people's intuitive goodness and not to their actual reason. Reason only developed once a civilized society was established. The intuitive goodness was easily overwhelmed, however, by arguments for institutions of social control, which likened rulers to father figures and extolled the virtues of obedience to such figures. To a remarkable extent, strong leaders have, in Rousseau's judgment, already succeeded not only in extracting obedience from the citizens that they ruled, but also more importantly, having managed to justify such obedience as necessary.

Rousseau's most direct influence was upon the **French Revolution** of 1789. In the *Declaration of the Rights of Man and of the Citizen*, he explicitly recognizes the sovereignty of the general will as expressed in the law. In contrast to the American **Declaration of Independence**, it contains explicit mention of the obligations and duties of the citizen, such as assenting to taxes in support of the military or police forces for the common good. In modern times, ideas such as Rousseau's have often been used to justify the ideas of authoritarian and totalitarian systems. During America's colonial era, Rousseau and other philosophers of the Enlightenment influenced the path American's took toward independence and the formulation of a new government under the Constitution.

DOMAIN VI   ECONOMICS AND SCIENCE, TECHNOLOGY AND SOCIETY

COMPETENCY 20: ECONOMIC CONCEPTS AND TYPES OF ECONOMIC SYSTEMS

THE TEACHER UNDERSTANDS BASIC ECONOMIC CONCEPTS, MAJOR DEVELOPMENTS IN ECONOMIC THOUGHT, AND VARIOUS TYPES OF ECONOMIC SYSTEMS.

SKILL 20.1   **Demonstrate knowledge of the concepts of scarcity and opportunity costs and their significance.**

Scarcity

The scarcity of resources is the basis for the study of economics. Some define **economics** as a study of how scarce resources are allocated to satisfy unlimited wants. Others define it as the production, distribution, and consumption of goods and services.

Production is creating a commodity suitable for exchange. **Resources** refer to the four factors of production—labor, capital, land, and entrepreneurship. **Labor** refers to the production process and to anyone who sells his or her ability to produce goods and services. **Capital** is the wealth that can be used to generate productivity or income. **Land** refers to the land itself and everything occurring naturally on it, such as oil, minerals, and lumber. **Entrepreneurship** is the ability of an individual to combine the three inputs with his or her own talents to produce a viable good or service. The entrepreneur takes the risk and experiences the losses or profits.

It is assumed that supply of these resources is finite. That means that society cannot have as much of everything that it wants and that there is a constraint on production and consumption and on the kinds of goods and services that can be produced and consumed. Scarcity means that choices have to be made. If society decides to produce more of one good, this means that there are fewer resources available for the production of other goods.

Opportunity Costs

Assume a society can produce two goods—good X and good Y. The society uses resources in the production of each good. If producing one unit of good X results in an amount of resources used to produce three units of good Y then producing one more unit of good X results in a decrease in three units of good Y. In effect, one unit of good X "costs" three units of good Y. This cost is referred to as **opportunity cost.**

Opportunity cost is the value of the sacrificed alternative, the value of what had to be given up in order to have the output of good X. Opportunity cost does not just refer to production. Your opportunity cost of studying with this guide is the value of what you are not doing because you are studying, whether it is watching TV, spending time with family, working, or whatever. Every choice has an opportunity cost. In other words, opportunity cost is the value of the next best purpose the asset could have been used for.

If wants were limited or if resources were unlimited, then the concepts of choice and opportunity cost would not exist, and neither would the field of economics. There would be enough resources to satisfy the wants of consumers, businesses and governments, and the allocation of resources would not be a problem. Society could have more of both good X and good Y without having to give up anything. There would be no opportunity cost. But this is not the situation that societies are faced with.

It is assumed that because resources are scarce, society does not want to waste them. Society wants to obtain the most satisfaction it can from the consumption of the goods and services produced with its scarce resources. The members of the society do not want their scarce resources wasted through inefficiency. This means producers must choose an efficient production process, which is the lowest cost means of production.

High costs may mean wasted resources. Consumers do not want society's resources wasted by producing goods that they do not want. How do producers know what goods consumers want? Consumers buy the goods they want and vote with their dollar spending. A desirable good, one that consumers want, earns profits. A good that incurs losses is a good that society does not want its resources wasted on. This signals the producer that society wants its resources used in another way.

Arbitrage is an item or service that an industry produces. The dictionary definition of *arbitrage* is the purchase of securities on one market for immediate resale on another market in order to profit from a price discrepancy.

SKILL 20.2   Understand the circular-flow model of the economy.

The circular-flow diagram is the simplest model of the economy that there is. It shows the flow of inputs, outputs, and money through the economy. Households, businesses, and government are related through the circular-flow diagram. They are all integral parts of the macro economy. There are two markets. The **input market** is where factor owners sell their factors and employers hire their inputs. The **output market** is where firms sell the output they produce with their inputs. It's where factor owners spend their incomes on goods and services.

There are two factor sectors, households and businesses. Households sell their factors in the input market and use their income to purchase goods and services in the output market. So wages, interest, rents, and profit flow from the business sector to the household sector. Households that earn their factor incomes in the factor market spend their incomes on goods and services produced by businesses and sold in the output market. Receipts for goods and services flow from households to businesses.

Government receives tax payments from households and businesses and provides services to businesses and households. Each of the three is a component of the aggregate sectors of the economy and as such makes a contribution to the Gross Domestic Product (GDP).

SKILL 20.3   **Analyze interactions among supply, demand, and price and factors that cause changes in supply, demand, and price, and interpret supply-and-demand graphs.**

Interactions among Supply, Demand, and Price

In a market economy the markets function on the basis of **supply and demand** and, if markets are free, the result is efficient allocation of resources. The seller's supply curve represents the different quantities of a good or service the seller is willing and able to bring to the market at different **prices** during a given period of time. The seller has to have the good and be willing to sell it. If either of these is not true, then the seller is not a part of the relevant market supply.

The **supply graph,** or supply curve, represents the selling and production decisions of the seller and is based on the costs of production. The **costs of production** of a product are based on costs of the resources used in its production. The **costs of resources** are based on the scarcity of the resource. The scarcer a resource is, relatively speaking, the higher its price. A diamond costs more than paper because diamonds are scarcer than paper is. All of these concepts are embodied in the seller's supply curve.

The same thing is true on the buying side of the market. The buyer's preferences, tastes, income—all of his or her buying decisions—are embodied in the **demand graph,** or demand curve. The demand curve represents the various quantities of a good or a service the buyer is willing and able to buy at different prices during a given period of time. The buyer has to want the good and be willing and able to purchase it. The buyer who wants a Ferrari but cannot afford one is not a part of the relevant market demand.

The demand side of the market shows what buyers are willing and able to purchase, and the supply side of the market shows what sellers are willing and able to supply. But we do not know anything about what buyers and sellers actually do buy and sell without putting the two sides together. If we compare the buying decisions of buyers with the selling decisions of sellers, the place where they coincide represents the **market equilibrium.**

This is where the **demand and supply curves** intersect. At this one point of intersection, the buying decisions of buyers are equal to the selling decisions of sellers. The quantity that buyers want to buy at that particular price is equal to the quantity that sellers want to sell at that particular price. This is the market equilibrium. At this one point, the quantity demanded is equal to the quantity supplied. This price—**quantity combination**—represents an efficient allocation of resources.

How Supply, Demand, and Price Can Change

Consumers are basically voting for the goods and services that they want with their dollar spending. When a good accumulates enough dollar votes, the producer earns a profit. The existence of profits is the way the market signals the seller that he or she is using society's resources in a way that society wants them used. Consumers are obtaining the most satisfaction that they can from the way their society's scarce resources are being used.

When consumers do not want a good or service, they do not purchase it, and the producers do not accumulate enough dollar votes to have profits. Losses are the market's way of signaling that consumers do not want their scarce resources used in the production of that particular good or service. They want their resources used in some other manner. Firms that incur losses eventually go out of business. They either have a product that consumers do not want or they have an inefficient production process that results in higher costs, and therefore higher prices. Having higher costs than the competitors' costs means that there is inefficiency in production. All of this occurs naturally in markets in a market economy.

SKILL 20.4   **Demonstrate knowledge of the historical origins of contemporary economic systems (e.g., capitalism, socialism, communism), including the influence of various economic philosophers such as John Maynard Keynes, Karl Marx, and Adam Smith.**

Contemporary Economic Systems

Capitalism

In a system of capitalism, private individuals control commerce and the means of production. Markets are competitive, and people are involved in trade to accumulate capital. When goods and services are exchanged, the individuals who are part of the business transaction determine the prices.

There are different types of capitalism, and the degree of government intervention varies in each type. Some countries that have a capitalist system have a mixed economy—an economy that is market-driven but also is planned. (See Skill 20.5 for more information on mixed economies.)

Laissez-faire economics, or **pure capitalism,** is based on free markets without government interference in the marketplace. The role for government was to establish the framework for the functioning of the economy, determining things like standards of weights and measures and providing public goods.

Socialism

There are various theories of socialism, but generally it means a collective ownership and administration of the production and distribution of goods.

Communism

The economic doctrine of communism involves government ownership and control of the major means of production. Usually, the government control of natural resources is also present in a communistic economy.

Economic Theorists

John Maynard Keynes

The theories of John Maynard Keynes form the basis theories for modern **macroeconomics**. Keynesian theory is **demand-side** theory. Keynes felt that the level of aggregate spending determines the level of economic activity in an economy. If there is excess aggregate demand, or spending, then the economy cannot produce enough output to satisfy that demand, and the result is rising prices or inflation.

According to Keynes, the way to cure the inflation is for government to implement **contractionary** fiscal policy—raising taxes or lowering government spending—to slow down an economy that is expanding too quickly. Keynes believed that if there is a deficiency in aggregate demand, then there is not enough spending in the economy to cause suppliers to produce enough output to employ the labor force. The Keynesian solution is to stimulate the economy with expansionary fiscal policy, to lower taxes and/or increase spending. In the Keynesian framework, government policy action is required to rid the economy of inflation and unemployment because the economy will not self-correct.

Karl Marx

Karl Marx viewed economics in a different perspective. He felt that labor was the value-determining factor. Since it was labor that gave a commodity value, labor was entitled to the value of what it produced, or the surplus. The capitalist did not do anything to earn the surplus, Marx believed. The capitalist appropriated it from labor and, therefore, exploited labor. This is the basis for Marxist economics. Marx went on to apply the doctrine of historical necessity and the **Hegelian triad** to history and predicted a revolution based on the exploitation of labor. Marxist theories were the basis for the former Soviet and Eastern-bloc economies. He believed there should be a central banking system; that government own and control labor, transportation, and factors; and that private property should be eliminated.

Adam Smith

Adam Smith, the author of *The Wealth of Nations,* believed that free markets should exist without government interference because that would interfere with the rights and liberties of the market participants even though laissez-faire economics results in an unequal distribution of income. According to Smith, the economy, if left alone, would function as if an invisible hand guided it to an efficient allocation of resources.

SKILL 20.5   Understand free enterprise, socialist, and communist economic systems in different places and eras.

The traditional economy is one based on custom. This term usually describes the situation that exists in many less developed countries. The people are not technologically advanced. Since their mindset is directed toward tradition, they are not interested in technology, equipment, or new ways of doing things. Technology and equipment are viewed as a threat to the old ways. There is little upward mobility for the same reason.

The model of capitalism is based on private ownership of the means of production and operates on the basis of **free markets,** on both the input and output sides. The free markets function to coordinate market activity and to achieve an efficient allocation of resources. Laissez-faire capitalism is based on the premise of no government intervention in the economy. The market will eliminate any unemployment or inflation that occurs. Government needs only to provide the framework for the functioning of the economy and to protect private property.

The role of **financial incentives** is crucial, for it results in risk taking and research and development. Capitalist economies tend to have democratic forms of government because the system is based on competition and individual freedoms.

Command Economies and Mixed Economies

A **command economy** is almost the exact opposite of a market economy. A command economy is based on government ownership of the means of production and the use of planning to take the place of the market. Instead of the market determining the output mix and the allocation of resources, the bureaucracy fulfills this role by determining the output mix and establishing production target for the enterprises, which are publicly owned. The result is inefficiency. There is little interest in innovation and research because there is no financial reward for the innovator. A command economy is often found in conjunction with an authoritarian form of government because a planning mechanism that replaces the market requires a planning authority to make decisions supplementing the freedom of choice of consumers and workers.

A **mixed economy** uses a combination of markets and planning, with the degree of each varying according to country. The real world can be described as mixed economies, each with varying degrees of planning. The use of markets results in the greatest efficiency since markets direct resources in and out of industries according to changing profit conditions. However, government is needed to perform various functions.

The degree of government involvement in the economy can vary in mixed economies. Government is needed to keep the economy stable during periods of inflation and unemployment.

All of the major economies of the world are mixed economies. They use markets but have different degrees of government involvement in the functioning of the markets and in the provision of public goods. For example, in some countries health care and education are provided by government and are not a part of the private sector.

Examples of Capitalist, Communist, and Socialist Economic Systems

In the United States, most health care and higher education is private and at the expense of the consumer. The United States is an example of a **capitalist** country and has had this type of economic system from the colonial days.

The Soviet **communist** economy began in the early 1900s and continued until late in the twentieth century when its inhabitants wanted free-market economies and democracies and caused the breakup of the Soviet government.

European countries such as Denmark have an economic system of **socialism.**

SKILL 20.6 Understand and compare types of market structures (e.g., pure competition, monopolistic competition, oligopoly, monopoly).

The fundamental characteristics of the U.S. economic system are the uses of competition and markets. Profit and competition go together in the U.S. economic system. Competition is determined by market structure. Since the cost curves are the same for all the firms, the only difference comes from the revenue side. The existence of economic profits, an above-normal rate of return, attracts capital to an industry and results in expansion. Whether or not new firms can enter depends on barriers to entry.

Pure Competition

The most competitive of all market structures is **perfect competition,** characterized by numerous buyers and sellers, all with perfect knowledge. It is also referred to as pure competition. No one seller is big enough to influence price, so the firm is a price taker. Products are homogenous so buyers are indifferent as to whom they buy from. The absence of barriers to entry makes it easy for firms to enter and leave the industry. Perfect competition exists where the products are so similar that consumers see little differences in them and a large number of buyers and sellers. Because these goods have little differences, they are called homogeneous goods. Homogeneous goods must compete by price and availability.

Monopolistic Competition

A monopolistic completion exists where there are many producers, with products that are different from one another in quality or because of brand. Clothing is an example of a good that is a rival in monopolistic competition. A consumer will find many types of shirts or slacks on the market. All of them are similar but different because of brand or price. They would not have identical substitutes but provide options for the consumer.

Oligopoly

An oligopoly is a market structure with a few large firms selling heterogeneous or homogeneous products in a market structure with the strength of barriers to entry varying. Each firm maximizes profit by producing at the point where marginal cost equals marginal revenue. Oligopolies reduce competition and their products bear higher price tags. When one member of an oligopoly follows a specific course or takes action, the other oligopolists are likely to respond in the same manner. Companies in the cellular phone market are examples of oligopolists.

Monopoly

A seller who is the only seller of a unique one-of-a-kind product has a monopoly. Barriers to entry are significant enough to keep firms from entering or leaving the industry. The significant barriers to entry in a monopoly serve to keep firms out so the monopolist continues to earn an above-normal rate of return.

SKILL 20.7 **Demonstrate knowledge of concepts and issues related to international trade (e.g., absolute and comparative advantage, effects of changes in the exchange rate of world currencies, free trade and the effects of trade barriers).**

Absolute and Comparative Advantage

Trade theory is based on prices and costs. A nation has an **absolute advantage** in the production of a good when it can produce that good more efficiently than the other nations can. It is **comparative advantage** that is the basis for international trade. Trade that takes place on the basis of comparative advantage results in lower output prices and higher resource prices.

According to trade theory, nations or regions should **specialize** in the production of the good that they can produce at a relatively lower cost than the other country can.

In other words, if in country A one unit of X costs one unit of Y, and in country B one unit of X costs three units of Y, good X is cheaper in country A and good Y is cheaper in country B. It takes only one-third of a unit of X to produce one unit of Y in country B, whereas it takes one unit of Y in country A. Therefore, country B has the comparative advantage in the production of Y, and country A has the comparative advantage in the production of good X. Trade theory says that each country should specialize in the production of the good in which it has the comparative advantage and trade for the other good. This means country B should use all of its resources to produce good Y and trade for good X.

Country A should do the opposite and specialize in the production of good X and trade for good Y. Specialization and trade on this basis results in lower prices in both countries or regions and greater efficiency in the use of resources. Each country will also experience increased consumption since it is getting the maximum amount of output from its given inputs by specializing according to comparative advantage. Each country or region can consume its own goods and the goods it has traded for.

Trade Barriers and Free Trade

The introduction of national or international competition into a market can result in greater efficiency if the trade is without restrictions, with tariffs or quotas. **Trade barriers** cause inefficiencies by resulting in higher prices and lower quantities.

A **tariff** is a tax that is added to the price of the import or export. The purpose is to raise the price of the import so people buy the domestic good. This leads to higher employment levels in the domestic industry and possible unemployment in the foreign industry. Resources have shifted due to the tariff. Tariffs are a way of exporting unemployment to a foreign country.

Import quotas are one method of trade restriction. The amount of goods imported is regulated in an effort to protect domestic enterprise and limit foreign competition. Both the United States and Japan, two of the world's most industrialized nations have import quotas to protect domestic industries.

Quotas are limits set on the physical number of units on imports or exports. An import quota limits the number of units entering a country and an export quota limits the number of units leaving the country. The result of limiting the quantity is to cause a higher price. Whether the trade barrier is a tariff or a quote, the result is to lower the volume of international trade. All of the benefits that were achieved with free trade are being lost. The results of trade barriers are lower levels of production, consumption, employment and income. However, under certain conditions, restrictions on trade can promote growth in a developing country.

Trade theory says that **free trade** is best. It results in the highest level of efficiency for the world and the greatest levels of output, production, consumption, income, and employment. Any form of interference with free trade, such as tariffs and quotas, deters from the highest level of efficiency. The world has less output from its available inputs. There are lower levels of income and employment. This is why there is a movement on for trade liberalization.

Changes in Exchange Rates of World Currencies

When nations trade, the traded goods and services must be paid for. This involves the use of foreign exchange. The **exchange rates** of most currencies today are determined in a **floating exchange rate** regime.

In a **clean float,** supply and demand factors for each currency in terms of another are what determine the equilibrium price or the exchange rate. A clean float is a market functioning without any government interference, purely on the basis of demand and supply.

Sometimes nations will intervene in the market to affect the value of their currency compared with the other currency. This situation is referred to as a **managed or dirty float.** A government is not required to intervene to maintain a currency value, as they are under a regime of fixed exchange rates. A government that intervenes in the currency market now does so because it wants to, not because it is required to intervene to maintain a certain exchange rate value. For example, if the U.S. government thinks the dollar is depreciating too much against the Canadian dollar, the U.S. government will buy U.S. dollars in the open market and pay for them with Canadian dollars. This increases the demand for U.S. dollars and increases the supply of Canadian dollars. The U.S. dollar **appreciates,** or increases in value, and the Canadian dollar **depreciates,** or decreases in value, in response to the government intervention. A stronger U.S. dollar means Canadian goods are cheaper for Americans, and American goods are more expensive for Canadians.

COMPETENCY 21: STRUCTURE AND OPERATION OF THE U.S. FREE ENTERPRISE SYSTEM

THE TEACHER UNDERSTANDS THE STRUCTURE AND OPERATION OF THE U.S. FREE ENTERPRISE SYSTEM; THE ROLE OF GOVERNMENT, BUSINESS, CONSUMERS, AND LABOR IN THE SYSTEM; AND BASIC CONCEPTS OF CONSUMER ECONOMICS.

SKILL 21.1   **Analyze the origins and development of the free enterprise system in the United States and understand the basic principles of the free enterprise system (e.g., profit motive, voluntary exchange, private property rights, competition).**

Origins and Development of Free Enterprise

The U.S. free enterprise system began during the colonial era. Individual goals and work ethics promote the concept of doing well and earning profits. Small businesses existed in the colonies and when the Constitution was drafted, the framers limited regulations on commerce and taxing to interstate commerce. The principles of private property rights were also provided for in the Constitution.

Principles of Free Enterprise

Financial incentives and certain basic freedoms are the key to a functioning market economy. Economic agents have the right to use their resources in whatever way they want within the confines of the legal system.

All market participants are willing to take a risk for the opportunity of being financially successful. Entrepreneurs are willing to undertake the risk of new business ventures for the purpose of monetary gain. Resources move into higher than normal rate-of-return industries because they are attracted by the **profit potential**. Inventors are willing to take the risk of spending time and money trying to come up with new products in the hope of monetary gain. All of these represent the ways financial incentives operate in a market economy.

Consumers vote for the products they want with their dollar spending. Goods acquiring enough dollar votes are profitable, signaling to the producers that society wants their scarce resources used in this way. This process is known as consumer sovereignty. The producer then hires inputs in accordance with the goods consumers want, looking for the most efficient or lowest cost method of production. The lower the firm's costs for any given level of revenue, the higher the firm's profits. If a good does not acquire enough dollar votes, then the firm is not profitable. Consumers are letting producers know that they do not want society's scarce resources used for the production of the good.

The existence of economic profits in an industry functions as a market signal to firms to enter the industry. Economic profits means there is an above-normal rate of return in this industry. As the number of firms increases, the market supply curve shifts to the right. Assuming cost curves stay the same, the expansion continues until the economic profits are eliminated and the industry is earning a normal rate of return. Depending on the level of capital intensity, this process might take a few years or it might take many years.

The easier it is to shift resources from one industry to another, the faster the process will be. But the expansion will continue as long as there are economic profits to attract firms. Resources will go where they earn the highest rate of return, especially if they are in a situation earning a lower than normal rate of return. Firms are free to use their resources in any way they want within the confines of the prevailing legal system.

Profit Motive

Profit motive is the willingness of entrepreneurs and investors to take risks on the chance that a business venture will succeed. Without a profit incentive, there would be no reason for firms to spend millions and billions on research and development, and technological progress would be almost nonexistent.

The entrepreneur is willing to take the risks. He or she knows there is a good probability that the business will fail, but there is also a chance that it will succeed—and there is a remote chance that it will be as successful as Microsoft. Given this chance, entrepreneurs are willing to risk their own money, and investors are also willing to risk money on the chance that the business venture will be successful. If the venture is not successful, meaning it is not receiving those dollar votes that make it profitable, the consumers are telling that business that they do not want their scarce resources used in that way. Profits are the market signal that entrepreneurs and firms look for.

Voluntary Exchange

When people voluntarily exchange goods in a free enterprise system, the consumers receive the goods they want and the supply of goods continues. If the supply continues and people are satisfied with the exchange, then it is likely the business will survive.

Private Property Rights

Private property is an important concept in free enterprise. The opposite of private ownership is collective ownership. Private ownership means that the individual owns resources and controls the production of resources.

Competition

Competition is an important element of free enterprise. Individuals try to produce products that are better than similar products and then set their own prices. Competition spurs the economy to provide better products at lowest possible prices.

SKILL 21.2   Analyze issues and developments related to U.S. economic growth from the 1870s to the present (e.g., antitrust acts, tariff policies, the New Deal; economic effects of World War I, World War II, and the Cold War; increased globalization of the economy).

Antitrust Acts

Once the Industrial Revolution occurred, the economic growth and expansion led to the formation of **trusts**. These were monopolies that were controlling large industrial groups of companies. Even though they represented a concentration of power in the hands of a few people, they contributed to the growth of the nation with large efficient corporations. But there were many unfair business practices with smaller businesses being forced out of business. This led to the enactment of the **Sherman Antitrust Act**, which made trusts or any combination that existed to restrain trade illegal. The government dissolved the huge trusts, such as Standard Oil. The economy continued to grow and prosper in the years approaching World War I. The **Robinson-Patman Act** and the **FTC Act** were other antitrust measures passed by Congress.

Tariff Policies

Tariff policies fluctuated after the 1870s. Agricultural interests favored lower tariffs and industrial interests favored higher tariffs. The political parties included planks in their platforms relating to tariffs. The Republicans supported high tariffs because many who belonged to that party were industrialists. The Democrats, on the other hand, generally supported lower tariffs.

Economic Effects of World War I

The World War I years resulted in a wartime economy with heavy reliance on the banking system to assist with finances. After the war, the European nations' economies were devastated, and the U.S. helped with the reconstruction.

There had been changes in the social structure of the economy with the formation of unions and women's rights. The 1920s were known as the Roaring Twenties and represented an era of prosperity. During this period there was increased urbanization as people left the farms to move to the cities for jobs. There was massive investment in building, the expansion of the automobile industry, and excessive stock market investment. Much of this investment represented **buying on margin.**

The New Deal

Buying on margin allowed people to control huge amounts of stock with a minimal cash outlay. This is what led to the stock market crash in 1929 and eventually to the Great Depression. The massive unemployment during the Depression led the government to focus on policies to relieve the misery and stimulate the economy. As part of the New Deal, the government enacted the National Recovery Act with a variety of agencies to try to stimulate the economy and provide jobs. President Franklin Roosevelt instituted a number of program designed to put people back in the workforce. Programs such as the Works Progress Administration and the Civilian Conservation

Corps allowed people to work and, at the same time, contribute to the betterment of society (see Skill 9.2).

Economic Effects of World War II and the Cold War

With the outbreak of World War II and the U.S. entry into the war, the Great Depression ended. The United States and the Soviet Union emerged from World War II as world powers. Veterans returned to the United States and a peacetime economy. The country was experiencing economic prosperity. Housing construction increased and prefabricated homes became popular. Banks loaned money for mortgages and veterans returned to colleges to complete and/or obtain an education for better job prospects. The automobile industry began increased production and more automobiles were purchased.

Following the end of World War II to 1990, the Cold War represented a tense situation for the world as the United States and the Soviet Union built up an arsenal of nuclear weapons. The U.S. economy continued to experience overall growth, interrupted at times by recession and inflation. Government spending was focused on the "space race" and outshining the Soviet Union in technological advances.

Increased Globalization of the Economy

The period of European peace after the defeat of Napoleon and the reliance upon the gold standard in that time is often referred to as "The First Era of Globalization." This period began to disintegrate with the crisis of the gold standard in the late 1920s and early 1930s. This period of globalization included Europe, several European-influenced areas in the Americas, and Oceania. The exchange of goods based upon the common gold standard resulted in prosperity for all countries involved. Communication and the exchange of ideas between these countries also prospered. Since World War II, globalization of trade has been accomplished primarily through trade negotiations and treaties.

The global economy expanded rapidly in the early twentieth century with the advent of the **airplane,** which made travel and trade easier and less time-consuming. From the Roman Empire to the recent advent of the Internet, the world today might be better termed a global neighborhood.

The concept of globalization has made large strides since the invention of the computer and the introduction of the Internet and World Wide Web. For further discussion of globalization during the twentieth and twenty-first centuries, see Skill 22.7.

SKILL 21.3   **Understand and compare types of business ownership (e.g., sole proprietorships, partnerships, corporations).**

Three basic types of business structure in the United States are the sole proprietorship, the partnership, and the corporation.

22

A **sole proprietor** is the owner of his or her own business. The proprietor is responsible for the performance of all of the business functions of that business. He or she provides all of the capital and receives all of the profits. The big drawback of this form of business is that the sole proprietor faces unlimited liability. The owner is personally responsible for all of the debts of the business, and there is no difference between the debts and assets of the business and the owner. The sole proprietor has a difficult time raising capital for the business, although there are entities such as the **Small Business Administration** that help. The sole proprietorship is the most prevalent form of business in the United States.

A **partnership** is an arrangement in which two or more people own and operate a business for a profit. They share in all of the business's functions and are responsible for the business's functions. They provide all the capital and receive all the profits. They also face unlimited liability in that each partner is responsible for the business debts incurred by the other. They may or may not face an easier time raising capital than the sole proprietor does.

A **corporation** is a legal entity in its own right. It has all of the legal rights and liabilities of a legal person. There is usually a separation between management and ownership since the corporation is owned by its stockholders. The advantage of the corporation is that it can resort to forms of financing not available to the sole proprietorship and partnership. The corporation can issue stocks or bonds to finance its growth instead of just using retained earnings.

Of the three forms of business, the corporation has the easiest time raising capital. The corporation faces limited liability because the shareholders have limited liability. The company is responsible for its own debts. Creditors cannot attach the assets of the stockholders unless the corporate veil has been pierced. Piercing the corporate veil only occurs in rare cases as when, for example, the corporation is the alter-ego of a shareholder.

SKILL 21.4   Demonstrate knowledge of the role of financial institutions in saving, investing, and borrowing.

Savings, investing, and borrowing take place through financial institutions. The money that is saved by households and businesses is then available as funds for borrowing. The banks and other institutions make loans with the funds that are saved. These represent funds that are spent in the economy, leading to higher levels of aggregate demand. If there is not enough money for loans, there is a lower level of spending and a lower level of aggregate demand. This is the manner in which the Federal Reserve implements monetary policy (see Skill 21.5).

Financial institutions are also active in underwriting new stock and bond offerings for corporations. This raises capital for the firm and represents investment opportunities for investors. These investors buy the stocks and bonds. The money they pay for them represents money the corporation can use for expansion. Investors buy stocks and bonds because they expect a return on their investment.

SKILL 21.5   **Analyze the role of government in the U.S. free enterprise system (e.g., significance of government rules and regulations, impact of fiscal and monetary policy decisions, role and function of the Federal Reserve System, relationship between government policies and international trade).**

Government Rules and Regulations

Government policies, whether federal, state, or local, affect economic decision making and, in many cases, the **distribution of resources.** This is the purpose of most economic policies imposed at the federal level. Governments do not implement monetary and fiscal policy at the state or local level, only at the national level. Most state and local laws that affect economic decision making and the distribution of resources have to do with taxation. If taxes are imposed or raised at the state or local level, the effect is less spending. The purpose of these taxes is to raise revenues for the state and local government, not to affect the level of aggregate demand and inflation. At the federal level, the major purpose of these policies is to affect the level of aggregate demand and the inflation rate or the unemployment rate.

Government at all three levels affects the distribution of resources and economic decision making through transfer payments. This is an attempt to bring about a redistribution of income and to correct the problem of income inequality. Programs such as **Food Stamps, Temporary Assistance to Needy Families (TANF),** unemployment compensation, and Medicaid all fall into this category. Technically, these government transfer programs result in a rearrangement of private consumption, not a real reallocation of resources. Price support programs in agriculture also result in a redistribution of income. The imposition of artificially high prices results in many resources going into agriculture and can lead to product surpluses.

Laws can be enacted at all three levels to correct for the problem of **externalities.** An externality occurs when uninvolved third parties are affected by some market activity. For example, in pollution, dumping obnoxious and/or poisonous wastes into the air and water means that the air and water are being treated as a free input by the firm that is engaged in polluting. The market does not register all costs of production because the firm does not have to pay to use the air or water.

The result of the free inputs is lower production costs for the firm and an over-allocation of resources into the production of the good the firm is producing. The **role for government** then is to cause a redistribution of resources by somehow shifting all or part of the cost on to the offending firm by such measures as imposing fines, taxes, requiring pollution abatement equipment, and selling pollution permits. Whatever method is chosen will raise the costs of production for the firms and force them to bear some of the costs.

Fiscal and Monetary Policy Decisions

Government policies can be enacted in order to encourage labor to migrate from one sector of the economy to another. This is primarily done at the national level. The U.S. economy is so large that it is possible to have unemployment in different areas while the economy is at full employment. The purpose then is to cause unemployed labor in one area to migrate to another area where there are open jobs. State unemployment and labor agencies provide information to the unemployed.

U.S. economic policy is based on promoting full employment and stable prices in the economy. The economy needs a stable environment in which to function. With this end in mind, monetary policy or fiscal policy is used to fine-tune the economy and to steer it toward its goals. **Contractionary** monetary or fiscal policies are used to slow an economy that is expanding too quickly. **Expansionary** monetary or fiscal policies are used to stimulate a sluggish economy to eliminate unemployment.

Fiscal policy consists of changing the level of taxes and government spending to influence the level of economic activity. Contractionary fiscal policy consists of decreasing government spending and/or raising taxes and is intended to slow down a rapidly expanding economy to curb inflation. Contractionary policies result in a lower level of trade and spending. Expansionary fiscal policy consists of lowering taxes and raising government spending to stimulate a sluggish economy and generate higher levels of employment. Expansionary fiscal policy results in a higher level of spending and trade.

Federal Reserve System

The **Federal Reserve** is involved in deciding monetary policy for the United States by changing levels of reserves in the banking system. The Federal Reserve System has three tools available: the reserve ratio, the discount rate, and open-market operations.

The **reserve ratio** refers to the portion of deposits that banks are required to hold as vault cash or on deposit with the Federal Reserve. When the Federal Reserve changes the reserve ratio, it changes the money creation and lending ability of the banking system.

When the Federal Reserve wants to expand the money supply it lowers the reserve ratio, leaving banks with more money to loan. This is one aspect of expansionary monetary policy and leads to more spending or trade. When the reserve ratio is increased, this results in banks having less money to loan, which is a form of contractionary monetary policy and leads to a lower level of spending or trade in the economy.

Another way in which monetary policy is implemented is by changing the **discount rate**. When banks have temporary cash shortages, they can borrow from the Federal Reserve. The interest rate on the borrowed funds is called the discount rate. Reducing the discount rate encourages banks to borrow from the Federal Reserve, instead of restricting their lending to deal with the temporary cash shortage. By encouraging banks to borrow, their lending ability is increased and this results in a higher level of spending and trade in the economy.

Lowering the discount rate is a form of expansionary monetary policy. Discouraging bank lending by raising the discount rate is a form of contractionary monetary policy.

The final tool of monetary policy is called **open-market operations**. This consists of the Federal Reserve buying or selling government securities with the public or with the banking system. When the Fed sells bonds, it is taking money out of the banking system, which is a form of contractionary monetary policy that leads to a lower level of spending and trade in the economy.

The Federal Reserve is expanding the money supply when it buys bonds from the public or the banking system because it is paying for those bonds with dollars that enter the income-expenditures stream. The result of the Federal Reserve's buying bonds is an increase in the level of spending and trade in the economy.

Government Policies and International Trade

Markets today are international. All nations are a part of a global economy. No nation exists in isolationism or is totally independent of other nations. Isolationism is referred to as "autarky" or a closed economy. Membership in a global economy means that what one nation does affects other nations because economies are linked through **international trade**, commerce, and finance. International transactions affect the levels of income, employment, and prices in each of the trading economies.

The relative importance of trade is based on what percentage of **Gross Domestic Product (GDP)** trade constitutes. In the United States, trade represents only a small percentage of GDP. In other nations, trade may represent more than 50 percent of GDP, and for those countries, changes in international transactions can cause many economic fluctuations and problems.

Trade barriers are one way in which economic problems are caused. Suppose a nation is confronted with rising unemployment in a domestic industry due to cheaper foreign imports. Consumers are buying the cheaper foreign import instead of the higher-priced domestic good. In order to protect domestic labor, government imposes a tariff, thus raising the price of the more efficiently produced foreign good. The result of the tariff is that consumers buy more of the domestic good and less of the foreign good.

The problem is that the foreign good is the product of the foreign nation's labor. A decrease in the demand for the foreign good means foreign producers do not need as much labor, so they lay off workers in the foreign country. The result of the trade barrier is that unemployment has been exported from the domestic country to the foreign country.

Treaties such as the North American Free Trade Agreement (NAFTA) are one way of lowering or eliminating trade barriers on a regional basis. As trade barriers are lowered or eliminated, this causes changes in labor and output markets. Some grow; some shrink. These adjustments are taking place now for Canada, the United States, and Mexico. Membership in the global economy adds another dimension to economics—in terms of aiding developing countries and in terms of implementing national policies.

The exact same thing can happen through the exchange rate. Nations can affect their exchange rate values buy buying and selling foreign exchange in the currency markets. Suppose the United States decides that a lower-valued dollar will stimulate its exports which will lead to higher employment levels in the United States. The United States then sells dollars on the open market, thus increasing the supply of dollars on the world market. The effect is a depreciation of the dollar.

The lower-valued dollar makes U.S. exports more attractive to foreigners who buy the relatively cheaper U.S. exports instead of the now relatively higher-priced domestic goods. The increased demand for U.S. exports leads to higher employment levels in the export industries in the United States. The lower demand for domestic products in the foreign country leads to unemployment in their domestic industries. Each nation's actions will have an effect on other nations.

SKILL 21.6   **Demonstrate knowledge of the goals of economic growth, stability, full employment, freedom, security, equity, and efficiency as they apply to U.S. economic policy.**

Goals of Economic Growth

All government policy is geared toward the attainment of the government's goals. Policies are a way of leading to those goals. The goals of economic growth are stability, full employment, freedom, security, equity, and efficiency, and they are the reasons for the policies that the U.S. government implements.

Economic growth can be defined as increases over time in real output. The growth rate is computed as the difference between the growth rates in two periods divided by the growth rate in the first period. Nations want to see their growth rates increase. Nations experience economic growth when there is an increase in the supply of resources or when they use their existing resources more efficiently. In other words, total output will increase whenever there is an increase in labor and a corresponding increase in productivity. There are many factors that enter into this.

Supply factors are factors that affect the physical capabilities of the economy. They involve the quantity and quality of resources. The first factor is **natural resources.** This involves the quantity and quality of natural resources that a country has. Government establishes policies for conservation of scarce resources. **Human resources** are the second factor. This factor involves the quantity and quality of the labor force. The quality of the labor force has to do with productivity or how much output labor produces.

Factors affecting productivity include **education and training, health and nutrition, government policies in health, safety, and environment, and the amount and quality of capital** such as equipment and machinery available for accomplishing work. Many policies are geared toward human capital. Programs help with training and employment, and workers can learn where available jobs are in the country and what skills they require.

The last growth factor is determined by the level of investment and is called the **stock of capital**. Here, the capital-labor ratio is important because this shows the amount of capital a worker has to work with. If a nation has a growing labor force, it needs growth in its capital stock in order to experience growth. Higher levels of investment lead to higher growth rates. At the same time the economy needs public investment in order to improve and expand the infrastructure.

The last factor that determines an economy's ability to grow is **technological progress.** Technological progress results in new and better ways of doing things, and it is the creation of new and more efficient production processes.

The other side of the growth rate has to do with the **demand side of the economy**. There must be sufficient demand in the economy to generate economic growth. Aggregate demand has to grow steadily to absorb the increased output that comes with growth. The economy must have full employment and full production in order to experience growth. Deviations from full employment are dealt with by monetary and fiscal policy.

All of the above discussion is illustrated as an outward shift of the **production possibility curve,** which represents economic growth. This is the curve that shows the maximum amount of output that an economy can achieve given its supply of resources and its technology. Technological progress and increases in the quality of labor result in economic growth or outward shifts of the curve.

Stability

Stability refers to the evenness or amount of fluctuations in a nation's financial economy. Developed countries strive for stability and little inflation. Government policy is often implemented to achieve stability.

Full Employment

A country's economy experiences full employment when all or nearly all of the persons who want to work and can work are able to do so at the wages offered and in work conditions that are offered. Realistically, there may never be 100 percent per full employment because seasonal unemployment needs to be factored in to the situation. However, higher employment numbers and percentages are indicators of a society that is not experiencing inflation.

Freedom

Freedom is an economic goal. Freedom to select work, own and use resources, and select the type of work are important economic factors for a nation. The degree of freedom often depends upon the level of society and the degree of government involvement in the economy.

Security

Security is a goal of economic growth. The degree of stability of a country can be seen by the security of its people. Often, security relates to income levels and methods of making changes in government policy. Countries that experience coups usually have a lesser degree of security than democratic societies where governmental decisions are made by elected representatives or agencies within the government with the approval of one of the branches of government.

Equity

In the area of economic growth, equity relates to fairness and equality. The process of distributing goods in an economy is related to the principle of equity. Governments in developing nations often seek to address questions such as whether all people have access to all goods and services. In countries with close to full, or full, employment, more people will have access to goods and services.

Efficiency

Efficiency relates to the use of resources. When a nation makes wise use of resources, it is said to make efficient use of resources. An efficient use of resources help assist in maintaining a supply of resources and eliminating waste.

SKILL 21.7 **Understand the rights and responsibilities of consumers, labor, and business in the U.S. free enterprise system.**

Financial incentives and certain basic freedoms are the key to the functioning of a market economy. Economic agents or firms have the right to use their resources in whatever way they want within the confines of the legal system. All market participants are willing to take a risk for the opportunity of being a financial success.

Consumers

In a free enterprise system, consumers need to make responsible choices. Anyone can make a choice, but a consumer needs to be informed to make a responsible and correct choice. Consumers are an important part of the free enterprise system because when they make purchases they are encouraging economic growth. When consumer spending decreases, supplies of goods increase and the economy can become sluggish. The consumer index of spending is a guide of how well the economy is performing and provides an outlook for the future. Consumers in the United States can purchase whatever they want provided they can pay for it and they are not acquiring a good or service in violation of local, state, or federal laws. Consumers vote for the products they want with their dollar spending. Goods acquiring enough dollar votes to be profitable signal to the producers that society wants scarce resources used in this way. This is the process of **consumer sovereignty.**

Labor

A free enterprise system depends on labor. Labor produces the products that consumers purchase. The costs of labor factor into economic development and free enterprise. Privately owned industry employs labor at rates that are acceptable to the workers. Labor unions negotiate the work contract with the employer to establish a procedure for grievances and to acquire a larger share of income for their members. In a free market economy, some of the labor may be performed outside of a country because of reduced costs. The quality, quantity, and cost of products must all be considered as an aspect of labor in a free market economy.

Business

The role of business in a free-market system is to make profits. Its role is also to produce a supply of goods for consumers. Businesses base prices on costs of products their intended profit. They are free to determine and set their own prices and use materials of their choice. If the supply and demand are equal, then businesses can thrive. If a supply exceeds demand, then prices will often be reduced and the economy may not grow as intended. If demand exceeds supply, it is likely the economy will grow at a faster rate. Businesses in a free market economy have a greater control over supply and demand than businesses to in other types of economies.

The fundamental characteristics of the U.S. economic system are the uses of competition and markets. Profit and competition all go together in the U.S. economic system as all economic agents act in their own interests within the confines of the legal environment. Competition is determined by market structure. The absence of barriers to entry makes it easy for firms to enter and leave the industry. At the other end of the spectrum is monopoly, the only seller of a unique one-of-a-kind product. Barriers to entry are significant enough to keep firms from entering or leaving the industry. The competitiveness of the market structure determines whether new firms or capital can enter in response to profits.

Profit functions as a financial incentive for individuals and firms. The possibility of earning profit is why individuals are willing to undertake entrepreneurial ventures and why firms are willing to spend money on research and development and innovation. Without financial incentives, there wouldn't be much new product development or technological advancement.

SKILL 21.8   **Demonstrate knowledge of basic concepts of consumer economics (e.g., factors involved in decisions to acquire goods and services, means by which savings can be invested, risks and rewards of various investment options).**

Consumers rarely have enough time and money to do everything that they want and to buy everything that they want. Time and money are scarce resources. If a consumer spends time doing one activity, he or she is sacrificing another activity. For example, if a consumer spends the afternoon playing golf, he is sacrificing doing the garden work. If a consumer decides to enroll in evening classes, she has less time to spend with family and friends. Devoting time to one activity means that there is another activity that has to be sacrificed.

Scarcity is evident in personal financial management. Scarcity here refers to dollars and paying bills. The buying of one good means sacrificing another good. This is the concept of opportunity cost. This is why consumers have to make choices. The consumer has to decide which goods give him the most satisfaction for his dollars. Just as consumers have to choose how to spend their time, they also have to choose how to spend their dollars.

Scarcity means that consumers cannot have all of the goods that they want or participate in all of the activities that they want to do. This is true on both a micro and a macro level. All of these choices involve opportunity costs.

The consumer needs enough of an income to engage in savings. If his or her income does not cover expenditures, the consumer borrows. Much of this borrowing is through the use of credit cards. If consumers have extra income, they can invest in various ventures in the hope of profiting from that investment. Taking risks may be easier and less harmful to individuals with many assets than those who cannot afford to take a risk and lose.

There are various ways to invest and various ways to take risks. Consumer economic options are similar to the elements of becoming an informed consumer. Consumer economic options such as investing and risk taking are choices. These choices can be made in various ways. Although there is no certainty that any specific choice is the correct choice, it is important that the consumer is informed and makes a reasonably intelligence choice based on all information that is available.

COMPETENCY 22: SCIENCE, TECHNOLOGY, AND SOCIETY

THE TEACHER UNDERSTANDS MAJOR SCIENTIFIC AND MATHEMATICAL DISCOVERIES AND TECHNOLOGICAL INNOVATIONS AND THE SOCIETAL SIGNIFICANCE OF THESE DISCOVERIES AND INNOVATIONS.

SKILL 22.1   **Demonstrate knowledge of how major scientific and mathematical discoveries and technological innovations have affected societies throughout history.**

Scientific and Mathematical Discoveries through the Ages

In Germany, Gutenberg's invention of the **printing press** with movable type facilitated the rapid spread of Renaissance ideas, writings, and innovations, thus ensuring the enlightenment of most of Western Europe. Contributions were also made by Paracelsus in science and medicine.

Prince Henry the Navigator of Portugal encouraged, supported, and financed the Portuguese seamen who led in the search for an all-water route to Asia. A shipyard was built along with a school that taught navigation. New types of sailing ships were built to carry the seamen safely through the ocean waters. Experiments were conducted with newer items such as maps, navigational methods, and instruments. With the use of items such as the **astrolabe** and the **compass** sailors could determine direction as well as latitude and longitude for exact location.

The **microscope** first appeared about 1590, and was steadily improved upon. The microscope revealed an entire world of invisible activity of bacteria and fungus and it laid bare the cell structure of complex organisms. Advancements in microscopy led directly to important discoveries concerning germs, viruses, and the cause of disease, greatly aiding the field of medicine.

Electrical power is a phenomenon that has been known about for centuries, but it was not until the late nineteenth century that understanding and technology had advanced to the point where it could be reliably produced and transmitted. The ability to transmit power by wire over distances changed the nature of industry that previously had relied on other sources, such as steam plants or waterpower to move machinery.

The **Theory of Relativity** was proposed by Albert Einstein, and revolutionized physics. Einstein proposed that the measurement of time and space changed relative to the position of the observer, implying that time and space were not fixed but could warp and change. This had radical implications for Newtonian physics, particularly as it related to gravity, and it opened new fields of scientific study.

Penicillin was developed in the mid-twentieth century and rapidly became an important drug, saving countless lives. Penicillin is derived from a mold, which, it was discovered, inhibited and even killed many kinds of germs. In drug form, it could be used to fight infections of various kinds in humans. Penicillin and similarly derived drugs are called antibiotics.

The **microchip** was developed in the 1950s as a way to reduce the size of transistor-based electronic equipment. By replacing individual transistors with a single chip of semiconductor material, more capability could be included in less space. This development led directly to the microprocessor, which is at the heart of every modern computer and most modern electronic products.

The **religious beliefs and institutions** of a culture can greatly influence scientific research and technological innovation. During the Renaissance in Italy, for example, science was interpreted and dictated by Catholic religious doctrine, and theories that contradicted this doctrine were dismissed and their proponents sometimes punished.

Political factors have affected scientific advancement, as well, especially in cultures that partially support scientific research with public money. Warfare has traditionally been a strong driver of technological advancement as cultures strive to outpace their neighbors with better weapons and defenses. Technologies developed for military purposes often find their way into the mainstream. Significant advances in flight technology, for example, were made during the two world wars.

The Impact of Technological Innovation

Socially, many cultures have come to value innovation and welcome new products and improvements to older products. This desire to always be advancing and obtaining the latest, newest technology creates economic incentive for innovation.

New technologies have made production faster, easier, and more efficient. People found their skills and their abilities replaced by machines that were faster and more accurate. To some degree, machines and humans have entered an age of competition. Yet these advances have facilitated greater control over nature, lightened the burden of labor, and extended human life span.

The advances in science, knowledge, and technology have also called into question many of the assumptions and beliefs that have provided meaning for human existence. The myths that provided meaning in the past have been exposed, and there are no new structures of belief to replace them. Without the foundational belief structures that have given meaning to life, an emptiness and aimlessness has arisen. Technology and science have extended life and made life easier. Science has provided power and knowledge, but not yet the wisdom to know how to eliminate prejudice, cruelty, violence, crime, or wars.

The extraordinary advances in science and technology have opened new frontiers and pushed back an ever-growing number of boundaries. These influences have had a profound effect in shaping modern civilization. Each discovery or machine or insight built upon other new discoveries or insights or machines.

By the twentieth century, the rate of discovery and invention grew dramatically. The results have, in most cases, been beneficial. Advances in biology and medicine have decreased infant mortality and increased life expectancy dramatically. Antibiotics and new surgical techniques have saved countless lives. Inoculations have essentially erased many dreadful diseases.

New technologies have changed the way of life for many. Tremendous progress in communication and transportation has tied all parts of the earth and drawn them closer. This is the computer age, and around the world, computers are found even in elementary schools. Technology makes the world seem a much smaller place. The existence of television and modern technology has people all over the world watching events unfold in "real time."

Outsourcing is now popular because of technological advances. Call centers for European, American and other large countries are now located in India and Pakistan. Multinational corporations locate plants in foreign countries to lower costs.

In many places technology has resulted in a mobile population. Popular culture has been shaped by mass production and the mass media. Mass production and technology has made electronic goods affordable to most. This is the age of the cell phone and the portable device. The Internet and email allow people anywhere in the world to be in touch with one another and allow people to immediately know about current events.

The Soviet Union was the first nation to successfully begin a program of space flight and exploration, launching *Sputnik* and putting the first human in space. Space exploration continued to grow with the United States successfully landing space crews on the moon, the development of the space shuttle and the Hubble space telescope, and continual exploration of the solar system with probes and robotic rovers.

SKILL 22.2   **Trace the origin and diffusion of major ideas in mathematics, science, and technology that occurred in river valley civilizations, classical Greece and Rome, classical India, the Islamic Caliphates between 700 and 1200, and China from the Tang to Ming dynasties.**

Major ideas in mathematics, science, and technology have been discussed in other sections throughout this guide. The following is a summary of the ideas in the following civilizations.

The early **river valley civilizations** in Mesopotamia developed tools that were made with metals such as bronze. They also invented a plow and the wheel. They used their scientific knowledge in farming but later their inventions were spread with trade. They used a number system and were involved in mapmaking. Their scientific and mathematical knowledge extended to the planets and stars and to dividing the year into two seasons.

There were major science, technology, and mathematical advances in **classical Greece and Rome.** The mathematical skills of the Greeks allowed them to develop a calendar from studying the stars and constellations. Rome's major technological accomplishments were in the area of architecture and building design. They built bridges, theaters, and aqueducts in addition to buildings. Their skills in science led to the invention of concrete and its use as a building material.

During the early part of the history of India, the Indians developed farming tools and equipment such as wheel barrows from metals. In **classical India,** their mathematical skills became famous. One mathematician developed the concept of zero.

The **Islamic Caliphates** were knowledgeable in the areas of mathematics and science. They studied algebra and the induction theory.

China was the source of many technological inventions. Some of the inventions included printing, gunpowder, and cast iron. The Chinese also developed a compass and decimal mathematics.

SKILL 22.3   **Demonstrate knowledge of the contributions of significant scientists and inventors (e.g., Copernicus, Galileo, Isaac Newton, Marie Curie, Thomas Edison, Albert Einstein).**

The following is a brief summary of contributions of scientists and inventors who have been discussed in other sections of this guide.

Nicolaus Copernicus lived during the fifteenth and sixteenth centuries. He was an astronomer and theorized that the sun was the center of the universe and that the earth revolved around the sun. He has been known as the father of the scientific revolution.

Galileo has been called the father of modern science. He improved the telescope and agreed with Copernicus's beliefs about the placement of the sun and the earth.

Sir Isaac Newton, aside from being considered a key figure in science, was also a mathematician, philosopher, astronomer, and alchemist. He described universal gravitation and the three laws of motion.

Marie Curie was a scientist. She became a professor of physics and was appointed director of a laboratory in the Radium Institute of the University of Paris. She and her husband, Pierre Curie, isolated radium in laboratory experiments and they used radium to ease the suffering of soldiers during World War I. She received the Nobel Prize in Physics and in Chemistry.

Thomas Edison is best remembered for his development of the light bulb. He also developed the phonograph and the motion picture camera. He is believed to have had the first industrial research laboratory and is credited with holding more than one thousand patents.

Albert Einstein was a physicist who developed the theory of relativity. He received the Nobel Prize in Physics. The work that was the basis for the prize later was important in establishing the quantum theory. He was a German who was in the United States at the time of Hitler's rise to power. He became an American citizen before the United States entered World War II. He led what would become known as the Manhattan Project.

SKILL 22.4   **Analyze connections between major developments in science and technology and the growth of industrial economies and societies in the eighteenth, nineteenth, and twentieth centuries.**

Eighteenth-Century Developments

Many of the scientific and technological developments of the 1700s were inventions that paved the way for the Industrial Revolution and improved transportation. The steam engine and steamboat were two such inventions.

Inventions that moved the economy from a farm society to an urban industrial society included the steam engine and steamboat. **Robert Fulton's** *Clermont* was the first commercially successful steamboat, and it led the way to fast shipping of goods. Later, steam-powered railroads rivaled the steamboat as a means of shipping, eventually opening the West. Inventions that moved the country to an industrial economy included the power loom, cotton gin, and spinning jenny. The lightening rod, telegraph, threshing machine, and battery were also eighteenth-century developments.

Nineteenth-Century Developments

Developments and inventions during the 1800s improved transportation, communication, and home life. Improvements were made to the steam engine and the internal combustion engine was invented. Gas lights and electric lights beautified cities and gave homes a new source of lighting. The sewing machine became a useful device for the home and for industry, and the washing machine saved time and energy. The typewriter became a device that was used as the concept of offices was developed. Farming was made easier with the invention of the reaper and barbed wire divided property as the country expanded west.

Twentieth-Century Developments

Developments in the 1900s allowed society to advance at a rapid rate. People had more leisure because of the improvement of the vacuum cleaner and microwave ovens. Radios provided a source of entertainment as did the talking motion pictures. The invention of the airplane, helicopter, and jet engine allowed transportation to enter a modern age.

The twentieth century is also noted for the development of the atomic and hydrogen bombs. Perhaps the most far-reaching invention with the most significant impact on society was the microchip.

Impact on Modern Daily Life

Science and technology have increasing effects on our daily lives, as we use the scientific and technological research to more fully understand many of the phenomena around us. In each of the areas listed below, there are several examples of scientific principles at work.

In **health care** we can see many of the fruits of science and technology in nutrition, genetics, and the development of therapeutic agents. We can see an example of the adaptation of organisms in the development of resistant strains of microbes in response to use of antibiotics. Organic chemistry and biochemistry have been exploited to identify therapeutic targets and to screen and develop new medicines. Advances in molecular biology and our understanding of inheritance have led to the development of genetic screening and allowed us to sequence the human genome.

There are two broad trends in **environmental science and technology**. First, many studies are being conducted to determine the effects of changing environmental conditions and pollutions. New instruments and monitoring systems have increased the accuracy of these results. Second, advances are being made to mitigate the effects of pollution, develop sustainable methods of agriculture and energy production, and improve waste management.

Development of new technology in **agriculture** is particularly important as we strive to feed more people with less arable land. Again we see the importance of genetics in developing hybrids that have desirable characteristics. New strains of plants and farming techniques may allow the production of more nutrient rich food and/or allow crops to be grown successfully in harsh conditions. However, it is also important to consider the environmental impact of transgenic species and the use of pesticides and fertilizers. Scientific reasoning and experimentation can assist us in ascertaining the real effect of modern agricultural practices and ways to minimize their impact.

SKILL 22.5   **Demonstrate knowledge of how specific developments in science, technology, and the free enterprise system have affected the economic development of the United States (e.g., cotton gin, Bessemer steel process, electric power, telephone, railroad, petroleum-based products, computers).**

The development of the United States has been affected by the development of various items and processes, including but not limited to the ones that are summarized here.

The **cotton gin** was developed in the late 1700s and was able to remove unneeded seeds from cotton fiber. Before this invention, the seed removal was done by hand. The invention allowed for more fabric to be made more quickly from the cotton fiber and this process resulted in the development of more textile factories.

Henry Bessemer was an Englishman who learned how to convert pig iron to steel. This process made a strong metal because the carbon and silicon in the iron were oxidized. The first steel plant in the United States was built in 1865. The **Bessemer steel process** made harder metal, and the steel was used to replace the iron railroad rails and was used in the building industry and other areas of business that needed strong metals. Steel was also used in equipment needed for World Wars I and II. Pittsburgh, Pennsylvania, became a steel center in the United States. The Bessemer steel process was later superseded by a process that was called the "open hearth" process.

Electric power, the **telephone,** and **railroad** helped develop cities and industry, provide more luxury to homes, and was important in the geographic expansion of America. Electric power was used to light home and for interurban transportation systems. The telephone provided better communication and was a way families and friends could stay connected. The railroads became transcontinental lines that helped speed food and agricultural products to market and provide the country with fresher foods and a greater quantify of products.

Mail order became a popular way to purchase items. Company catalogs were distributed to families in rural areas who could purchase items that would be delivered by rail.

Petroleum-based products became available in the 1950s and 1960s. Clothing made of nylon and similar products were popular because they were easy to care for and did not wrinkle, like natural fiber fabrics. Plastic products were made from petroleum and many were used in the home. Plastic dishes and silverware were less expensive than china or pottery dishes, were available in more modern designs, and were usually lighter weight. Sports equipment was also made from petroleum-based products. As the cost of oil increased, some of the popularity of these produces declined because the costs of products increased. However, there are still thousands of products made today from petroleum.

Computers may be the most significant invention of modern times. The computer has changed the way people communicate, transact business, and learn.

SKILL 22.6   **Analyze moral and ethical issues related to changes in science and technology.**

Changes in technology and science can alter lifestyles and raise ethical and moral issues.

Nuclear energy was once hailed as a cheap and relatively clean alternative to fossil fuels, but concern rose after accidents at nuclear plants. Nuclear technology has continued to advance, and the crucial consideration is safety. Nuclear waste sites are a conflictive issue since the waste is highly radioactive. Internationally, there is concern that nuclear power plants may be outfitted to produce material for nuclear weapons, creating another level of controversy over the spread of nuclear technology.

Biotechnology is another area that shows promise but also brings controversy. Cloning and genetically altering organisms raise serious ethical issues, especially when it relates to human beings or human tissues.

Ethical issues arise in connection with **information technology**. The computer and Internet facilitate business transactions and ease communication. Many medical providers currently correspond to patients by the Internet and patient records are frequently placed on the medical facility's Web site. When confidential information is misdirected, ethical issues can arise because technology may be a threat to a person's privacy rights.

Globalization refers to the complex of positive and negative social, political, technological, and economic changes that result from increasing contact, communication, interaction, integration and interdependence of peoples of disparate parts of the world. The term is generally used to refer to the process of change or as the cause of turbulent change. Globalization may be understood in terms of positive social and economic change, as in the case of a broadening of trade resulting in an increase in the standard of living for developing countries.

Globalization may also be understood negatively in terms of the abusive treatment of developing countries in the interest of cultural or economic imperialism. These negative understandings generally point to cultural assimilation, plunder and profiteering, the destruction of the local culture and economy, and ecological indifference.

SKILL 22.7   **Analyze the impact of scientific discoveries, technological innovations, and the free enterprise system on the standard of living in the United States (e.g., radio, television, automobile, vaccines).**

Innovations in the Standard of Living

Although the British patent for the **radio** was awarded in 1896, it was not until World War I that the equipment and capability of the use of radio was recognized. The first radio program was broadcast August 31, 1920. The first entertainment broadcasts began in 1922 from England. One of the first developments in the twentieth century was the use of commercial AM radio stations for aircraft navigation. In addition, radio was used to communicate orders and information between army and navy units during World War I. Broadcasting became practical in the 1920s after radio receivers were introduced on a wide scale.

The relative economic boom of the 1920s made it possible for many households to own a radio. The beginning of broadcasting and the proliferation of receivers revolutionized communication. The news was transmitted into every home with a radio. Rather than obtaining filtered information, people heard the actual speeches and information that became news. By the time of the stock market crash in 1929, approximately 40 percent of households had a radio. With entertainment broadcasting, people were able to remain in their homes for entertainment.

Another innovation of the 1920s was the introduction of **mass production,** the production of large amounts of standardized products on production lines. The method became very popular when Henry Ford introduced mass production to build the Model T Ford. The process facilitates high production rates per worker. Thus, the method reduced the price of products. The process is, however, capital intensive. It requires expensive machinery in high proportion to the number of workers needed to operate it. Using mass production, American manufacturers developed new products, such as refrigerators, bicycles, cameras, and automobiles.

Automobiles transformed American society. When Henry Ford implemented the assembly line, his company increased the number of available vehicles and reduced the cost of ownership. As more families purchased automobiles, the demand continued. Today, many families have multiple automobiles. Many areas of the country lack public transportation systems and people drive to work and other places they would not have been able to reach easily before the invention of the automobile. Automobiles have resulted in better roads and more traffic. Urban areas now face shortages of parking facilities for vehicles driven to work. Automobiles also cause problems in urban areas during "rush" hour, making travel slow. Automobiles have provided people with ore opportunities to appreciate their surroundings. Leisurely drives are part of some families' routine to relax and spend time together.

The **motion picture industry** began with the motion picture camera. Cecil B. DeMille and Charles Chaplin were among the first commercial movie makers. Weather was one of the main reasons the industry grew in Hollywood, California. From the era of the silent film through World War II, Metro-Goldwyn Mayer (MGM) was the leading studio in Hollywood, releasing a new movie every week for more than a quarter of a century. The industry has changed with movies now available to watch at home on DVDs.

Television has revolutionized the way people spend leisure time and become aware of current events in the world. Technology has improved from the early days of television when the pictures had grainy black-and-white images. Today, high definition is a norm for many television owners. Television can be learning tools because many students enroll in "distance-learning" classes. Widespread problems related to obesity have been blamed partially on television.

Vaccines have been an important development for the betterment of lives throughout the world. Polio was a serious problem in the 1950s but with the development of the polio vaccine, polio has almost been eradicated. Vaccines provide children with healthier lives because they provide protection from dreaded diseases.

Impact of Globalization on Standards of Living

Globalization involves exchange of money, commodities, information, ideas, and people. Much of this has been facilitated by the great advances in technology in the last one hundred fifty years. The effects of globalization can be seen across all areas of social and cultural interaction. Economically, globalization brings about broader and faster trade and flow of capital, increased outsourcing of labor, the development of global financial systems, the introduction of common currencies such as the Euro, the creation of trade agreements, and the birth of international organizations to moderate the agreements.

From a social and cultural point of view, globalization results in greater exchange of all segments of the various cultures, including ideas, technology, food, clothing, fads, and culture. Travel and migration create multicultural societies. The media facilitates the exchange of cultural and social values. As values interact, a new shared set of values begins to emerge.

Trucks, trains, and ships carry cargo all over the world. Trains travel faster than ever as do ships. Roads are prevalent and enable distribution of cargo by trucks an efficient process.

With all of this capability has come increasing demand for products. People traditionally obtained their goods using their own means or from traders who lived nearby. As technology improved, trade routes became longer, and the demand for items from overseas grew. This demand fed the economic imperative of creating more supply, and vice versa. As more people discovered goods from overseas, the demand for those foreign goods increased. Because people could get goods from overseas with relative ease, they continued to get them and demand more.

Globalization has brought about welcome and unwelcome developments in the field of **epidemiology.** Vaccines and other cures for diseases can be shipped relatively quickly all around the world. For example, this has made it possible for HIV vaccines to reach the remotest areas of the world. Unfortunately, the preponderance of global travel has also meant a threat of spreading a disease by an infected person traveling on an international flight.

Technology contributed to globalization with the development of the **Internet.** Instant communication between people thousands of miles apart is possible just by plugging in a computer and connecting to the Internet. The Internet is an extension of the telephone and cell phone revolutions. All three are developments in communications that have brought faraway places closer together. All three allow people to communicate, no matter the distance. This communication can facilitate friendly chatter, remote business meetings, and distant trade opportunities. Cell phones and the Internet are often required to do business in today's society. Computer programs enable the tracking of goods and receipts quickly and efficiently.

Globalization has also brought financial and cultural exchange on a worldwide scale. Many businesses have investments in countries around the world. Financial transactions are conducted using a variety of currencies. The cultures of the countries of the world are increasingly viewed by people throughout the world via multimedia developments. Not only goods but also belief systems, customs, and practices are being exchanged.

DOMAIN VII   SOCIAL STUDIES FOUNDATIONS, SKILLS, RESEARCH, AND INSTRUCTION

COMPETENCY 23: SOCIAL STUDIES FOUNDATIONS AND SKILLS

THE TEACHER UNDERSTANDS SOCIAL STUDIES TERMINOLOGY AND CONCEPTS, THE PHILOSOPHICAL FOUNDATIONS OF SOCIAL SCIENCE INQUIRY, RELATIONSHIPS AMONG AND BETWEEN SOCIAL SCIENCE DISCIPLINES AND OTHER CONTENT AREAS, AND SKILLS FOR RESOLVING CONFLICTS, SOLVING PROBLEMS, AND MAKING DECISIONS IN SOCIAL STUDIES CONTEXTS.

SKILL 23.1   Demonstrate knowledge of the philosophical foundations of social science inquiry.

The social sciences are built upon the philosophy that human movements and interactions can be measured, studied, and ultimately predicted using a variety of methods and research techniques. By studying how humans act individually and within their societies, the social sciences seek to discover and explain common motivations and reactions among humans.

The body of knowledge generated by the social sciences has great influence on both the individual and societal levels. Methods of individual psychological treatment, for instance, are based on ongoing research in the social science of psychology. In the larger scheme, a country bases its foreign policy largely on the analyses of political scientists and other social researchers.

Social sciences include several philosophical foundations. Anthropology, economics, history, sociology, political science, and psychology are examples. Researchers also study the social sciences from the perspectives of positivism, normativism, and pragmatism. All three philosophies may be used in research. The exact philosophy that is used will depend upon the type of research being conducted. Researchers also use empiricism in research and the scientific approach to solving problems.

Positivism is based on the foundation that information that is obtained from logical or scientific material is the exclusive source of all authoritative knowledge. **Auguste Comte**, a philosopher and sociologist, was the first to develop this approach during the nineteenth century.

Normativism describes laws as being independent of social factors or behaviors of society that may influence legislatures and courts. Normativism requires the study of law be in a "pure" form, meaning that the law is what the law is and not what it ought to be. This philosophy was important in Europe until after World War II but is still important in Latin American countries.

Pragmatism describes the method of dealing with situations in a practical, reasonable, and logical manner. It is contrary to earlier ideas that dealt with problems on the basis of ideas and theories. The theory of pragmatism was developed by Americans **C. S. Pierce** and **William James.**

SKILL 23.2   Use social studies terminology correctly.

Social sciences, like other fields, have a set of terminology and vocabulary. For instance, an economist is concerned with supply, demand, and factors of production. The other areas of the social sciences, including history, geography, government, anthropology, sociology, and psychology, also have their own sets of terminology.

Each set of terminologies or vocabularies helps the student learn more information correctly about whichever subject is being taught. Terminologies are fundamental to the learning process. The terminologies the students are expected to learn begin at a basic level in the lower grades and increase in detail and content as students progress through high school. Terminology should include a word and a definition for the word.

When social studies terminology is used correctly, it provides the student with an increased vocabulary but also helps the student become more aware of the world around him or her. This awareness, in turn, will hopefully lead to better citizens, more effective citizens, and citizens who are more aware of the background of their country and the world.

As you review each section of this guide, become familiar with the terms used in each of the areas of social studies.

SKILL 23.3   Know how knowledge generated by the social science disciplines affects society and people's lives, understand practical applications of social studies education, and know how to use social studies information and ideas to study social phenomena.

Knowledge generated by the social studies disciplines may be in many forms. Research projects and academic learning in the classroom are two examples. This knowledge can affect society in several ways. It may identify problems that society is facing, introduce the significance of problems facing society, or may promote objectives that society may want to consider to better living conditions or problems that the society faces.

The knowledge generated by the social studies disciplines benefit individuals as well as society. In addition to adding to a person's intellect, the knowledge can help individuals learn about society's problems and develop goals for attempting to correct the problems. The knowledge can also help individuals lead better personal lives because the knowledge should make the person aware of the goals of society.

Social science knowledge has practical application in society because it helps people understand past problems and present problems in addition to considering how to alleviate problems in the future.

Knowledge learned as the result of social studies disciplines has impact locally, nationally, and globally. Becoming better citizens locally is a goal of educated people, but in today's society of expanded international contact through communications, technology, and travel, obtaining knowledge of the social sciences is a way to become a better national and international citizen.

SKILL 23.4 Understand how social science disciplines relate to each other and to other content areas.

The disciplines within the social sciences, sometimes referred to as social studies, include anthropology, geography, history, sociology, psychology, economics, and political science. The subjects of civics and government may be a part of an educational curriculum as separate from political science. The study of archaeology may be an extension of the study of anthropology. Some programs also include philosophy, religion, law, and criminology.

Anthropology is the scientific study of human culture and humanity or the relationship between human beings and their culture. Anthropologists study different groups and how they relate to other cultures, patterns of behavior, similarities, and differences. Their research is two-fold—cross-cultural and comparative. The major method of study is referred to as "participant observation." The anthropologist studies and learns about the people being studied by living among them and participating with them in their daily lives. Other methods may be used, but this is the most characteristic method.

Archaeology is the scientific study of past human cultures by studying the remains they left behind—objects such as pottery, bones, buildings, tools, and artwork. Archaeologists locate and examine any evidence to help explain the way people lived in past times. They use special equipment and techniques to gather the evidence and make special effort to keep detailed records of their findings because a lot of their research results in destruction of the remains being studied.

The first step is to locate an archaeological site using various methods. Next, surveying the site takes place starting with a detailed description of the site with notes, maps, photographs, and collecting artifacts from the surface. Excavating follows either by digging for buried objects or by diving and working in submersible decompression chambers, when underwater. Archaeologists record and preserve the evidence for eventual classification, dating, and evaluating their find.

Geography involves studying locations and how living things and the earth's features are distributed throughout the earth. It includes where animals, people, and plants live and the effects of their relationship with earth's physical features. Geographers also explore the locations of earth's features, how they got there, and why it is so important.

History is the study of past events and developments, often in chronological sequence, specifically how they relate to human beings. The word history comes from a Greek word meaning "inquiry."

Political science is the study of the processes, principles, and structure of government and political institutions. **Civics** is the study of the responsibilities and rights of citizens with emphasis on such subjects as freedom, democracy, and individual rights. Students study local, state, national, and international government structures, functions, and problems. Related to this topic are other social, political, and economic institutions. As a method of study, students gain experience and understanding through direct participation in student government, school publications, and other organizations. They also participate in community activities such as conservation projects and voter-registration drives.

Economics generally is the study of the ways goods and services are produced and the ways they are distributed. It also includes the ways people and nations choose what they buy and what they want. Some of the methods of study include research, case studies, analysis, statistics, and mathematics.

Sociology is the study of human social behavior, especially the study of the origins, organization, institutions, and development of human society. For more information, see Skill 16.4.

Psychology is the study of human behavior and mental processes. For more information, see Skill 16.8.

SKILL 23.5   **Know how to use problem-solving processes to identify problems, gather information, list and consider options, consider advantages and disadvantages, choose and implement solutions, and evaluate the effectiveness of solutions.**

Problem-Solving Processes

A clearly presented description of research results will spell out what question the researchers hoped to answer. Analyzing research results includes comparing the information given as it relates to this initial question. One must also consider the methods used to gather the data, and whether they truly measure what the researchers claim they do.

A research project that sets out to measure the effect of a change in average temperature on the feeding habits of birds, for instance, should use appropriate measurements such as weather observations and observations of the birds in question. Measuring rainfall would not be an appropriate method for this research because it is not related to the primary area of research. If, during the experiment, it appears that rainfall might be affecting the research, a researcher may design another experiment to investigate this additional question.

The Scientific Approach

The central scientific methodology (not a single "scientific method") has the following general steps:

1. Identify the problem/issue/question
2. Define research objectives
3. Develop approaches for achieving objectives (including hypotheses of expected outcomes)
4. Conduct the analysis (testing the hypothesis)
5. Interpret the results and draw conclusions

These steps are common to all disciplines.

Identifying the Problem/Issue/Question

Identifying the problem is an important step because it allows you to investigate further to determine what needs to be resolved. The more clearly a person can identify a problem, the easier the person will find it is to use the remaining steps and draw conclusions. It is important to look for the cause of a problem and not the symptoms of a problem.

Defining Research Objectives

It is important to decide the type of problem that needs to be resolved. You will need to decide whether there is a hurdle or barrier to overcome or whether you need to use a certain approach to reach an objective. In the first step, the question that is to be asked is "What is the problem?" The second step of defining research objectives must ask, "What is it that you want to accomplish?" In this step you are looking at your ultimate goal.

Developing Approaches for Achieving Objectives

In this step of problem solving, the question should be, "How do we approach the problem to achieve the desired objective?" A cause-and-effect diagram may be helpful. This step should include identifying as many approaches as possible. For each possible approach, it may be helpful to identify a hypothesis for each expected outcome. Identify as many possible solutions as possible. If you are creative in considering possible approaches, you may find that an analysis is easier and that the results are easier to interpret because you have considered all types of approaches.

Conducting the Analysis (Testing the Hypothesis)

When conducting analysis, it is important to test each hypothesis. Some testing may be by trial and error but some may be tested by using a cause-and-effect diagram that you constructed earlier. The testing of some of the hypotheses will have expected results whereas other testing may have unexpected results.

Interpreting the Results and Drawing Conclusions

The goal of interpreting results is to obtain the best solution possible. As you interpret the results, you may find that other options present themselves for testing. If this is the case, then begin the process again for each of the new options. Once you have interpreted all results, it is important to draw conclusions from those results. After the conclusions have been reached, it is possible to decide the actions, if any, that need to be taken. As the plan is implemented, it is important to remember that obtaining a solution may be an ongoing process. The first plan of action may or may not be effective. Therefore, it is important to retain the information from each of the steps to have them available in the event one or more solutions do not work.

SKILL 23.6   **Know how to use decision-making processes to identify situations that require decisions, gather and analyze information, identify options, predict consequences, and take action to implement decisions.**

Decision-Making Steps

Decision making can be broken down into methodical steps that will result in sound decisions based on the relevant facts.

Identify Situations That Require Decisions

The first step in decision making is to identify situations that require decisions. These situations often present themselves in daily life. One decision that faces many people is whether to buy a home or rent an apartment.

Gather and Analyze Information

Before making a decision to buy or rent, a person should gather information. Information including availability of apartments and homes for sale in the city where one lives and the relative monthly costs of each option are important facts that must be taken into account.

Identify Options

The third step—identifying options—organizes the facts gathered in the second step into clear potential decisions.

Predict Consequences

Predicting the consequence of a decision is an important step in the process. In this example, forecasting the effect of buying vs. renting on one's monthly income would be a crucial step. One choice might be less expensive but may be farther from work, increasing commuting expenses, for example. Predicting how a decision will affect other areas of one's life is essential before arriving at a final decision, which is the last step in the process.

Implementing the Decision

Arriving at a final decision and taking action to implement the decision complete the process. Sometimes this is an experimental phase. If the first choice of an answer does not reach the desired result, then the steps can be reviewed, ultimately reaching another decision as to which action to implement.

COMPETENCY 24: SOURCES OF SOCIAL STUDIES INFORMATION; INTERPRETING AND COMMUNICATING SOCIAL STUDIES INFORMATION

THE TEACHER UNDERSTANDS SOURCES OF SOCIAL STUDIES INFORMATION AND KNOWS HOW TO INTERPRET AND COMMUNICATE SOCIAL STUDIES INFORMATION IN VARIOUS FORMS.

SKILL 24.1   Demonstrate knowledge of characteristics and uses of primary and secondary sources (e.g., databases, maps, photographs, documents, biographies, interviews, questionnaires, artifacts).

Primary Sources

Primary sources include interviews, focus groups, surveys, questionnaires, and experiments. Advantages of primary research are that the research is computer accessible for rapid analysis. Coding enables multiple comparisons among all the variables in the research, and it can be generalized to a larger population. It is verifiable because it can be replicated. The respondents can be re-questioned. Of course, validity is dependent on the random sample and its size.

Primary sources also include original records created at the time, original records in the form of memoirs, diaries, journals, and oral histories. Primary sources may include letters, manuscripts, newspapers, speeches, interviews, documents produced by Congress or the Office of the President, photographs, audio recordings, moving pictures, video recordings, research data, and objects or artifacts such as works of art or ancient roads, buildings, tools, and weapons.

Secondary Sources

Secondary sources are generally easy to obtain, and they include the following kinds of materials:

- Books written on the basis of primary materials about the period of time
- Books written on the basis of primary materials about persons who played a major role in the events under consideration
- Books and articles written on the basis of primary materials about the culture, the social norms, the language, and the values of the period
- Quotations from primary sources
- Statistical data on the period
- Conclusions and inferences of other historians
- Multiple interpretations of the ethos of the time

Guidelines for the use of secondary sources include the following:

- Do not rely upon only a single secondary source.
- Check facts and interpretations against primary sources whenever possible.
- Do not accept the conclusions of other historians uncritically.
- Place greatest reliance on secondary sources created by the best and most respected scholars.
- Do not use the inferences of other scholars as if they were facts.

- Ensure that you recognize any bias the writer brings to his/her interpretation of history.
- Understand the primary point of the book as a basis for evaluating the value of the material presented in it to your questions.

Specific Types of Sources

Databases

Databases are used for collecting information. For example, a history project may include databases for names of witnesses to an event in history and authors of primary and/or secondary sources.

Maps

Maps, graphs, and charts are examples of illustrations that are used in social sciences. They may be primary sources if they are contemporaneous to the time being discussed. Maps may be flat or relief. They can show a variety of information, including levels of terrain, population, landforms, and shapes and sizes of countries and land areas.

For more extensive discussion of maps, graphs, charts, and other visual representations of social science data, see Skills 24.5, 24.6, and 25.5.

Photographs

Photographs are often used as primary sources because they provide evidence of political figures and events of a time that is being discussed, visualized, or learned about. They illustrate what the actual time period was like or show how a person looked in a certain time and place. A photograph is an illustration because it may provide a better understanding of an event or time than a written description would.

Documents

A document is written and represents and idea or a thought. Source documents can take many formats. A document may be minutes of a meeting or a statement of reasons for action, such as the Declaration of Independence. Documents may also consist of court opinions and speeches given by famous people.

Biographies

A biography is the life story of an individual written from another's perspective. Biographies are secondary sources. A life's story written by the person whose story is being told is an autobiography and is a primary source.

Interviews

Interviews are conversations between two or more people. If two people are involved, one person asks questions to elicit information from the other person. Interviews may be primary or secondary sources. If the person being interviewed has witnessed an event and the interview is taking place near the time of the event, the interview is likely a primary source. If an author is being interviewed about a biography that he or she has written, the interview is a secondary source because the information elicited is a compilation of the writer's research.

Questionnaires

Questionnaires are sources of information and are usually in the form of written questions that are expected to be answered. Questionnaires may seek facts, opinions, or a combination of the two.

Artifacts

An artifact is an object made by a person. Artifacts are important in social studies research because they tell about the culture or time period in which a person lived/lives. Pieces of Roman pottery that are found in the earth can help provide information about life during the times the Romans lived. If the pottery found in England is different from pottery found in Italy, then social scientists can make determinations about why there are differences. If the pieces are similar, then social scientists can make comparisons and draw conclusions about similarities of life between the two areas.

SKILL 24.2   **Evaluate the validity of social studies information from primary and secondary sources and be able to identify bias (e.g., assessing source validity on the basis of language, corroboration with other sources, and information about the author).**

Making a decision based on a set of given information requires a careful interpretation of the information to decide the strength of the evidence supplied and what it means.

For example, a chart showing that the number of people of foreign birth living in the United States has increased annually over the last ten years might allow one to make conclusions about population growth and changes in the relative sizes of ethnic groups in the United States. The chart would not give information about the reason the number of foreign-born citizens increased nor would it address matters of immigration status. Conclusions in these areas would be invalid based on this information.

Evaluating Validity of Social Studies Information

When evaluating sources, it is important to first **look at the time period** in which the article was written. Was the author a participant or an observer of the event? Did the author interview witnesses to the event or did the author introduce evidence that related directly to the event? The time period can tell the researcher whether the information was contemporary with the event. It can also tell whether the article should be considered as a primary or secondary source.

If more than one account of an event is available, read each account to **determine the factual similarities and differences.** If there are differences in the accounts, analyze why there are differences. From whose point of view is the account written? The fact that there are differences may not make one primary source more reliable than another, but the writer may have seen the event from a different perspective.

Secondary sources need to be evaluated, also. However, because these sources were not written contemporaneously with the occurrence of an event, they need to be evaluated differently. One of the first questions that should be asked in an evaluation is **how much distance is there between the event and the author** of the source he or she is writing about. Is the writing based on primary sources, secondary sources, or the author's opinions or conclusions from having read other sources about the subject?

Many secondary sources are based on primary sources and may be good sources to use. However, other secondary sources may be based on opinion or other secondary sources, such as the Internet. Those secondary sources may not be the best researched materials. Sources from government Websites, libraries, and museums may be good sources even though the information is found on the Internet. It is also important to **check the accuracy of the material** in the secondary source and evaluate bias.

Identifying Bias

Bias is the showing of prejudice in the account of an event or happening. Bias can occur in any account of an event, whether the account is a primary source or a secondary source. It may be in favor of or against someone or some group. Its purpose is to persuade the reader to believe as the writer believes. Bias usually results in an unfair portray of a person or event.

Most documents, whether primary sources or secondary sources, may include bias. The bias may be purposefully included or unconsciously included by the author as he or she expresses a point of view. Has the material been interpreted in one way or another for a specific purpose? What are the credentials of the writer? Does the writer have bias? Has the writer stated his or her purpose in providing the account?

It is important to evaluate bias before utilizing a researched source of information. Learn as much as you can about the qualifications and credibility of the writer and decide whether those qualifications make him or her a good reference source. Consider why the author presented the material in a certain way and whether the audience was attempting to influence thought or whether the source was to be used for a specific audience.

SKILL 24.3   **Assess multiple points of view and frames of reference relating to social studies issues, and know how to support a point of view on a social studies issue or event.**

Assessing Points of View and Frames of Reference

Analyzing an event or issue from multiple perspectives involves seeking out sources that advocate or express those perspectives and comparing them with one another. Listening to the speeches of Martin Luther King, Jr., for example, provides insight into the perspective of one group of people concerning the issue of civil rights in the United States in the 1950s and 1960s. Public statements of George Wallace, an American governor opposed to integration, provide another perspective from the same time period. Looking at the legislation that was proposed at the time and how it came into effect offers a window into the thinking of the day.

Comparing perspectives on the matter of civil rights provides information on the key issues that each group was concerned about and provides a fuller picture of the societal changes that were occurring at that time. Analysis of any social event, issue, problem, or phenomenon requires that various perspectives be taken into account in this way.

Supporting Points of View

Historical concepts are movements, belief systems, or other phenomena that can be identified and examined individually or as part of a historical theme. Capitalism, communism, democracy, racism, and globalization are all examples of historical concepts. Historical concepts can be interpreted as part of larger historical themes and provide insight into historical events by placing them in a larger historical context.

One way to analyze historical events, patterns, and relationships is to focus on historical themes. Many themes repeat throughout human history, and they can be used to make comparisons between different historical times as well as between nations and peoples. By comparing sources, patterns, and reports of history, one can determine whether the points of view can be supported, and if so, to what extent. A few of the widely recognized historical themes are as follows:

Politics and political institutions can provide information on prevailing opinions and beliefs of a group of people and how they change over time. Historically, Texas produced several important political figures and was a traditional supporter of the Democratic Party for nearly a century. This has changed in recent years, with the Republican Party gaining more influence and control of Texas politics. Looking at the political history of the state can reveal the popular social ideals that developed in Texas and how they have changed over time.

Race and ethnicity is another historical theme that runs through the history of Texas and the nation. Texas was formerly part of Spanish territory and then part of Mexico, and Hispanic settlers have been present from the earliest days of settlement. European Americans began moving into the area in the early nineteenth century and soon made up most of the Texas population. This has changed recently, with ethnic minority groups in Texas now outnumbering those described as Caucasian. Researching the history of how people of different races treated one another reflects on many other social aspects of a society and can be a fruitful line of historical interpretation.

The study of **gender** issues is a theme that focuses on the relative places men and women hold in a society and is connected to many other themes such as politics and economics. In the United States, women were not allowed to vote until 1920, for example. In economic matters, married women were expected not to hold jobs. For women who did work, a limited number of types of work were available. Investigating the historical theme of gender can reveal changes in public attitudes, economic changes, and shifting political attitudes, among other things.

Economic factors drive many social activities such as where people live and work and the relative wealth of nations. As a historical theme, **economic history** can connect events to their economic causes and explore the results. Mexican immigration is a national political issue currently. Economic imbalances between the United States and Mexico are driving many Mexicans to look for work in the United States. As a border state with historic ties to Mexico, Texas receives a large number of these immigrants and has the second largest Hispanic population in the country, which plays a crucial role in the current economy of Texas. The subject of immigration in Texas is an example of how the historical themes of politics, economics, and race can intersect, each providing a line of historic interpretation into the state's past.

The historic concept of **colonialism,** for example, is one that is connected to the history of Texas. Colonialism is the concept that a nation controls areas outside of its borders for economic and political gain by establishing settlements and controlling the native inhabitants. Beginning in the seventeenth century, the nations of France and Spain were both actively colonizing North America, with the French establishing a colony at the mouth of the Mississippi River. Spain moved into the area to contain the French and keep them away from their settlements in present-day Mexico. These colonial powers eventually clashed, with Spain maintaining its hold over the region. France finally sold its holdings to the United States in its sale of the Louisiana Purchase, which positioned the United States at New Spain's frontier. The eighteenth and early nineteenth centuries were a time of revolutionary movements in many parts of the world.

The American and French revolutions had altered the balance of world power in the 1770s and 1780s, and by the 1820s Mexicans living under Spanish colonial control won independence and Texas became part of the new, independent state of Mexico. Texas would itself declare independence from Mexico and survive as an independent country for a decade before being annexed by the United States as a state.

SKILL 24.4 Organize and interpret information from outlines, reports, databases, narratives, literature, and visuals including graphs, charts, timelines, and maps.

Social studies provide an opportunity for students to broaden their general academic skills in many areas. When students are encouraged to ask and investigate questions, they gain skill in making meaningful inquiries into social issues. Providing students with a range of resources requires them to make judgments about the best sources for investigating a line of inquiry and helps them develop the ability to determine authenticity among those sources. Collaboration develops the ability to work as part of a team and to respect the viewpoints of others.

Historic events and social issues cannot be considered in isolation. People and their actions are connected in many ways, and events are linked through cause and effect over time. Identifying and analyzing these social and historic links is a primary goal of the social sciences. The methods used to analyze social phenomena borrow from several of the social sciences. Interviews, statistical evaluation, observation, and experimentation are just some of the ways that people's opinions and motivations can be measured. From these opinions, larger social beliefs and movements can be interpreted, and events, issues and social problems can be placed in context to provide a fuller view of their importance.

Organization

Organizing information is important in research because it provides a more orderly and systematic approach to problem solving and reaching objectives of the research. The organization of information can be done by separating, for example, outlines, reports, and visuals into their own separate categories. There may be a subdivision within that organization, too. If narratives include more than one aspect of a research inquiry, for example, then those should be organized separately and stored according to topic or time period. Organization can also be done by topic where various sources are placed together.

Interpretation

Interpreting information is important to reach conclusions and provide evidence for those conclusions. It is important to determine whether the information is relevant to your research and whether it is consistent with earlier research or shows a change in evidence from earlier research. If the social studies research project involves, for example, the causes of World War II, then the information that has been collected needs to show that a causal relation exists between the events that are indicated as reasons for the war and the actual war.

SKILL 24.5   **Know how to use maps and other graphics to present geographic, political, historical, economic, and cultural features, distributions, and relationships.**

Maps and graphics are important resources for the social studies because they record information. They perform several functions, such as showing the positions of countries and continents, climates, terrain, and population densities. They are useful because:

- Maps identify the location of places. The places may be countries or continents, oceans or seas, or other territories and regions.

- Maps provide visual descriptions of areas. The borders between states, or countries, can be viewed on a map. Also, if an area has mountain ranges or rivers, these geographical features can be viewed.

- Maps can show different boundaries of an area for different times in history. For example, maps of various years during World War II can show Axis and Allied control of areas and how those areas decreased or increased.

- In election years, maps of the United States can show "red" and "blue" states to show the political alignment for the national election.

- Graphics are images that may be computer generated, graphs, or other drawings.

- Graphics are designed to show comparisons. For example, if the demographics of a community are the focus of a project, a graph or chart can show percentages of population by ethnicity, number, or age.

SKILL 24.6   **Use maps to obtain and analyze data for solving locational problems and to answer questions, infer relationships, and analyze spatial change.**

Geography involves studying location and how living things and the earth's features are distributed. It includes where animals, people, and plants live and the effects of their relationship with earth's physical features. Geographers also explore the locations of earth's features. Maps can be used to show themes of geography and to analyze spatial change.

Themes of Geography

Location includes absolute and relative location. **Absolute location** is the exact whereabouts of a person, place, or thing, according to any kind of geographical indicators you want to name. Absolute location refers to a specific point, such as 41 degrees North latitude, 90 degrees West longitude, or 123 Main Street.

Every point on earth has a specific location that is determined by an imaginary grid of lines denoting latitude and longitude. Parallels of latitude measure distances north and south of the line called the Equator. Meridians of longitude measure distances east and west of the line called the Prime Meridian. Geographers use latitude and longitude to pinpoint a place's absolute, or exact, location.

To know the absolute location of a place is only part of the story. It is also important to know how that place is related to other places—in other words, to know that place's relative location. **Relative location** refers to the surrounding geography, e.g., "on the banks of the Mississippi River." Relative location is *always* a description that involves more than one thing. When you describe a relative location, you tell where something is by describing what is around it. The description of where the nearest post office is in terms of relative location might be this: "It's down the street from the supermarket, on the right side of the street, next to the dentist's office." Relative location deals with the interaction that occurs between and among places. It refers to the many ways—land, water, and even technology—that places are connected.

All places have characteristics that give them meaning and character and distinguish them from other places on earth. Geographers describe places by their **physical and human characteristics.** Physical characteristics include such elements as animal life. Human characteristics of the landscape can be noted in architecture, patterns of livelihood, land use and ownership, town planning, and communication and transportation networks.

Languages, as well as **religious and political ideologies,** help shape the character of a place. Studied together, the physical and human characteristics of places provide clues to help students understand the nature of places on the earth.

A basic unit of geographic study is the **region,** an area on the earth's surface that is defined by certain unifying characteristics. The unifying characteristics may be physical, human, or cultural. In addition to studying the unifying characteristics of a region, geographers study how a region changes over times. Using the theme of regions, geographers divide the world into manageable units for study.

Spatial Organization and Change

Spatial organization is a description of how things are grouped in a given space. In geographical terms, this can describe people, places, and environments anywhere and everywhere on the earth. The most basic form of spatial organization for people is where they live. The vast majority of people live near other people, in villages, towns and cities, and settlements. These people live near others in order to take advantage of the goods and services that naturally arise from cooperation. These villages, towns and cities, and settlements are, to varying degrees, near bodies of water. When **spatial change** takes place, it is important to understand the reasons for the change. An analysis of spatial organization and diffusion can result in answers.

A **place** has both human and physical characteristics. Physical characteristics include features such as mountains, rivers, and deserts. Human characteristics are the features created by human interaction with their environment such as dams, canals, and roads.

The theme of **human-environmental interaction** has three main concepts. First, humans adapt to the environment. Wearing warm clothing in a cold climate is an example. Second, humans modify the environment. An example is planting trees to block a prevailing wind. Third, humans depend on the environment for food, water, and raw materials.

The theme of **movement** covers how humans interact with one another through trade, communications, emigration, and other forms of interaction.

A **region** is an area that has some kind of unifying characteristic, such as a common language or a common government. There are three main types of regions. **Formal regions** are areas defined by actual political boundaries, such as a city, county, or state. **Functional regions** are defined by a common function, such as the area covered by a telephone service. **Vernacular regions** are less formally defined areas that are formed by people's perceptions. Terms such as "the Middle East" and "the South" are examples.

SKILL 24.7 **Communicate and interpret social studies information in written, oral, and visual forms, and translate information from one medium to another.**

Social studies is a broad field of study that incorporates many kinds of research and results. The different types of research lend themselves to varying types of **communication**. Geographic material might best be communicated with a map, for instance, while historical material might be best conveyed through writing. Population changes might be displayed in a chart or graph. It is important to make students familiar with appropriate ways to communicate diverse types of information. Giving several options will keep students' interest level high. Examples of written, oral, and visual forms of information are atlases, surveys, and opinion polls.

An **atlas** is a collection of maps usually bound into a book that contains geographic features, political boundaries, and perhaps social, religious, and economic statistics. Atlases can be found at most libraries, and they are widely available on the Internet. The United States Library of Congress holds more than 53,000 atlases, most likely the largest and most comprehensive collection in the world.

Statistical **surveys** are used in social sciences to collect information on a sample of the population. With any kind of information, care must be taken to accurately record information so the results are not skewed or distorted.

Opinion polls are used to represent the opinions of a population by asking a number of people a series of questions about a product, place, person, or event and then using the results to apply the answers to a larger group or population. Polls, like surveys are subject to errors in the process. Errors can occur based on who is asked the question, where they are asked, the time of day, or the biases one may hold in relevance to the poll being taken.

Interpreting information learned from various means of communication permits the researcher to determine whether the research has reached the anticipated or correct result(s). **Translating** the information from one medium to another can be accomplished in various ways. One method is through the use of graphs and charts. Another method may be the summarization of the information and the inclusion in written form into the final research document.

SKILL 24.8 **Analyze various economic indicators to describe and measure levels of economic activity.**

Economic Indicators

The major **indicators** used to describe and measure levels of economic activity are the **unemployment rate** and the **inflation rate.** When the economy is functioning smoothly, the amount of national output produced or the aggregate supply is just equal to the amount of national output purchased, or aggregate demand. Then we have an economy in a period of prosperity without economic instability.

Market economies, however, experience the fluctuations of the business cycle, the ups and downs in the level of economic activity. There are four **phases of economic activity**—**boom** (period of prosperity), **recession** (a period of declining GDP and rising unemployment), **trough** (the low point of the recession), and **recovery** (a period of lessening unemployment and rising prices).

There are no rules pertaining to the duration or severity of any of the phases. The phases result in periods of unemployment and periods of inflation. **Inflation** results from too much spending in the economy. Buyers want to buy more than sellers can produce and bid up prices for the available output. **Unemployment** occurs when there is not enough spending in the economy. Sellers have produced more output than buyers are buying, and the result is a surplus situation. Firms faced with surplus merchandise lower their production levels and lay off workers, resulting in unemployment. These are situations that may require government policy actions.

A deficiency in aggregate spending results in unemployment. There is not enough aggregate demand in the economy to cause producers to produce enough output that requires the full labor force to be employed. Unemployment is measured by the unemployment rate, which is the percentage of the labor force that is unemployed. The labor force consists of people aged sixteen or older who are working, want to work, and are actively seeking employment. It does not include people who cannot work because they are too young or institutionalized, or those who do not want to work, such the retired population or the parents who stay home with the children.

Analysis

There are certain situations that cause these figures to be inaccurate. First of all, the figures do not account for underemployment, which refers to people who are working part-time while looking for full-time employment. The figures-keepers just asks if the person is employed and it does not matter if it is full-time employment or part-time employment.

This practice tends to understate the unemployment rate. The figures also do not account for the discouraged worker who has given up trying to find employment. The figures treat that worker as being out of the labor force because he or she is not actively looking for employment.

This practice also understates the published unemployment figures. The last problem is people who give false information. People may claim to be actively seeking employment when they really aren't, just to collect unemployment compensation. This tends to overstate the published figures.

The overall macroeconomic instability problems of inflation and unemployment are, for the most part, caused by the inequality of **aggregate demand** and **aggregate supply**. They are referred to as the twin evils of capitalism.

Inflation results from excess aggregate demand. Buyers want to buy a larger quantity of national output at a given price level than sellers can produce and sell. An economy that is growing too rapidly and has too high a level of spending has inflation, a period of rises in the price level as buyers bid up prices to obtain the given supply of goods and services.

Inflation results in a dollar with less purchasing power. When there is, for example, 5 percent inflation, this means the $100 that purchased $100 of goods last year, only buys $95 of goods this year. Goods and services are more expensive.

The inflation rate is computed from index numbers. The formula is very simple.

$$\text{Price Index} = \frac{\text{Price in any year}}{\text{Price in base year}} \times 100$$

Any year in the series can be selected as the base year and it is then used to compute the index number for the rest of the years, as given in the above formula.

The index numbers are then used to compute the inflation rate using the formula below:

$$\text{Inflation Rate} = \frac{\text{This year's index \# - Last year's index \#}}{\text{Last year's index \#}}$$

Inflation affects different people in different ways and in different degrees. People on fixed incomes feel the effects of inflation more than people who have flexible incomes. Social Security benefits are an example of a fixed income.

Inflation is caused by the economy expanding too quickly. There is excess aggregate demand that is fueling the inflation. This is a situation where governmental action may attempt to slow down the economy by implementing policies that result in less spending in the economy to end the inflation. These will be contractionary monetary and fiscal policies.

Contractionary monetary policy will result in the banking system having less money available for loans. Aspects of contractionary monetary policy consist of raising the reserve ratio, raising the discount rate, and selling bonds.

Contractionary fiscal policy consists of raising taxes and/or decreasing government spending. If there is less money to spend in the economy, it takes the pressure off prices because there is a decrease in aggregate demand which slows down the economy and stops the rising price level.

SKILL 24.9   **Use economic models such as production-possibilities curves, circular-flow charts, and supply-and-demand graphs to analyze economic data.**

Economic data can be presented in a variety of ways. This is what is illustrated in the production possibilities curve, circular-flow charts, and supply-and-demand graphs. Each is a method of presenting and analyzing an economic situation.

Production-Possibilities Curve

Scarcity affects the decision making of all economic agents. Scarcity means that choices have to be made by all. No economic agent can have more of all goods. Producing more of one good means that there aren't enough resources to produce other goods. That is the constraint of a fixed supply of resources. This is the relationship given in the **production-possibilities curve**.

Every point on the curve represents the different combinations that the economy can have of the two goods, given their supply or resources and that they are producing efficiently. The curve shows the trade-off between the two goods, or the opportunity cost imposed on society by the fact that resources are scarce. Producing more of one good means shifting resources from the production of the other good so there are fewer units of the second good. Having more of both goods is not feasible because it would put society at a point beyond the curve, a point that is unattainable given the supply of resources.

Circular-Flow Charts

The **circular-flow chart** is the simplest model of the economy that there is. It shows the flow of inputs, outputs, and money through the economy.

Supply-and-Demand Graphs

Graphs can be used to represent a variety of situations. Consider a graph showing **supply and demand** and an equilibrium price. Consumers buy the goods and services that give them satisfaction or utility. They want to obtain the most utility they can for their dollar. The quantity of goods and services that consumers are willing and able to purchase at different prices during a given period of time is referred to as demand.

Aggregating all of the individual demands yields the market demand for a good or service. Since consumers buy the goods and services that give them satisfaction, this means that, for the most part, they do not buy the goods and services that they do not want that or that do not give them satisfaction.

Consumers are, in effect, voting for the goods and services that they want with the dollars, i.e., dollar voting. Consumers are signal firms as to how they want society's scarce resources used with their dollar votes. A good that society wants acquires enough dollar votes for the producer to experience profits—a situation where the firm's revenues exceed the firm's costs.

The existence of profits indicates to the firm that it is producing the goods and services that consumers want and that society's scarce resources are being used in accordance with consumer preferences. When a firm does not have a profitable product, it is because that product is not tabulating enough dollar votes of consumers.

Consumer sovereignty is the process in which consumers vote with their dollars. Consumers are basically directing the allocation of scarce resources in the economy with the dollar spending. Firms that are in business to earn profit then hire resources, or inputs, in accordance with consumer preferences. This is the way in which resources are allocated in a market economy. This is the manner in which society achieves the output mix that it desires.

Price plays an important role in a market economy. Supply is based on production costs, and the supply of a good or service is defined as the quantities of a good or service that a producer is willing and able to sell at different prices during a given period of time.

Market equilibrium occurs when the buying decisions of buyers are equal to the selling decision of seller, or where the demand and supply curves intersect. At this point the quantity that sellers want to sell at a price is equal to the quantity the buyers want to buy at that same price. This is the **market equilibrium price.**

The price of an input or output allocates that input or output to those who are willing and able to transact at the market price. Those who can transact at the market price or better are included in the market and those that cannot or will not transact at the market price are excluded from the market.

Prices are rational and based scarcity of inputs. Inputs and outputs that are scarce carry higher prices than those that are more frequently occurring. Diamonds are higher priced than water because diamonds are scarcer than water. This is the way in which consumer sovereignty and the market result in an efficient allocation of resources in accordance with consumer preferences. All of this information is represented in a graph with supply, demand, and an equilibrium price.

COMPETENCY 25: SOCIAL STUDIES RESEARCH

THE TEACHER UNDERSTANDS SOCIAL SCIENCE AND HISTORICAL RESEARCH METHODS, INCLUDING PROCEDURES FOR FORMULATING RESEARCH QUESTIONS AND FOR ORGANIZING, ANALYZING, EVALUATING, AND REPORTING INFORMATION.

SKILL 25.1   Know how to formulate research questions.

Identifying a Topic for Research

There are many different ways to find ideas for **research problems**. One of the most common ways is through experiencing and assessing relevant problems in a specific field. Researchers are often involved in the fields in which they choose to study, and thus encounter practical problems related to their areas of expertise on a daily basis. They can use their knowledge, expertise, and research ability to examine their selected research problem.

For students, all that this entails is being curious about the world around them. Research ideas can come from one's background, culture, education, readings, or experiences.

Another way to get research ideas is by exploring literature in a specific field and coming up with a question that extends or refines previous research.

Once a **topic** is decided, a research question must be formulated. A research question is a relevant, researchable, feasible statement that identifies the information to be studied.

Framing the Research Question

Formulating meaningful questions is a primary part of any research process, and providing students with a wide variety of resources promotes this ability by making them aware of a wide array of social studies issues. Encouraging the **use of multiple resources** also introduces diverse viewpoints and different methods of communicating research results. This practice promotes the ability to judge the value of a resource and the appropriate ways to interpret it, which supports the development of meaningful inquiry skills.

Framing the question is important because the question will serve as a road map for obtaining information about the subject posed by the question. When you frame a question you are indicating what you want to find out about the subject. For example, if you are researching the effectiveness of the New Deal, the focus of the question should be the creation of the programs and their successes and failures. Framing a question about the causes leading up to the New Deal will not help you reach your goal of finding out what sources tell you about the success or failure of New Deal programs.

Research questions need to be **relevant to the goal** you are trying to accomplish. If you want to learn about events leading up to American independence, then the question needs to be focused on what types of acts were passed by Parliament, the responses of the colonists, and the results of those responses. Research questions need to be refined until the exact question that you want answered can be answered with research. However, the sources of information need to be available. If research materials cannot be obtained easily and if research materials are not within your ability to evaluate, the research question should be redefined.

The research question **should be interesting and should be able to be answered.** If the question is vague, the result of the research will not be conclusive or will not lend itself to an adequate interpretation of the sources used for the research. If the question is not interesting, the research and resulting conclusions may not accomplish the intended purpose.

The research question that is formulated **should be specific.** If it is too broad, the result will most likely not be definitive. A question relating to the success or failure of recovery programs in Europe after World War II may be too broad for a research question, but a question relating to the Berlin airlift or to the success of the Marshall Plan in Germany after the war may be more specific and, thus, a better question to research.

SKILL 25.2   **Use appropriate procedures to reach supportable judgments and conclusions in social studies.**

Once the initial research question is formulated, it is a good idea to think of specific issues related to the topic. This approach will help to create a hypothesis.

Developing a Hypothesis

A research **hypothesis** is a statement of the researcher's expectations for the outcome of the research problem. It is a summary statement of the problem to be addressed in any research document. A good hypothesis states, clearly and concisely, the researcher's expected relationship between the variables that he or she is investigating.

The Scientific Method

The scientific method is the process by which researchers over time endeavor to construct an accurate (that is, reliable, consistent and non-arbitrary) representation of the world. Recognizing that personal and cultural beliefs influence both our perceptions and our interpretations of natural phenomena, standard procedures and criteria minimize those influences when a theory is being developed.

The scientific method has four steps:

- Observation and description of a phenomenon or group of phenomena
- Formulation of a hypothesis to explain the phenomena
- Use of the hypothesis to predict the existence of other phenomena or to predict quantitatively the results of new observations
- Performance of experimental tests of the predictions by several independent experimenters and properly performed experiments

Although the researcher may bring certain biases to the study, it's important that bias not be permitted to enter into the interpretation. The researcher must not rule out data that will not fit the hypothesis. This is unlikely to happen if the researcher is open to the possibility that the hypothesis might turn out to be null. Another important caution is to be certain that the methods for analyzing and interpreting are flawless. Abiding by these mandates is important if the discovery is to make a contribution to human understanding.

SKILL 25.3 **Understand social studies research and know how social scientists and historians locate, gather, organize, analyze, interpret, and report information using standard research methodologies.**

Locating Information

After the research question has been posed, it may be helpful to identify all aspect of the question by writing an outline or listing sub-points relating to the topic. Read as many primary and secondary sources as possible. It is important to locate information that is accessible.

Historical societies and libraries are two obvious options for locating information related to social studies. Libraries may be connected by a system from which research materials may be loaned. If a lending library is not available, then locating information may be more difficult. The Internet may provide access to information or may provide a source for obtaining the information, but special care must be taken to use reliable sources. Photographs, surveys, polls, and interviews may also be available from libraries or historical societies.

Gathering Information

The best way of gathering information is reading as much as possible about the subject that has been chosen. **Taking notes** or keeping track of the information is equally important. Each person may use a different system for gathering information, but whether the system includes taking notes on the computer, using file cards, or writing notes on paper, note taking is an important aspect of gathering information because it is a method of keeping track of it.

Careful documentation is extremely important, particularly with regard to which particular edition is being read in the case of written sources and the date, location, and source of information obtained from the Internet. The link that shows the source of Internet information and the last date the information was accessed is useful in research. If the conversation, interview, or speech is live, then the date, circumstances, and location must be indicated.

Organizing Information

There are various ways of organizing information. The key to successful organization is to make it meaningful to the researcher and representative of what the research is attempting to prove.

No one way of organizing information is better than another. Each researcher must develop a way that is best for him or her. **Separating primary sources from secondary sources** is one method. Developing a **cross-referencing system** will make the organization more complete.

Some researchers develop **charts and numbering systems** to identify information that has been organized. For example, a photograph of the opening of the Great Lakes to ocean traffic may be entered as a source on an information list and might be identified by a number. It may be catalogued as a primary source, and notations may be made relating to its possible use in a specific part of the research document. If an outline or listing of points is available, the documents may be assigned to those parts of the paper.

Analyzing and Interpreting Information

Analyzing an event or issue from multiple perspectives involves seeking out sources that advocate or express those perspectives, then comparing them with one another. After you have gathered and organized information, it is important to determine whether the information will help you reach the desired research goal.

Interpreting information will lead to the decision of whether or not to include the information in the research project. Is the information relevant? Why? Why not? How is it relevant? How will the information help reach the research answer? The important focus of interpreting information should be to determine whether the information helps answer the research question that has been asked. When these questions are asked about each part of the research project and how they relate to the desired or anticipated answer, it will become apparent whether or not the information will be useful in writing the project or reporting the information.

Reporting Information

Reporting information is more efficient when the researcher has taken time to be detailed in the work of researching the subject. Detailed gathering, organizing, analyzing, and interpreting of information makes the reporting simpler and more accurate as well as making the research goal easier to accomplish.

Reporting is the last step in the research project. There are two types of research papers—analytical and argumentative.

Analytical Research Papers

Analytical papers focus on examining and understanding the various parts of a research topic and reformulating them in a new way to support your initial statement. In this type of research paper, the research question is used as both a basis for investigation as well as a topic for the paper. Once a variety of information is collected on the given topic, it is coalesced into a clear discussion.

Argumentative Research Papers

Argumentative papers focus on supporting the question or claim with evidence or reasoning. Instead of presenting research to provide information, an argumentative paper presents research in order to prove a debatable statement and interpretation.

SKILL 25.4 **Know how to analyze social studies information by sequencing, categorizing, identifying associations and cause-and-effect relationships, comparing, contrasting, finding the main idea, summarizing, making generalizations, and drawing inferences and conclusions.**

Knowing How to Analyze

The purpose of analysis is to understand the works of others and to use that work in shaping a conclusion. The writer or speaker must clearly differentiate between the ideas that come from a source and those ideas that are his or her own.

A synthesis of information from multiple sources requires an understanding of the content chosen for the synthesis. The writer of the synthesis will wish to incorporate his or her own ideas, especially in any conclusions that are drawn, and show relationships to those of the chosen sources. That can happen only if the writer has a firm grip on what others have said or written. There is less focus on documentary methods than on techniques of critically examining and evaluating the ideas of others.

Recognizing Errors in Reasoning

Helping students to become critical thinkers is an important objective of the social studies curriculum. History, geography, and political science classes provide many opportunities to teach students to recognize and understand reasoning errors. Common reasoning errors tend to fall into two categories: a) inadequate reasons, and b) misleading reasoning. Following are examples of each.

Inadequate Reasons

- **Faulty analogies:** The two things being compared must be similar in all significant aspects if the reasoning is to be relied upon. If there is a major difference between the two, then the argument falls apart.

- **False cause:** It is sometimes helpful to use the Latin phrase *Post hoc ergo propter hoc* means "after this, therefore because of this." There must be a factual tie between the effect and its declared cause.

- *Ad hominem:* The Latin phrase *Ad hominem* refers to attacking the person instead of addressing the issues.

- **Slippery Slope:** The domino effect is usually prophetic in nature—predicting what will follow if a certain event occurs. This is only reliable when it is used in hindsight—not in predicting the outcome.

- **Hasty conclusions:** One example of leaping to conclusions when not enough evidence has been collected was the set of accusations made in the 1996 bombing at the Summer Olympics in Atlanta. Not enough evidence had been collected, and the wrong man was arrested.

Misleading Reasoning

- **The red herring:** The phrase "red herring" refers to a smoked fish being dragged across a trail to distract hunting dogs. It is a technique that is often used in politics to get an opponent on the defensive about an issue that is different from the one under discussion.

- *Ad populum* or **"jumping on the bandwagon":** "Everybody's doing it, so it must be right." In research, biggest is not necessarily best when it comes to following a crowd.

- **Appeal to tradition:** "We've always done it this way." This type of reasoning is often used to squelch innovation.

- **The false dilemma or the either/or fallacy:** No other alternative is possible except the extremes at each end. This type of reasoning is used in politics frequently, but the creative researcher finds other alternatives.

SKILL 25.5   **Analyze social studies data using basic mathematical and statistical concepts and other analytical methods.**

Social scientists draw on a variety of mathematical and statistic concepts to present their observations. This involves analyzing data in a variety of ways—from simple construction of charts to complex analysis requiring knowledge of advanced calculus and statistics.

Demography

Demography is the branch of science of statistics most concerned with the social well-being of people. **Demographic tables** may include:

- Analysis of the population on the basis of age, parentage, physical condition, race, occupation, and civil position, giving the actual size and the density of each separate area
- Changes in the population as a result of birth, marriage, and death
- Statistics on population movements and their effects and relationship to given economic, social, and political conditions
- Statistics of crime, illegitimacy, and suicide
- Levels of education and economic and social statistics

Such information is also similar to that area of science known as **vital statistics** and is indispensable in studying social trends and making important legislative, economic, and social decisions. Such demographic information is gathered from census and registrar reports. By various laws such information is kept by physicians, attorneys, funeral directors, members of the clergy, and similar professional people.

Collecting and Organizing Statistical Data

It is typically not possible to secure data on a full **population.** Social scientists routinely collect data on **samples** that are based on measurements or observations of a portion of a population. Samples ideally are collected **randomly,** meaning that each observation in a population had an equal chance of being selected.

The samples are described using measures of central tendency but also by the range from the low score to the high score.

Measures of central tendency are ways of finding the average in a sample. There are three statistical measures of central tendency. The **mean** is routinely calculated by summing the value of observations and dividing by the number of observations. The **median** is the middle item in a series of observations, and the **mode** is the item or score that occurs most often.

Hypothesis Testing

Hypothesis testing involves analyzing the results of a sample to show support for a particular position. A social scientist will establish a hypothesis regarding some pattern in the world. This may be, for example, that a particular counseling approach is better than another or that the president has greater support than other candidates running for office.

The scientist will collect data and analyze it against a **null hypothesis** to show that there is no difference in counseling strategies or preferred presidential candidate. Using the standard normal curve, the scientist is able to evaluate if there is a **significant difference** allowing the acceptance or rejection of the null hypothesis. More advanced forms of analysis include regression analysis, modeling, and game theory.

Social scientists need to be concerned about **bias** in a sample. Bias can be caused by sample selection problems, ambiguous questions, or simply by some people refusing to answer some or all of the questions. An **asymmetrical distribution** is one that is skewed because of some factor in the distribution.

Visual Presentation of Data

Social scientists utilize a variety of ways to present data visually. Maps perform several important functions (see Skills 24.5 and 24.6). There are also many formats for presenting results from studies and surveys, including bar graphs, pictographs, histograms, line graphs, pie charts, scatter plots, and stem and leaf plots.

Bar Graphs and Pictographs

Bar graphs and pictographs are useful comparing data about two or more similar groups of items. They can summarize relative amounts, trends, and data sets, and are helpful in comparing quantities. A **bar graph** uses bars to convey information about categorical data where the horizontal scale represents nonnumeric attributes such as cities or years. A **pictograph** uses small figures or icons to represent data.

To read a bar graph or a pictograph, read the explanation of the scale used in the legend. Compare the length of each bar with the dimensions on the axes, and calculate the value that each bar represents. On a pictograph, count the number of pictures used in the chart and calculate the value of all the pictures.

Histograms

Histograms are visually similar to bar graphs and are used to summarize information from large sets of data that can be naturally grouped into intervals. The vertical axis indicates **frequency** (the number of times any particular data value occurs), and the horizontal axis indicates data values or ranges of data values. The number of data values in any interval is the **frequency of the interval**.

Line Graphs

A line graph compares two variables, and each variable is plotted along an axis. A line graph highlights trends by drawing connecting lines between data points. This representation is particularly appropriate for data that will vary continuously.

Pie Charts

A pie chart, also known as a **circle graph,** is used to represent relative amounts as parts of a whole. The pie chart is useful in comparing amounts or sizes, especially when each wedge is labeled with a percentage amount.

Scatter Plots

Scatter plots compare two characteristics of the same group of things or people and usually consist of a large body of data. They show how much one variable is affected by another. The relationship between the two variables is their **correlation**. The closer the data points come to making a straight line when plotted, the closer the correlation.

Stem and Leaf Plots

Stem and leaf plots are best suited for small sets of data and are especially useful for comparing two sets of data. The **stems** are the digits in the greatest place value of the data values, and the **leaves** are the digits in the next greatest place values.

For example, a stem and leaf plot can be used to represent a set of test scores. The following test scores are represented in the plot given below.

49, 54, 59, 61, 62, 63, 64, 66, 67, 68, 68, 70, 73, 74, 76, 76, 76, 77, 77, 77, 77,
78, 78, 78, 78, 83, 85, 85, 87, 88, 90, 90, 93, 94, 95, 100, 100

4	9
5	4 9
6	1 2 3 4 6 7 8 8
7	0 3 4 6 6 6 7 7 7 7 8 8 8 8
8	3 5 5 7 8
9	0 0 3 4 5
10	0 0

COMPETENCY 26: SOCIAL STUDIES INSTRUCTION AND ASSESSMENT

THE TEACHER UNDERSTANDS THE TEXAS ESSENTIAL KNOWLEDGE AND SKILLS (TEKS) IN SOCIAL STUDIES; KNOWS HOW TO PLAN AND IMPLEMENT EFFECTIVE SOCIAL STUDIES INSTRUCTION, INCLUDING HELPING STUDENTS MAKE INTERDISCIPLINARY CONNECTIONS AND DEVELOP RELEVANT READING SKILLS; AND KNOWS PROCEDURES FOR ASSESSING STUDENTS' PROGRESS AND NEEDS IN SOCIAL STUDIES.

SKILL 26.1   Know state content and performance standards for social studies that comprise the Texas Essential Knowledge and Skills (TEKS), and understand the vertical alignment of social studies in the TEKS from grade level to grade level, including prerequisite knowledge and skills.

The Texas Essential Knowledge and Skills (TEKS) are the state standards for Texas K-12 education in public schools. These are detailed descriptions of the teaching objectives: topics students are expected to know and skills that they are expected to perform at each grade level.

The following section from the Texas Education Agency's Website details the vertical alignment of the social sciences for TEKS from grade level to grade level, including prerequisite knowledge and skills:

http://ritter.tea.state.tx.us/rules/tac/chapter113/index.html

The State of Texas Assessments of Academic Readiness (STAAR) testing program is aligned with the TEKS curriculum to measure students' progress and acquisition of the TEKS. The STAAR program emphasizes readiness standards that are considered necessary for grade-level success as well as supporting standards necessary for preparation for the next grade level. Each STAAR question may address two or more TEKS objectives and is more complex in construction, often requiring students to synthesize information from a given passage or content information and complete two or more steps to solve a problem while using deductive and logical reasoning.

The STAAR program annually assesses grades 3–8 in reading and mathematics, grades 4 and 7 in writing, grades 5 and 8 in science, and grade 8 in social studies. It also includes end-of-course assessments for English I, English II, Algebra I, biology and U.S. history.

In 2012, STAAR replaced the **Texas Assessment of Knowledge and Skills (TAKS)** as the state's assessment program. The STAAR program is more rigorous than the TAKS program, placing more emphasis on the integration of the state curriculum, classroom instruction, and state-mandated assessment.

(Adapted from Texas State's media toolkit at www.tea.state.tx.us/index2.aspx?id= 2147504081)

For additional information, refer to the Texas Education Agency's website at: http://www.tea.state.tx.us/student.assessment/staar/.

Please refer to http://www.tea.state.tx.us/rules/tac/chapter113/index.html for the vertical alignment of the social sciences for Texas Essential Knowledge and Skills from grade level to grade level.

SKILL 26.2   Select and use developmentally appropriate instructional practices, activities, technologies, and materials to promote student knowledge, skills, and progress in social studies.

The interdisciplinary curriculum planning approach to student learning creates a meaningful balance inclusive of curriculum depth and breadth. Take, for instance, the following scenario:

> Mr. Hansel presents his 9A social studies class with an assignment for collaborative group work. He provides students with the birth date and death date of the civil rights activist Susan B. Anthony and asks them to decide how old she was when she died. He gives them five minutes as a group to work on the final answer. After five minutes, he asks each group for their answer and writes the answers on the board. Each group gives a different answer. When Mr. Hansel comes to the last group, a student asks, "Why do we have to do math in a social studies class?"

The application of knowledge learned from a basic math class would have problem-solved the social studies question. Given the date of Susan B. Anthony's birth and the date of her death, all students needed to do was subtract her birth year from her death year to come up with a numerical answer for the age when she died. Providing students with a constructivist modality of applying knowledge to problem-solve pertinent information for a social studies class should be an integral part of instructional practice and learning in an interdisciplinary classroom.

Historically, previous centuries of educational research have shown a strong correlation between the need for interdisciplinary instruction and cognitive learning application. Understanding how students process information and create learning was the goal of earlier educators.

Developmentally appropriate instruction provides students with optimal learning and development in a specific area. Learning the basic information about westward expansion may be appropriate for children in earlier grades whereas a more detailed approach, including the philosophy and effects of Manifest Destiny, would be more appropriate for older students. If the instruction is developmentally appropriate, children can be challenged and achieve goals individually and in groups.

Instructional materials that are developmentally appropriate should be appropriate for individual children. They should also be relevant to the children's cultural backgrounds, their ages, and their intellectual abilities.

SKILL 26.3   **Understand the appropriate use of technology as a tool for learning and communicating social studies concepts, and provide instruction on how to locate, retrieve, and retain content-related information from a range of texts and technologies.**

Using Technology for Research

The Internet and other research resources provide a wealth of information on thousands of interesting topics for students preparing presentations or projects. Using search engines such as Google, Yahoo, and Infotrac allow students to search multiple Internet resources or databases on one subject search. Students should have an outline of the purpose of a project or research presentation that includes:

- Purpose: an identification of the reason for the research information
- Objective: a clear thesis for a project that will allow the students opportunities to be specific on Internet searches
- Preparation: using resources or collecting data and creating folders for sorting through the information. Providing labels for the folders will create a system of organization that will make construction of the final project or presentation easier and less time-consuming
- Procedure: an organization of folders and a procedural list of what the project or presentation needs to include that will create A+ work for students and A+ grading for teachers
- Visuals: a selection of data or visual aids specific to the subject content or presentation. Make sure that poster boards or PowerPoint presentations can be seen from all areas of the classroom. Teachers can provide laptop computers for PowerPoint presentations

Having the school's librarian or technology expert as a guest speaker in classrooms provides another method of sharing and modeling proper presentation preparation using technology. Teachers can also appoint technology experts from the students in a classroom to work with other students on projects and presentations. In high schools, technology classes often provide students with teacher assistants who fulfill the role of technology experts.

The Importance of Evaluating Internet Sources

It is important to train the student to evaluate Internet sources that they are considering using. In using the Internet to obtain information, researchers must take special care to evaluate the sources they are consulting and try to use only reliable sources. Because the Internet offers quick access to a variety of information that might be helpful, especially for current events, it is very tempting to use the Internet frequently for research. Yet because anybody can post information on the Internet, it is important consider the source carefully before deciding whether use it. The following are a few questions the student might ask as part of this evaluation:

- Who are the author and publisher of the source? Does the author have an academic affiliation?
- Why was this information posted? Is there potential for bias? Is the author trying to analyze a situation objectively or presenting a strongly held personal opinion?

- How recent is the source? Has the Website been updated in response to current events?

In addition, the researcher must carefully document the use of these sources. Any Internet source that is used must be cited fully in the bibliography or references section of the research paper.

SKILL 26.4 **Use a variety of instructional strategies to ensure all students' reading comprehension of content-related texts, including helping students link the content of texts to their lives and connect related ideas across different texts.**

The number of social science instructional strategies is unlimited. The important thing to remember is to match the strategy with the skills and content you, as a teacher, want the students to learn. Learning is more fun and more rewarding for the student and the teacher if the process, or at least some of the process, is interactive. Regardless of which types of instructional strategies a teacher uses, if the strategy links personal experiences and backgrounds of the students with the content, learning will be more meaningful and, hopefully, lasting.

Asking Questions

Students may have background information about a subject that can be shared and used as a springboard for other discussions. For example, in a high school history class discussing the Vietnam War, questions about what students have learned from their families may provide in-depth discussions about democracy, colonialism, or the cultures of other countries.

Problem Solving

Problems can be presented for students to evaluate and reach a solution. For example, a problem might be presented relating to contemporary actions, such as a parent taking away something a student believes to be a right. Various solutions can be presented by the students, and after the "contemporary" problem is presented or solved, it can be discussed in relation to the solutions the American colonists used when the British took away rights they believed they were entitled to, such as being taxed without representation.

Role Playing

Younger students like to be involved in a class project. Providing young students with the opportunity to reenact an important historical event can provide them with a more in-depth understanding of the concerns and problems of society of a given era or time frame. Recreating the Lewis and Clark journey and its trials, tribulations, successes, and accomplishments can bring history to life and make the learning about westward expansion more meaningful.

Teaching Concepts and Generalizations

The use of maps, the Internet, and resources materials can be a good instructional strategy for individual learners and for group projects. Specific information will be learned from the research of each student but generalizations and concepts can be drawn from the collective information.

Primary and secondary resources and be used and conclusions can be drawn from the use of research materials in addition to the content itself.

SKILL 26.5   Provide instruction on how to locate the meanings and pronunciations of unfamiliar content-related words using appropriate sources.

Dictionaries are useful for spelling, writing, and reading. It is very important to expose and habituate students to enjoy using the dictionary to develop a lifelong comfort level with the dictionary and vocabulary acquisition.

Requesting or suggesting that students look up a word in the dictionary should be an invitation to exploration, not a punishment or busy work that has no reference to their current reading assignment. Model the correct way to use the dictionary. Do not routinely require students to look up every new spelling word in the dictionary.

How to locate the meanings of unfamiliar content-related words:

1. Turn to the letter your target word starts with. For example, "physics" begins with "p."
2. Look for guide words at the top of dictionary pages to help locate your word.
3. Read what is said about the word, and pay attention to any related neighbors.

Depending on the dictionary, you may find:

*   Definition
*   Pronunciation
*   Synonyms and/or antonyms
*   Etymology, derivation, or history of the word
*   Examples of how the word may be used
*   Idioms associated with the word

If there are multiple definitions, decide which one matches the context you're seeking. Try using the word in a sentence. To correctly pronounce a word, it can help to be familiar with the current phoneme set the dictionary uses. Today also you can go to Websites and find dictionaries that provide the pronunciation of words in an audio format.

Encourage students to use glossaries that provide information in the books they're reading. Having students explore atlases not just for the maps but for the glossaries that explain what words used in the atlas refer to will help them better understand geography.

During writing assignments, using a thesaurus to choose the best word will help students to build their vocabulary and help them become better communicators.

SKILL 26.6   **Know how to provide instruction that makes connections between knowledge and methods in social studies and in other content areas.**

It is important for teachers to consider students' development and readiness when deciding instructional decisions. If an educational program is child-centered, then it will surely address the developmental abilities and needs of the students because it will take its cues from students' interests, concerns, and questions. Making an educational program student-centered involves building on the natural curiosity students bring to school, and asking them what they want to learn.

Teachers help students to identify their own questions, puzzles, and goals, and then structure widening circles of experience and investigation of those topics. Teachers manage to infuse all the skills, knowledge, and concepts that society mandates into a child-driven curriculum. This does not mean teachers should be passive teachers and only respond to students' explicit cues.

Teachers also draw on their understanding of children's characteristic developmental needs and enthusiasms to design experiences that lead children into areas they might not choose, but that they do enjoy and that engage them. Teachers also bring their own interests and enthusiasms into the classroom to share and to act as a motivational means of guiding children.

Implementing such a **child-centered curriculum** is the result of very careful and deliberate planning. Planning serves as a means of organizing instruction and influences classroom teaching.

Well thought-out planning includes specifying behavioral objectives, specifying students' entry behavior (knowledge and skills), selecting and sequencing learning activities so as to move students from entry behavior to objective, and evaluating the outcomes of instruction in order to improve planning.

SKILL 26.7   **Provide instruction that models and promotes understanding of various points of view.**

Teachers must have a good understanding of theories in order to implement various practices in teaching and classroom management. Some techniques will be effective only at certain stages during childhood.

Major Theories of Child Development

Early in the twentieth century the study of child development began to explode. In previous studies, children were merely described as tiny adults. It was the expectation that a child's success was the result of the parents who had passed on the genes. Studies began to recognize the advances in cognitive abilities, language usage, and physical growth, in addition to atypical development.

The following are just a few of the many theories of child development that have been proposed by theorists and researchers. More recent theories outline the developmental stages of children and identify the typical ages at which these growth milestones occur.

Psychoanalytic Theories

Sigmund Freud presented theories that stressed the importance of childhood events and experiences. These theories focus on the mental disorder side of functions rather than that of the normal functioning of students. According to Freud, there is a series of **psychosexual stages** that he outlined in *Three Essays on Sexuality* in 1915. He proposes that at each stage a satisfaction of desire is necessary because it later plays a role in adult personality.

Erik Erikson's development theory included development throughout the entire human lifespan. Erikson believed that each stage of development is involved in conflict resolution. Impact of overall functioning throughout childhood into adulthood would determine either success or failure. Erikson's **theory of psychosocial development** is one of the best-known theories of personality in psychology. Similar to Freud, Erikson believed that personality develops in a series of stages. Unlike Freud's theory of psychosexual stages, Erikson's theory describes the impact of social experience across the whole lifespan.

One of the main elements of Erikson's psychosocial stage theory is the development of **ego identity**. Ego identity is the conscious sense of self that we develop through social interaction. According to Erikson, our ego identity is constantly changing due to new experiences and information we acquire in our daily interactions with others. In addition to ego identity, Erikson also believed that a sense of competence also motivates behaviors and actions.

Each stage in Erikson's theory is concerned with becoming competent in an area of life. If the stage is handled well, the person will feel a sense of mastery. If the stage is managed poorly, the person will emerge with a sense of inadequacy. Erikson believed that in each stage people experience a **conflict** that serves as a turning point in development. In Erikson's view, these conflicts are centered on either developing a psychological quality or failing to develop that quality. During these times, the potential for personal growth is high, but so is the potential for failure.

Jean Piaget is the theorist credited for recognizing that children think differently than adults do. He proposed a **theory of cognitive development.** He is credited for the idea that children hold the vital keys to gaining their own knowledge of the world.

Theories based upon behavior and interactions with the environment are considered **behavioral theories.** Several theorists contributed to the ideas of behavioral learning. Noted theorists are **Watson, Pavlov,** and **Skinner.** Behavioral theories deal only with observable behaviors. Development is considered a reaction to rewards, punishments, stimuli, and reinforcement. These behavioral processes are known as *operant conditioning* and *classical conditioning.*

Social Development Theories

Social development theories are still growing in popularity. There is a great deal of research being performed regarding the theories of early development, specifically regarding relationships with caregivers and role models. The idea is that these relationships continue to grow and influence social relationships throughout life. **John Bowlby** proposed one of the earliest theories of social development. His theory is known as the **attachment theory.**

SKILL 26.8   Demonstrate knowledge of forms of assessment appropriate for evaluating students' progress and needs in social studies.

The Importance of Assessment

The process of collecting, quantifying, and qualifying student performance data using multiple assessment information on student learning is called **assessment.**

With today's emphasis on student learning accountability, the public and legislature demands for school community accountability for effective teaching, and assessment of student learning outcomes will remain a constant mandate of educational accountability.

It is vital for teachers to track students' performances through a variety of methods. Teachers should be able to assess students on a daily basis using **informal assessments** such as monitoring during work time, class discussions, and note taking. Often these assessments are a great way to determine whether or not students are "on track" for learning selected objectives.

During class discussion, participation points may be offered, especially to those students who have special needs and participate well in class but may struggle with alternative assignments. More **formal assessments** are necessary to ensure students fully understand selected objectives. Making use of grading rubrics that break down the variety of learning tasks is important.

Assessment results from creating tests that cover the presented materials. Tests may be multiple choice, true-false, fill-in-the-blank, or essay questions or any combination thereof.

Assessment methods determine if the student has sufficiently learned the required material. Assessment essentially means asking a question and receiving a response from the student.

Forms of Assessment

Effective classroom assessment can provide educators with a wealth of information on student performance and teacher instructional practices. Using student assessment can provide teachers with data in analyzing student academic performance and making inferences on student learning planning that can foster increased academic achievement and success for students.

A comprehensive assessment system must include a diversity of assessment tools. In evaluating school reform improvements for school communities, educators may implement and assess student academic performance using norm-referenced, criterion-referenced, and performance-based assessments.

Norm-Referenced Assessments

Norm-referenced tests (NRTs) are used to classify student learners for homogenous groupings based on ability levels or basic skills into a ranking category. In many school communities, NRTs are used to classify students into Advanced Placement (AP), honors, regular, or remedial classes that can significantly impact students' future educational opportunities or success.

NRTs are also used by national testing companies and other major test publishers to test a national sample of students to norm against standard test takers. NRT ranking ranges from 1 to 99 with 25 percent of students scoring in the lower ranking of 1–25, and 25 percent of students scoring in the higher ranking of 76–99.

Criterion-Referenced Assessments

Criterion-referenced tests (CRTs) look at specific student learning goals and performance compared to a norm group of student learners. CRTs are generally used in learning environments to reflect the effectiveness of curriculum implementation and learning outcomes.

Many school districts and state legislation use CRTs to ascertain whether schools are meeting national and state learning standards. The latest national educational mandate of the No Child Left Behind Act and Adequate Yearly Progress use CRTs to measure student learning, school performance, and school improvement goals as structured accountability expectations in school communities.

Performance-Based Assessments

Performance-based assessments are currently being used in a number of state testing programs to measure the learning outcomes of individual students in subject areas. In today's classrooms, performance-based assessments in core subject areas must have established and specific performance criteria that start with pre-testing in a subject area and maintain daily or weekly testing to gauge student learning goals and objectives. To understand a student's learning is to understand how a student processes information.

A test is the usual method in which the student answers questions on the material he or she has studied. Tests, of course, can be written or verbal. Tests can be game-like. Students can be asked to draw lines connecting various associated symbols or selecting a picture representing a concept. The test could require creating graphs or drawing maps. Other assessment methods involve writing essays on various topics. Verbal reports can accomplish the same goal.

Examples of assessment items for social studies students could include identification questions, explanation questions, writing assignments, and speaking assignments.

"Identify freedoms guaranteed in the Bill of Rights" is an identification assessment that draws upon the student's factual knowledge. For younger students, the statement may be more general, such as in this example. Older students will have studied the amendments in more depth, and the

assessment item can be geared to more specific amendments, the freedoms identified in the First Amendment, or to the rights of an accused.

"Explain" questions challenge the students to examine the depth of their understanding. For example, an assessment item that asks the student to *"Compare and contrast the power of the central government under the Articles of Confederation with the powers given to the central government under the Constitution"* is a question that requires students to apply knowledge from more than one lesson plan or unit of learning. This type of assessment item develops critical thinking because the student must understand the concepts of government provided for in both documents and appreciate the differences between the two forms of government.

An assessment can be requested in nonconventional ways. For example, a student may be asked to assume the role of a member of the committee that was appointed to write the Declaration of Independence and be asked to write a letter to the king of England explaining one of various parts of the Declaration—reasons why he or she has a belief that people in general have a right to change governments, why (and/or which) specific acts and events have taken place that have resulted in the need for independence, or the choices the colonists have in situations such as the one that exists.

A variation of a nontraditional assessment may be, for example, an assignment to assume the role of a colonist who has been asked to present a speech before Parliament, pleading the case of "representation" for the colonists.

Effective performance assessments will show the gaps or holes in student learning, which allows for an intense concentration on providing fillers to bridge nonsequential learning gaps. Typical performance assessments include oral and written student work in the form of research papers, oral presentations, class projects, journals, student portfolio collections of work, and community service projects.

SKILL 26.9   **Use multiple forms of assessment and knowledge of the TEKS to determine students' progress and needs and to help plan instruction in social studies (e.g., Freedom Week).**

Using TEKS and STAAR

The TEKS, the state standards for Texas K-12 education in public schools, are detailed descriptions of the teaching objectives, and the STAAR testing program is aligned with the TEKS curriculum to measure students' progress and acquisition of the TEKS.

In 2012, STAAR replaced the Texas Assessment of Knowledge and Skills (TAKS) as the state's assessment program. The STAAR program is more rigorous than the TAKS program, placing more emphasis on the integration of the state curriculum, classroom instruction, and state-mandated assessment.

The following tests from the STAAR program are most common in middle school and high school social studies:

- **STAAR:** State of Texas Assessments of Academic Readiness is for all students who do not qualify for one of the other STAAR assessments.

- **End-of-Course Exams:** Currently, End-of-Course (EOC) exams are given for English I, English II, Algebra I, biology, and U.S. history. However, these are subject to change as the state is reevaluating frequency and topics of the EOC exams.

(Adapted from the State of Texas Assessments of Academic Readiness Assessments Comparison Chart for the 2012–13 academic year)

For more information on TEKS and STAAR, see Skill 26.1.

Instruction and Assessment of English Language Learners

Teaching **English language learners (ELLs),** or students who are learning **English as a Second Language (ESL),** poses some unique challenges, particularly in a standards-based environment. The key is realizing that no matter how little English a student knows, the teacher should teach with the student's developmental level in mind. This means that instruction should not be "dumbed-down" for ELLs. Different approaches should be used, however, to ensure that these students get multiple opportunities to learn and practice English and still learn content.

Instruction of ELLs

Many ESL approaches are based on social learning methods. By being placed in mixed-level groups or by being paired with a student of another ability level, students will get a chance to practice English in a natural, nonthreatening environment. Students should not be pushed in these groups to use complex language or to experiment with words that are too difficult. They should simply get a chance to practice with simple words and phrases.

In teacher-directed instructional situations, visual aids, such as pictures, objects, and video are particularly effective at helping students make connections between words and items they are already familiar with.

ESL students may need additional accommodations with assessments, assignments, and projects. For example, teachers may find that written tests provide little to no information about a student's understanding of the content. Therefore, an oral test may be better suited for ELLs. When students are somewhat comfortable and capable with written tests, a shortened test may actually be preferable. If this is the type of test that is given, the teacher should take note that the student will need extra time to translate.

Assessment of ELLs

The **Texas English Language Proficiency Assessment System (TELPAS)** is an exam that tests the proficiency level of each ELL. TELPAS assesses the English-language proficiency of K-12 ELLs in compliance with the No Child Left Behind Act in the domains of speaking, reading, listening, and writing in English. As an annual assessment, TELPAS provides data that indicate an ELL's progress, not mastery of content, with a pass or fail score. Students' progress is measured into four proficiency levels: beginning, intermediate, advanced, and advanced high.

Monitoring Assessment of ELLs

Each public school or academic facility in Texas that services ELLs must have a **Language Proficiency Assessment Committee (LPAC).** Whenever an educator has a question or concern about an ELL's educational placement, the LPAC can provide historical background information about the student, as well as help make decisions for future interventions and testing procedures.

The LPAC may consist of administrators, teachers, and community representatives. The committee monitors the academic needs and progress of ELLs and oversees assessment and accommodation decisions on a per-student basis, basing decisions upon state procedures and requirements. Should the student also receive special education services, then the Admissions, Review, and Dismissal Committee, another state-mandated committee, will work with the LPAC to make state assessment decisions for STAAR, TELPAS, and TEKS.

Celebrate Freedom Week

Each year Texas schools have the opportunity to celebrate the importance of documents that are fundamental in the development of the United States. State law mandates a variety of celebrations and observances, including Celebrate Freedom Week.

As of 2013, Texas was one of five U.S. states to observe Celebrate Freedom Week. Texas designates this observance for the week that includes September 17, the date the U.S. Constitution was signed.

During this week, each social studies class must include appropriate instruction concerning the intent, meaning, and importance of the Declaration of Independence and the U.S. Constitution, including the Bill of Rights, in their historical contexts. The study of the Declaration of Independence must include the study of the relationship of the ideas expressed in that document to subsequent American history, including the relationship of its ideas to the rich diversity of the U.S. people as a nation of immigrants, the American Revolution, the formulation of the U.S. Constitution, and the abolitionist movement, which led to the Emancipation Proclamation and the women's suffrage movement.

Each school district must require that, students in grades 3–12 study and recite the following: "We hold these Truths to be self-evident, that all Men are created equal, that they are endowed by their Creator with certain unalienable Rights, that among these are Life, Liberty and the Pursuit of

Happiness—That to secure these Rights, Governments are instituted among Men, deriving their just Powers from the Consent of the Governed."

Juneteenth Celebrations

Another day of celebration Texas is the U.S. holiday of **Juneteenth,** which is observed each year on June 19. Juneteenth commemorates the announcement of abolition in Texas in 1865 and the emancipation of African Americans throughout the United States. Celebrations range from traditional readings of Lincoln's Emancipation Proclamation to festive picnics with songs and readings of African American writers.

SAMPLE TEST

1. **How did the Agricultural Revolution impact lives in the period between 10,000 and 5000 BCE? (Easy) (Skill 1.1)**

   A. It supported small rural communities.
   B. It resulted in greater trade of raw materials.
   C. It lessened cooperation between members of society.
   D. It became less communal and more individualized.

2. **How did Alexander's empire differ from the Chinese Empire between 500 BCE and 500 CE? (Average) (Skill 1.2)**

   A. Alexander's empire transitioned from the Republic to the Empire.
   B. Alexander's empire was larger than the Chinese Empire.
   C. The Chinese Empire united people previously isolated from each other.
   D. The Chinese Empire was the largest when the Tang dynasty ruled.

3. **What role did Greek culture have in Etruscan society? (Rigorous) (Skill 1.3)**

   A. It had no role.
   B. It was accepted in its entirety.
   C. It was absorbed and modified.
   D. It had a limited role.

4. **Which is not a way ancient civilizations contributed, at various levels, to the government of the United States? (Average) (Skill 1.4)**

   A. Direct democracy
   B. Philosophy of government
   C. Indirect democracy
   D. Checks and balances

5. **How were Charlemagne and Genghis Khan alike? (Average) (Skill 2.1)**

   A. They were both European leaders.
   B. They both conquered Western European areas.
   C. They both conquered lands in Asia.
   D. They both amassed large empires before their deaths.

6. **Which Africans were responsible for the spread of Islam throughout Africa? (Average) (Skill 2.2)**

   A. Mali scholars
   B. Egyptian traders
   C. Slave traders
   D. The Mamluk military

7. **How was the Catholic church involved with feudalism during the Middle Ages? (Easy) (Skill 2.3)**

   A. It prohibited feudalism in Japan.
   B. It was a large land owner.
   C. It prohibited feudalism in Europe.
   D. It owned the homes in which lords lived.

8. **The Byzantines made contributions to society after 476 CE in all of the following ways except: (Average) (Skill 2.4)**

   A. Preservation of Greek architecture.
   B. The Code of Justinian.
   C. Preserving Roman law.
   D. Avoiding conflict with the Roman Catholic Church.

9. The reign of _____ is an example of "divine right" of kings. (Rigorous) (Skill 2.5)

   A. King James I
   B. King George III
   C. King Edward
   D. King William

10. How did the Crusades benefit the Roman Catholic Church? (Average) (Skill 2.6)

    A. They permanently recaptured Jerusalem.
    B. They eliminated the military threat of the Muslims.
    C. They prevented the massacre of individuals.
    D. They established small states along the way.

11. What was the result of exploration by the Portuguese in Africa? (Rigorous)(Skill 3.1)

    A. They took over the caravan trade.
    B. They established the "Slave Coast."
    C. They built forts in South Africa.
    D. They established trading posts in East Africa.

12. Which of the following was not a native South American tribe? (Average) (Skill 3.2)

    A. Aztec
    B. Inca
    C. Minoans
    D. Maya

13. What potential economic benefits did the Protest Reformation have on ruling monarchs? (Rigorous) (Skill 3.3)

    A. They could become "divine right" monarchs.
    B. They could possess church lands.
    C. They could stifle the rise of the middle class.
    D. They could promote the growth of nationalism.

14. The Atlantic slave trade lasted approximately how many years? (Average) (Skill 3.4)

    A. 400
    B. 300
    C. 200
    D. 100

15. European nations controlled all parts of Africa except _____ during the Age of Imperialism. (Average) (Skill 3.5)

    A. Morocco
    B. South Africa
    C. Ethiopia
    D. the Congo

16. The Americans were thrown into the Great Depression in which year? (Average) (Skill 4.1)

    A. 1920
    B. 1929
    C. 1935
    D. 1941

17. Which revolutionary group set up the first Marxist state? (Average) (Skill 4.2)

    A. Communists
    B. Bolsheviks
    C. Socialists
    D. Juntas

18. The French Revolution was a revolution against all of the following except: (Rigorous) (Skill 4.2)

   (A) Political prisoners.
   B. Excesses.
   C. Economic abuses.
   D. Extreme taxation.

19. The belief that the United States should control all of North America was called: (Easy) (Skill 4.3)

   A. Westward Expansion
   B. Pan Americanism
   (C) Manifest Destiny
   D. Nationalism

20. How did the Industrial Revolution impact society? (Rigorous)(Skill 4.4)

   A. It caused England to revert to an agriculture economy.
   B. It cured the social evils that had developed before industrialization.
   (C) It was the beginning of a period of colonialism.
   D. It caused the prices of products to increase.

21. Which of the following beliefs is an example of the concept of fascism? (Rigorous) (Skill 4.5)

   A. Isolationism
   (B) Social hierarchy
   C. Rule by the masses
   D. Individual interests are paramount

22. How were the causes of World War I different from the causes of World War II? (Average) (Skill 4.6)

   (A) World War I was caused by the desire of countries to obtain natural resources.
   B. World War I was the result of problems with the Treaty of Versailles.
   C. World War II was caused by the New Deal's slowing worldwide recovery due to the Depression.
   D. World War II was caused by the rise of isolationism.

23. How did the Truman Doctrine and the Marshall Plan differ? (Average)(Skill 4.7)

   A. The Truman Doctrine focused on the Soviet Union whereas the Marshall Plan focused on Europe. The Truman Doctrine speeded up the recovery of war-torn Europe and the Marshall Plan focused on limiting the spread of communism.
   B. The Truman Doctrine assisted with economic recovery of Eastern Europe and the Marshall
   C. Plan provided funding to defeat communist aggression in Greece and Turkey.
   (D) The Truman Doctrine focused on limiting the spread of communism and the Marshall Plan focused on European economic recovery.

24. **How were the goals of Mohandas Gandhi and Nelson Mandela similar? (Rigorous) (Skill 4.8)**

A. Both worked for the freedom of South Africans and independence of the people in India.

B. Both led a struggle against apartheid taught methods of civil disobedience.

C. Gandhi led India's movement for independence from the French and Mandela led South Africa's movement for independence from the Dutch.

D. Both worked to end discrimination and both pursued a policy of nonviolent civil disobedience.

25. **Early French settlement gave the French control over which two rivers? (Average)(Skill 5.1)**

A. The Missouri and Mississippi

B. The St. Lawrence and the Hudson

C. The Hudson and Missouri

D. The Mississippi and the St. Lawrence

26. **How did the Treaty of Paris of 1783 affect the Native Americans? (Average) (Skill 5.2)**

A. It did not.

B. It set aside areas for them to live.

C. Native American land was ceded to the United States

D. Native American land was ceded

27. **Geographically, how were the New England and Middle colonies different? (Easy) (Skill 5.3)**

A. New England had an abundance of good soil but the Middle colonies did not.

B. New England's farms produced a large supply of food but Middle colonies imported most of their foodstuffs.

C. The Middle colonies had a rocky shoreline and the New England colonies had large seaports.

D. The Middle colonies had a less severe climate than the New England colonies.

28. **In what ways are the Mayflower Compact and Fundamental Orders of Connecticut similar? (Rigorous) (Skill 5.4)**

A. They both pledged loyalty to the king of England.

B. They were joint resolutions of various communities.

C. They were expressions of views and forms of government.

D. They were created in the late 1700s before statehood.

29. **In what way did spatial exchange influence the development of colonial society? (Rigorous) (Skill 5.5)**

A. Population was diffused throughout the colonies.

B. It affected the settlement of inland colonies.

C. It was the reason colonists settled the Midwest.

D. Population focused on its importance in forming towns.

30. **What effect did the passage of acts such as the Sugar Act, the Stamp Act, and the Townshend Acts have on colonial America? (Rigorous) (Skill 6.1)**

    A. The acts polarized the colonists.
    B. The acts were accepted with dignity.
    C. The colonists tolerated the acts.
    D. The colonists resisted the acts.

31. **Why did King George III repeal the Stamp Act? (Easy) (Skill 6.2)**

    A. He feared rebellion.
    B. He no longer needed funds.
    C. Parliament recommended repeal.
    D. Parliament amended the act.

32. **How did England benefit from the Navigation Acts? (Average) (Skill 6.3)**

    A. The acts were revenue producing.
    B. The acts assured England's economic supremacy.
    C. The acts required the use of English ships.
    D. The acts monitored colonial commerce.

33. **All of the following are reasons why the government under the Articles of Confederation was not retained except: (Rigorous)(Skill 6.4)**

    A. It did not provide for a strong chief executive.
    B. It lacked power to enforce legislation.
    C. It lacked the ability to regulate finances.
    D. It lacked the power to enforce treaties.

34. **The Federalists: (Average) (Skill 6.5)**

    A. supported states' rights.
    B. desired a weak central government.
    C. favored a strong central government.
    D. were also called Loyalists.

35. **Generally, _____ favored low tariffs. (Rigorous) (Skill 6.6)**

    A. Democratic-Republicans
    B. the Supreme Court
    C. Federalists
    D. Congress

36. **What event sparked a great migration of people from all over the world to California during the mid-1800s? (Easy) (Skill 7.1)**

    A. The birth of labor unions
    B. Manifest Destiny
    C. The invention of the automobile
    D. The Gold Rush

37. **After the settlers inhabited _____, they believed they were destined to settle the North American continent. (Rigorous) (Skill 7.2)**

    A. the Louisiana Territory
    B. the Northwest Territory
    C. the Piedmont of Virginia
    D. Texas

38. **Which area was acquired last by the United States? (Average) (Skill 7.3)**

    A. The Gadsden Purchase
    B. Annexation of Texas
    C. Acquisition of Oregon
    D. The Louisiana Purchase

39. **Why did Northerners first oppose the admission of Texas to statehood? (Average) (Skill 7.4)**

    A. Texas was controlled by Mexico
    B. Texas did not have the required population.
    C. Texas wanted to allow slavery.
    D. Texas owed debts to the U.S. government.

40. **Which was not an issue that caused sectionalism? (Rigorous) (Skill 7.5)**

    A. Mechanization of farming
    B. Tariffs
    C. Slavery
    D. Land speculation

41. **The principle of "popular sovereignty" that allowed people in any territory to make their own decisions concerning the slavery issue was first stated by: (Average)(Skill 7.6)**

    A. Henry Clay
    B. Daniel Webster
    C. John C. Calhoun
    D. Stephen A. Douglas

42. **Who was a Confederate commander? (Average) (Skill 7.6)**

    A. J. E. B. Stuart
    B. Burnside
    C. McClellan
    D. McDowell

43. **Which statement is true about the Radical Republicans? (Rigorous) (Skill 7.6)**

    A. They favored Andrew Johnson's plan of Reconstruction.
    B. They established the Freedmen's Bureau.
    C. They opposed "black codes."
    D. They favored harsh measures of Reconstruction.

44. **Which doctrine was invoked to intercede in affairs of Latin American countries in the late nineteenth and early twentieth centuries? (Rigorous) (Skill 8.1)**

    A. Monroe Doctrine
    B. Imperialism
    C. Manifest Destiny
    D. Expansionism

45. **Which of the following is not correct about the Fourteen Points? (Average) (Skill 8.2)**

    A. They were drafted by Woodrow Wilson.
    B. They were considered at the Paris peace talks.
    C. The fourteenth point called for the creation of the United Nations.
    D. The program applied to post-World War I.

46. **The use of atomic bombs in 1945 was justified as a way to: (Average) (Skill 8.3)**

    A. defeat Japan
    B. defeat Germany
    C. show America's power
    D. stop World War II

47. **Why were Alfred Mahan's theories important in shaping U.S. foreign policy? (Rigorous) (Skill 8.4)**

    A. He believed America should "speak softly and carry a big stick."
    B. He believed a strong army would avoid confrontations.
    C. He believed the use of the atomic bomb would end war.
    D. He believed a strong navy showed a strong foreign policy.

48. **The international organization established to work for world peace at the end of World War II is the: (Easy) (Skill 8.5)**

    A. League of Nations
    B. United Federation of Nations
    C. United Nations
    D. United World League

49. **The space race began: (Average) (Skill 8.5)**

    A. in 1963.
    B. after the Soviets developed the atomic bomb.
    C. after the Soviets placed missile bases in Cuba.
    D. after the Soviets launched Sputnik.

50. **President Carter believed the oil fields of the Persian Gulf were threatened when the Soviets entered which country? (Rigorous) (Skill 8.6)**

    A. Iraq
    B. Iran
    C. Kuwait
    D. Afghanistan

51. **Which of the following is not an example of an advancement of transportation that took place during the post-Civil War period? (Average) (Skill 9.1)**

    A. Rail passenger service
    B. Completion of the transcontinental railroad
    C. Jet planes
    D. Automobile

52. **Which political philosophy is concerned with the commonsense needs of the average person? (Average) (Skill 9.2)**

    A. Popular sovereignty
    B. Populism
    C. Progressivism
    D. Protectionism

53. **All of the following are causes of the Industrial Revolution except : (Average) (Skill 9.3)**

    A. Immigrants from southeast Europe.
    B. Inventions.
    C. Machines.
    D. Extensive rail service.

54. **The late-nineteenth social worker who established a settlement house, known as Hull House, in Chicago was: (Easy) (Skill 9.4)**

    A. Betty Friedan
    B. Susan B. Anthony
    C. Jane Addams
    D. Elizabeth Cady Stanton

55. The passage of the Civil Rights Act of 1964 took place during which U.S. president's administration? (Average) (Skill 9.5)

A. John F. Kennedy
B. Lyndon Johnson
C. Jimmy Carter
D. Richard Nixon

56. How has the Hispanic civil rights movement differed from the African American civil rights movement? (Rigorous) (Skill 9.5)

A. The African American movement focused on social integration whereas the Hispanic movement focused on educational integration.
B. The African American movement focused on economic integration whereas the Hispanic movement focused on preventing discrimination based on color.
C. The two movements did not differ.
D. The two movements differed in their focus but not their goal of integration into American society.

57. Which Native American tribes moved west of the Mississippi in the early nineteenth century? (Average) (Skill 10.1)

A. The Cherokee, Choctaw, and Shawnee
B. The Wichitas, Comanches, and Caddoes
C. The Coahuiltecans, Lipans, and Kiowas
D. The Tonkawas, Wichitas, and Caddoes

58. What was the cause of friction between the United States and Spain after the Louisiana Purchase in 1803? (Average) (Skill 10.2)

A. Both nations disputed the boundary between Texas and Louisiana.
B. Spain resented American involvement in the Cuban War of Independence.
C. Mexico wanted to buy the Louisiana Territory from France.
D. Spain angered the United States by sinking the American battleship The Maine.

59. Why did missionaries abandon east Texas in 1693? (Rigorous) (Skill 10.4)

A. Tensions with Native Americans over a smallpox outbreak scared them away.
B. The Mexican War of Independence forced abandonment.
C. They moved their mission into the sunny beaches of Spanish Florida.
D. American citizens began to settle in the region.

60. Which domestic animals existed in the Texas region before the arrival of Europeans? (Average) (Skill 10.5)

A. Cattle
B. Pigs
C. Horses
D. None

61. Who was the first American allowed to obtain a colonial grant to settle in Texas? (Average) (Skill 10.6)

A. Stephen F. Austin
B. Agustin de Iturbide
C. Moses Austin
D. Fray Damián Massanet

62. What was one of the causes of the Mexican War of Independence? (Average) (Skill 11.1)

    A. Confiscation of church property
    B. Taxation of the Thirteen Colonies
    C. Abdication of Napoleon
    D. Debt from the War of 1812

63. What was the final battle of the Texas Revolution? (Average) (Skill 11.2)

    A. Battle of the Alamo
    B. Battle of San Jacinto
    C. Battle of Gonzales
    D. Battle of Gettysburg

64. What early Texas pioneer documented daily life during the Republic of Texas and early statehood? (Average) (Skill 11.3)

    A. Sam Houston
    B. Stephen F. Austin
    C. Mary Maverick
    D. Joshua Houston

65. Which event motivated Texas to hold a secessionist vote in 1861? (Average) (Skill 11.4)

    A. South Carolina's secession from the Union.
    B. Battle of Palmito Ridge
    C. Battle of Galveston
    D. Texas Revolution

66. Which Comanche leader was an important leader in both warfare against Texan settlers and reservation life? (Easy) (Skill 11.6)

    A. Quanah Parker
    B. Joshua Houston
    C. Sacagawea
    D. Jack Coffee Hays

67. Texas was the leading supplier of which product during the late nineteenth century? (Average) (Skill 11.7)

    A. Cattle
    B. Cottonseed
    C. Packaged meats
    D. Petroleum

68. What government agency was formed in 1890 as a result of deforestation in Texas? (Easy) (Skill 11.8)

    A. Forestry Association
    B. Farmer's Alliance
    C. Eleventh Legislature
    D. Texas Rangers

69. Which two teams played the first college football game in the state of Texas in 1894? (Average) (Skill 11.9)

    A. University of Texas vs. Prairie View A & M College
    B. Texas A & M vs. Prairie View A & M College
    C. University of Texas vs. Texas A & M
    D. University of Texas vs. University of Oklahoma

70. Who was the first native Texan to serve as governor? (Average) (Skill 12.1)

    A. James Hogg
    B. Jane McCallum
    C. George W. Bush
    D. Manuel C. Gonzales

71. **What was the main contribution that Texas citizens made during World War II? (Average) (Skill 12.2)**

    A. Rationing food, gas, rubber, and mechanical parts
    B. Building bomb shelters
    C. Women joining the workplace
    D. Both A and C

72. **What popular Democratic Texas governor did George W. Bush defeat in 1994 to become the 46th governor of Texas? (Average) (Skill 12.3)**

    A. Albert Gore, Jr.
    B. Ann Richards
    C. Lyndon B. Johnson
    D. James Allred

73. **What were the reasons for the growth of the agricultural industry in Texas during the beginning of the twentieth century? (Average) (Skill 12.4)**

    A. Urbanization of Texas
    B. World War I
    C. Widespread use of the tractor
    D. All of the above

74. **What Texas airport is the largest in the state and the second largest airport in the nation? (Easy) (Skill 12.5)**

    A. San Antonio International Airport
    B. Dallas/Fort Worth International Airport
    C. George Bush Intercontinental Airport
    D. Austin-Bergstrom International Airport

75. **Which of the following is a characteristic of peat? (Rigorous) (Skill 13.1)**

    A. It is compressed.
    B. It is fine and sandy.
    C. It has a high content of salt.
    D. It has a low water content.

76. **A(n) _____ is formed when plants and animals interact with the physical environment. (Easy) (Skill 13.4)**

    A. terrain
    B. steppe
    C. atmosphere
    D. ecosystem

77. **Language is a unifying cultural characteristic because: (Rigorous) (Skill 14.1)**

    A. belief systems are introduced into society in a number of ways.
    B. it defines the relationship between a culture's government and its people.
    C. it studies the characteristics and influences on varied cultures.
    D. it creates and explains ideas and information.

78. **How did the federal government demonstrate that education was important in the westward expansion movement? (Average) (Skill 14.4)**

    A. Congress required students to attend school until the age of 15.
    B. Congress provided funds for agricultural colleges.
    C. Congress required each township establish schools.
    D. Congress established teacher-training colleges.

79. **How did the history of Christianity have an impact on the building of the Shrine of Guadalupe? (Rigorous) (Skills 14.7, 14.8)**

    A. Because Christianity is not completely unified, the people of Mexico were unable to persuade the Church to contribute to the funding of the shrine.

    B. Because Christianity was begun around 1500 BCE, the shrine could not be used to   convert the natives.

    C. The vision of a native Mexican was used to teach other Mexicans to become a follower of Jesus Christ.

    D. The schism in Western Christianity affected the construction of the shrine.

80. **What was the main reason early humans moved from place to place? (Rigorous) (Skill 15.1)**

    A. Agriculture expanded the types of foods that were available.

    B. They were required to move with their food sources.

    C. Clothing enabled them to adapt to a wider range of climates.

    D. Wool-bearing animals became domesticated.

81. **Which of the following was not a cause of the Dust Bowl? (Rigorous) (Skill 15.4)**

    A. Droughts
    B. Dust storms
    C. Winds
    D. Resettlement

82. **How do raw materials affect the economic activities of a location? (Rigorous) (Skill 15.7)**

    A. Availability of raw materials requires availability of nearby transportation.

    B. Lack of raw materials inhibits growths of communities.

    C. Management of raw materials can affect the survival of a community.

    D. Loss of raw materials can affect the viability of a community.

83. **Which of the following is not a common characteristic of an ethnic group? (Rigorous) (Skill 16.2)**

    A. Religion
    B. Genetic lineage
    C. Background
    D. Language

84. **The role of a(n) _____ in meeting basic societal needs is to develop good citizens. (Rigorous) (Skill 16.5)**

    A. religion
    B. educational system
    C. family
    D. mass media

85. **Which of the following individuals developed the method called psychoanalysis? (Easy) (Skill 16.8)**

    A. Wilhelm Wundt
    B. F. Skinner
    C. Edward Thorndike
    D. Sigmund Freud

86. _____ is the fundamental law of the U.S. republic. (Rigorous) (Skill 17.1)

    A. Separation of powers
    B. Checks and balances
    C. Federalism
    D. The Constitution

87. Federal taxation legislation must originate in: (Rigorous) (Skill 17.4)

    A. the House of Representatives.
    B. the Senate.
    C. either the House or the Senate.
    D. both the House and Senate simultaneously.

88. The Thirteenth, Fourteenth, and Fifteenth Amendments were called the "Civil War" amendments because they: (Rigorous) (Skill 17.7)

    A. provided due process, direct election of U.S. senators, and voting rights regardless of race, color, or previous condition of servitude.
    B. provided equal protection, prohibited the poll tax, and abolished slavery.
    C. abolished slavery, gave voting rights to former slaves, and provided for equal protection.
    D. prohibited the poll tax, provided for direct election of U.S. Senators, and guaranteed due process.

89. The American governmental system is a federal system because: (Rigorous) (Skill 17.10)

    A. there are fifty states and one national government.
    B. the national and state governments share powers.
    C. state governments have three branches of government.
    D. the federal government has administrative agencies.

90. How does policy making affect influence decision making? (Rigorous) (Skill 18.3)

    A. It formulates public opinion.
    B. It is an alternative to adoption.
    C. It requires interaction.
    D. It identifies a problem.

91. The temperance movement resulted in: (Easy) (Skill 18.6)

    A. women gaining the right to vote.
    B. the increased manufacture of alcohol.
    C. enactment of the Prohibition Amendment.
    D. reduction of abuses of drunkenness.

92. The Mayflower Compact is an example of: (Average) (Skill 19.1)

    A. a social contract theory document.
    B. a resistance to illegitimate government.
    C. the law of nature.
    D. a divine right theory document.

93. In which type of government system are coalition parties common? (Rigorous) (Skill 19.4)

   A. Monarchy
   B. Dictatorship
   C. Federalist
   D. Parliamentary system

94. What was dominant form of political organization in Europe during the Middle Ages? (Rigorous) (Skill 19.5)

   A. Democracy
   B. Nationalism
   C. Federalism
   D. Feudalism

95. Who was the most influential French political theorist before the French Revolution? (Easy) (Skill 19.6)

   A. Rousseau
   B. Champlain
   C. La Salle
   D. Hobbes

96. Which of the following is not a factor of production? (Average) (Skill 20.1)

   A. Opportunity cost
   B. Labor
   C. Capital
   D. Land

97. The circular-flow diagram is a model of: (Rigorous) (Skill 20.2)

   A. supply and demand.
   B. the business sector.
   C. the Gross Domestic Product.
   D. the economy.

98. Adam Smith believed that: (Rigorous) (Skill 20.4)

   A. labor was a value-determining factor.
   B. free markets should exist without government interference.
   C. aggregate spending determined the level of economic activity.
   D. collective ownership and administration of goods was necessary.

99. Private ownership of production a characteristic of which type of economic system? (Easy) (Skill 20.5)

   A. A mixed economy
   B. Socialism
   C. Communism
   D. Capitalism

100. The most competitive of market structures is: (Rigorous) (Skill 20.6)

   A. Monopoly
   B. Pure competition
   C. Oligopoly
   D. Monopolistic competition

101. What is meant by a nation's absolute advantage in the production? (Rigorous) (Skill 20.7)

   A. There will be lower output prices and higher resource prices.
   B. Restrictions such as tariffs will be implemented to raise prices.
   C. Quotas will be set on the physical number of permitted imports.
   D. One country can produce goods more efficiently than others.

102. **What is the term describing situations in which individuals try to produce products that are better than similar products and set their own prices? (Average) (Skill 21.1)**

    A. Voluntary exchange
    B. Private property rights
    C. Competition
    D. Profit incentive

103. **What was the first federal antitrust legislation? (Average) (Skill 21.2)**

    A. Sherman Act
    B. FTC Act
    C. Robinson-Patman Act
    D. CCC Act

104. **Which form of business organization provides the most protection for its member(s)? (Average) (Skill 21.3)**

    A. Partnership
    B. Sole proprietorship
    C. Joint venture
    D. Corporation

105. **NAFTA is a: (Easy) (Skill 21.5)**

    A. trade organization.
    B. trade agreement.
    C. series of regional trade barriers.
    D. foreign trade barrier.

106. **At which level or levels of government are policies generally enacted to encourage labor to migrate from one sector of the economy to another? (Average) (Skill 21.5)**

    A. National
    B. State
    C. Local
    D. National, state, and local

107. **What is an example of a scarce resource? (Easy) (Skill 21.8)**

    A. Market choices
    B. Time
    C. Consumer options
    D. Raw materials

108. **The discovery of _____ by Albert Einstein revolutionized the study of physics. (Easy) (Skill 22.1)**

    A. the microchip
    B. the microscope
    C. the theory of relativity
    D. electrical power

109. **Where was gunpowder invented? (Easy) (Skill 22.2)**

    A. India
    B. China
    C. River valley civilizations
    D. Classical Greece and Rome

110. **The most significant invention of modern times may be: (Easy) (Skill 22.5)**

    A. the computer
    B. the telephone
    C. electric power
    D. petroleum-based products

111. How does the correct use of social studies terminology demonstrate the philosophical foundations of social science inquiry? (Rigorous) (Skills 23.1, 23.2)

   A. Social sciences seek to discover and explain common motivations and reactions among humans.
   B. Social sciences include several philosophical foundations, such as economics and history.
   C. Students can become more aware of the world around them and become better citizens.
   D. The teacher needs to be aware of correct terminology to better understand the philosophical foundations.

112. How should historical concepts be interpreted? (Rigorous) (Skill 24.3)

   A. They should be interpreted as movements.
   B. They should be identified as belief systems.
   C. They should focus on historical themes.
   D. They should provide insight into historical events.

113. Organization of information provides _____ whereas interpretation of information provides _____.
   (Average) (Skill 24.4)

   A. conclusions; reaching objectives
   B. reaching objectives; separation
   C. an orderly approach; evidence for conclusions
   D. evidence for conclusions; reaching objectives

114. Which of the following is major indicator that is used to measure levels of economic activity? (Average) (Skill 24.8)

   A. The unemployment rate
   B. Periods of prosperity
   C. Economic instability
   D. Surplus merchandise

115. Why is it important to encourage the use of multiple research resources? (Easy) (Skill 25.1)

   A. They will serve as a road map for further research.
   B. They will promote the ability to judge the value of the resource.
   C. They will be relevant to the research goal.
   D. They will make the research project definitive and successful.

116. **What is the difference between an argumentative paper and an analytical paper? (Average) (Skill 25.2)**

A. An argumentative paper examines the various parts of a research topic to support the initial statement whereas an analytical paper supports a question or claim.

B. An argumentative paper focuses on understanding the research topic to reformulate the parts in a way to support the initial statement whereas an analytical paper focuses on the scientific method.

C. An argumentative paper examines the various parts of a research topic to support its conclusions whereas an analytical paper challenges a question or claim.

D. An analytical paper presents research to provide information whereas an argumentative paper presents research to prove a debatable statement.

117. **A demographic table may show which of the following? (Rigorous) (Skill 25.5)**

A. Vital statistics
B. A null hypothesis
C. Levels of education
D. Census reports

118. **Which acronym represents the state standards for Texas K-12 education in public schools? (Easy) (Skill 26.1)**

A. TAKS
B. TEKS
C. TELPAS
D. STAAR

119. **Why is developmentally appropriate instruction important? (Average) (Skill 26.2)**

A. It provides interdisciplinary instruction.
B. It eliminates cognitive learning.
C. It provides problem-solving knowledge.
D. It provides students with optimal learning.

120. **The purpose of assessments is to determine whether the student has: (Easy) (Skill 26.8)**

A. sufficiently learned the required material.
B. performed well according to a norm group.
C. met a school's graduation requirements.
D. All of the above

ANSWER KEY FOR SAMPLE TEST

1. B	25. D	49. D	73. D	97. D
2. B	26. C	50. D	74. B	98. B
3. C	27. D	51. A	75. A	99. D
4. D	28. C	52. B	76. D	100. B
5. D	29. B	53. A	77. D	101. D
6. A	30. D	54. C	78. B	102. C
7. B	31. A	55. B	79. C	103. A
8. D	32. D	56. D	80. B	104. D
9. A	33. B	57. A	81. D	105. B
10. D	34. C	58. A	82. C	106. A
11. D	35. A	59. A	83. B	107. B
12. C	36. D	60. D	84. C	108. C
13. B	37. B	61. C	85. D	109. B
14. A	38. A	62. A	86. D	110. A
15. C	39. C	63. B	87. A	111. C
16. B	40. A	64. C	88. C	112. D
17. B	41. D	65. A	89. B	113. C
18. A	42. A	66. A	90. C	114. A
19. C	43. D	67. B	91. C	115. B
20. C	44. A	68. A	92. A	116. D
21. B	45. C	69. C	93. D	117. C
22. A	46. D	70. A	94. D	118. B
23. D	47. D	71. D	95. A	119. D
24. D	48. C	72. B	96. A	120. D

RIGOR TABLE FOR SAMPLE TEST

Rigor Level	Questions
Easy (20%)	1, 7, 19, 27, 31, 36, 48, 54, 66, 68, 74, 76, 85, 91, 95, 99, 105, 107, 108, 109, 110, 115, 118, 120
Average (44%)	2, 4, 5, 6, 8, 10, 12, 14, 15, 16 , 17, 22, 23, 25, 26, 32, 34, 38, 39, 41, 42, 45, 46, 49, 51, 52, 53, 55, 57, 58, 60, 61, 62, 63, 64, 65, 67, 69, 70, 71, 72, 73, 78, 92, 96, 102, 103, 104, 106, 113, 114, 116, 119
Rigorous (36%)	3, 9, 11, 13, 18, 20, 21, 24, 28, 29, 30, 33, 35, 37, 40, 43, 44, 47, 50, 56, 59, 75, 77, 79, 80, 81, 82, 83, 84, 86, 87, 88, 89, 90, 93, 94, 97, 98, 100, 101, 111, 112, 117

RATIONALES FOR SAMPLE TEST

1. **How did the Agricultural Revolution impact lives in the period between 10,000 and 5000 BCE? (Easy) (Skill 1.1)**

    A. It supported small rural communities.
    B. It resulted in greater trade of raw materials.
    C. It lessened cooperation between members of society.
    D. It became less communal and more individualized.

Answer: B. It resulted in greater trade of raw materials

The Agricultural Revolution enabled trade in raw materials and finished goods to develop between communities. Option A is incorrect because communities actually increased in size. Options C and D are incorrect because the revolution had the opposite effect in both cases.

2. **How did Alexander's empire differ from the Chinese Empire between 500 BCE and 500 CE? (Average) (Skill 1.2)**

    A. Alexander's empire transitioned from the Republic to the Empire.
    B. Alexander's empire was larger than the Chinese Empire.
    C. The Chinese Empire united people previously isolated from each other.
    D. The Chinese Empire was the largest when the Tang dynasty ruled.

Answer: B. Alexander's empire was larger than the Chinese Empire

Alexander's empire was larger because it encompassed most of the known world. Options A and C describe other civilizations. Option D is incorrect because the Tang dynasty in China ended internal struggles.

3. **What role did Greek culture have in Etruscan society? (Rigorous) (Skill 1.3)**

    A. It had no role.
    B. It was accepted in its entirety.
    C. It was absorbed and modified.
    D. It had a limited role.

Answer: C. It was absorbed and modified

Options A, B, and D are incorrect. The Etruscans adopted elements of Greek culture such as writing, some religious practices, and engineering skills. They modified the Greek culture to fit their needs and passed these skills to the Romans.

4. **Which is not a way ancient civilizations contributed, at various levels, to the government of the United States? (Average) (Skill 1.4)**

    A. Direct democracy
    B. Philosophy of government
    C. Indirect democracy
    D. Checks and balances

Answer: D. Checks and balances

Options A, B, and C are incorrect because direct democracy is part of the town meeting process, Congress is an example of indirect democracy, and the philosophy of government was that one person had one vote.

5. **How were Charlemagne and Genghis Khan alike? (Average) (Skill 2.1)**

    A. They were both European leaders.
    B. They both conquered Western European areas.
    C. They both conquered lands in Asia.
    D. They both amassed large empires before their deaths.

Answer: D. They both amassed large empires before their deaths

Charlemagne was called the "father of Europe," and Genghis Khan conquered large areas in Eastern Europe and Asia. Option A is incorrect because Genghis Khan was a Mongol horseman. Option B is incorrect because Genghis Khan captured lands in Eastern Europe. Option C is incorrect because Charlemagne brought most of Western Europe into a single kingdom.

6. **Which Africans were responsible for the spread of Islam throughout Africa? (Average) (Skill 2.2)**

    A. Mali scholars
    B. Egyptian traders
    C. Slave traders
    D. The Mamluk military

Answer: A. Mali scholars

Scholars from the kingdom of Mali who had converted to Islam preserved the history of Mali and spread Islam throughout Africa. Options B, C, and D are incorrect because these groups were focused on economic and military expansion rather than the expansion of religion.

7.   **How was the Catholic church involved with feudalism during the Middle Ages? (Easy) (Skill 2.3)**

   A. It prohibited feudalism in Japan.
   B. It was a large land owner.
   C. It prohibited feudalism in Europe.
   D. It owned the homes in which lords lived.

Answer: B. It was a large land owner

The Catholic church controlled approximately one-third of the useable land in Europe during the Middle Ages. Option A is incorrect because the church was not involved in Japanese feudalism. Option C is incorrect because it owned land upon which feudalism was carried out. Option D is not the best answer because the church also owned land.

8.   **The Byzantines made contributions to society after 476 CE in all of the following ways except: (Average) (Skill 2.4)**

   A. preservation of Greek architecture.
   B. the Code of Justinian.
   C. preserving Roman law.
   D. avoiding conflict with the Roman Catholic Church.

Answer: D. avoiding conflict with the Roman Catholic Church

Options A, B, and C are incorrect because the Byzantines preserved many Greek and Roman achievements. They also preserved Roman law and the Code of Justinian.

9.   **The reign of ____ is an example of "divine right" of kings. (Rigorous) (Skill 2.5)**

   A. King James I
   B. King George III
   C. King Edward
   D. King William

Answer: A. King James I

Options B, C, and D are incorrect because these monarchs did not rule during the Age of Absolutism. King George III ruled during the American colonial era. William and Mary were dual monarchs. King Edward ruled in the late nineteenth and early twentieth centuries.

10.   How did the Crusades benefit the Roman Catholic Church? (Average) (Skill 2.6)

  A. They permanently recaptured Jerusalem.
  B. They eliminated the military threat of the Muslims.
  C. They prevented the massacre of individuals.
  D. They established small states along the way.

Answer: D. They established small states along the way

Option A is incorrect because Jerusalem was captured and lost in different Crusades. Option B is incorrect because the Muslims occupied part of Spain but the expulsion of Moors from Spain occurred later. Option C is incorrect because the crusaders massacred people as they marched into Jerusalem.

11.   What was the result of exploration by the Portuguese in Africa? (Rigorous)(Skill 3.1)

  A. They took over the caravan trade.
  B. They established the "Slave Coast."
  C. They built forts in South Africa.
  D. They established trading posts in East Africa.

Answer: D. They established trading posts in East Africa

Option A is incorrect because the caravan trade took place in parts of Africa the Portuguese did not explore. Option B is incorrect because the "Slave Coast" was the area of West Africa. Option C is incorrect because although the Portuguese explored South Africa, they were interested in establishing trading posts and exploring beyond the Cape. Option D is correct because they were the first to establish trading posts in this area of Africa.

12.   Which of the following was not a native South American tribe? (Average) (Skill 3.2)

  A. Aztec
  B. Inca
  C. Minoans
  D. Maya

Answer: C. Minoans

The Minoans lived in Greece. Options A, B, and D are the names of native South American groups. Option C is correct because they lived in Greece.

13. **What potential economic benefits did the Protest Reformation have on ruling monarchs? (Rigorous) (Skill 3.3)**

    A. They could become "divine right" monarchs.

    B. They could possess church lands.

    C. They could stifle the rise of the middle class.

    D. They could promote the growth of nationalism.

Answer: B. They could possess church lands

Option A is incorrect because "divine right" is a political concept, not economic. Option C is incorrect because the middle class was rising in society and clashed with the Church. Option D is incorrect because nationalism is a political, not economical, concept.

14. **The Atlantic slave trade lasted approximately how many years? (Average) (Skill 3.4)**

    A. 400

    B. 300

    C. 200

    D. 100

Answer: A. 400

Options B, C, and D are incorrect because the Atlantic slave trade took place between the 1300s and 1700s.

15. **European nations controlled all parts of Africa except _____ during the Age of Imperialism. (Average) (Skill 3.5)**

    A. Morocco

    B. South Africa

    C. Ethiopia

    D. the Congo

Answer: C. Ethiopia

Options A, B, and D are incorrect. France controlled Morocco. The English and Dutch were involved in South Africa, and Belgium colonized the Congo.

16. The Americans were thrown into the Great Depression in which year? (Average) (Skill 4.1)

    A. 1920
    B. 1929
    C. 1935
    D. 1941

Answer: B. 1929

Only Option B is correct. Option C is close, but although the Great Depression affected lives during the 1930s, it began in the year 1929 when the stock market crashed.

17. Which revolutionary group set up the first Marxist state? (Average) (Skill 4.2)

    A. Communists
    B. Bolsheviks
    C. Socialists
    D. Juntas

Answer: B. Bolsheviks

Option B is the best answer because Bolsheviks were extreme Marxists who had a majority in Russia's Socialist Party and took over the government after the Russian Revolution of 1917. The communists and socialists are political parties, and the juntas were South American groups involved in their independence movements.

18. The French Revolution was a revolution against all of the following except: (Rigorous) (Skill 4.2)

    A. political prisoners.
    B. excesses.
    C. economic abuses.
    D. extreme taxation.

Answer: A. political prisoners

The capture of the prison was symbolic. Mobs stormed the French prison, the Bastille, to release the few prisons who were housed there. Options B, C, and D were reasons for the French Revolution of 1789.

19. **The belief that the United States should control all of North America was called: (Easy) (Skill 4.3)**

    A. Westward Expansion
    B. Pan Americanism
    C. Manifest Destiny
    D. nationalism

Answer: C. Manifest Destiny

Option A is incorrect because westward expansion was how America carried out its policy of Manifest Destiny. Option B is incorrect because Pan Americanism involves mutual understandings and feelings for Latin countries. Option D is incorrect because nationalism is a feeling of pride for one's country

20. **How did the Industrial Revolution impact society? (Rigorous)(Skill 4.4)**

    A. It caused England to revert to an agriculture economy.
    B. It cured the social evils that had developed before industrialization.
    C. It was the beginning of a period of colonialism.
    D. It caused the prices of products to increase.

Answer: C. It was the beginning of a period of colonialism

England was moving from an agricultural to an industrial economy. Therefore, Option A is incorrect. Option B is not correct because the Industrial Revolution caused, than cured, social evils. Option D is incorrect because prices decreased as the result of mechanization and greater production.

21. **Which of the following beliefs is an example of the concept of fascism? (Rigorous) (Skill 4.5)**

    A. Isolationism
    B. Social hierarchy
    C. Rule by the masses
    D. Individual interests are paramount

Answer: B. Social hierarchy

Options A, C, and D are incorrect because fascist movements encompass the ideas of nationalism, a rule of the elite, and a belief that individual interests are of less importance than the welfare of the nation.

22. **How were the causes of World War I different from the causes of World War II? (Average) (Skill 4.6)**

    A. World War I was caused by the desire of countries to obtain natural resources.
    B. World War I was the result of problems with the Treaty of Versailles.
    C. World War II was caused by the New Deal's slowing worldwide recovery due to the Depression.
    D. World War II was caused by the rise of isolationism.

Answer: A. World War I was caused by the desire of countries to obtain natural resources

The early 1900s saw the rise of countries such as England, France, the United States, Germany, and Japan seeking additional territories. One of the benefits of gain territory was the natural resources to be gained from the acquisitions. Option B is incorrect because the Treaty of Versailles was signed after World War I. Option C is incorrect because the New Deal sped up recovery from the Depression in the United States. Option D is incorrect because countries became aggressive for land control.

23. **How did the Truman Doctrine and the Marshall Plan differ? (Average)(Skill 4.7)**

    A. The Truman Doctrine focused on the Soviet Union whereas the Marshall Plan focused on Europe.
    B. The Truman Doctrine speeded up the recovery of war-torn Europe and the Marshall Plan focused on limiting the spread of communism.
    C. The Truman Doctrine assisted with economic recovery of Eastern Europe and the Marshall
    D. Plan provided funding to defeat communist aggression in Greece and Turkey.
       The Truman Doctrine focused on limiting the spread of communism and the Marshall Plan focused on European economic recovery.

Answer: D. The Truman Doctrine focused on limiting the spread of communism and the Marshall Plan focused on European economic recovery

Option A is incorrect because the Truman Doctrine focused on an area greater than the Soviet Union. Options B and C are both incorrect because the choices are reversed.

24. How were the goals of Mohandas Gandhi and Nelson Mandela similar? (Rigorous) (Skill 4.8)

    A. Both worked for the freedom of South Africans and independence of the people in India.
    B. Both led a struggle against apartheid taught methods of civil disobedience.
    C. Gandhi led India's movement for independence from the French and Mandela led South Africa's movement for independence from the Dutch.
    D. Both worked to end discrimination and both pursued a policy of nonviolent civil disobedience.

Answer: D. Both worked to end discrimination and both pursued a policy of nonviolent civil disobedience

Both men pursued a policy of nonviolent civil disobedience in working for the end of discrimination; Gandhi encouraged nonviolent civil disobedience and Mandela spoke against South Africa's policy of apartheid. Option A is not correct because Gandhi worked for the independence of India and Mandela sought to end apartheid in South Africa. Option B is not correct because Mandela led the fight against apartheid. Option C is incorrect because the Indian movement for independence was against the British and Mandela fought against apartheid.

25. Early French settlement gave the French control over which two rivers? (Average)(Skill 5.1)

    A. The Missouri and Mississippi
    B. The St. Lawrence and the Hudson
    C. The Hudson and Missouri
    D. The Mississippi and the St. Lawrence

Answer: D. The Mississippi and the St. Lawrence

The French were interested in the fur trading areas near the Great Lakes and the Ohio Valley. When the French had control of the Mississippi and St. Lawrence rivers, they could ship the pelts and hides to Europe. Options A, B, and C are incorrect because the Hudson is in New York and the Missouri is in the Great Plains area.

26. How did the Treaty of Paris of 1783 affect the Native Americans? (Average) (Skill 5.2)

    A. It did not.
    B. It set aside areas for them to live.
    C. Native American land was ceded to the United States
    D. Native American land was ceded to the British.

Answer: C. Native American land was ceded to the United States

The Treaty of Paris of 1783 ended the American Revolution. It affected the Native Americans because land they had lived on was given to the new nation of the United States. Therefore, Options A, B, and D are incorrect.

27. Geographically, how were the New England and Middle colonies different? (Easy) (Skill 5.3)

    A. New England had an abundance of good soil but the Middle colonies did not.
    B. New England's farms produced a large supply of food but Middle colonies imported most of their foodstuffs.
    C. The Middle colonies had a rocky shoreline and the New England colonies had large seaports.
    D. The Middle colonies had a less severe climate than the New England colonies.

Answer: D. The Middle Colonies had a less severe climate than the New England colonies

New England had rocky soil and rocky shorelines. The Middle colonies had good soil and produced an abundance of food.

28. In what ways are the Mayflower Compact and Fundamental Orders of Connecticut similar? (Rigorous) (Skill 5.4)

    A. They both pledged loyalty to the king of England.
    B. They were joint resolutions of various communities.
    C. They were expressions of views and forms of government.
    D. They were created in the late 1700s before statehood.

Answer: C. They were expressions of views and forms of government

Options A and B are incorrect because the Mayflower Compact pledged loyalty to the king of England but the Fundamental Orders are considered to be the first written constitution in the colonies. Option D is incorrect because both documents were written in the 1600s.

29. In what way did spatial exchange influence the development of colonial society? (Rigorous) (Skill 5.5)

    A. Population was diffused throughout the colonies.
    B. It affected the settlement of inland colonies.
    C. It was the reason colonists settled the Midwest.
    D. Population focused on its importance in forming towns.

Answer: B. It affected the settlement of inland colonies

The terms spatial exchange and spatial diffusion refer to the way people are distributed in an area. Option A is incorrect because spatial diffusion is the same as spatial exchange. Option C is incorrect because spatial exchange explains the reason for settlement and migration rather than being a reason for settlement. Option D is incorrect because spatial exchange is not considered in inhabiting areas.

30. **What effect did the passage of acts such as the Sugar Act, the Stamp Act, and the Townshend Acts have on colonial America? (Rigorous) (Skill 6.1)**

    A. The acts polarized the colonists.
    B. The acts were accepted with dignity.
    C. The colonists tolerated the acts.
    D. The colonists resisted the acts.

Answer: D. The colonists resisted the acts

Option A is incorrect because these acts were early legislation to recoup debt from the French and Indian Wars. At this point, the people were not polarized. Option B is incorrect because some of the resistance took the form of burning British officials in effigy. Option C is incorrect because resistance resulted from the passage of the acts.

31. **Why did King George III repeal the Stamp Act? (Easy) (Skill 6.2)**

    A. He feared rebellion.
    B. He no longer needed funds.
    C. Parliament recommended repeal.
    D. Parliament amended the act.

Answer: A. He feared rebellion

Option B is incorrect because Parliament passed more acts to recoup war expenses and exert control over the colonies. Option C is incorrect because at the same time of the repeal, Parliament passed more acts to tighten England's control over the colonies. Option D is incorrect because the act was repealed, not amended.

32. **How did England benefit from the Navigation Acts? (Average) (Skill 6.3)**

    A. The acts were revenue producing.
    B. The acts assured England's economic supremacy.
    C. The acts required the use of English ships.
    D. The acts monitored colonial commerce.

Answer: D. The acts monitored colonial commerce

The benefit of the acts was to monitor colonial commerce by requiring the use of English ships and the use of English ports for export to other nations. Options A, B, and C are incorrect because the acts were passed for the purpose of maintaining English economic supremacy.

33. **All of the following are reasons why the government under the Articles of Confederation was not retained except: (Rigorous)(Skill 6.4)**

    A. It did not provide for a strong chief executive.
    B. It lacked power to enforce legislation.
    C. It lacked the ability to regulate finances.
    D. It lacked the power to enforce treaties.

Answer: B. It lacked power to enforce legislation

The government had the power to legislate but it did not have a strong executive to enforce the legislation. Therefore, Option A is incorrect. Options C and D are incorrect because these were weaknesses of the Articles of Confederation.

34. **The Federalists: (Average) (Skill 6.5)**

    A. supported states' rights.
    B. desired a weak central government.
    C. favored a strong central government.
    D. were also called Loyalists.

Answer: C. favored a strong central government

Options A and B describe the Democratic-Republicans. Option D is incorrect because Tories were called Loyalists.

35. **Generally, _____ favored low tariffs. (Rigorous) (Skill 6.6)**

    A. Democratic-Republicans
    B. the Supreme Court
    C. Federalists
    D. Congress

Answer: A. Democratic-Republicans

Option B is incorrect because the Supreme Court would interpret laws made by Congress but would not issue policy decisions. Option C is incorrect because Federalists favored a strong central government and protective tariffs. Option D is incorrect because Congress passed high and low tariffs at different times in history.

36. **What event sparked a great migration of people from all over the world to California during the mid-1800s? (Easy) (Skill 7.1)**

    A. The birth of labor unions
    B. Manifest Destiny
    C. The invention of the automobile
    D. The Gold Rush

Answer: D. The Gold Rush

Labor unions were not first organized in California. Therefore, Option A is incorrect. Option B is incorrect because Manifest Destiny is the theory behind westward expansion. Option C is incorrect because the automobile was invented later.

37. **After the settlers inhabited _____, they believed they were destined to settle the North American continent. (Rigorous) (Skill 7.2)**

    A. the Louisiana Territory
    B. the Northwest Territory
    C. the Piedmont of Virginia
    D. Texas

Answer: B. the Northwest Territory

Option A is incorrect because the Louisiana Territory was purchased after the Northwest Territory had been opened to settlement. Option C is incorrect because small farmers lived in the Virginia Piedmont during colonial times. Option D is incorrect because Texas belonged to Mexico and was settled after the Louisiana Territory.

38. **Which area was acquired last by the United States? (Average) (Skill 7.3)**

    A. The Gadsden Purchase
    B. Annexation of Texas
    C. Acquisition of Oregon
    D. The Louisiana Purchase

Answer: A. The Gadsden Purchase

The Gadsden Purchase, which included New Mexico and Arizona, was made in 1853. Options B, C, and D are incorrect. The Louisiana Territory was acquired from France in 1803. Texas was annexed in 1845. Oregon became part of the United States in 1846.

39. **Why did Northerners first oppose the admission of Texas to statehood? (Average) (Skill 7.4)**

    A. Texas was controlled by Mexico

    B. Texas did not have the required population.

    C. Texas wanted to allow slavery.

    D. Texas owed debts to the U.S. government.

Answer: C. Texas wanted to allow slavery

The Northerners wanted to maintain a balance of slave and free states in Congress. Option A is incorrect because Texas was no longer controlled by Mexico when it applied for statehood. Option B is incorrect because any requirements for population would have been met before applying for statehood. Option D is incorrect because Mexico, not Texas, owed debts to the U.S. government.

40. **Which was not an issue that caused sectionalism? (Rigorous) (Skill 7.5)**

    A. Mechanization of farming

    B. Tariffs

    C. Slavery

    D. Land speculation

Answer: A. Mechanization of farming

Options B, C, and D were all issues relating to sectionalism. The industrial North wanted high tariffs to protect their industries. Slavery became an issue when territories applied for statehood. Land speculation kept settlers out of areas while investors sold cheap land at high prices.

41. **The principle of "popular sovereignty" that allowed people in any territory to make their own decisions concerning the slavery issue was first stated by: (Average)(Skill 7.6)**

    A. Henry Clay

    B. Daniel Webster

    C. John C. Calhoun

    D. Stephen A. Douglas

Answer: D. Stephen A. Douglas

Stephen A. Douglas originated the term "popular sovereignty" and was in favor of the Kansas-Nebraska Act. Option B is incorrect because Daniel Webster was a Northerner. Options A and C are incorrect because Henry Clay and John C. Calhoun were Southerners.

42. **Who was a Confederate commander? (Average) (Skill 7.6)**

    A. J. E. B. Stuart
    B. Burnside
    C. McClellan
    D. McDowell

Answer: A. J. E. B. Stuart

J. E. B. Stuart was a Confederate. Burnside, McClellan, and McDowell were military leaders of the North.

43. **Which statement is true about the Radical Republicans? (Rigorous) (Skill 7.6)**

    A. They favored Andrew Johnson's plan of Reconstruction.
    B. They established the Freedmen's Bureau.
    C. They opposed "black codes."
    D. They favored harsh measures of Reconstruction.

Answer: D. They favored harsh measures of Reconstruction

Option A is incorrect because the Radical Republicans did not believe Andrew Johnson's plan of Reconstruction was strict enough. The Freedman's Bureau was not established by the Radical Republicans. Therefore, Option B is incorrect. Option C is incorrect because the Radical Republicans favored strict laws, and the "black codes" were not lenient.

44. **Which doctrine was invoked to intercede in affairs of Latin American countries in the late nineteenth and early twentieth centuries? (Rigorous) (Skill 8.1)**

    A. Monroe Doctrine
    B. Imperialism
    C. Manifest Destiny
    D. Expansionism

Answer: A. Monroe Doctrine

The Monroe Doctrine warned European powers to stay out of Latin America. Presidents believed it was appropriate for America to intercede when it appeared that European countries were going to try to exert influence in Latin America. Option B is incorrect because imperialism defines the reason countries were acquiring territories. Option C is incorrect because Manifest Destiny means a God-given right to expand territory. Option D is not correct because expansionism is the process of acquiring more land.

45.   Which of the following is not correct about the Fourteen Points? (Average) (Skill 8.2)

A. They were drafted by Woodrow Wilson.
B. They were considered at the Paris peace talks.
C. The fourteenth point called for the creation of the United Nations.
D. The program applied to post-World War I.

Answer: C. The fourteenth point called for the creation of the United Nations

The fourteenth point called for the creation of a League of Nations. The United Nations was formed in the World War II era.

46.   The use of atomic bombs in 1945 was justified as a way to: (Average) (Skill 8.3)

A. defeat Japan
B. defeat Germany
C. show America's power
D. stop World War II

Answer: D. stop World War II

President Truman justified the use of the atomic bomb because it would speed up the end of the war. Options A and B are incorrect because the using the bombs caused Japan, not Germany, to surrender. Option C is incorrect because although the use of atomic bombs showed America's strength, it was not a justification for their use.

47.   Why were Alfred Mahan's theories important in shaping U.S. foreign policy? (Rigorous) (Skill 8.4)

A. He believed America should "speak softly and carry a big stick."
B. He believed a strong army would avoid confrontations.
C. He believed the use of the atomic bomb would end war.
D. He believed a strong navy showed a strong foreign policy.

Answer: D. He believed a strong navy showed a strong foreign policy.

Option A refers to the foreign policy of President Theodore Roosevelt. Option B is incorrect because it was a navy, not an army, that Alfred Mahan believed was important. Option C is not correct because Alfred Mahan's theories were developed in the late nineteenth century.

48.   **The international organization established to work for world peace at the end of World War II is the: (Easy) (Skill 8.5)**

    A. League of Nations
    B. United Federation of Nations
    C. United Nations
    D. United World League

Answer: C. United Nations

Option A is incorrect because the League of Nations was established after World War I. Options B and D are incorrect because they are either not organizations or were not established after World War I.

49.   **The space race began: (Average) (Skill 8.5)**

    A. in 1963.
    B. after the Soviets developed the atomic bomb.
    C. after the Soviets placed missile bases in Cuba.
    D. after the Soviets launched Sputnik.

Answer: D. after the Soviets launched Sputnik

The first satellite to orbit the earth, Sputnik triggered a race relating to science and technology between the United States and the Soviets. Sputnik was launched in 1957.

50.   **President Carter believed the oil fields of the Persian Gulf were threatened when the   Soviets entered which country? (Rigorous) (Skill 8.6)**

    A. Iraq
    B. Iran
    C. Kuwait
    D. Afghanistan

Answer: D. Afghanistan

Although Iraq, Iran, and Kuwait are all located in the Persian Gulf area, it was the Soviet invasion of Afghanistan that President Carter believed threatened the oil reserves.

51. **Which of the following is not an example of an advancement of transportation that took place during the post-Civil War period? (Average) (Skill 9.1)**

    A. Rail passenger service
    B. Completion of the transcontinental railroad
    C. Jet planes
    D. Automobile

Answer: A. Rail passenger service

Options B, C, and D were advancements. Option A is correct because rail passenger service was available before the Civil War.

52. **Which political philosophy is concerned with the commonsense needs of the average person? (Average) (Skill 9.2)**

    A. Popular sovereignty
    B. Populism
    C. Progressivism
    D. Protectionism

Answer: B. Populism

Option A is incorrect because popular sovereignty involves the right of the people to make decisions for themselves. Option C is incorrect because progressivism was a movement to advance as a nation. Option D is incorrect because protectionism refers to views about tariffs.

53. **All of the following are causes of the Industrial Revolution except : (Average) (Skill 9.3)**

    A. immigrants from southeast Europe.
    B. inventions.
    C. machines.
    D. extensive rail service.

Answer: A. immigrants from southeast Europe

More immigrants were a result of the Industrial Revolution, not a cause. Options B, C, and D are reasons why there was an Industrial Revolution. New inventions made work easier and faster. Machines replaced hand labor. Extensive rail service linked areas of the country for transport of goods.

54. **The late-nineteenth social worker who established a settlement house, known as Hull House, in Chicago was: (Easy) (Skill 9.4)**

    A. Betty Friedan
    B. Susan B. Anthony
    C. Jane Addams
    D. Elizabeth Cady Stanton

Answer: C. Jane Addams

Option A is incorrect because Betty Friedan was founder of NOW. Options B and D are incorrect because Susan B. Anthony and Elizabeth Cady Stanton were advocates for women's suffrage.

55. **The passage of the Civil Rights Act of 1964 took place during which U.S. president's administration? (Average) (Skill 9.5)**

    A. John F. Kennedy
    B. Lyndon Johnson
    C. Jimmy Carter
    D. Richard Nixon

Answer: B. Lyndon Johnson

Option A is incorrect because President Kennedy was assassinated and Lyndon Johnson became president in 1963. Options C and D are incorrect because Carter and Nixon served after Johnson.

56. **How has the Hispanic civil rights movement differed from the African American civil rights movement? (Rigorous) (Skill 9.5)**

    A. The African American movement focused on social integration whereas the Hispanic movement focused on educational integration.
    B. The African American movement focused on economic integration whereas the Hispanic movement focused on preventing discrimination based on color.
    C. The two movements did not differ.
    D. The two movements differed in their focus but not their goal of integration into American society.

Answer: D. The two movements differed in their focus but not their goal of integration into American society

Options A and B address an incorrect focus of each group. Option C is incorrect because the movements differed in focus. The African Americans did not want to be discriminated against because of race. The Hispanics wanted to integrate socially and economically.

57. **Which Native American tribes moved west of the Mississippi in the early nineteenth century? (Average) (Skill 10.1)**

A. The Cherokee, Choctaw, and Shawnee
B. The Wichitas, Comanches, and Caddoes
C. The Coahuiltecans, Lipans, and Kiowas
D. The Tonkawas, Wichitas, and Caddoes

Answer: A. The Cherokee, Choctaw, and Shawnee

The Wichitas, Caddoes, Coahuiltecans, Lipans, and Tonkawas were Native American tribes indigenous to various parts of Texas. The Kiowas and Comanches migrated from Montana and Wyoming, respectively.

58. **What was the cause of friction between the United States and Spain after the Louisiana Purchase in 1803? (Average) (Skill 10.2)**

A. Both nations disputed the boundary between Texas and Louisiana.
B. Spain resented American involvement in the Cuban War of Independence.
C. Mexico wanted to buy the Louisiana Territory from France.
D. Spain angered the United States by sinking the American battleship The Maine.

Answer: A. Both nations disputed the boundary between Texas and Louisiana

The U.S.-Spanish boundary dispute was resolved after an agreement in 1819 in which the Sabine River became the geographical border between Texas and Louisiana. Spain's resentment of American involvement in the Cuban War of Independence and Spain angering the United States by attacking The Maine were both causes of the Spanish-American War in 1898. Mexico did not want to buy Louisiana nor were in the fiscal position to make such a purchase.

59. **Why did missionaries abandon east Texas in 1693? (Rigorous) (Skill 10.4)**

A. Tensions with Native Americans over a smallpox outbreak scared them away.
B. The Mexican War of Independence forced abandonment.
C. They moved their mission into the sunny beaches of Spanish Florida.
D. American citizens began to settle in the region.

Answer: A. Tensions with Native Americans over a smallpox outbreak scared them away

The Mexican Revolution occurred from 1810 to 1821. Spanish missionaries in Texas did not wanted to abandon their mission in favor of the sunny beaches of Florida. American citizens did not begin to settle in Texas until the 1820s.

60. **Which domestic animals existed in the Texas region before the arrival of Europeans? (Average) (Skill 10.5)**

    A. Cattle
    B. Pigs
    C. Horses
    D. None

Answer: D. None

Spanish settlers introduced cattle, pigs, and horses to the Americas in what is now called the Columbian Exchange. Native Americans living in Texas did not have access to domestic animals prior to the arrival of Europeans.

61. **Who was the first American allowed to obtain a colonial grant to settle in Texas? (Average) (Skill 10.6)**

    A. Stephen F. Austin
    B. Agustin de Iturbide
    C. Moses Austin
    D. Fray Damián Massanet

Answer: C. Moses Austin

Stephen F. Austin led 300 American families to settle in Central Texas, but his father, Moses Austin, had made the agreement for settlement. Agustin de Iturbide was a Spanish officer who helped negotiate the independence of Mexico. Fray Damián Massanet was a Spanish Franciscan priest who co-founded numerous missions in Texas.

62. **What was one of the causes of the Mexican War of Independence? (Average) (Skill 11.1)**

    A. Confiscation of church property
    B. Taxation of the Thirteen Colonies
    C. Abdication of Napoleon
    D. Debt from the War of 1812

Answer: A. Confiscation of church property

In 1804 a royal decree ordered the confiscation of some lands owned by the Catholic church. Some of the other reasons for the Mexican War of Independence were taxation of New Spain, abdication of Ferdinand, and war debt from the Napoleonic Wars.

63. **What was the final battle of the Texas Revolution? (Average) (Skill 11.2)**

    A. Battle of the Alamo
    B. Battle of San Jacinto
    C. Battle of Gonzales
    D. Battle of Gettysburg

Answer: B. Battle of San Jacinto

The Battle of the Alamo was a decisive defeat by Mexican forces against Texan forces that while a victory for the Mexicans; it was at a huge cost in terms of troops lost. The Battle of Gonzales was the first battle of the Texas Revolution. The Battle of Gettysburg was a Civil War battle rather than a battle of the Texas Revolution.

64. **What early Texas pioneer documented daily life during the Republic of Texas and early statehood? (Average) (Skill 11.3)**

    A. Sam Houston
    B. Stephen F. Austin
    C. Mary Maverick
    D. Joshua Houston

Answer: C. Mary Maverick

Sam Houston was the general of the Texas army that won independence from Mexico and the first president of the Republic of Texas. Stephen F. Austin brought the first American immigrants into Texas because of a contract between his father and the Mexican government. Joshua Houston was Sam Houston's personal servant and slave.

65. **Which event motivated Texas to hold a secessionist vote in 1861? (Average) (Skill 11.4)**

    A. South Carolina's secession from the Union.
    B. Battle of Palmito Ridge
    C. Battle of Galveston
    D. Texas Revolution

Answer: A. South Carolina's secession from the Union

Palmito Ridge and Galveston were both battles of the Civil War. The Texas Revolution was an armed conflict between Texas and Mexico that led to the establishment of the Republic of Texas.

66. **Which Comanche leader was an important leader in both warfare against Texan settlers and reservation life? (Easy) (Skill 11.6)**

    A. Quanah Parker
    B. Joshua Houston
    C. Sacagawea
    D. Jack Coffee Hays

Answer: A. Quanah Parker

Joshua Houston was the personal servant of Texas governor Sam Houston. Sacagawea was a Shoshone woman who assisted the Lewis and Clark expedition in 1805. Jack Coffee Hays was a Texas Ranger who led many battles against Native American groups.

67. **Texas was the leading supplier of which product during the late nineteenth century? (Average) (Skill 11.7)**

    A. Cattle
    B. Cottonseed
    C. Packaged meats
    D. Petroleum

Answer: B. Cottonseed

Options A and C are incorrect because although Texas ranchers were able to supply a large amount of cattle and packaged meats, Texas was the United States' largest supplier of cottonseed during this period. Option D is incorrect because petroleum was not an important aspect of Texas' economy until the twentieth century.

68. **What government agency was formed in 1890 as a result of deforestation in Texas? (Easy) (Skill 11.8)**

    A. Forestry Association
    B. Farmer's Alliance
    C. Eleventh Legislature
    D. Texas Rangers

Answer: A. Forestry Association

The Farmer's Association was formed to promote cooperative farming practices among Texas farmers. The Eleventh Legislature was a governing body that attempted to curtail Reconstruction efforts. The Texas Rangers fought Native Americans on the frontier.

69. **Which two teams played the first college football game in the state of Texas in 1894? (Average) (Skill 11.9)**

    A. University of Texas vs. Prairie View A & M College
    B. Texas A & M vs. Prairie View A & M College
    C. University of Texas vs. Texas A & M
    D. University of Texas vs. University of Oklahoma

Answer: C. University of Texas vs. Texas A & M

Options A and B are incorrect because of segregation in that Prairie View A & M College would not have been allowed to play a white college. Although the University of Texas versus the University of Oklahoma is a historically important rivalry game (Red River Rivalry), the first game between those two schools occurred in 1900.

70. **Who was the first native Texan to serve as governor? (Average) (Skill 12.1)**

    A. James Hogg
    B. Jane McCallum
    C. George W. Bush
    D. Manuel C. Gonzales

Answer: A. James Hogg

Option A is correct because Hogg became the first native-born governor of Texas in 1890. Jane McCallum was a women's suffrage leader. George W. Bush was governor of Texas during the 1990s. Manuel C. Gonzales was a Mexican American civil rights leader.

71. **What was the main contribution that Texas citizens made during World War II? (Average) (Skill 12.2)**

    A. Rationing food, gas, rubber, and mechanical parts
    B. Building bomb shelters
    C. Women joining the workplace
    D. Both A and C

Answer: D. Both A and C

Option D is correct because it includes options A and C, rationing and women joining the workplace during World War II. Option B is incorrect because many Texans built bomb shelters in their backyards in response to fears of nuclear annihilation during the Cold War.

72. **What popular Democratic Texas governor did George W. Bush defeat in 1994 to become the 46th governor of Texas? (Average) (Skill 12.3)**

    A. Albert Gore, Jr.
    B. Ann Richards
    C. Lyndon B. Johnson
    D. James Allred

Answer: B. Ann Richards

George W. Bush defeated Ann Richards in the gubernatorial election. Bush defeated vice president Al Gore during the 2000 presidential election. Lyndon Johnson was the first Texas-born president of the United States. James Allred was Texas governor during the presidency of Franklin Roosevelt.

73. **What were the reasons for the growth of the agricultural industry in Texas during the beginning of the twentieth century? (Average) (Skill 12.4)**

    A. Urbanization of Texas
    B. World War I
    C. Widespread use of the tractor
    D. All of the above

Answer: D. All of the above

The urbanization of Texas and the start of World War I created a larger demand for agricultural goods, which drove up prices. The widespread use of the tractor made farming more efficient, thus easier to accommodate the larger demand.

74. **What Texas airport is the largest in the state and the second largest airport in the nation? (Easy) (Skill 12.5)**

    A. San Antonio International Airport
    B. Dallas/Fort Worth International Airport
    C. George Bush Intercontinental Airport
    D. Austin-Bergstrom International Airport

Answer: B. Dallas/Fort Worth International Airport

Option B is correct because DFW is larger and receives significantly more air traffic than the airports listed in the other options.

75. **Which of the following is a characteristic of peat? (Rigorous) (Skill 13.1)**

    A. It is compressed.
    B. It is fine and sandy.
    C. It has a high content of salt.
    D. It has a low water content.

Answer: A. It is compressed

Peat is a type of soil that has a high water content and lots of organic matter. Therefore, Option D is incorrect. Option B is incorrect because fine and sandy soil describes silt. Option C is incorrect because the description is of saline soil.

76. **A(n) _____ is formed when plants and animals interact with the physical environment. (Easy) (Skill 13.4)**

    A. terrain
    B. steppe
    C. atmosphere
    D. ecosystem

Answer: D. ecosystem

Option A is incorrect because terrain is a synonym for land. Option B is incorrect because a "steppe" is an example of an ecosystem. Option C is incorrect because the atmosphere surrounds the earth.

77. **Language is a unifying cultural characteristic because: (Rigorous) (Skill 14.1)**

    A. belief systems are introduced into society in a number of ways.
    B. it defines the relationship between a culture's government and its people.
    C. it studies the characteristics and influences on varied cultures.
    D. it creates and explains ideas and information.

Answer: D. it creates and explains ideas and information

Option D best describes language as a unifying cultural force. Language is a way of preserving culture and passing it to future generations. As a result, it is an important characteristic of culture. Option A describes religion. Option B defines political culture. Option C describes cultural geography.

78. **How did the federal government demonstrate that education was important in the westward expansion movement? (Average) (Skill 14.4)**

    A. Congress required students to attend school until the age of 15.
    B. Congress provided funds for agricultural colleges.
    C. Congress required each township establish schools.
    D. Congress established teacher-training colleges.

Answer: B. Congress provided funds for agricultural colleges

Option B describes the dedication of Congress to education. Congress did not require students to attend school. It set aside a section within each township for public education but did not require that schools be built there even though most schools were built there. Congress did not establish teacher-training colleges.

79. **How did the history of Christianity have an impact on the building of the Shrine of Guadalupe? (Rigorous) (Skills 14.7, 14.8)**

    A. Because Christianity is not completely unified, the people of Mexico were unable to persuade the Church to contribute to the funding of the shrine.
    B. Because Christianity was begun around 1500 BCE, the shrine could not be used to convert the natives.
    C. The vision of a native Mexican was used to teach other Mexicans to become a follower of Jesus Christ.
    D. The schism in Western Christianity affected the construction of the shrine.

Answer: C. The vision of a native Mexican was used to teach other Mexicans to become a follower of Jesus Christ

The Shrine of Guadalupe commemorates the vision of the Virgin Mary that Catholics believe was experienced by a native peasant in the sixteenth century. The story was used by the Spanish church to convert further Mexican natives. Option A is incorrect because the people of Mexico built the shrine. Option B has an incorrect date. Option D is incorrect because the schism in Western Christianity occurred before the building of the Shrine of Guadalupe.

80. **What was the main reason early humans moved from place to place? (Rigorous) (Skill 15.1)**

    A. Agriculture expanded the types of foods that were available.
    B. They were required to move with their food sources.
    C. Clothing enabled them to adapt to a wider range of climates.
    D. Wool-bearing animals became domesticated.

Answer: B. They were required to move with their food sources

Options A, C, and D are true statements but are not the reason why early humans moved from place to place. They were required to move because they hunted and gathered food from wild sources. Since their basic support was from nature, they needed to move to maintain a food supply.

81. **Which of the following was not a cause of the Dust Bowl? (Rigorous) (Skill 15.4)**

    A. Droughts
    B. Dust storms
    C. Winds
    D. Resettlement

Answer: D. Resettlement

Resettlement was an effect, not a cause, of the Dust Bowl. Droughts, dust storms, and winds were all causes of the Dust Bowl.

82. **How do raw materials affect the economic activities of a location? (Rigorous) (Skill 15.7)**

    A. Availability of raw materials requires availability of nearby transportation.
    B. Lack of raw materials inhibits growths of communities.
    C. Management of raw materials can affect the survival of a community.
    D. Loss of raw materials can affect the viability of a community.

Answer: C. Management of raw materials can affect the survival of a community

Option C is correct because the key word is survival. Option A is incorrect because modern transportation methods can carry resources, such as oil, to refineries thousands of miles away. Option B is incorrect because there are multiple factors for establishing and creating growth in a community. Option D is incorrect because viability of a community depends on leadership, not raw materials.

83. **Which of the following is not a common characteristic of an ethnic group? (Rigorous) (Skill 16.2)**

    A. Religion
    B. Genetic lineage
    C. Background
    D. Language

Answer: B. Genetic lineage

Option B is correct because an ethnic group does not necessarily share a common genetic lineage. Options A, C, and D are incorrect because they describe common characteristics of an ethnic group.

84. **The role of a(n) _____ in meeting basic societal needs is to develop good citizens. (Rigorous) (Skill 16.5)**

    A. religion
    B. educational system
    C. family
    D. mass media

Answer: C. family

Option C is correct because the development of good citizens and preserving society are primary family roles. The other options are incorrect because religion can make society a better place, education can help people to become better citizens, and mass media communicates events important to a society.

85. **Which of the following individuals developed the method called psychoanalysis? (Easy) (Skill 16.8)**

    A. Wilhelm Wundt
    B. F. Skinner
    C. Edward Thorndike
    D. Sigmund Freud

Answer: D. Sigmund Freud

Freud developed psychoanalysis as a method of interpretive and introspective psychology. Wundt developed a laboratory to study psychology. Skinner and Thorndike developed behaviorism.

86. **_____ is the fundamental law of the U.S. republic. (Rigorous) (Skill 17.1)**

    A. Separation of powers
    B. Checks and balances
    C. Federalism
    D. The Constitution

Answer: D. The Constitution

Option D is correct because the Constitution is the document that is the supreme law of the land. There is no national power superior to it. Options A, B, and C are theories included within the Constitution.

87. **Federal taxation legislation must originate in: (Rigorous) (Skill 17.4)**

     A. the House of Representatives.
     B. the Senate.
     C. either the House or the Senate.
     D. both the House and Senate simultaneously.

Answer: A. the House of Representatives

The Constitution provides that federal tax legislation must originate in the House of Representatives.

88. **The Thirteenth, Fourteenth, and Fifteenth Amendments were called the "Civil War" amendments because they: (Rigorous) (Skill 17.7)**

     A. provided due process, direct election of U.S. senators, and voting rights regardless of race, color, or previous condition of servitude.
     B. provided equal protection, prohibited the poll tax, and abolished slavery.
     C. abolished slavery, gave voting rights to former slaves, and provided for equal protection.
     D. prohibited the poll tax, provided for direct election of U.S. Senators, and guaranteed due process.

Answer: C. abolished slavery, gave voting rights to former slaves, and provided for equal protection

Option C is correct because the Thirteenth Amendment abolished slavery, the Fourteenth Amendment guaranteed due process and equal protection, and the Fifteenth Amendment gave voting rights to former slaves. The other options are incorrect because the Seventeenth Amendment provided for direct elections of U.S. senators and the Twenty-Fourth Amendment prohibited poll taxes.

89. **The American governmental system is a federal system because: (Rigorous) (Skill 17.10)**

     A. there are fifty states and one national government.
     B. the national and state governments share powers.
     C. state governments have three branches of government.
     D. the federal government has administrative agencies.

Answer: B. the national and state governments share powers

Option B is correct because a federal system of government is one in which the state and federal government share powers. The other options are true statements but are not correct definitions of a federal system of government.

90.   How does policy making affect influence decision making? (Rigorous) (Skill 18.3)

    A.   It formulates public opinion.
    B.   It is an alternative to adoption.
    C.   It requires interaction.
    D.   It identifies a problem.

Answer: C. It requires interaction

Option C is correct because policy making involves groups and more than one individual. Therefore, interaction is required. Option A is incorrect because policy making may or may not formulate public opinion. Option B is incorrect because policy must be adopted to be implemented. Option D is incorrect because identification of the problem is the first step in policy making.

91.   The temperance movement resulted in: (Easy) (Skill 18.6)

    A.   women gaining the right to vote.
    B.   the increased manufacture of alcohol.
    C.   enactment of the Prohibition Amendment.
    D.   reduction of abuses of drunkenness.

Answer: C. enactment of the Prohibition Amendment

Leaders of the temperance movement wanted to gain the prohibition of sale, manufacture, and consumption of alcoholic beverages. The other options are incorrect because the suffrage movement secured the right for women to vote, Prohibition did not increase the sale or manufacture of alcohol, and the temperance movement could not control drunkenness.

92.   The Mayflower Compact is an example of: (Average) (Skill 19.1)

    A.   a social contract theory document.
    B.   a resistance to illegitimate government.
    C.   the law of nature.
    D.   a divine right theory document.

Answer: A. a social contract theory document

The Pilgrims entered into the Mayflower Compact to form a government in the New World. The other options are incorrect because no government had been established at the time the Pilgrims executed the Mayflower Compact, the Compact was not discussing natural rights, and it did not discuss a "divine right" ruler.

93. **In which type of government system are coalition parties common? (Rigorous) (Skill 19.4)**

    A. Monarchy
    B. Dictatorship
    C. Federalist
    D. Parliamentary system

Answer: D. Parliamentary system

Option D is correct because a parliamentary system usually has many parties. The other options are incorrect because a king or queen rules a monarchy, a dictator rules a dictatorship, and in the federalist system there are two main parties.

94. **What was dominant form of political organization in Europe during the Middle Ages? (Rigorous) (Skill 19.5)**

    A. Democracy
    B. Nationalism
    C. Federalism
    D. Feudalism

Answer: D. Feudalism

Option D is correct because the king, a noble, or a church owned the land and the people worked for the owner with a guarantee of protection. The other options are incorrect because they were not concepts of political organization during the Middle Ages.

95. **Who was the most influential French political theorist before the French Revolution? (Easy) (Skill 19.6)**

    A. Rousseau
    B. Champlain
    C. La Salle
    D. Hobbes

Answer: A. Jean-Jacques Rousseau

Jean-Jacques Rousseau wrote The Social Contract. Samuel Champlain and René-Robert de la Salle were explorers, and Thomas Hobbes was English.

96. Which of the following is not a factor of production? (Average) (Skill 20.1)

A. Opportunity cost
B. Labor
C. Capital
D. Land

Answer: A. Opportunity cost

Option A is correct because opportunity cost is the value of a sacrificed alternative. Land, capital, and labor are all factors of production.

97. The circular-flow diagram is a model of: (Rigorous) (Skill 20.2)

A. supply and demand.
B. the business sector.
C. the Gross Domestic Product.
D. the economy.

Answer: D. the economy

Option D is correct because the circular-flow model shows the flow of inputs, outputs, and money through the economy. The other options are various aspects of the economy.

98. Adam Smith believed that: (Rigorous) (Skill 20.4)

A. labor was a value-determining factor.
B. free markets should exist without government interference.
C. aggregate spending determined the level of economic activity.
D. collective ownership and administration of goods was necessary.

Answer: B. free markets should exist without government interference

Adam Smith described this theory in The Wealth of Nations. Option A was a belief of Karl Marx. Option C is John Maynard Keynes's theory, and option D describes socialism.

99. Private ownership of production a characteristic of which type of economic system?   (Easy) (Skill 20.5)

A. A mixed economy
B. Socialism
C. Communism
D. Capitalism

Answer: D. Capitalism

Private ownership of the means of production and a free market economy are characteristic of capitalism. The other options are incorrect because a mixed economy uses a combination of markets and planning, and socialism and communism have government ownership of the means of production.

100. The most competitive of market structures is: (Rigorous) (Skill 20.6)

    A. Monopoly
    B. Pure competition
    C. Oligopoly
    D. Monopolistic competition

Answer: B. Pure competition

Option B is correct because a pure competition has many buyers and sellers. A monopoly has one main seller of a unique product, an oligopoly has a few large firms selling products, and a monopolistic competition exists where there are many similar products sold at different prices.

101. What is meant by a nation's absolute advantage in the production? (Rigorous) (Skill 20.7)

    A. There will be lower output prices and higher resource prices.
    B. Restrictions such as tariffs will be implemented to raise prices.
    C. Quotas will be set on the physical number of permitted imports.
    D. One country can produce goods more efficiently than others.

Answer: D. One country can produce goods more efficiently than others

Option A is incorrect because it describes comparative advantage. Option B describes the result when tariffs are imposed. Option C is incorrect because the definition of "quote" is the limit that is placed on the physical number of units of permitted imports or exports.

102. What is the term describing situations in which individuals try to produce products that are better than similar products and set their own prices? (Average) (Skill 21.1)

    A. Voluntary exchange
    B. Private property rights
    C. Competition
    D. Profit incentive

Answer: C. Competition

Competition is an important element of free enterprise. The other options are incorrect because they describe other terms involved in a free enterprise system.

103. What was the first federal antitrust legislation? (Average) (Skill 21.2)

A. Sherman Act
B. FTC Act
C. Robinson-Patman Act
D. CCC Act

Answer: A. Sherman Act

The Sherman Act was passed in 1890. Options B and C are incorrect because the FTC and Robinson-Patman acts were passed later. Option D is incorrect because the CCC refers to the Civilian Conservation Corps, a New Deal program.

104. Which form of business organization provides the most protection for its member(s)? (Average) (Skill 21.3)

A. Partnership
B. Sole proprietorship
C. Joint venture
D. Corporation

Answer: D. Corporation

A corporation provides limited liability to its owners. A sole proprietorship and partnership result in unlimited liability for the owners. A joint venture is an undertaking by two or more groups (usually countries) to construct major facilities (such as hotels or power plants).

105. NAFTA is a: (Easy) (Skill 21.5)

A. trade organization.
B. trade agreement.
C. series of regional trade barriers.
D. foreign trade barrier.

Answer: B. trade agreement

NAFTA stands for the North American Free Trade Agreement. The United States, Canada, and Mexico have signed the agreement, so it is not an organization. The purpose is to lower trade barriers.

106. **At which level or levels of government are policies generally enacted to encourage labor to migrate from one sector of the economy to another? (Average) (Skill 21.5)**

    A. National
    B. State
    C. Local
    D. National, state, and local

Answer: A. National

The national government can view the needs of the entire country. The state and local governments usually provide information to the unemployed.

107. **What is an example of a scarce resource? (Easy) (Skill 21.8)**

    A. Market choices
    B. Time
    C. Consumer options
    D. Raw materials

Answer: B. Time

Consumers rarely have enough time to do everything they want. The other options are weaker answers because they may or may not be scarce.

108. **The discovery of _____ by Albert Einstein revolutionized the study of physics. (Easy) (Skill 22.1)**

    A. the microchip
    B. the microscope
    C. the theory of relativity
    D. electrical power

Answer: C. the theory of relativity

Option C is correct because the study implied that time and space were not fixed. Options A, B, and D are incorrect because they were not discovered by Albert Einstein.

109. Where was gunpowder invented? (Easy) (Skill 22.2)

    A. India
    B. China
    C. River valley civilizations
    D. Classical Greece and Rome

Answer: B. China

China was the center of many inventions such as printing, cast iron, and gunpowder India developed metal tools and mathematical concepts; the river valley civilizations made development in scientific knowledge about farming, science, and mathematics; and classical Rome and Greece developed calendars, architectural accomplishments, and other technological concepts.

110. The most significant invention of modern times may be: (Easy) (Skill 22.5)

    A. the computer
    B. the telephone
    C. electric power
    D. petroleum-based products

Answer: A. the computer

Option A is correct because the computer has changed the way people communicate, transact business, and learn. Options B and C are incorrect because they are older inventions and have not had the same impact as the computer. Option D was more significant when the price of oil was less.

111. How does the correct use of social studies terminology demonstrate the philosophical foundations of social science inquiry? (Rigorous) (Skills 23.1, 23.2)

    A. Social sciences seek to discover and explain common motivations and reactions among humans.
    B. Social sciences include several philosophical foundations, such as economics and history.
    C. Students can become more aware of the world around them and become better citizens.
    D. The teacher needs to be aware of correct terminology to better understand the philosophical foundations.

Answer C. Students can become more aware of the world around them and become better citizens

The purpose of knowing the correct terminology is to teach students the terminology and have the students become more aware of their world and develop into better citizens. Options A and B do not explain the importance of terminology. Option D is incorrect because the question asks about use of terminology, not the awareness of terminology.

112. How should historical concepts be interpreted? (Rigorous) (Skill 24.3)

    A. They should be interpreted as movements.
    B. They should be identified as belief systems.
    C. They should focus on historical themes.
    D. They should provide insight into historical events.

Answer: D. They should provide insight into historical events.

Option D is correct because historical concepts can be interpreted as part of larger historical themes and provide insight into historical events by placing them in a larger historical context. Options A, B, and C are incorrect because historical concepts are movements and belief systems that can be examined as part of a historical theme.

113. Organization of information provides _____ whereas interpretation of information provides _____. (Average) (Skill 24.4)

    A. conclusions; reaching objectives
    B. reaching objectives; separation
    C. an orderly approach; evidence for conclusions
    D. evidence for conclusions; reaching objectives

Answer: C. an orderly approach; evidence for conclusions

Organization provides a systematic approach to storing information whereas interpretation of the information results in conclusions. Options A, B, and D are presented in reversed order.

114. Which of the following is major indicator that is used to measure levels of economic activity? (Average) (Skill 24.8)

    A. The unemployment rate
    B. Periods of prosperity
    C. Economic instability
    D. Surplus merchandise

Answer: A. The unemployment rate

The unemployment rate and inflation rate are two major indicators used to describe and measure levels of economic activity. Options B and C describe characteristics of the economy, and Option D describes a situation that may affect the economy.

115. Why is it important to encourage the use of multiple research resources? (Easy) (Skill 25.1)

    A. They will serve as a road map for further research.
    B. They will promote the ability to judge the value of the resource.
    C. They will be relevant to the research goal.
    D. They will make the research project definitive and successful.

Answer: B. They will promote the ability to judge the value of the resource

Multiple resources introduce diverse viewpoints that can be judged as to value. Option A is not correct because it is the framing of the question that provides the road map. Option C is incorrect because resources may or may not be relevant. Option D is incorrect because multiple resources will not necessarily make the project successful.

116. What is the difference between an argumentative paper and an analytical paper? (Average) (Skill 25.2)

    A. An argumentative paper examines the various parts of a research topic to support the initial statement whereas an analytical paper supports a question or claim.
    B. An argumentative paper focuses on understanding the research topic to reformulate the parts in a way to support the initial statement whereas an analytical paper focuses on the scientific method.
    C. An argumentative paper examines the various parts of a research topic to support its conclusions whereas an analytical paper challenges a question or claim.
    D. An analytical paper presents research to provide information whereas an argumentative paper presents research to prove a debatable statement.

Answer: D. An analytical paper presents research to provide information whereas an argumentative paper presents research to prove a debatable statement

An argumentative paper focuses on supporting a claim with evidence or reasoning. An analytical paper presents a discussion about a specific topic. Options A, B, and C are incorrect because they state the reverse.

117. A demographic table may show which of the following? (Rigorous) (Skill 25.5)

    A. Vital statistics
    B. A null hypothesis
    C. Levels of education
    D. Census reports

Answer: C. Levels of education

Demographic tables may include levels of education and economic and social statistics. Demography is the branch of science of statistics most concerned with the social well-being of people. The other options are incorrect because vital statistics is another area of science, a null hypothesis is the result of testing, and census reports are sites for gathering demographic data.

118. Which acronym represents the state standards for Texas K-12 education in public schools? (Easy) (Skill 26.1)

  A. TAKS
  B. TEKS
  C. TELPAS
  D. STAAR

Answer: B. TEKS

Only Option B, the Texas Essential Knowledge and Skills (TEKS), refers to educational standards. The TEKS are the state standards for Texas K-12 education in public schools. STAAR, TAKS, and TELPAS are current or former assessment programs used in the Texas educational system.

119. Why is developmentally appropriate instruction important? (Average) (Skill 26.2)

  A. It provides interdisciplinary instruction.
  B. It eliminates cognitive learning.
  C. It provides problem-solving knowledge.
  D. It provides students with optimal learning.

Answer: D. It provides students with optimal learning

Optimal learning is the goal of teaching. Options A and C are aspects of student learning in various types of situations but are not the reasons why developmentally appropriate instruction is important. Option B is incorrect because this kind of instruction increases cognitive learning.

120. The purpose of assessments is to determine whether the student has: (Easy) (Skill 26.8)

  A. sufficiently learned the required material.
  B. performed well according to a norm group.
  C. met a school's graduation requirements.
  D. All of the above

Answer: D. All of the above

Assessments are tools that have various purposes. These may include determining whether the student has sufficiently learned the material, performed well according to a norm group, or met graduation requirements.

Jobs
for
Teachers

Find out more at
XAMonline.com

XAMonline.com

CPSIA information can be obtained at www.ICGtesting.com
Printed in the USA
BVOW04s0020200116
433467BV00020BA/159/P